CLOSED CIRCUITS

GARRETT STEWART

CLOSED CIRCUITS

SCREENING NARRATIVE SURVEILLANCE

UNIVERSITY OF CHICAGO PRESS
CHICAGO AND LONDON

Garrett Stewart is the James O. Freedman Professor of Letters in the Department of English at the University of Iowa and the author of numerous books on fiction and film.

The University of Chicago Press, Chicago 60637
The University of Chicago Press, Ltd., London

Printed in the United States of America
24 23 22 21 20 19 18 17 16 15   1 2 3 4 5

ISBN-13: 978-0-226-20121-4 (cloth)
ISBN-13: 978-0-226-20149-8 (paper)
ISBN-13: 978-0-226-20135-1 (e-book)
DOI: 10.7208/chicago/9780226201351.001.0001

Library of Congress Cataloging-in-Publication Data
Stewart, Garrett, author.
Closed circuits : screening narrative surveillance / Garrett Stewart.
pages ; cm
Includes bibliographical references and index.
ISBN 978-0-226-20121-4 (cloth : alk. paper)— ISBN 978-0-226-20149-8 (pbk. : alk. paper)—
ISBN 978-0-226-20135-1 (ebook) 1. Electronic surveillance in motion pictures.
2. Motion pictures—United States—History and criticism. I. Title.
PN1995.9.E38S74 2015
791.430973—dc23
2014016861

♾ This paper meets the requirements of ANSI/NISO Z39.48–1992 (Permanence of Paper).

For D.A. Miller,

whose "too close reading"
takes us to the inner limit of screen viewing

CONTENTS

PREFACE: RETURNS OF THEORY

All montage is espionage. This is either too easy to be true or too true to be useful. Specifying each pole of the conjectural equation—rephrased, for starters, as the difference between film viewing and motivated surveillance in cinematic narrative—is one aspect of the coming task. Viewing invisibly vs. sighting unseen: watching versus spying. What follows takes its own medium-long look at the sporadically compromised look of screen viewing in (but also beyond) certain identifiable narrative genres. Formulated at a broader level, the purpose is to consider how cinema, from its celluloid origins in the age of photography down through its digital reconstitution in an electronic era, tends to rework—across different stylistic periods, narrative forms, and technological innovations—the shifting ratios, ethical as well as epistemological, between screen visibility and the impulses of human vision.

On each of these several fronts, the questions that need answering are roughly the same to begin with: How may editing tacitly operate in this or that film to embroil the communal spectator (beyond some general fictional license) in a quasi-illicit audiovisual purchase on another populated space? And how might this optical implication (both senses) be further bound up, in given films, with the apparatus of technological surveillance? How, and exactly where, might this happen in the cinematographic management of narrative and its transitions? In considering a diverse range of potentially intersecting evidence, what patterns emerge about the work (and material support) of audiovisual mediation in the full array of its application from voyeurism to informatics, from invaded privacy to military invasion, the latter including the relays of panoptic reconnaissance and targeted spycraft? What might comparative evidence reveal in everything from a police dragnet film by German master Fritz Lang through the "telescreen" ethos of Orwellian scenarios down through film treatments of our current "wired wars," with their digital surveillance as well as drone targeting? And how most recently should we understand—beyond, and building on, this quasi-ballistic arsenal of video facilitation in the latest spate of nonepic war films—the further reach of scopic prognostication in the latest sci-fi plots? For these include treatments of audiovisual virtuality that offer, in national defense fables of counterterrorism, the newest technological update of a futurist (if only day-after-tomorrow) surveillance motif.

From the promotional taglines of 1954's *Rear Window* ("In deadly danger . . . because they saw too much!") through 1998's *Enemy of the State* ("In God we trust. The rest we monitor") through 2013's epitomizing British title *Closed Circuit* (and its almost redundant "They See Your Every Move"), this book is meant to chart the mutation from detective eyewitnessing to machinic surveillance in the postwar era, with an initial historical grounding in Lang's masterpiece of pretechnological but cinematically articulated (rather than just visually pictured) surveillance from 1931, *M* (short in German both for *Murder* and its resulting *Manhunt*). As I say: to chart—rather than to chronicle. This is not a history, let alone an exhaustive one, but rather a graph of pressure points (often intertextual) in the evolution of a motif and the genres it reshapes in the process by selective adaptation. Of course, from the dragnet in *M* to James Bond's fatal use of "M" as surveillance bait in entrapping the computer-genius villain of *Skyfall* (Sam Mendes, 2012), the covert tracking of a moving human agent has been the mainstay of the thriller plot. But this book is about something even more foundational in the relation of narrative technique to the thematics of furtive record and pursuit, visual search and potential seizure—something surfaced increasingly in the common axis of montage and electronic spycraft (or e-spionage): namely, the shared logistics of editorial cross-cutting and a surveillance hub's channel switching. And about the place of this in our understanding of a wired globe where one is occasionally moved to remember that a web, World-Wide or otherwise, is spun from fibers, however enabling, meant ultimately to ensnare.

Replacing human duration with clocked electronic activity, our zeitgeist has come to be determined in large measure by the time log. Every digital memory is datelined. And, more to the point, every time we sit at our computer screens, it is we who are subject to their electronic "monitors," webcams or not. The apparatus has finally justified its once strictly televisual and one-way name. Beyond monstration, in itself it tracks the activity of its user. Filmic cinema, of course, pictures differently from the platforms of computational electronics and its often unwitting data banks, but what it pictures has regularly foreseen such closed circuits of informatic flow, optic well before fiberoptic, in precisely their closing in on us. And not just in sci-fi film, and not just lately. As the opening chapter will show, as early as cinema's third decade, Fritz Lang's edited motion-capture and "networked" montage establish a cross-genre prototype for screen surveillance while his camera and lab work also anticipate, even before the audiovisual spyware imagined by Orwell's *1984*, certain postfilmic (that is, digitized) ramifications of a surveillance culture—and certainly its paranoia. In the wired network, even a directly visual (rather than data) tracking is no longer a matter, as in *M*, of following at a safe but embodied distance. The already figurative footprint of the subject to be tailed (and whose movements need tallying) is now electronic rather than corporeal to begin with—or, even at its most somatic, traced not by a motion across space but by a remote "positioning system" linked to satellite feeds.

Moreover, and more often all the time, sighting itself, even remote, can now seem relatively obsolete. The very notion of spatial position, let alone of site, has lost much of its visual sense under the new and broader rubric of dataveillance, where a panoptic regime is largely figurative—and "spying" little more than metaphoric. In most contemporary "walks of life," as they used to be called, with their new shadowing by a vast electronic cloud (determining our localized preferences if not our geographic position), the onetime etymon of the verb *survey* (the sighting of *sur-veiller*) has itself become, half a millennium after its introduction into English, a nearly dead metaphor. Monitoring is no longer necessarily rooted in things *over*-seen, *super*-vised. This new idea of surveillance taps a generalized source of anxiety about what can instead be intercepted in its coded digital form, mined, tabulated, aggregated. Privacy has found new ways to be violated, both by military-industrial and by corporate prying, all eyes aside.

Paper trails were one thing, once. Now the pathways of electronic detection are all but simultaneous with the intentional activity they trace. Call nothing mine that can be data mined. There is, for instance, no dead letter office for e-mail. And deletion (even when you've answered yes to whether you want the deleted items further deleted) is only another name to indicate the trash bin for tertiary storage. Everything is up for grabs, to be fished by institutional uploading. Yet all the while, lest so-called evidence of the senses be entirely forsworn, the unverbalized trace of your life—your body in motion—is peeled off from live time for potential attention, saved in digitized larval form, awaiting its rebirth as actual image on demand. What we say to each other out loud and on the move, unless bugged, may evade immediate capture, but little that we say in writing, even visibly do in public, will be safe from being cached for later scrutiny in dataveillant files or optically recorded for either kinetic replay or stop-action excerpt.

Film plots are naturally fascinated with this whole panoply of informatic intrigue, scopic and otherwise. But it is with the technics of audiovisual surveillance in particular, albeit a mere subset of a current global panoptic far from narrowly visual, where cinema nonetheless has most to say—simply by letting the variant modes of secret sighting be seen: viewed, reframed, displaced, hypermediated, and sometimes recontained. And not just seen, but seen in distinction from, relation to, or complicity with the narrative screen. The medial bias is built in. Movies about surveillance tend to be about surveillance by moving images, however much rounded out by other gumshoe throwbacks or electronic data manipulation. Where "enhanced interrogation" is the new euphemism for torture, the often facilitated violence of "enhanced surveillance" finds its most photogenic exposure (and at times suspect cinematic affinity) in the purview of remote and mobile spyware—in everything from the global machinations of big-budget political thrillers to the spate of so-called "found footage horror films" (plotted out by either handheld camcorder or mounted CCTV images) from 1999's *The Blair Witch Project* to the Spanish-made *[REC]* or the American *Paranormal Activity,* both from 2007, together with their several remakes and sequels.

Sight *Geist*

As the spirit of an age, invisible surveillance is indeed the sign of our times—and the timed record of our signals to each other, in act or gesture or electronic text. Dispiriting or not, it marks one outer limit of a supposed human autonomy already willingly attenuated. Beginning with our own wired affordances, we are part of the body-machine complex at once by election and by an exponentially potential detection. Every motion, contact, or communication may well, at any given moment, be ghosted by its computerized trace. If CCTV had been called "reality TV" at its origin, leaving the low-budget docudramas of exhibitionism spawned under that rubric to cast about for an alternate genre brand, the designation would certainly have been less of a misnomer. For much of the real is now on hold for electronic and televisual replay.

There is a genealogical irony in this automatized doubling of the world. Let's accept for a moment one credible metahistory proffered by intermedia approaches to literature and film. Say, then, that cinema arose in silence from the Romantic century of the literary doppelganger. It thus arrived to render the fantastic mechanical. But what has followed? After its audiovisual hegemony for most of another century, including the coming of sound and color, only now has modernity's dominant medium—as if by a strange reversion within technological advance—

yielded place to a digital phantom double of the human body's routine motions in 24/7 silent black-and-white record. This ghostly seconding is an audio-free computerized text (or otherwise strictly optic file)—when not including an actual voice intercept. One thing is hard not to notice: in this historical and technological transformation, motion pictures have been overshadowed by the ubiquitous picturing of motion. Incorporating as well the electronic imprints of motion-activated keypad discourse consigned to so-called deep storage, much of conscious life is now led on unconscious file.

Though the topic of surveillance is therefore even timelier than when I began these chapters, it is in the nature of this study that it can't be brought up to date. Instances multiply too quickly, inside the theater and out, many of them not just topical and passing but standing for the whole culture of surveillance in compressed terms. The main inference of such molested privacy is clear. Any action, whether knowingly recorded or not, may operate in the eerie, almost spectral zone—and potential frame of incrimination, sometimes even line of fire—of its electronic capture. In theatrical and broadcast formats alike, visual narrative is obsessed lately with the politics and psychology of electronic rescreening under one degree or another of a police regime. *The Wire*, one of the most acclaimed television series in the medium's history (2002–2008), is directly named for the surveillance network of urban Baltimore where its crime dramas unfold—and by which its incidents are frequently relayed: a title evoking everything from the synecdochic "wire" (for an undercover agent strapped with a secret recorder or transmitter) through the online cameras of an urban video network to the deployment of remote trackers and portable surveillance vans.

Synecdoche: repeatedly in these narratives, the instance representing both itself as technological fact and the encompassing social syndrome it pinpoints. Another organizing synecdoche for a later TV series—though in this case seemingly whole-for-part—appears in the title *Homeland*, with the entire US nation as justificatory shorthand for the plot's relentless surveillance operation. But in ironically identifying the narrative's unspoken "Homeland Security" protocols, the title suggests at the same time an institutional part-for-the-whole of a "terrorized" country whose borders are shored up in supposed defense against covert infiltration. And with another synecdochic irony, that recent British thriller mentioned above, *Closed Circuit* (John Crowley, 2013), turns its title metaphoric for the plot that encloses it. This is a film in which the ubiquitous CCTV surveillance of modern London records a truck-bomb attack, instigated under cover by a government counterterrorist scheme gone wrong. As the double-cross plot is brought to light, the title's freestanding phrase comes to figure the vicious circle resulting from an attempt to short-circuit—and so foreclose—the investigations of lawyers assigned to the case. They are themselves tracked and wiretapped while the innocent terror suspect and government fall guy is murdered in a prison "guarded" by spycam monitors, one of which has been briefly intercepted and shut down to mask all transmit of his fake suicide by secret service agents.

On the heels of so much, and in the midst of much more like it, there is, of course, the ultimate real-world synecdoche in the notorious case of the NSA defector Edward Snowden, with one operational link in the computerized data chain breaking open an entire nexus of electronic surveillance. As if it were the script for yet another Hollywood thriller in the odd-man-out mold, a single government agent—part-for-the-whole, cog in the machine—breaches US cybersecurity by hacking the evidence of the government's own privacy violations by way of electronic data mining. As is repeatedly the case with film versions of this synecdochic pattern, clandestine interception and its medial channels are caught in just such a closed circuit of cause and effect, perpetration and resistance. The same US public up in arms about the government's covert infractions of civil liberties has certainly seen it coming on the fictional screen for years. In the Snowden case, as in a film over a decade earlier like *Enemy of the State*, three talismanic words are exposed in political disconnect: national, security, agency—with patriotic retrenchments either summarily curtailing the freedom of personal agency or being defied by the criminal violations of a whistle-blower's principled solo insurgency.

Among fictional representations coterminous with the Snowden affair, the series *Homeland* has carried the logic furthest—or say deepest (somatically at least), beginning with its "troubled" heroine as a CIA agent *too* paranoid and *too* bipolar even for an antiterrorist operative. Before her lust for the truth has turned her prey into her lover, she authorizes a diverse battery of surveillance cameras to monitor every other move of this American citizen and suspected traitor: an Iraq war hero of widespread TV exposure—and resulting elevation to US Congress—whom she discovers to be a secret Islamic (perhaps jihadi) convert. But finally the kind of undercover technology (rather than broadcast media) shadowing him is turned, at the climax of the second season, against the CIA network itself and its former director, the sitting vice president, in revenge for Mideast drone strikes. In an ironic reversal of the warrantless and illegal cameras both hidden in the veteran's home and following him by wired van or satellite feed, such covert monitoring—in the hands of the terrorist cell he may still be working for (or is perhaps merely blackmailed by, to save the undercover heroine's life)—becomes an invasive access of a uniquely "biopolitical" sort.

It is a stratagem, in fact, whose technical plausibility has been stressed by bloggers and TV reviewers in consultation with medical engineers. For what comes to pass is that the suspected traitor has located the serial number of the vice president's pacemaker and texted it to the terrorist leader, whose computer technician (introduced out of the blue, as if out of the ether) can hack into the digital circuits of this prosthesis and cause its lethal misfire. In yet another synecdochic shift from macro to micro, and bypassing the external physical torture played out in counterpoint to this plotline, something like the heart-pounding rush of an electronically tracked car chase, staple of the genre, has here been diverted to the interception of the body's organic pulse itself. Even internal organs are no longer safe from surveillance and targeting. Such benign procedures as "multiple resonance imaging" (MRI), not to mention the electroshock treatments administered to relieve the heroine's psychotic tendencies at the end of season one, have been digitally retooled in this case—turned involuntary, remote, and homicidal. And the series still continues: both *Homeland* and the narrative cycle it represents. Without knowing what's next on either front, it is enough for now to allow that TV productions as well as mainstream cinema have rarely, at the level of both topic and technical execution, been more tightly in stride with contemporaneous social and political debate. Screen narrative's own evolved medium as cable-delivered broadcast video or digitally projected cinema is certainly inseparable, as such, from any cultural angst over our new digital ambience that it may choose to explore or exploit. The coming pages investigate the cinematic prehistory of this lockstep convergence.

The Theater of "Espials": A "Seeing Unseen"

Which is why, with this topic, any gestures at a preface or foreword must begin by looking backward. Very far back for a moment, pre-"media": to the aesthetics of surveillance at stake in advance of any representational apparatus whatsoever. For a philosopher like Stanley Cavell—concerned as he is with the relation of stage to film, and of each to the world it enacts—Shakespearean theater is an art born in exactly the moment of Cartesian epistemological skepticism. This is a questioning of the senses whose aesthetic testings reach all the way through to our suspended disbelief in "the world viewed" of cinema (a concept entitled by his first film book).[1] As such, tragic theater's purgative dynamic anticipates one central definition of film for Cavell: a world "complete without me" (indeed impervious to me) but yet "present to me."[2] Similarly, as Cavell demonstrates, one pressure point in the affect of Shakespearean tragedy is our incapacity for intervention. In our pity and fear, we could leap to the stage, but although we'd be ruining an actor's scene, we'd be doing nothing to spare the eyes of the *character* from being gouged out. Theater teaches us, from within its constrained identifications, the very limits of such sympathy and its urges. And not just in obvious cases. It is not merely in the "play within the play" in *Hamlet*, as rethought by Cavell, that we see our relation to enactment played out as surveillance-with-a-difference.[3] Earlier, in a scene not discussed by Cavell, with Claudius as watcher of reactions rather than watched for his own, this agent of what the usurper himself calls "lawful espials" is bent on stage-managing a scene of audiovisual eavesdropping by which he and Polonius will "so bestow" themselves that, "seeing unseen," they may judge of the encounter between Hamlet and Ophelia to determine—to *see whether* (as we say)—it is prompted by mad desire or otherwise: a derangement either erotic or (as Claudius suspects) more dangerously political.[4] Standing in for our own curiosity about the coming rendezvous, and those rights of trespass theater "bestows" on us, these self-authorized snoops ("stowed" out of sight) are poised to become either sexual voyeurs or state spies.

Yet "seeing unseen" is, of course, a condition of surveillance that is also the nature of attended performance, live or screened. Configured at the level of perception itself rather than affect, such unseen sighting helps establish that so-called aesthetic distance whose remove is to be rendered not just literal but strategic, and anything but aesthetic, under the complementary mandates of surveillance. Spectatorial emplacement is often revealed in this way as the structural opposite, but also the first cause, of a so-called covert operation. What the dramatic audience can't do to prevent or mitigate an onstage disaster is what distinguishes theater from a surveillance whose real-time purpose may in fact be intervention—whether forensic or even, today, electro-ballistic. And when, further, over historical time, one adds to enactments at the Globe not just the apparatus of record and projection, advancing from phonography through cinema to digital video, but, further, the new remote relays of global panoptics—developed for our latest "theaters" of war and proliferating mostly unchecked since for "securitizing" our subways and garages, our parks and hallways—a broad lineage is apparent. From Cartesian doubt about the existence of the world and other minds—therapized in theatergoing according to Cavell, and later in movie viewing—we have arrived at the bursting electronic archive of the world's populated duration awaiting not belief but forensic assessment via screen interface.

The passive optical data of a worldwide security network is not a simulacrum of social space (except in the final sci-fi turns of the last two chapters) so much as a latency lifted to image only on demand: as if to say the "world viewed" only on a need-to-know basis. By contrast with a previous and manifold culture of the image, this new dispensation both *is* and, in narrative terms, *makes* a difference almost ineffable. For what is quietly compromised in every way by video surveillance is the very status of the image on which it depends—depends, without being materially based. Or put it that what must be distinguished in the digital backlog of surveillance video is the passive data bank from the active picture. The time log (and resultant lag) of space and action passes indiscriminately into storage until retrieved ad hoc as retroactively motivated visuals. The present disappears from instant to instant on the way to its selective re-presentation—unless of course the optical data feed is accessed in real time, more like theater than film, for the purpose of interception. At which point image vanishes into actionable sighting—and in some cases into immediate bull's-eye.

In light of this, one needs a long view of screen viewing: a kind of telephoto framing meant to bring certain distant contours frontward for a clearer sense of continuity amid difference. From chapter to chapter we will look to exemplary episodes in the cross-cut logic of film montage, from its dormancy as an engine of narrative through its classic proliferation in parallel editing to its latest variants in those alternate realities and parallel worlds that structure the computerized time-travel surveillance of recent sci-fi. At certain turning points in this intermittent technological history of the cinematic medium, three terms can seem like one: screening, narrative, surveillance. In my subtitle, they are meant to read not just topically, as a list of keywords, but syntactically: telescoped into a single network of linked visualizations whenever—most obviously, though not exclusively—the image system of plot locks down on a secondary screening device. My subject is indeed the screening of narrative surveillance—but with surveillance being not just a subtheme within the ventures of the medium but a lurking synonym (or call it another synecdoche) both for a certain kind of narrative vantage point and for its received projection by the audience. All novelists, as one among them has said, "are spies."[5] All readers too. And, hence, all narrative viewers. And yet . . . .

Montage and espionage don't of course use each other up as categories. In certain screen realizations, they instead question each other. One result of this interrogation is that "surveillance film" unravels under scrutiny into surveillance on film, which in turn can suggest either the material base or medium of strategic (often secret) sighting in moving-image form or instead (and my dominant topic here) scenes of such sighting narrated on film—even while "film" has come increasingly to mean digital video. This last is a transformation with which any approach to recent onscreen fables of surveillance must come to grips. My attempt at this is to hold up only a few representative samples under a certain degree of sustained pressure, a pressure applied not just from their cultural moment and its dominant technology but from the media history of their narrative technique. And applied, as well, from the audiovisual theory returned here—returned from neglect or rejection—to differentiate the phases of that history as well as the sampled impact of its artifacts.

From Time-Based to Time-Coded

Identifying literature along with film as time-based media is not yet to have named the medium of either—just one perceptual quality they share. Call it the serial disappearance of their increments. A film can of course be rescreened, a page reread. But reading as much as viewing must go at first with the flow, alphabetic, photogrammatic: the former dissolved into word recognition, then syntax, the latter a subliminal flicker assimilated—more automatically (or unconsciously) yet—to optical, then scenic, manifestation. It is one curious "bonus feature" of the transfer of film to DVD, not in the latter's marketed add-ons but as an inbuilt effect of digitization, that the disk format has rendered its platform more like a page than a filmic projection: available in its lateral access, that is, for immediate reverse and replay—as well for the freezing and slowing that were formerly rhetorical for film, but are now operational, a matter of mediation rather than narrative technique.

A committed "reader" of film might once have enthusiastically sided with Roland Barthes in hopes for the rescinded rivalry of the sibling arts and the bundling of everything together under the umbrella of text.[6] But that was then: then when—with no seeming risk of losing our sense of film as such (as not just an auteurist but an inalienably cinematographic art)—it seemed reasonable enough that an alternate semiotic imperative could offer a useful resistance to that brand of strictly appreciative commentary not yet operating, for film and other media as well, under the sanction of the textual turn. All that changed quickly, and twice over. Under the subsequent thumb of a diffuse historicist and cultural studies model—including most often in cinema studies an emphasis on the modes of production and distribution in the movie industry and their "culture of reception"—any textualist premise has been all but wholly overthrown in most quarters.[7] And all this has been transpiring while so-called medium specificity, let alone its theorized inferences, has lost its hold on attention as well—and not just in the exchanges of cultural studies scholarship but in those cross-disciplinary efforts of a general narratology looking for the rudimentary functions of storytelling apart from their featuring forth in a given plastic or scriptive form.

This has a third and markedly untimely result as well, given our media-historical moment. At just the point in technological history when the photomechanical basis of cinematic processing and projection was surrendering ground to digitizations of various sorts, from editing to simulated imaging—and when whatever difference this might make, this turn to the postfilmic image, should have been most compelling to estimate—institutional film studies (already transformed instead to cinema studies, and already in large part "post-theory" in persuasion) wasn't broadly poised for rising to any such materialist optical occasion. The task has been left instead mostly to new media studies, which has a tendency to leave narrative cinema far behind for its preferred evidentiary base in experimental video. Though downplayed in thematic cinema studies, however, and even in its subsequent recasting as screen studies, the technological occasion of a newly hybrid cinematic medium, exponentially digital in production and distribution, was (and is) real—and has seemed to me of immediate narrative import.

That sense of things is already on record. My two previous books, and several intervening articles, can be filed together as one selective account of this medial transition.[8] I would propose them as a "before and after shot," except that the picture, as such, was always in motion and the transition is scarcely over yet. So why another book while still in midstream? Beyond the question of why me? (the erstwhile "textualist"), there looms, that is, the why now? Given that paired studies of mine straddle the digital watershed, one looking back on film's photo genealogy, the other toward an already encroaching postfilmic system, why, then, a third while still under the sway of the second's assessed moment? It's not just that there is suddenly new evidence (isn't there always?). It's that something new has happened, to which narrative cinema has been variously, dubiously, and sometimes deviously responding. I think of it as the hypertrophic instrumentalization of a time-based medium reduced to the new time-coded digital tapes or disks of security cams, whose spatiotemporal coordinates—as in "Terminal 3 men's room 8/3/12

1:40 am"—have now been so often folded back into conventions of narrative cinema and spun out as scenic captioning, even when no surveillance thematic is immediately on tap.

But before exploring the deliberately theoretical ramifications still extant (still viable, that is, as I count on showing) concerning these films—especially in their narrative imbrication with closed-circuit video—let me note a related experiment in simulated surveillance equally topical, even though non-narrative. This, from the realm of installation rather than cinematic art: a piece of conceptual video from an artist elsewhere interested in photographic exposures of covert as well as public space. Thomas Demand is a German conceptualist sculptor-photographer who, in his most famous works, constructs cardboard replicas of instantly recognized settings, typically based on photographic extracts from previous media—and often from scenes of visual (even mediatized) scrutiny in themselves. The resulting "sites," not human scenes, might actually seem, as part of a specifically German tradition, to invoke or even travesty the precision-tooled sterilized geometries of the New Objectivist (Neue Sachlichkeit) images that, as we are to find, so much influenced Lang's 1931 set design in *M*. (See especially the 1995 stairwell reconstruction called simply *Staircase*.) Demand's riveting series of works features at one point a life-size mockup of a TSA security checkpoint (*Gate*, 2004), scanners blank, trays empty of human evidence. Demand has also produced a handmade and then rephotographed "stage set" of the ransacked Stasi headquarters after 1989: a case of surveillance surveyed, where every unearthed file is composed merely of blank sheets of paper, their onetime use effaced by the very turn of history. This exacting sculptural artist then photographs these simulacral spaces with such high-definition clarity that the tertiary reproduction works against the uneasy illusionism of the "mise-en-scène." As if in a parody of real surveillance technology, hyperdefinition probes no secrets except the artifice of the scene itself.

This whole procedure is brilliantly reversed in a video work of Demand's installed for an exhibition at SFMOMA in 2010, mostly on still photography, called *Exposed: Voyeurism, Surveillance, and the Camera Since 1870*. There, to my surprise, knowing as I did only Demand's photographic work—and there to the deliberate surprise of every gallerygoer in transit—was the museum looker looked upon: but also, yet again, only by simulacrum. This resulted from a high-definition video loop that lasted approximately a minute and a half and repeated the sweep of an airport CCTV cam installed high on its own neutral wall—a closed-circuit mounting recorded by Demand in medium close-up as it scans the traffic of (unseen) bodies spread out below it: a loop that was itself projected, homologously, near the gallery's own ceiling and identified by discreet wall plaque below simply as *Camera*. Not *lucida* or *obscura* but rather *simula*—yet ironically elucidating as such.

This ontologically gutted but no less cautionary work, the very image of monitoring turned monitory, thereby conveys the peripheral sense at first of the museum's own security apparatus rather than an object of display. And it was not just a video, but an audiovisual, installation as well, whose ambient stereo sound, even if you were alone in the gallery, sutured you back into the public space of passers-by as passers spied. Hovering above the other photos and videos exposed to our view in the *Exposed* show, this image had the effect of exposing us. But doing so as artifice, not as real technology. The logic: all it takes for surveillance to work, in general, is for you to see a sign of yourself being seen. That's the piece's final irony: even the dummied mechanical eye operates as an instrumental object of constraint.

The rest of this book, of course, is concerned not with looking, in museum display, at the moving image of a camera, but, instead, with looking at moving images through such a monocular apparatus—in its cinematic rather than CCTV variant. But before turning first and at length to Lang's *M*, his surveillance thriller from 1931, the coming Introduction needs to frame his camera's own logic within the broad range of screen issues—first media-historical, then theoretical—that offer the fullest context for the montage initiatives of that first of Lang's sound films. And, not least among those issues, to show what film theory might help highlight, reorient, or set straight. Film theory in particular, not cinema studies (or screen studies) more generally (institutional rather than medial)—and, again, film theory in its most exhaustive form as apparatus theory. Why? Exactly for what has been lost sight of lately in too much film writing: the film medium itself, in various degrees of digital eclipse. Without paradox, then, an argument for certain local returns to theory can be advanced on entirely *practical* grounds: theory getting retrieved for discussion whenever a viewer is on the lookout for its unique audiovisual dividends, the true conceptual yield of its analytic returns.

INTRODUCTION: NARRATIVE SPYCAMS—A FORE-SHORTENED VIEW

Our topic: the convergence of a time-based medium, narrative film, with a time-coded recording technology that in various ways both parodies and contaminates narrative cinema. This collision, at times a mutant crossbreeding, registers in the very style of contemporary filmmaking. It does so not only in the switch-screen cuts or click-and-drag zooms from one video feed to another on inset monitors or control room panels, with their frequent equivalent in the narrative's own full-screen montage. It manifests itself, as well, in the ubiquitous return of the silent film intertitle in geographic captions for scene changes—as if episodic narrative omniscience had found a new model for its versatility in the auto-identification of retrieved surveillance footage and its video datelines, punched out letter-by-letter across the screen. But these subtitles are only the explicit tip of an iceberg in the relation—medium-deep and several genres wide—between the narrative establishing shot and the fixed-position POV of time-imprinted surveillance footage, where duration is automatic rather than, as in narrative, selective and elliptical. And where detection is intrinsic, internally engineered: not a genre but a search function.

Any such time log of latently incriminating evidence is a flashpoint in contemporary societal (as well as cinematic) terms. Narrative films that know and show this are not just topical, not even the one called *Look* (Adam Rifkin, 2007, discussed in chapter 3) that begins with an intertitle to the effect that the four billion hours of digital video laid down each week under surveillance protocols include, via diverse security cams, roughly two hundred unbidden images of each of us, on average, every day. Films about electronic searches, verbal or especially visual—films increasingly electronic in their own production—are also films about the medium-defining relation between viewing and spying, between optical overview and social control. That is my most immediate subject: narratives filming surveillance, or vice versa (as in the case of *Look*, whose emplotment purports to be the mere sampling of security cam footage).

Other topics impinge, of course, but remain sidelined. I won't be considering in any detail the flip side of optic inspection fostered by our image culture: the rampant desire for video self-display, as symptomatized in the so-called "reality" of television shows like *Big Brother* (with its collective household surveillance, 24/7) or *The Bachelor* (where every sexy date might as well be datelined along the bottom of the "live," however intrinsically factitious, footage that purveys it). In all of this programming, the very idea of privacy must be *performed* for the camera by the knowing show-off (or sacrificial victim, as in *The Hunger Games* film [Gary Ross, 2012]) rather than by some honestly unsuspecting subject.[1] Instead of these extrusions of privacy for protonarrative spectacle, I'll be looking to that unique homology between agents in the world, unwittingly recorded, and characters in a film who act as if they weren't being (until they are sometimes made to know otherwise). These are subjects whose very being as fictional people, in fact, depends on our suspended disbelief in just this regard: this matter of primary (if not secondary) camera regard.

Nor will the coming discussion be much concerned, except when the topic is raised by individual films, with the wider erosion of privacy induced by the blandishments of electronic interactivity and covered elsewhere in new media scholarship under, in one monograph, the rubric of "iSpying."[2] Directed at narrative cinema, this book's consideration gravitates instead, it might be said, to the self-conscious and remediated zone, the cinematographic leeway, between poetic license and search warrant. Such is the zone staked out—almost from the beginning of the medium—in the drift from an entirely documentary image to the recording of a staged scene. In the continued spirit of this rearward-as-forward glance, we return, this time, not to cinema's precedents in Shakespeare's early modern theater but to film technology's coincidence with the dawning of electric modernism: to its machinic place, that is, in the new ethos of techno-aesthetics whose narrative entailments for the spectator—rapt, lured, sutured, and even implicitly scrutinized—the remainder of this Introduction will sketch out.

Animatography and Genre

A year after the Lumière brothers unveiled to Parisian acclaim their legendary "Cinématographe," Robert W. Paul exhibited his own "Theatrograph" at Finsbury Technical College in London (20 February 1896) before eventually moving a retooled version to the Alhambra Music Hall in Leicester Square (25 March 1896) under the rebranded and eventually dominant name "Animatograph."[3] Traced between these two venues, in compressed form, is the giant step of the medium not just from experimental science to commercial spectacle but from laboratory to the former site of live theater. Indeed, one of the short film sequences at the Alhambra involves a "lightning cartoonist" filmed in a recreation of his theatrical act: drawing, in the case of this brief documentary snippet, a rapid caricature of Bismark. Cinema thus greeted London audiences in the partly acknowledged form of a glimmering photographic cartoon under the cover of an unbroken representational gesture.

But Paul recognized the need for "adding interest to wonder"—as if to say the human interest of storytelling—and thus filmed "a comic scene called The Soldier's Courtship."[4] The lightly voyeuristic "story" (a clinch and kiss) in a single strip might remind us that film historians' insistence on the "interest" in the "wonder" of the lifelike "attraction" itself, vivid enough at the outset, should not lead us to overlook the latent distinction between spectacle and at least a rudimentary plot.[5] For this was a distinction that indeed dawned upon the commercial imagination almost coterminously with the first projector lamp. And if this is true of a simple wordless romance, it's equally true of another perdurable genre: cops and robbers. The film Paul had made the year before, in 1895, with photographer Birt Acres, called *Arrest of a Pickpocket*—with its low-keyed chase and apprehension "plot" in a single shot—is perhaps a better inaugural candidate for the dubious (since at the time unused) category of British "fiction film."[6] But something else slips in there, through the cracks of sprocketed motion. For this is a brief slice-of-police-life episode whose mise-en-scène puts into regress not only still images in the form of flyers and wanted posters on the wall behind the characters (anticipating the ambient signage of Lang's *M*) but also two stick figure drawings to the left and right of the triangulated principals. Chalked in prefilmic time by child vandals, no doubt, these are images that—in the unmistakable flicker-effect of early projection—become, in their minimal spastic animation, among the first cartoons.

One historical trajectory of the screen image to be isolated in this book by the ironies of surveillance is thus encapsulated here with earliest implementations of the narrative impulse: as a function, in this case, of overseen criminology and its medial friction. Original viewers of films like *Arrest of a Pickpocket* would have had no real trouble reconciling the stroboscopic flicker of the medium's unprecedented magic with the enthrallment of narrative event, however simplistic—since both are what they came for in that newly virtual pay-per-view spectacle of recorded purview. They eagerly accepted the medium along with the message. As we do today, but in a different sense—one almost wholly recuperated by narrative. Think of the repeated digital static, the medial "interference" in that sense, that roughens again and again the optic surface of surveillance thrillers—usually, but not always, in the form of transmissions on an embedded video screen: this as a mode of narrative remediation, or technological interface, rather than, as in 1896, an inevitability of the cinematic apparatus.

Whether or not that quaint and accidental metafilmic distraction of flickering stick figures once put a minor drag on the narrated (apart from incidental) motion of that earliest "police procedural," whether or not it troubled in the least the transparency of its incipient genre action, it is certainly the case that another facet of cinematography and its popular convictions was successfully installing itself at the turn of that first cinematic century. For what is clear from those early British examples—the stolen kiss, the apprehended thief—is that we find there, in embryonic form, not so much two aborning genres as two abiding modalities of invested camerawork: eroticism ogled, transgression framed for capture. Claudius and Polonius might still be at their invisible watch, waiting to see either a peepshow or a scene of revealed sedition. On offer to a British audience there at the end of a later century, in other words, are two sides of exactly that coin on whose narrative payout this book is to concentrate. My topic, in short, is a constitutive cinematic voyeurism attended to in narratives that render this condition more or less explicit—but do so under genre conventions that may work to de-eroticize, sublimate, deflect, or even mask it. For among the long-term results of adding interest to wonder, apart from the particulars of romance or crime scenarios, is exactly that mode of surveillance narrative where plot, subsumed to complot, focuses any *dis*interested optical wonder on—or through—the wholly tactical (rather than libidinal) gaze. More than pickpockets have come under arrest by inferred (and increasingly explicit) camerawork. Numerous genre variants soon arose to detect, corner, and inspect the action of characters imaged on-screen—and sometimes to investigate the imaging agency such plots themselves deploy and manipulate.

That investigation can of course remain tacit, often disingenuous. Even the on-screen injunctions to turn off any of your myriad electronic devices at the theater, where the same trailers you've just watched are also incidentally available, is a kind of subliminal commercial, just short of named product-placement: a reminder of this ubiquitous technology for those few who haven't yet purchased theirs. And in the genre plot of not just defied digital surveillance but mastered electronic countersurveillance—the kind of plot that so often follows, these days, from this friendly reminder as the lights go down—you may well identify (you're certainly cued to) with the justly paranoid and computer-savvy protagonists in their insurgent raids against a more coercive data profiling in all its forms, everything from the remote sampling of CCTV through biometric facial identification to satellite transmits. It is precisely because you can't ultimately beat them that you've got to join them in the closed circuits of monitored action and technological pushback. Powerless to escape, the heroes repeatedly hack back into the system, playing as if to win. This makes for films offering a salving parable of enhanced audiovisual affordance. Victory comes from seizing the keypad of power. And there lies the latent ideological surcharge of the counter-surveillance mode. Removed from the arena of on-screen heroic exploit—operating across the horizontal ground of daily human commerce—one new and unusually deceptive form of alienation (an alienation figured on-screen in hyperbolic genre terms as lethal surveillance and, fitful at best, the brave-hearted miracles of its defeat) is the need to stay perpetually tuned in, at once online and on alert.

For the screen audience, part of what gets circulated by such plots is the lurking inherence of the already *watched* within the merely *visualized*. Here is one version of the fall into spectatorship (from a purer viewing) posited and debunked at once, as originary myth, by apparatus theory. Even before the historical development of screen storytelling per se, this involves the audience's founding disenchantment with the visual medium as such, as a mechanism for projecting and framing rather than simply manifesting the world. Among other potential narrative formats, the image no longer conveyed in its unmotivated purity suggests surveillance cinema in gestation, Lang waiting in the wings. Lang, with his explicit conflation of aggressive looking and narrative drive, including the long shadow this casts over the history of film montage—right down to the electronic ingenuities of our current thriller plots in the surveillance mode.

Current—and politically overdetermined. Operating as immediate historical prologue to this book are the escalations of both optical technology and its surveillance protocols in these years of the War on Terror—including the continuous risk of such a campaign turning into that perpetual war, that perennial state of emergency (and exception), presaged by George Orwell in *1984*, whose novel leads off discussion in the wake of Lang. As if answering to the global broadcast of the 9/11 catastrophe, its images disseminated (as everyone recognized) in a nightmarish montage hard to distinguish from a "disaster pic," the United States has since taken our postfilmic technology to war in response—at first with a "shock and awe" strategy in the War on Terror borrowed in fact from the negative sublime of the Hollywood action thriller in an apocalyptic mode. But there is a complementary optic at stake, beyond the *spectacle* of destruction, whereby visual technology itself is actually recruited in the prosecution of these conflicts. In proliferating ways on any number of shifting fronts, we have outfitted our troops—and in part our unmanned attack planes—with audiovisual prosthetics: digital helmet cams, telephoto and infrared sights, remote launching software, and the like, even while our martial science has been answered by the enemy in low-tech kind: as, for instance, by the video record of our aggression on Arab camcorders, for anti-imperialist propaganda, or by the cell-phone detonation of improvised bombs whose damage can be captured visually and then transmitted from the same remote hand-held unit. Our digito-video war is the enemy's as well.

The Hollywood fallout for the war film scenario has been rapid and unmistakable—faster than in any of Friedrich Kittler's previous research-and-development cycles, whereby military experiment in encrypted communication regularly precedes, as his evidence so consistently shows, all commercial media advance.[7] Instead, action plots now upgrade real-world ballistic optics with fantastic redeployments of every sort. In cinematic terms, a once venerable genre has imploded like a self-detonated sabotage device, and in place of the mangled and enervated war film we have a roster of Homeland Security thrillers. These are narratives whose implicit work is to recover the reconnaissance and surveillance technology from the narrative debris of the war picture and turn it to new plots of covert picturing in the stateside War on Terror. This genre displacement has made for its own cycle in mainstream narrative formats, so familiar by now, so ubiquitous, so emergently generic in their own right, that, for instance, the TV series *Homeland* doesn't even need "Security" in its title, as we've seen, to strike the note of national paranoia and preventive spyware. Such are the new narratives in which reconnaissance and targeting, surveillance and the lethal erasure of "take out," share with overseas assault the same viewfinders and computer grids, even at times the same drone deployment.

War films, of course, by genre mandate, normally elide any clear distinction between surveillance and violence. In these films, what sightings are unmistakably after is a hit. In the high-tech manhunts and spycraft backfire narratives that have developed alongside—and especially since—the openly ballistic use of the same electronic technologies in recent overseas war plots, it is also the case that *coming into view* may in and of itself be fatal. And across the decades from Lang's surveillance masterworks to, say, the *Bourne* films, the steady formal preparation for screening per se as a postfilmic—but still metacinematic—spy machinery has therefore involved, as well, a set of formal constraints and adjustments. These include a crossfeed of genre expectations and technical options determined by the overlapping coordinates of two main modes of classic plotting. Detection is one function of surveillance; surveillance is one mode of detection. Thought of in terms of Venn diagrams, the correlated operations overlap whenever an identified person crosses the line into an apparent (visible or audible) transgression: becomes not just a subject but a suspect. Or, in the title of the all-too-predictable CBS series a *Person of Interest*: a person subject, in the case of this series, to a routinized technique by which an electronic surveillance program's computer-zoom function is taken up as the very rhythm of editing—in and beyond actual narrated sightings. The genre consequences of the broader tendency are obvious enough in the rough, though in a given case sometimes elusive, with the detective figure morphing into surveillance engineer—and vice versa. And not just elusive, but at times ethically as well as epistemologically dubious.

This troubled stance has a rather pointed narrative history. So ingrained is surveillance in the nature of narrative that it is, as "reconnaissance," the fourth function mentioned by Vladimir Propp, out of thirty-one permutable ingredients of the folktale.[8] But it was the surveillance, there, of hero (or his precincts) *by villain*, rather than the other way around: the located target sniffed out (and sometimes snuffed out) by an external threat. To turn that inherent aggression of spying and oversight into a badge of honor or a brandished weapon of heroic defense requires a deliberate narrative rechanneling of the folktale via the new nineteenth-century invention (Edgar Allan Poe and Charles Dickens) of the detective quester narrative, mutating eventually into the surveillance film, whether its plot involves the military-technological bureaucracy bent on locating a defector or the odd-man-out bent on hacking back in—or of course, repeatedly, both. After Poe and Dickens, that is, the manifold apparatus of the new medium, cinema, and since then digital imaging, complicates—not beyond recognition exactly, but beyond clean segregation—the linked *techne* of surveillance (before the fact) and detection (after).

If this isn't the stuff of cinema theory as well as media theory, and precisely because of how postfilmic the latest cinematic execution of such narratives often is, then theory really is dead. There, I've said it. And, alas, you didn't hear it here first, and certainly not only in the conjectural mode either. Where D.N. Rodowick brings to bear his best philosophical perspective on the question so as to deliver a conjoint eulogy and elegy for theory, the present argument, by contrast, in regard to the rigors of "suture theory" in particular, offers more of a recovery operation.[9] Not exactly *Saving Private Ryan*, but not *Letters from Iwo Jima* either. Not a disciplinary battle scene at all, in fact, doomed or recuperative, but just a venture in renewed deployment—freed, at least briefly, from methodological contestation. If it works out in practice, then it still works, as it were, in theory. And the proof of suture is always in the texture of shot transition itself, as subsequent discussion will recover at several climactic points across separate chapters.

Apparatus / *Cyberopsis*: Narratography and the Fate of Suture

With its focused recourse in this way to apparatus theory, this book is not a history of surveillance in film, let alone on film. It is a book of selected examples that invite our lingering over the very distinction: surveillance effected by an image system like film when recorded *in* it (as narrative) or *on* it (as document). The motive, and the hope, is unabashedly theoretical, but not predominantly. Analysis chooses to reanimate the theoretical canon, where necessary, in order to spur its continued potential: the always renewable *application* of things theoretical as an interpretive appliance—ad hoc, exploratory, localized rather than blanketing. But given the evidence here, or any I might have amassed in a longer and more historically definitive survey, the effort would never primarily have been to reinvigorate apparatus theory in the merely passing light of given film texts, still less to demonstrate their textuality—their signification rather than their mimesis—in the light of such theory. The partners are equal in this effort at restored collaboration. On the one hand, media theory proves its utility on the narrative proof text. On the other, cinematic narrative engages us beneath and beyond plot, at the level of medium (as well as cultural milieu), and is soonest seen to do so under the analytic auspices of theory.

A longstanding commitment of this sort on my part has been sorely tried by the desiccating scorched-earth policies of so-called post-theory, leaving supposedly arid what was once fertile ground: namely, cinematographic analysis. This is what I have tried reviving in *Framed Time* under the modal parameters and medium specificity of filmic (and now digital) "narratography." As distinct from the morphology of a term like cinematography, but at the same level of pictographic (and audiovisual) detail, narratography is not what is done to the view to produce it as image, sound-synced or otherwise, but what is done with the image in reception, to understand it as such—as well as to get some medial standing beneath the obvious (or sometimes overtly tricky) plot momentum that propels it. Suture theory thus offers one way of realizing how deeply unstable this standing is. One doesn't need the Lacanian figure of cognition flickering-in-eclipse to explain the groundlessness of the cinematic image in the exchange of shots. One simply has to look—look hard. At which point, at least after a fuller discussion in the coming chapter, one can appreciate how suture theory's stress on the move from cinema (as manifest image) to "the cinematic" (as system) might illuminate as well, and in some detail, the later shift from the photomechanical to the postfilmic. Including, in surveillance, the subsumption of seeing to sighting.

Few books are less nostalgic for Lacanian abstractions than this one, yet few less inclined to boast of having moved beyond them in the gloating lassitude of the "post." Isn't there some middle ground between proselytizing and anathematizing? And what occupies our attention when we occupy it? Surely something more than cultural generalizations or cognitive positivisms—meant to cleanse viewing from the impositions of psychoanalysis and Marxism, in all their supposed ideological subterfuges. But repression and interpellation were only the marching cry of high theory—say, its strategy. Its tactics were more trenchant and flexible. To my eye, the power of suture theory—to take that quintessential instance of apparatus study—already resided, to begin with, in its cinematographic analysis, its precision about montage and about the dialectical relation of camerawork to image and of image to audience. This was what its proponents got so indisputably right before the further theorization (via Lacan and/or Althusser) of a viewer's disempowerment by each shot change, a slap in the absent interface that must be repressed, sublimated, converted to a more nervous and ultimately perverse scopophilia that interpellates us (in Althusser's concept of ideological acquiescence) into, for instance, a masculinist regime of the look or a consumerist passivity before the image stream.

If remembering, or elegizing, the suture in this way—in an obituary for its political as well as metapsychological ambitions, and with the intent instead of salvaging its optical rigor—could be said, in objection, to pare away the theory per se from its retained formalist exactitude, then at least what we have left is what we always had. This is film writing's most cogent analysis of a serial privation in the world viewed, as much at the level of the framed view on-screen as of the photo-frames in motion. This is an absence, a gapping—lateral and frontal both, enchained by the image strip as well as at right angles to it in imagined space—that is made manifest at times in narrative: an account of which, an account if not a theory, would as a result be part of any closely textured response (if "reading" itself is too text-theoretical a term) to a given film.

But what kinds of films? It's not only the masterpiece that can take the medium to pieces in revealing ways. Even routine screen narratives are often more interesting as film than as films, or now as digitized cinema more than as movies—interesting for the way their medium facilitates or defies the logic of their plots, abets or shreds it. Not every motion picture can test and stretch the outer limits of cinema's possibility. Many screen narratives, however, instructively test the medium's inner limits: the pliability of editing and focus, the options of camera angle, the techniques of transition. Call it the grammar of montage rather than the rhetoric or stylistics of vision. And this grammatical testing is all the more suggestive in our increasingly postfilmic moment when those inner limits, like the outer ones now, are typically hybrid: a combination of electronic compositing and digital editing in a variable mix with the almost vestigial photomechanics of the celluloid frame line.

No apology conceivably needed for dwelling (yet again) on Lang's benchmark film *M*. But none is in order, either, for taking up the minor contemporary sci-fi and espionage thrillers with which I conclude, especially the time-loop fantasies *Déjà Vu* (Tony Scott, 2006) and *Source Code* (Duncan Jones, 2011). For each of these, like *M*, closes in on itself and its materialization, its availability to view, in direct response to the narrative content of invasive surveillance. In case after case, analysis is productively drawn to films that are in themselves works of medial analysis. Which means in part works of historical perspective. The reign of photo-indexical cinema may be behind us, but the projector still is as well, even in digital projection. We are there on the outside (where the image is assembled and manifested), looking on—if not really in. Whether or not there's a curtain to part, the lights go down as the lit image, thrown forward, comes up. And from the variable patchwork occlusion of that pure beam of light (all the more mosaic, though imperceptible as such, in the epoch of the pixel), a rapid play of shadows—and their differential pigmentation—chops up the plane into a picture. Forgetting or ignoring this, we may incline to take it (in) simply as a view. But not for long.

So begins, according to apparatus theory, as we will soon pursue it more closely, the first of two degrees of separation. Cinema (image kinesis) becomes cinematic (selected and framed) on its way to the possibility of narrative. And as soon as the recognized framing cuts away from the inaugural view into a positioned new sighting, we begin to forget the wonder of the moving image as such in our wonder about motivation—about the *what next?* Enter the narrative impetus. But even a fully developed plot, later in this history of cinema, may have need to remember the cinematic for us, to revert to it, to drop away from the filmed discourse to the framed awareness of filming, to make the work of the medium itself as telling as the story—indeed, a part of the story. Such a plot may, in other words, make a roughening of the representation—some glitch, perhaps, in the continuity of vision—over into a narrative supplement: convert some exposed impasse or trespass at the inner limit of montage into a quotient of story.[10]

When one speaks of "the reveal" in the recent popularity of the trick-ending film, at the same time (as the final two chapters should serve to exemplify and summarize with their attention to the fantasy twist of digital teleportation and its temporal quantum leaps) one is often speaking of a revealed filming, a probed trick of camera (or lab) as well as plot. No matter how cheaply earned, or sometimes contradictory and disabling, this kind of rhetorical inflection may seem in a given film, still any such irrelevant stylistic fillip, in its slack default to filming itself—however transient, and though not necessarily a lesson learned and internalized by the narrative itself—may appear instructive. What it educes in us takes place at the vital overlap between narratology, as discipline of response, and cinematography as means of production. This is the meeting ground of plot and its audiovisual medium whose further and textured registration (by narratography)—intuitive and subliminal at times—awaits whatever added analysis such filming might appear to elicit. Commentary at this point is not appreciation, not even criticism necessarily, but a certain charged attention (hence precision) of response.

Narratography: like cartography, a measured assessment of a given optic terrain rather than the geographic shape, the material contour, so charted. In application to a film text, the term designates not its cinematographic status per se but a secondary mapping thereof. It indicates a mode or degree (more than procedure) of response—of response, not of production; a close-grained apprehension of structure, whose only system is location-bound, medium-specific, narratively situated, granular and cumulative. In terms of the difference, for instance, between slow motion as a photomechanical rhetoric and slow motion as a remote-control DVD function, the Preface distinguished between the rhetorical and the operational, between technique and its technical basis. In each medium separately, of course, the distinction exists—and at a deeper level yet as well, concerned with the already inscribed or encoded operations of photogram and pixel. Such is the multiple (multi-*ply*) distinction that narratography would rearticulate. Insofar as it attempts a symptomatic reading, it diagnoses the cultural assumptions of screen stories as in part diagnostic of the medium that conditions their production, where, to borrow medical lingo, an irony may "present as" filmic or digital effect. Any hermeneutic circle of analytic checks and corrections is looped back through the audiovisual substrate of plot, just as any interpretation of a literary text along similar (typographic) lines refuses the transcendence of syntax by sense, the disappearance of lexeme into narrative event, of syllable into implication. The architecture of meaning is kept in touch with its own engineering. And in particular, on-screen, with its own imageering.

Testing message against medium in this way, a cinematic narratography reads the microplot of framing and shot, camera and lab work, image and editing. That's the method—or say the scale—of registration. Its spirit is immersive and reversible. It engages screen plots in view of their visual conditions, the medium in view of a given narrative. It sees the framed image on-screen in light of its material base, even as it understands the latter in the light of the former. This is because the light is the same in each case, going or coming, generated or received. It is the light of projection itself, through whose function the racing frame line or lightning-fast pixel scan, either one, leaves its traces, makes its mark, takes its emotional toll, accretes its aesthetic impact—in the process divulging at times its own ingredient pulse across the very framework of transition in either kind of optical system, photomechanical or digital. By which I mean in particular—at key turns in almost every film I will be taking up—the system of transition, the very logic of spatial traverse and enfolded attention, named suture.

Hence, above and beyond both narrative and technical developments in the mediated view on-screen, from a 1931 dragnet melodrama like *M* to current digital sci-fi—encircling their consideration one might say—is a heuristic return here, full circle, from new media studies to the investigations of apparatus theory. This revisitation, this hindsight, is methodological more than technological, hearkening back to a mechanics of the edited gaze that precedes all computerized electronic affordances. It is one thing, for instance, to say that, on its new monitors, what electronics generate for display is something that was essentially binary and quasi-digital about cinema all along, its motion strictly differential on the strip, one frame on, then off again, across the occluded blank between each (a point made by Kittler in *Optical Media*).[11] As it happens, that rough-hewn optical (and transmedial) proposition seems to me more applicable in fact to the photographic frame line than to any real common denominators it shares with the electronic scan, whose linear compositing of the image is very different from the film strip's integral sequencing of the/n/ow—as those previous paired books of mine have meant to show. More to the point here, however, would be the ways in which the new mobilization of electronic screening in recent film plots casts attention back not so much to the rudimentary toggle of the celluloid photogram as to that psychoanalytically inflected theory of masked discontinuity one level up in the domain of interchanged shots, with their resulting inference of an engulfing rather than a planar space. This is the theory of the sutured view, at its most obvious in the case of shot/countershot patterns: the viewer's look at her, in full narrative swing (and pivot), being no more than a placeholder for an unseen character's own looking. But then, all of a sudden, vice versa as well. According to suture theory, the torn seams between the visible and the viewed are in a constant and reciprocal state of repair, though the gap is never quite sewn closed.

Suture theory has, as granted above, its clear and often strained limits, especially when waxing monolithic in its psychoanalytic and ideological overreaching: castration of the gaze, political interpellation of the spectator, and so forth.[12] But the tightly observed medial determinations of this approach through the apparatus have lost no force in outlasting its far wider currency in the poststructuralist moment. Its rigor and utility have scarcely been exhausted with time, nor, still less, sidelined by new media and their own apparatuses. Indeed, suture gives us unusual current purchase on many a fine line (and frayed border) between human subjects on screen and the sightlined vectors of their electronic manifestation within the narrative scene—right down to the on-screen inclusion of web-fed interfaces in the so-called "sky peer-to-peer" system (shortened to Skype with a no doubt welcome loss of a latent and awkward verb/noun play on peering as well as user reciprocity). Certainly the surveillance scenario is not incidental to these overarching questions. It is exemplary. But what it crystallizes as scopic drama cuts to the quick of the medium. Put it this way: for an overview of narrative technique in screen images centered on medial technology and its delegated and vicarious optics, plots of surveillance work to survey and distill a broad field of consideration.

A dominant pattern has been established, in which Thomas Demand's *Camera* is an epitomizing work. No longer holding up the mirror to nature or our place in it, art now pictures back to us, in automated form, the way we are automatically pictured. So in cinema too, not just video art, with narrative film continually reframing the inner ports and portals of clandestine imaging. Which brings me to what is absent here, and may, at a thumb-through, seem curiously missing: illustrations, frame grabs. After some five hundred painstaking ones in my last two books—and this before they were easy to do at one's own keyboard—I was steeling myself again, in distant prospect, for that labor of love while beginning to draft these pages, sometimes in earlier forms for separate reviews and articles. When an expedience, by way of experiment, occurred to me. Why not write so as to evoke a given image, in its framing or digital effects, without counting on there being space or budget for its insert as figure, or without being sure the reproduction would do it contextual justice? The question stayed put—especially since so much of what I was beginning to say depended on the uncapturable dynamism of shot exchange in the study of montage and the theory of suture, as well as less often, though crucially, the disjunctive effects of voice-over. What began as a descriptive challenge and a stopgap measure evolved—one can only hope for a reader's agreement here—into something more. Such exacting description seemed over time more than just potentially compensatory. I found that talking my way into the images was a way of thinking them through. It started to feel Deleuzian: the image itself taking thought, but only by being met with it in words. To comment thoroughly on what was there in and between frames was to speak of such mediations, bespeak their impact, rather than just alluding to something figured and numbered alongside for illustration (and in the process artificially frozen and silenced).

Moreover, even in the few years since my second film book, the web has made so many more of these images available via stills and clips anyway (as is the case for representative images by Demand as well, not to mention the art of Weimar's New Objectivity movement seen flanking and inflecting the aesthetic of *M* in the first chapter), that the deficit here, if felt to be one, is easily mitigated. But beyond that practical fallback, I'm hoping for something more—by way, if you will (and it certainly is in part up to you), of an enacted narratography of conceptual uptake. If I'm right, the most interesting of these films, at least in the most interesting of their images, have already translated some medial schema into narrative shot plan. Depicting shot or shot change in conceptual language, rather than just reproducing it in one or more stills, is a kind of reverse translation: a reading. If the shots come alive for a reader, whether or not you've seen the films in question, or whether or not you skim the web for them (or their close approximations in a given film), then they've somehow been imprinted in this transferred reading, worked back from abstracted inference to its original manifestation, in the first place, as image: not as picture, but as *image of*, as figuration. If these films are thinking in images, then the thought of their images, close-grained enough, might close a circle without the instancing frame enlargement. If this works, then it is reception's own version of cinematic thinking. Let's hope so, each of us. For everything formalist about the theoretical commitment reiterated here depends on the dynamics—the cinematics—of framing and transition, glimpse and impetus, gape and suture.

"We've become a race of Peeping Toms," complains the incapacitated photographer's cynical nurse in Hitchcock's *Rear Window*. The problem is an old one. But voyeurism is something new when it's a two-way street. Peeping Tomism has become, as it were, Peering Camism. And more. If you're not reading this Introduction in an e-book, your reactions eavesdropped upon when your underscorings and demurrals are logged in for potential cloud-sourced tabulation, then your own face was probably either on camera while buying it in a bookstore or your interests profiled on the web when submitting your electronic order. Topical certainly, these issues, but there'd be no such book as this if the questions weren't also historical, and in particular media-historical, which means in part formal as well. The latest films of surveillance—in the hypertrophic mode of futurist computerization—are so fully keyed to the fantastic videography they narrate, given the cinematic distance from its electronics that their critique attempts to achieve, that the very plan of camerawork and editing can seem at times folded back into their plots as a quasi-magical intervention in space-time continuity. *Déjà Vu, Source Code*: these films, in short, stage montage as not just narratological but ontological, a wondrous instrumentation of cerebral transport and telepresencing as well as a seasoned screen technique.

Tertiary Identification

So the *what* of this phenomenon in its latest phase, before the "so what?": namely, global as well as local surveillance narratives involving often freakishly powerful technological adjuncts to the human audiovisual sensorium—or if not that, then films working to emplot the violence of more normative mediation under the imperative of surveillance. While we're at it, the *where*: in international productions from Asia to the West, Israel to Germany, the UK to the United States. The *when*: more and more often, especially in Hollywood narratives under the banner of a War on Terror in both its overseas and homeland forms. The *how*: by computerized optics tending increasingly to outstrip familiar video tech (even that which generates a film's own special effects) into the specular marvels of time-travel sci-fi. The *what next*: hard to say. Even within the same quasi-generic cycle, it's unusually difficult to fantasize such new levels of audiovisual fantasy. But the premises will grow more and more cyborgian, no doubt, at least at the level of plot (if not by some further reach of 3-D prosthetics in the theater seat), with human cognition progressively enhanced for characters, at least—if only much later for viewers—by computer machination. But apart from the *what next*, there is the *what for* of these films on their own discursive and visual terms. Often they seem participating in a rather typical maneuver of genre: to raise (by exaggerating) intractable social or political problems, but raise only to vaporize them by even more exaggerated and fantastic solutions.

And the *so what* for cinema analysis? Quite apart (though never wholly) from contemporary urgency, these narratives have a media-historical relevance. Even if they didn't flow so directly from a widespread cultural paranoia in which threat and prevention take the same (reversible) form of stealth record, and so even if they didn't in the process speak directly to a contemporary unease about stolen freedoms and policed rather than unchecked movements, these films would be of notable interest to cinema studies. For they round out at a new level (even as they keep pushing past) over a century's worth of montage practice in the once photochemical, now computer-juiced, plasticity of image generation. They do so by virtualizing a constructed scene as the function no longer just of camerawork but of electronic feeds that in fact can now starve the diegesis of all spatiotemporal materiality, or at least of all autonomy. In these digitized films of mediated ocular access across separate time frames, the world itself is becoming a mere and recursive data stream, with duration inseparable from instant replay.

Short of these sci-fi time-warp plots, the exploration to follow operates very much in the spirit of Thomas Y. Levin's work on the surveillance modalities of cinema as contributing to a "rhetoric" whose persuasive force results from its having replaced the discredited index of the cinematic photogram with a real-time verisimilitude closer to that of live TV.[13] Whereas traced space is subject to digital manipulation under the regime of Photoshop and its lab of illusions, we might say that the surveillant image—especially when offered as intermittent surrogate for narrative discourse—vouches at least for the *now* before the *there* (or the doctorable *here*) of the pictured world, with the result that "surveillance has become *the condition of the narration itself*" (583; Levin's emphasis). Despite the medial watershed of late, the historical roots of this go far back. Levin sees even Louis Lumière's landmark 1895 film of workers leaving his factory as a precursor of the managerial CCTV image: forerunner, in other words, of the closed-circuit imaging whose look transforms those cinematic narratives of the 1990s to which Levin's exemplification turns—and a device all the more prevalent, as we are to see, in the post–9/11 decade since his 2002 commentary.

Levin wishes to single out such specific cinematic functions—as this book likewise needs to do—from the broader concerns of global surveillance, including all manner of telephonic and electronic intercepts, dataveillance, traffic security, retinal scans, etc. Hence his emphasis on mainstream cinema's "move away from a *thematic* to a *structural* engagement of surveillance" (582), so that "surveillance becomes one of the topoi of a certain kind of intermedially-displaced cinematic reflexivity" (581). Nonetheless, it is within both this broad tendency and its salient recent trends that the present book concentrates on a recurrent *conjunction* of the structural and the thematic, especially given the way a problematical (if not nefarious) surveillance has returned to the thematic foreground in recent sci-fi variants. It is there that the "rhetoric of the temporal index" (from Levin's title) is in itself as much equivocated as is the spatial trace—but where "suture," with its primal service to the construction of space on screen, is now recruited for certain ironies of the time-image instead, that category of filmic "thinking" so crucial in the film-philosophy of Gilles Deleuze to which we'll later be turning.[14]

In Levin's account, the most notable development across the evolving prominence of surveillant narrative (rather than just surveillance plots) is the epistemological move from retrieved tapes in playback to live-feed temporality. For this marks the narratological convergence he means to chart between, one might say, techne and *syuzhet*, mediation and narrative structure. Though discussion will be reframed in the coming chapters by film-historical questions of spatial (and, more recently, temporal) suture and by certain post-Deleuzian ramifications of temporal semiotics in screen manifestation, nonetheless it sets out from an assumption very much like Levin's about "the semiotic deflation" of cinema's "photogrammatic indexicality" (584)—or, in other words, very much like the premise of my own previous investigation (*Framed Time*) of the post-filmic moment. Yet the overlap of theme into structure held out for there, as in fact the very instigation of narratography, remains uppermost as we proceed. The narrative films in question are those that cast surveillance into question in some suggestive way—as a topic rather than a passing plot device. Analysis thus gravitates to screen narratives *about* surveillance in order to grasp what surveillance in cinema is all about.[15]

I began summarizing above the explicitly cinematic issues at stake in all this as standing in their own right "quite apart" from contemporary social urgency. But only (as qualified at the time) kept apart for analytic distinction, not in everyday experience. The pervasive immediacy of the mediations thematized by such films is in fact never far from, and closer all the time to, the very texture of modern urban existence. As I was drafting this introduction, an October 2012 headline in our campus daily, "UI Installs New Surveillance Policy"—with its passing metonymic wordplay—got right to a point the article itself never really made. The institutional decision to effect such installation *is* the ideological apparatus already at work. The wired eyes stare unblinking at us everywhere, but for the most part, one assumes, they are never looking, just set to record the aberrant veer from routine. What is *seen* comes only later if at all, and elsewhere. The oculus in question is really that of a reverse projector throwing over us the faint shadow of *being seen*. Only the shadow, only the potential—but it's meant as a deterrent against the very deviance that it could only later reference.

Whether or not the cameras are really wired to an electronic data bank, we act in good faith, as it were, that they are. We internalize. This interpellating ideology of oversight (discussed below with reference to literary theories of free indirect discourse) is, for one thing, a radical secularization of divine purview. Deference to the panoptic has other ontological ramifications as well—and ones that film itself can address. The idealism or subjective materialism (*esse est percipi*: "to be is to be perceived") is famously adapted from Bishop Berkeley in so many Latin words by Samuel Beckett for his movie *Film* (Alan Schneider, 1965), starring the former agent/viewer (actor/director) Buster Keaton. Berkeley's proposition is shifted by Beckett from an epistemological axiom about sensible objects to a crisis of the human subject's internalized visibility. The result is an onset of panic about one's self-constitution only in the eye of the other. A sense that one is never truly alone: paranoia. Onscreen: justified. "The horror" here, in the last shot, is Keaton's meeting the narrativie camera's gaze face on.

From Lang to Orwell to Beckett and beyond: that's one trajectory for violations to the rule of the unseen look. There are numerous screen narratives whose plots come to crisis or climax in this way, plots often distilled and rechanneled by the next film to take up the theme. When, in the 2001 remake (and tech upgrade) of *Ocean's Eleven,* Steven Soderbergh, converting to comic caper his obsession with machinic voyeurism from *Sex, Lies, and Videotape* (1989), narrates a surveillance subterfuge in a Las Vegas casino heist, he also narrates something about the mechanics of optical security systems in relation to screen narration. A decoy vault has been built and videotaped in a faux robbery by the thieves, and this recorded enactment has been smuggled in to replace the live feed of the casino camera, beating the house for once at its own game. Two lines of thought are inscribed here, for story and medium both. At the level of plot twist, this ruse puts the security guards on the wrong scent while, in real time, a different version of the robbery is taking place, unrecorded, right under their wired noses. At the level of media analysis, however, the deceit works to distinguish staged filming from live (rather than delayed) versions of onsite security: the one watched (ordinarily) as a fiction, the other surveyed for possible intervention. Simulated surveillance is cinematography turned inside out. The surveillance s/cam, in its deviance, reframes the norm. So that movies about robotic surveillance, genuine or faked, tell something of their own medial story as well. Screen narrative exists to be seen, and only if seen. Lives exist to be lived. In between, a perennial theme—and recurrent plot crux—of the movies in a certain genre lineage: the self under inspection.

And a recurrent stress point, it should be added, for an apparatus theory understood to extend beyond camerawork to spectatorship, beyond the lens of vision to the focal subject. In operation at such filmic moments is a complication of what Christian Metz famously distinguished as the difference between primary and secondary identification: a psychomotor alignment with the camera first, then the possibility of a psychological one opened between view/er and characters.[16] Each depends exactly on the lines of sight that, in the case of the shot/countershot pattern, suture tends to finesse in its serial alternation between POV and its displaced source in the absent human eye. So that the difference between first- and second-order identification depends on—indeed makes for—a perceptual gap that gapes all the more widely in the surveillance aesthetic of numerous recent films, with all their myriad remediations on laptops, cellular devices, control room monitors, and the rest. These are films where secondary identification, perforce redefined at times, seems activated as something like a *tertiary* alignment with the monitored spycam—and only then, if at all, with either the transmitted agency of a character on screen or that of the surveillant viewer. The effect of this, when ramified across an entire plot, is not a prismatic gaze, not even a kaleidoscopic one, but a distribution of image sources more arbitrarily decentered and vexed. As a result, Metz's sense of disavowal operates in overdrive, but against new odds: a denial not just of the cinematographic camera (that we readily pretend isn't there) but of its now suspect relation—privileged though we want it to remain in its narrative authority—to the partial, discontinuous, and tactically motivated optics of surveillance unveiled. Film after recent film pivots on the equivocations that result.

So now—surveyed along these suggested sightlines—let me give the book's structure in one panning scan, with the zoom function temporarily turned off: After Lang's archetypal *M* (chapter 1), a brief study of cinematic prose in novelistic treatments of surveillance and its suspicious imaging systems (chapter 2) leads to an extended treatment of surveillance camerawork in screen narrative: those "feedback loops" of motivated inspection within a rendered "technopticon" (chapter 3) whose action is conveyed, in Levin's terms, by the "surveillant enunciation" (582) of screen rhetoric "as such" (582), its intercut and optically adjusted shots. Attention moves from there to films in which the stakeout mentality tends to surrender its technological emphasis to a more psychological register—films characterized by an implacable vivisection of the surveillant libido and its perpetrated psychic violence. This involves us (chapter 4) in an almost inevitable pairing of voyeurism in Alfred Hitchcock's 1954 *Rear Window* with Michael Powell's case study of the syndrome in the eponymous *Peeping Tom* six years later. In such plots, being seen is both the condition of screen narratability and a narrated site for the subject's most threatening objectification. From these psychodramas of the invasive gaze (continued in chapter 5), we move forward to sagas of a more explicitly machinic technophobia that round out the lineage of this surveillance mode at a new level of ocular totality and "globallistics," where satellite positioning and remote triggering are part of the same closed circuit. After this survey (chapter 6) devoted to the electronic valence of reconnaissance sightings in screen treatments of wired and videographed warfare, we turn to sci-fi extrapolations from this pervasive visual technology (chapters 7 and 8) in which cyborgian optics—in the pun of one forgettable film title in this line, a new species of *Eyeborgs* (Richard Clabaugh, 2010)—serve to extend the sensory perception of the human subject beyond prosthesis into disembodied time-travel magic. Again and again, screen plots of this kind seem participating in a uniquely post–9/11 fantasy of retroactive surveillance and prevention even while redefining the cognitive sensorium of human epistemology in the process.

With this much in the viewfinder, though pitched all too generally so far, it is time, with Fritz Lang's *M* next, for a first phase of more exacting analysis. Screening / narrative / surveillance: three facts, at times one activation; three features of visual technology, one effect; three conditions, one emplotted theme; three words, one phrase. Hence the gist of a book about screening narrative surveillance in classic and contemporary film. This is a loose, mixed mode—and current sci-fi cycle—whose given plots are entangled at once with mediated optics, furtive vision, violated privacy, and compromised screen viewing. And not least when surveillance has itself become weaponized. What follows in these eight chapters, in the brevity of their sampling, can offer no more than one version of the cross-genre story such a film catalog tends to exemplify, but with their insistence on technique, no less than a good look at that story's evolving medial dynamic.

1 THE PRYING "I" OF MONTAGE

Fritz Lang's way of making visible in *M* (1931) the often fierce prying of the film's own optical prowess typifies not only his cinematic temper but the long tradition of camerawork it influenced. Cinema, like surveillance, is a dialectic between the seen and its seeing—as well as, from the late 1920s on, between the uttered and the overheard. And surveillance, like cinema, is often the work of mediation. Surveillance had already taken paper form, often photographically imprinted paper form, in the plotted paranoias of Lang's narratives (in wanted posters and forensic photos, for instance) long before the director introduced his own projective technology into given screen plots as an explicit instrument of moving-image capture and accusation: the heavenly filmic archive of Judgment Day in *Liliom* (1934), the incriminating courtroom footage in *Fury* (1936).[1] Yet his filmmaking was always implicitly just that: a form of cornering and exposure.

In this sense, the broad place of cinema in the panoptic regimes of modernity, rather than its secondary narrative emplacement in particular storylines, had been an undertheme in his work from the first time Lang trained his monocular lens on the supposedly unsuspecting actor overseen in role. And with Lang in mind, surveillance needs also to be located on a conceptual axis with its opposite (or complement) in disguise, impersonation, eluded recognition. In the first scene of the 1922 seedbed film, *Dr. Mabuse: the Gambler*—beginning an auteurist cycle ending only four decades later with the eponymous *Thousand Eyes* of the same mastermind—the criminal overlord at first fans out and reshuffles photographs of himself (in various disguises) like playing cards in the game of deception, choosing which one to deal out next for his on-camera (rather than, for the actor, behind the scenes) makeup artist. One of these photos is soon brought to life in the second sequence of the film when Mabuse appears to full view, though no longer *in propria persona*, to prosecute his anarchist schemes. The transition is medial as well as dramatic: from photograph to the kinetic mirage known as cinema. Almost a decade later in *M*, one may sense the same material tension between still and moving images linked in more subterranean ways to the epistemology of the photographic index and the tracking operations of the moving-image apparatus.

In this discussion's original setting as a conference paper under the umbrella notion of "Moving Modernism" (at Oxford University in the spring of 2011), I had trusted my title, "Frame-Advance Modernism: the Case of Fritz Lang's *M*," to ring a bell—or, better, throw a projector switch. Yet the case for the frame in this sense, as transparent photograph (or photogram) on the backlit spinning reel, is one that repeatedly needs advancing, rather than being taken as axiomatic—and all the more, I find, in the spreading intermedia landscape of new modernist studies, where theory is going to the movies as never before. Faced with the kinetic hypothesis of modernist mobility, certainly cinema comes to mind right away: moving pictures. Not so-called at first, though. Too candid, that transferred epithet, displaced from motor process to visible motion. What moves are indeed only the pictures, in order to picture movement. The *actual* moving of single transparencies, single backlit photograms, yields *virtual* movement. This is what people came for at first: the new magic, even before the specific attractions. In some of the earliest projection venues, in fact, the first image was held like a slide (made possible by water cooling) so as to highlight the subsequent wonder of its launch into action. Each screening thus served to bear forth the medium from its own genetic origin in the still.

Like moving pictures, the term motion pictures came later too: also true to the apparatus, at least in a roundabout way. The motion of anything on-screen is what the projector's own *motion pictures*, pictures in the thrown beam of change itself. This transition per se between celluloid frames or increments is then transferred to spatial transit across the screen frame. The *real* advance (pun allowed) of the flickers was the frame advance. Which is what encourages Friedrich Kittler, in *Optical Media*, to go so far as to subordinate cinema to the digital. For him, the necessary intermittence of the projected image in its syncopated pulsation of frame/[bar]/frame is thus discrete, binary, and in itself, though photographically composited, ultimately nonanalog in its motion effects.[2] This is exactly what the early modernist philosopher of time Henri Bergson disliked about film, its simulation rather than capture of *durée*, as did chronophotographer Étienne-Jules Marey, objecting to cinema's nonanalytic conflation of poses, its squandering of the properly discrete graphing of difference in the illusory spectacle of procession.[3] Assimilating a binary on/off to the internally traced difference (rather than sheer alternation) of cinema's cellular increments, each retaining the afterimage of the last and invaded in protention by the next, we might call this not the zero/one but the zer/o/ne effect. No anachronism is necessary to see this. I am therefore less concerned than Kittler to rethink cinema's material strip in the backward light of digital oscillation than to detect—in the narrative editing that exploits this original filmic microframe—one director's inadvertent forecast of an ocular mediation that characterizes the surveillance ethos of a whole (and now electronically implemented) rhetoric in contemporary cinema. This is what we might call Fritz Lang's perpetual modernism, the weird currency of his camerawork. In the grips of his shot logic, the future is now.

A Thousand Eyes

Tom Gunning's magisterial *The Films of Fritz Lang* certainly earns its broad and definitive title. At the same time, within its sustained variorum-like commentary on the interleaved themes of Lang's cinema is embedded, in effect, an entire stand-alone monograph on audiovisual surveillance as the destiny of the medium itself, a book-within-the book that might lay its own apt claim on the subtitle of the entire work: *Allegories of Vision and Modernity*.[4] In Gunning's auteurist scope almost no surveillance moment is overlooked, both in terms of POV camerawork and in regard to prosthetic technologies brought to bear on such a general epistemic framework. His commentary logs nearly every instance of this second-degree inflection of narrative optics (later audio) from as early as the silent urban thrillers whose theme is summed up by the 1928 title *Spies*: films that centrally reflect modernity's "new systems of social control through a panoptic system of surveillance" (94). In topic and technique, such narratives register a counterplay of violence, bottom-up versus top-down, that is most schematic in 1933's *The Testament of Dr. Mabuse*. Thus Gunning: "As the ordinary criminal threatens the state's monopoly on violence, the master criminal threatens the state's unique employment of the panopticon of surveillance and information-gathering" (95). What we'll come to in the Postface below, via Deleuze's sense of an overthrown panoptic model in "societies of control," cannot deny what Gunning is out to notice in these early sound films.

And the threat of coercive oversight in Lang often takes machinic form. From the simple "interlocking technologies" of "the railway, the pocket-watch, the telephone system" (98) in the opening episode of *Dr. Mabuse: The Gambler*, we move (with Gunning) across Lang's whole German and then American career—alongside nontechnological surveillance, for instance, in *You and Me* (1938), *Woman in the Window* (1944), and *House by the River* (1950)—from the incorporated function of cinema itself as a spying machine (in *Liliom* and *Fury*, again) through to the striking (almost literally arresting) use of television across the last half decade of Lang's screen work. In *While the City Sleeps* (1955), a newscaster's direct video address terrifies a criminal in hiding as if it were a private transmit rather than a broadcast dissemination (an effect quite possibly derived from Orwell's telescreen in *1984*, a device that might really be able to see the cornered subject during its invasive harangues). In Lang's last film, *The Thousand Eyes of Dr. Mabuse* (1960), with its new iteration of the title figure's posthumous power play, the ghost of the evil genius turns the criminal Cornelius into a master technician of closed circuit TV. This involves hidden automatic sound cameras spying in part on dialogue episodes whose intermediate transmission itself advances the plot. In a world that, for Lang, had come to seem increasingly "saturated with observation" (Gunning, 470), this new transmission technology moves—across these last two films—from intimidation to incrimination.

For Gunning, there is less media rivalry here than surveillance genealogy: "Television . . . simply realizes the role Lang had envisioned for it in his science-fiction scenarios" (471), as for instance with the closed-circuit surveillance screen communicating between factory floor and overlord in *Metropolis* (1936). The telos of all media optics: equally to show and to see. Mabuse's original out-of-body, beyond-the-grave effect has evolved into the instrumental telepathy of mediation as telepresence. So that, here again, this last "allegory of vision and modernity" is constellated as nothing less than the regime of surveillance. It is fully in view of, and in debt to, Gunning's broad grasp on this motif in Lang that I will be calling out certain cinematographic details—and even tacitly photogrammatic ones—that slip past notice in his account of *M*, even when in one case the shot in question is actually discussed in passing. This is to say that though Gunning's omnibus scope leaves no stone unturned in revealing the thematics of surveillance in film after film, the optical substrate of a given film, unearthed thereby, may still invite—and certainly in the foundational case of *M*—further cinemato/graphic notation regarding the implicature of its montage in the systems of coercion it articulates.

Much depends on scale. With Lang's *M*, the issue of fixity versus motion is not just, as Jacques Rancière sees it in *Film Fables*, a tension—in its own right quintessentially modernist—between mimesis and diegesis.[5] While for Rancière this formative division of labor pits image against plot, each reciprocally "thwarting" the other, a similar though invisible tension, one level down, is at work between photogram and frame line. What did Lang seem to know and to show about this underlying aspect of the image file—and its prehistory—at the very moment when, in his first sound film, he was double-timing silent cinema with his first audial track? What did the intermittent audial synchronizations he had budget for, or interest in, underscore about the fundamental intermittence of the strip? And how did he commandeer this apprehension for the pacing of narrative impact?

Medial premonitions aside, these are the historical questions that underlie this chapter—and that will direct our attention to images in the film that borrow their composition and framing from adjacent graphic arts of the period. The reasons for this are more than thematic. It's not just that Lang's montage aligns a time-based medium with the alternative pictorial formats it subsumes in the process. It does so with immediate technical as well as narrative repercussions, thus rendering inter-art comparisons less tangential than they may sometimes seem. Film is like sculpture in motion, like mobile panoramas, like large-scale narrative painting, and, increasingly in modernism, like dance, like cubism, like war and its mechanized sightlines, etc.—where the likeness serves to *keep* the very distance it would bridge. This is, of course, as it should be, for the most part. With one medial exception. My work concerning films previous to the digital advent—studying as it did the relation of film to photomechanical imaging—could reasonably dispense with the framework of similes. Film isn't like photography. Film *is* photography (or was, until computerized imaging), with the difference amounting mostly to internal differentials in high-speed sequencing. And, within narrative films, some photographs, printed rather than transparent, figure that fact—now genealogically, now elegiacally, now ironically.

But when one speaks about a certain photographic style more broadly, rather than simply the fact of photography, the axis of comparison widens once again. This is the case when contemplating an entire Weimar art movement, the Neue Sachlichkeit, as it inflects a contemporaneous film like *M*. How might this aesthetic practice, in painting as well as photography, be more than just a cultural ambience in Lang's film? More than a tacit intertext? How, that is, might on-camera satiric portraiture reminiscent of the canvases of George Grosz, for instance, alongside shots evoking still-life photographic treatments of urban industrial Germany and its merchandizing displays in the interwar years—with their stringent geometries rejecting in every way the inward urgencies of expressionism—be seen as developing in *M* something, for want of a better term, more inframedial? This is to ask: without actual photographs on camera until the film's climactic scene—where the serial child murderer, Beckert, is confronted with implausibly enlarged prints of his victims in the neutral photographic mode of studio portraits—how, building toward this, might the very different pictorial zeitgeist of the period find an impact *in*, rather than just *on*, Lang's narrative? An impact, that is—in this first (and perforce, in this respect, most experimental) of his sound films—on the narrative's own disclosures about the already "mixed medium" of speeding photo-transparencies (picture plus motorized projection) under the pressure of the new hybrid mediation of audio/visual synchronicity.

This is a synchronicity only fitfully secured in *M*—and often against the separate tread of image. Sound triggers an independent graphic pattern in the film's first extended sequence. Accompanying the forlorn mother's repeated shouting out of "Elsie" in this anguished missing-person episode (the first scream we hear in Lang's cinema), we see a veritable Neue Sachlichkeit portfolio of photo allusions processed in cinematically static (rather than optically frozen) fixed frames that step off the various architectural echo chambers, absent Elsie, of the mother's cry.[6] Much later, as if bookending this effect, we come upon serial images of the deserted corporate offices from which the killer has been removed—this, in another quasi-photographic dossier of depopulated and hence unmoving images redolent of the period's stripped-down, almost clinical aesthetic. These reveal the confines of an impersonal urban space, now ransacked, that is immediately recognized as typical of New Objectivist photography, including in the mix, this time, certain openly stop-action freeze-frames. In this optical episode, the less sound, in fact, the better. Thus isolated, these shots come forward as the recognizable photographic icons, and intrinsically silent film frames, that in fact they are. But their fixity italicizes more than that. For by this point Lang's spectator is wholly entailed, rhetorically, in the ocular articulation of plot that these images slow to a sprocket-driven crawl. So that what ultimately distinguishes the narrative's two phases of serial (photogrammatic) stasis, early and late—even while implicitly linking them at the level of allusive photographic composition—is the relation of the second series, by then, to a disembodied surveillance motif. More than just saturating Lang's work before and after *M*, this emphasis on motivated but invisible viewing is everywhere implicit, as well, in a certain lineage of film theory ("the system of the suture") that repeatedly queries the relation of optic frame to an invasive and disavowed spectatorial gaze.

The Implicated Spectator: *Sous(ra)ture*

A film like *M* can help remind us how that theoretical lineage has faded away in academic discourse without exhausting its full utility. In the related terms of literary deconstruction, the act of writing, like the ideology it sometimes explicitly inscribes, is the putting under erasure (*sous rature*)—in the name of meaning—of a text's basic lexigraphic operations. For apparatus theory in film studies, concerned instead with explicitly cinematographic erasure—and speaking English as well as French this time—"suture" names a related level of collaboration between text and ideology in the grip of disavowal, masking narrative cinema's essential gaps in service to diegetic coherence.[7] Implicit in this theory is the overridden action of the track as well as of editing. For what happens from frame to frame, subliminally, is also denied in the shot plan and its spatial discontinuities. This sense of denial or suppression derives in passing from the deepest mythographic self-consciousness of apparatus theory: a primal anxiety over the ruined illusory immediacy of all screen experience.

It goes this way, in the earliest formulation of the theory. With obvious (even when occasionally unstated) shades of the Lacanian imaginary stage, the original screen trauma is the recognition of sight as mechanically directed. The task of subsequent cinematic narrative is to assuage this anxious notice in an almost surgical fashion—through a masked pastiche whose own functional invisibility as such, once acceded to, in turn sutures the viewer into the piecemeal shots of montage in order to anchor their credibility as world space. Resisting the initial disenchantment of the gaze, suture arises to address, whatever its immediate local function, a utopian nostalgia for the pure seen. This is an optic not even yet demarcated as an image—just the sheer manifestation of the visible: apparatus disappeared unacknowledged into apparition. On this account, it is almost as if every movie, once its spools are set in motion, replays in projection—in the first wonder of its animation, subsequently undone by the machinations of framing and plot—the mirage of immanent life. Editing arrives to sustain, against all odds, this sense of presence.

But as soon, of course, as the screen figment is recognized (or say reconceived) as a manufactured image, which may of course be with the speed of simultaneity—or in other words as soon as the sighted picture, as image, is taken in as organized "scene"—the act of viewing (rather than just looking) has set in. The result is not to occlude the prospect, of course, but to bracket it as selective, worked, intentional, in short *framed*, and to this extent made rather than given, tainted with labor and artifice alike. The world no longer comes forward partially disclosed to us; instead, its separate aspects have been deliberately chosen from, for subsequent display. Recognizing this marks the primal fall from pure visibility into viewing, long before this loss is reinvested by either moving camera or edited shot-changes into a new narrative economy.

Suture theory understands the manifest manipulation of camerawork as serving always to reframe and (again its surgical sense) stitch over such a lost *jouissance*, because a fractured integrity, of the visible (ever and already vivisected). This is especially so, and most obviously, in the shot/countershot pattern of later narrative developments, where the very idea of the looked-at, an idea focused on the framed face before us, is a discovered illusion. For this looking happens within—how soon we forget—a wholly constructed interspace or interface (never a real human conjuncture) between detached framed images. To phrase it in the heuristic hyperbole of the discourse on suture, the prenarrative dream of immanent visibility, fallen into framing and spectatorship, has become the managed panic of continuous alternating evacuation, where the spliced wound between image and represented world, as well as between us and image, can never be owned to—and remains, as such, a cognitive prototype for bad faith.

One pattern above all is quintessential. In suture's basic format for a dialogue scene, her close-up, whatever seems signified by it, is the signifier of his looking at her, which action exists only by proxy in the viewer as "absent one." So be it—until, that is, the image of him looking (and talking) back offers the reversed signifier of her, this time, being there in our again-absent place: a place under erasure by complicit repression, time and again, if we are ever to give any credence to *their* cohabitation in a world apart. And if we bestow that credence, we are thus accepting the true signified of screen montage: the sign not of objects or people or vistas but of space itself, generated by redundancy (and so lent dimension) by being seen from (and across) more than one angle.

Further, this intercut denial of the camera's work, of framing itself, in the already degraded gaze finds, eventually, just the genres it needs for both the general massaging of spectation and its thematic ironies. Or, across genres, just the modes of optic purview required: voyeurism and surveillance (*The Soldier's Courtship* and *Arrest of a Pickpocket,* respectively). Each entails a mode of heavily invested spectatorial license (via absence) that redounds to the recognized mediations of certain vexed screen moments—and to the "narratography" of their potential notice.[8] Regarding Lang's *M* in particular, one main reason to call up again, in its full polemic extremity, the once dominant model of suture—explanatory paradigm for the lures and elisions of screen vision—is that its utopian backstory, mostly forgotten in its application as ideological critique, has tacitly resurfaced, though unnoted as such, in a revealing recent context. For suture theory's mythic prehistory and passive axiom—the lost primacy of vision despoiled by narrative scene—appears to inform a notable recent commentary on *M*, concentrating as that account by Rancière does, however, on the fixed-frame (and hence idealized) shot of a pivotal sequence whose ocular mood ends up wholly violated by the ensuing frame changes unexamined by Rancière, including the film's most aggressively sutured countershot. But before considering Rancière's attempt (contra suture) to extricate looking again from editing, ultimately vision from narrative, we need to explore the visual (rather than theoretical) preparation, indeed the inter-art context, for the scene on which he concentrates. This involves the broader skein of allusion to numerous motifs of contemporary photography and painting that this one scene participates in and explicitly foregrounds, both in its fixed-frame hold on a toyshop window (Rancière's defining moment) and in that same shot's mise-en-scène as mercantile display.

And even before that intermedia comparison, a further consideration of film's edited medium under the rule of suture is called for. Given the legacy of increasingly technologized surveillance in the dragnet optics derived from *M*, the place of suture in this lineage—with all its displacements—is important to foresee. My attempt is to retrieve the theoretical returns of suture for the ocular logic—before Lacanian psycho-logic—of the specular apparatus that both constitutes film as projective medium and concerns it in respect to the thematized viewing screens of its narratives. In this effort, however, I find myself anomalously aligned (if only up to a point) with Slavoj Žižek in his polemical Lacanian chapter "Back to the Suture."[9] The original power of suture theory, the force of its critique as we've just reviewed it, was to shatter the sense of a coherent-world optic in cinema, to lay bare the manufacture (rather than realism) of diegetic space. For Žižek, the exposed disjuncture of the system effected by such theorizing—the wedge driven into suture by its very recognition, the stake to its heart—was decisive in large part because it modeled a certain psychoanalytic rigor and disenchantment. His view of all this is in a sense the structural opposite of Stanley Cavell's "world viewed," which sees film training an epistemological acceptance, if not proof, of the world's otherness—and of others in it. From a reverse angle, though with no mention of Cavell, Žižek sees suture as the thin tissue of illusion used to secure our sense that some supervening POV, the Gaze of the big Other, might secure our relation to the world of desire and its objects. From Žižek's perspective, this more-than-optical blind spot in the visual system (and its analogic relation to the deceits of consciousness at large) is one that certain "art directors," from Welles through Godard to Kieślowski in his examples, will not always pander to or facilitate. Let alone, as we'll see in *M*, recruit, then vivisect, then thematize. By contrast, an alternate mode of imaging breaks entirely with suture's seamless logic, rips it to pieces, flattens traversable space to "interface." In so doing, films that explicitly exclude and hence rebuke the coherence of suture—the absent one of the shot exchange, the imaginary signifier of presence—can therefore be read, as Žižek does, to spotlight, in these lacunae of projection itself, the altogether imaginary nature of the Lacanian big Other. Our desires, including their sightlines, are not anchored outside us in the real. They oscillate only across their own structuring lack. No subjectification of this sort is stable or authenticating. Cinema (seen *through* in respect to the artifice of suture) would thus appear to brace one's skepticism—rather than, for Cavell, begin weaning one from it.

And among the most obvious way in which certain films accomplish this demystification, according to Žižek, is to collapse shot and its reverse shot into the same optic frame. Instead of the normal insinuated dovetailing of a framed human image and its answering human countershot across the sensorium of the viewer's bodily perception, what happens instead, in the breakdown of suture—its implosion to two rather than an imaginary three dimensions—is a duplicative two-shot of self and its image (by mirror or otherwise). He has in mind such doublings rather than exchanges as anamorphic reflections in Kieślowski or Citizen Kane dwarfed in frame by his own campaign banner: the "look" of the subject with no look back. This is what Žižek oddly calls an "interface," rather than reserving this term for the edited cross-cutting that one might more obviously consider a reversible interface-off of framed view[ing]s. In any case, and apart from whatever psychoanalytic leverage these optical departures from the norm may exert on the illusions of consciousness (via spectation), there is a further historical and political irony in this psychoanalytic focus of Žižek's on the self not Othered (and thus not rooted) from without but doubled by ocular projection as if from within: this flashpoint of the countershot system leveled instead to split-subjectivity. That irony has to do with the "real" interfaces, so to speak, that are sometimes focused on by a narrative cinema otherwise less concerned to break with the pivotal continuities of classic editing than are the resistant films Žižek champions. For in the absence of a big Other, there is, frequently enough, the instrumentalized Big Brother of equipmental interface, with the human subject (of surveillance) doubled, not from within but from without, by remote oversight or recording—and this in a line of technological descent from Lang's videophone in *Metropolis* (1926) and the telecontrol screens of the factory president in Chaplin's *Modern Times* (1936) through Orwell's telescreens in *1984* to the one-way cinemascopic "surveillance window" and its time-travel policing function in *Déjà Vu* (2006).

This is where one either departs from Žižek's whole template or brings his evidence correctively up to date. For well after Kieślowski's occasional and tactical deflation of countershot space, the moments of blocked or overthrown suture in contemporary plots of mediated surveillance are not an aesthetic vaunt. Instead, they represent either, or both, an electronic subterfuge within the narrative or the evocation of a vérité technique elicited by it. Under such audiovisual surveillance, action is often reduced to its mere "interfaced" traces. And getting "back to the suture" can, in exactly its palpable cancellation at such moments, get us back behind the otherwise ubiquitous optic determinants (or surveillant enunciaton) of these recent films to their intrinsic politics, the immanent power play behind their depicted control panels.

In the fullest cinematographic terms: the intrinsic politics of montage itself. And so another work whose title, though pointing not to screen technique per se, as does Žižek's term (and with no mention of Žižek in this regard, nor of suture) still arrives—from the clarifying margin of its concerns—at certain screen practices that directly intersect the questions in front of us. As the concluding chapter of Alexander R. Galloway's *The Interface Effect* (with earlier discussion concentrating primarily on the cultural implications of computer mediation and software technology), "Disingenuous Informatics" rounds out its reading of the TV series *24*, with its real-time narrative aesthetic, 24/7, by looking to cinematic counterparts of the same decade.[10] Galloway stresses the post-Altman effect in "millennial films"—films, here mentioned only in passing, for their independent and cross-braided storylines, as derived from the cross-cutting of the eponymous *Short Cuts* (Altman, 1993): a mixed array of Hollywood and European productions including *Magnolia* (Paul Thomas Anderson, 1999), *Code Unknown* (Michael Haneke, 2000), *Crash* (Paul Haggis, 2004), Babel (Alejandro González Iñárritu, 2006), as well as two films by Stephen Gaghan, *Traffic* (2000) and *Syriana* (2005). These are screen narratives whose structural reliance on "serendipity and concurrency" (118) have produced "a narrative structure of pure rhyzomatic imbrication" (118), a patterning "whose unique brand of narrative and visual simultaneity is one of the newly identifiable formal techniques in the control society" (118). Not exactly "pure" rhyzomatic articulation, perhaps—especially given the way (Galloway's ultimate point) that such narrative interplay becomes its own oblique symptom of control technologies. For in one of the films mentioned, though not in this regard, it is the diegetic (rather than narrative) cross-cut and closed circuit between drone optics and CIA assassination in *Syriana* that knots off at least three of its storylines under the surveillant "control" of a wired panoptic regime. Indeed, this might well be one of those gestures at "totality" (118) that Galloway goes on to acknowledge in these films, as they try binding themselves up with some degree of overarching unity that might pull together the narrative "network" (118) into a strained but somewhat more linear (hence his forced language) "global-single entrainment" (118). Diffusion comes together as fugue; things intercut read as interrelated; the disparate articulates itself as parallel. So there is an "entrainment," yes, but also an endemic political *entailment* linked to technology as well as to narrative technique. For in the most extreme of these films of radical "concurrency" (*Timecode* [Mike Figgis, 2000]), a title unmentioned in Galloway's roster, its four-way split-screen treatment renders in simulated adjacent "interfaces" (like monitored camcorder feeds in foursquare array, though with no other—or explicit—sense of recording devices or threats of surveillance) the multitasked aura of a fully mediatized narrative logic.

Such tech effects being more dramatically motivated elsewhere in the films Galloway adduces, we thereby approach a point where the analogy can be tightened a notch further between film technique and a culture of remote control. Through closer narratographic attention, we can look past something like an oblique symptom to a thoroughgoing montage syndrome. In the films that invite this scrutiny by way of an explicit surveillance theme, "serendipity and concurrency" (118) exacerbate the received aesthetic of parallel montage, turning it from narrational to operational device within the diegesis. The disjunctures of such montage are thus instrumentalized, we may say, not as plot transitions but from within the episodes themselves in their diagnosis of a control society and its new keystroked technoptics. This is to note that the narrative "network" Galloway mentions is no longer merely a dead metaphor, but rather a figurative allusion (cyberoptics its tenor) to the whole metonymic system—and covert instrumentation—of remediated shot exchange. The "interface," in this electronic manifestation, is right there on-screen at times, not simply evoked by it. Yet even when such an inset backlit monitor, upright or handheld, is absent from the frame, the manifold perspectivism of secondary transmission may seem inflecting many a film's entire shot plan quite apart from the explicit sightlines of remote POVs. So Galloway's closing point remains crucial. Screen narratives such as *Syriana,* or his own extended example in the TV series *24,* are not political first of all in regard to the inferred content of their ideological stance and its typifying dialogue. They are political in the very form of their narrative mapping. In this way, they can almost unconsciously mirror what they might intermittently resist or critique. Just because the "serendipity" of their scene changes seems aesthetic, more stylish than probing, even its "disingenuousness" may be political (Disingenuous Informatics," 101–119). Narrative control always is.

And if that sounds like it brings us back to Lang at last, you're right: Lang, where narrative cross-mapping within a montage "network," pivoted around the crisis of suture in *M,* sets the template for many decades of represented technological escalation in screen plots of social control, as bolstered en route by the coercive audiovisual mediations of *1984.* Brings us back to Lang first—and then, with his own interfaces and face-offs more fully assessed, forward to the films that follow his fierce initiatives in this mode, with all their unflinching grip on the spectator's lines of sight.

Lang's *Objectif*-ism

Few directors have been less "camera-shy," if you will, than Lang in exposing the cinematographic cast of their narratives. But in *M* he emphasizes the veritable lens (*objectif*) of his shots with, even for him, an unusual degree of pictographic self-consciousness. He does so precisely, I've suggested, by letting the image track revert by allusion to recognizable fixed-frame compositions in the contemporary art practice known as the New Objectivity. It is actually *The Testament of Dr. Mabuse,* rather than the earlier *M,* that makes this aesthetic self-consciousness almost comically explicit. Inspector Lohmann, trying to trap an accomplice to murder, places together on top of a file folder at the center of his desk a pistol and a small and unmarked cardboard box (opened later to reveal incriminating identical bullets retrieved from the bodies of separate victims). After this minimalist arrangement has been locked on by the camera, we hear in voice-over the beginning of Lohmann's interrogation: "What do you make of this still life?"

Very contemporary, he might have said. Cinema criticism has in fact been quick to note, for instance, the allusion to the Neue Sachlichkeit photographic still life in the reflected storefront cutlery of a passing shot in *M*—this, quite aside from the inevitable irony of knives as latent weapons in the homicide plot. But that's only the tip of the iceberg in the cool if not chilling network of the film's fine art intertexts from the Neue Sachlichkeit aesthetic. Under this new objectification, frontal images of buildings versus those of people show little difference in affect, including gleaming new industrial settings and postwar devastation alike. The depopulated office corridor from the architectonic vocabulary of Neue Sachlichkeit photography will turn up at a pivotal moment in *M*. So, too, the often listless window-framed cityscape, ubiquitous in this art style, as if in a kind of minimalist correction of German Romanticism's view from the open casement.

Most obvious perhaps of all the inter-art checkpoints in this film—especially given a sense (in Anton Kaes's work) of the child-murderer Beckert, Lang's tortured protagonist, standing in for a whole generation of shell-shocked victims grappling with their violent urges—is a well-known Otto Dix lithograph from 1919 that finds clear overtones in Peter Lorre's contorted facial performance as Beckert, whose traumatized expressionist gestures must be contained—stylistically as well as narratively—by the aesthetics of mise-en-scène and camerawork alike.[11] When not convulsed with trauma, however, humanoid forms in the New Objectivity tend, instead, to be reduced to marionettes, discarded dolls, or—in a related trope of spiritless form—the molded egg-like craniums of numerous automata in the works of painter George Grosz. These quasi-humanoid forms may be an influence on the film's first ominous balloon shot (that anthropomorphic plaything caught in telephone wires after the murder of Elsie Beckmann), including the close match between this shot and an iconic Neue Sachlichkeit still life of high-tension wires by Albert Renger-Patzsch. This ongoing relation of kinetic narration to fixed-frame plastic art saturates Lang's film and its manifest sense of its own serial celluloid medium even when there is no internal rear-projection, as sometimes there is, of the crime's indexical trace (the huge blowup of the killer's fingerprint) nor any overt allusion to the death masks of his victims as single and serial photo images (also pending in those portraits of his preteen victims in the film's penultimate scene). But what in particular do such earlier allusions to the New Objectivity import into (or impart to) Lang's narrative technique at this moment of his first venture into sound?

One possible answer lies fallow in an argument not concerned directly with *M* or Lang. For David Trotter, film's chief influence on modernist literature resides in the prenarrative *actualité* as view, as sheer sighting, rather than anything associated with its actualization of frame advance, so that the tactical blind spot in the gaze of recorded bodies before the camera is matched by the unblinking neutrality of their filmic capture.[12] On this showing, and in ways not unrelated to the originary image before suture, cinema thus approaches more nearly than otherwise possible, by way of a modernist epistemology, to a stringent aesthetics of record without representation. In this sense, montage aside, the Neue Sachlichkeit aura of Lang's mise-en-scène might seem, along with objectivism in poetry, a definitive realization of modernist optics. But I'll be asking why, in the midst of this inter-art ambience, we are nonetheless reminded by Lang's montage not just of the predominantly still life images from the latest Weimar art wave on which *M*'s set design and camera placement is based, but reminded as well—and partly by the same cross-medial inference—of the stilled life of the strip as it is openly and mechanically tracked into action, whether with or (as so often in *M*) without movement, but serialized nonetheless in its undertext. Or, putting the question more succinctly, why—and how—does Lang's film come to disclose its unique reflexive objectivism as a matter not just of the image composed but of the image serially composited?

In broader intermedial terms, of course, as seen with the Dix image from over a decade before, it is this aesthetic of New Sobriety (an alternate designation for the Neue Sachlichkeit movement) from which Lorre's performance is a backsliding to the externalized torments of the expressionist soul itself. So that when he is not on screen, it is as if the fixed-frame, quasi-photographic shots that interrupt and sanitize his polymorphous gestures take an entire art movement as their antiseptic counterweight. To note merely those motifs of the Neue Sachlichkeit movement that appear in the film's opening episode, there is the window-ledge or dormer-view still life—just before, in the least romantic of moments, Mrs. Beckmann calls out to (the evermore-offscreen) Elsie from the framing window. Next, there is the emptied site of architectural symmetry, a mainstay of photographs in the period, in the overhead shot down the geometric stairwell, empty of the returning girl. Then there is the prevalent visual trope of the deserted attic room (about which several art historians comment apart from Lang's film—perhaps most famously illustrated in a 1926 work by Ernst Thoms called simply *Attic*). As such, it is a paradoxically domestic space of nonhabitation (complete in Lang's shot, further matching the painting, with the line-drying undergarments of the girl's absent body). And finally there is the tabletop still life, as well as the related framings of more abstract geometries, often spheroid, including more than one still life with ball influenced by René Magritte's *The Secret Life* from 1927. Such are the specific optical motifs that converge not only on the Beckmann kitchen table with the circular shapes of the child's plate and glass, never to be filled again, but also on the subsequent discovery of Elsie's absent body survived only by its rocking ball and overhead balloon figure, the latter's tubular torso and limbs animated by the wind alone, no marionette strings attached.

Apart from any direct connection to Otto Rudolf Shatz's 1929 painting of a male balloon vendor and two teen girls, Lang's image of metonymy turned metaphor—with the breath-inflated object released by the dead body it lingers to figure—is thus very much of its visual moment. With Elsie's face-painted humanoid balloon form linked to the enigmatic doll and puppet motif of these same years—where, in the ultimate anti-expressionist gesture, the human form is reduced to mere curvatures of an unventriloquized objecthood, a hollow simulacrum—this topos of the Neue Sachlichkeit manner (prevalent a full decade before Hans Bellmer launched his ongoing work in the sculpting of doll forms) is related by Lang, as well, to a cutout harlequin operated as a mechanical automaton at a pivotal later moment. Doing its deep knee bends thanks to an unseen motor, this is the mobile object shot from behind in the toy store display, a kinetic focal point of the brief scene that goes strangely unmentioned when Rancière deliberates over what he takes to be the placid respite this setting affords.

Centered there amid the immobilities of commercial presentation—and spoiling from within, one might well think, any utopian interregnum (Rancière's point) from the killer's homicidal intentions—is the flat mechanical underside of the puppet's involuntary spasms framed together with its onlooker, a robotic murderer whose own strings are being pulled not by desire, he later explains, but by compulsion. "Not want to, must; not want to, must," he repeats about his killing in his last frenzied monologue, as if speaking there for an entire generation sent to war. It is an inference confirmed, in turn, by the mob's later threat not, in so many words, to execute him for the police crackdown his violence has visited upon them, but to put him, in military parlance, "out of commission." This threat emerges in a final scene where the balloon has come back—in the hands of its original salesman, the blind beggar who identifies Beckert's habitual whistle—not only to taunt the killer but to mock his expressionist rant. For his own tortured cranium keeps disappearing momentarily behind the inflated, vacant reminder of those lifeless bodies he leaves in his wake, yet by guilt over which, in his own tacit cinematic metaphors for self-surveillance, he is "shadowed" and "tracked."

At this point, there's no forgetting the opening instance of the balloon figure, as simulated human form, taking up the ball's cancelled momentum when—after being caught momentarily in the overhead wires—the weightless replica is released to invisibility in the ongoing flux of duration. In ways that obliquely anticipate the film's closure—when editing dismisses from view the apprehended killer without any judgment or extermination visited upon him beyond that of total displacement by plot and camerawork—death seems, in the earlier scene, almost brought to definition in optical terms. With the human body artificially imaged by toy figure to begin with, death takes graphically figured shape both as inanimate presence within frame and as removal from it—thus offering in resumé, as it happens, the film strip's own two motoring conditions in the artificial increments of its manufactured kinesis.

If we want to say that this early balloon image, perhaps the film's most famous shot—complete with its manifold Neue Sachlichkeit overtones—comes back to haunt Beckert in the accusations of the blind man, it does so only after Lang has brought off a bravura panning shot that deliberately reduces the mise-en-scène it sweeps past to a quasi-photographic tableau. This unfolds, once more, by way of an interext from Weimar graphic art, in this case large-format epic painting, where the film's underworld iconography seems crossed with the mass dissidence of leftist unrest as represented in the 1929 tableau of the Communist Internationale by German painter Otto Griebel. On view in that famous canvas is a wall of impassive faces like that which Beckert confronts in the criminal body of the kangaroo court. He is arraigned there in the deserted basement of bankrupt German industry—in particular, a failed brewery cellaring (and fermenting) only resentment—by a group portrait over which the camera edges left to right as if it were a scanned image in itself, the least ripple of human movement discernible only toward the end, and far right, of the travelling shot. Yet again at a critical narrative juncture in Lang, and with other two-dimensional media in mind, cinematography parses its own variable amalgam of framed stasis and motor advance.

From Objectivism to Abjection: Image vis-à-vis (or vs.) Narrative

Well before Beckert is sutured in as the pilloried object of this mass gaze (from a virtual theater's worth of spectators), his world, as we've seen, is already one of specular stereotypes and allusions. In his own terms from the coming monologue, he is hounded, haunted, by audiovisual ghosts, "the fire, the voices, the agony": a composite metaphor at once for his own raging incendiary torment and the frenzy of his victims, the self othered from within by guilt. To probe the killer's own imagery in this way is also to lay bare another latent link between contemporary image systems and the protagonist's own tacitly (or at least figuratively) postcombat torment, a link in particular between cinema and the front. It's not only that surviving trench veterans carried back movies in their heads from a drastically nonphotogenic war, as Kaes has detailed, where soldiers were dug-in and motionless for weeks and months on end, frustrating newsreel cameramen almost as much as themselves. It is also the case that they often returned, if not with real ocular damage, often with a psychosomatic blindness triggered by what they couldn't bear seeing even in their mind's eye. So that a soliloquy about inner rending voices in an innovative sound film featuring as the first and quintessential detective agent the blind beggar who overhears Beckert's telltale whistling has established a textual system that divides (in Barthes's sense) the figure of debilitation across two characters, the man who hears voices and the man who has lost all optic nerve.

Then, too, we may well elicit another militarist connection to Lang's editing style in particular from one of those moments of deadpan fanfare where Kittler announces that German entertainment television found its embryonic form in paramilitary police communiqués—this in the primitive linear scans of a protofax technology known as the "video phone."[13] Without mentioning *M* in regard to such forensic bureaucracy, Kittler dates this innovation from three years before: "In 1928, long before the Federal Criminal Police Office's computer surveillance, the Imperial Criminal Police were already able to slowly scan wanted posters and fingerprints, broadcast them with electrical speed, and then convert them slowly back into images again at distant police stations." TV, if you will, was a tool before it was a product, a potential weapon in the arsenal of overt social control before an informative (or pacifying) pleasure box.

No media-historical accident, then, that Lang used precisely such wanted posters (in their associated Neue Sachlichkeit cachet)—as well as such fingerprints—as pivotal transitions in two of *M*'s most intricate montage segues. The old-fashioned posters operate as prewired implements of public surveillance awaiting a noncommercial variant of the same electric technology—retooled for remote-transmit—that, in the form of our present cinematic narrative, pictures, first, the visual stasis of such postings and, eventually, the killer they can't identify. Then, too, in the longer historical view of surveillance machination, these are the very implements of disseminated vigilance that later yet, once the electric "video phone" has mutated into the electronic data streams of networked video, will generate what begins to seem like a new screen genre in the computational manhunt. En route, it is even less of an accident that Lang's last film, three decades later, *The Thousand Eyes of Dr. Mabuse*, would have incorporated in a Cold War setting one of the first instances in film history—inset precisely within commercial cinema's projected frame—of reframed CCTV surveillance via hidden cameras and sequestered monitors.

But as early as 1931, the marked absence of determinant visual evidence—the lack of Beckert's photograph for police tracking—can be seen (or, rather, not seen) by contrast, yet again, with *The Testament of Dr. Mabuse* (1933). One thinks of the presence there, not just of the villain's name in photographic reversal (written by one of his terrorized victims, Hoffmeister, on a pane of glass behind his own back, then passed through a police photographer's negative to reveal the secret of its cryptic inverted *esubaM*) but of Mabuse's actual admonitory photo portrait. Inspector Lohmann has just groaned that Hoffmeister "must have gone out of his mind with fear" when a match cut on dialogue jumps to Dr. Baum at the lectern, apologist for and tool of Mabuse, explaining that such madness (he means now Mabuse's) is not all that uncommon. His lecture to an academic theater finally grabs the audience's full attention when he flashes on a screen behind him a large transparency of the madman, in prisonlike pajamas, bedridden at the asylum. The students are thrown back in their seats with astonishment at this photo—which they glimpse before editing allows us to—in its image not just of derangement but of a self-induced mental incarceration: "He withdrew to the prison you see here." When it is our turn to register this abjection, the slide is not shown from the students' reactive point of view in their raked seating, but rather in a low-angle shot that seems, more from Baum's position at the bottom of the auditorium, to render the acute angle of Mabuse's persisting mesmeric dominance over his exegete and (we later discover) haunted alter ego. But photo it is, and to it as well as the man himself, the authorities have access. Not so in *M*, where the *Mörder* posters, and their reward in marks, have nothing to show for themselves by way of visual clues. In a world of allusive photographic evocation, the elusive photograph. It bears repeating: in *M* "cinematography parses its own variable amalgam of framed stasis and motor advance."

The pattern is as clear as it is cumulative. Time and again in *M*, from wide framing to tight, motion is either contrasted with or reduced to stillness within a lens-conscious geometry of bracketing and capture, where the look of a shot may then take its intermedial bearings from plastic rather than kinetic art. The same is true, though unnoted in this respect, for that earlier scene of a supposedly recovered ocular utopia that sustains Rancière's attention as one of his cinematographic parables. Articulating his dichotomy between image and narrative in *Film Fables*, Rancière does not explicitly mention the fabular origin of suture theory in a primal and uncontaminated field of view, though his claims do appear rooted—and less ironically, at that—in the discourse of suture, with a deliberate strain of medial nostalgia for a more innocent optic field before its diegetic framing. This seems especially the case in his reading of *M*, where the plot-deferring toy store idyll of pleasurable vision, almost haptic, but not prehensile—rather than, as it might also be understood, an infantilizing identification with the displayed objects of desire—is analyzed as a remission from motivation itself as well as from plot. For Rancière lays no stress on the way this scene of nonaggressive (however latently acquisitive) vision makes time for narrative to catch up with the specular agent—as stressed by Lang's editing in hyperbolically optical terms. Contra Rancière, the intrusive narrative effect can well be taken to submit any unfettered looking on the murderer's part, or on ours by association, to the concerted and unnerving scopophilia of the surveillance plot.

What Rancière wants from the scene is something else entirely, something for him definitive at this stage of Lang's career. In an essay mostly on the director's later 1955 film *While the City Sleeps*, where a murderer is climactically addressed in a private domestic space by the broadcast harangue of a TV reporter, Rancière introduces *M* by contrast. He sees it hailing (and presumably hailing us by way of medial if not ideological interpellation) from a different "age" of the image, a different "apparatus of visibility"(48)—as Rancière rather obscurely puts it, for it is certainly the cinematographic "apparatus," and its narrative entailments here, that his reading seeks to delimit. Under this earlier aegis, otherwise undefined, the murderer is granted a "moment of grace" understood "in the strong sense of the term" (49), the transient chance to "be human" just before the "hunt" (49) closes in. For Rancière, this is not a pocket of pleasure somehow naively free from narrative, but a moment intersected by a different modality altogether. It is a case, in his vocabulary, of *aisthesis* making autonomous room for itself within *mimesis* (50), where Beckert is allowed not only to "delight in a spectacle" (49) but also, in reciprocal specularity, to be liberated—in his own on-screen right—to an untrammeled "image" (49) of that delight.

Looking is thereby valorized for him and for us at once. The "issue is not one of narrative suspension, but of poetics" (49), thus drawing on, and renewing, the perennial tension in film between optics and plot. "The important point is not that the progression of the episodes has to be punctuated with moments of rest, but that the very meaning of episode has changed" (50), as if the concept were growing, one might add, closer to its etymology in the "epi"—always oblique, never dominant. In this sense of the episodic, *Film Fables* sounds most Deleuzian when—though stressing textual periodicity (rather than historical periodizing)—Rancière writes that, as a "new form of action," the "aesthetic plot" thus "breaks with the old narrative plot by its treatment of time" (50). Screen event opens to an "empty time" not of the post–WWII time-image (Deleuze's sweeping historical claim) but to the temporal rhythms of a more capacious flanerie, "the time of goals held in abeyance" (49). In any film exploring the boundaries of its own medium, its "fable" will therefore report in part on the uneven distribution of *opsis* and *diegesis* across the weave of sequence.

But how convincing is this claim for the counterplot of image over narration in *M*, especially in this particular narrative sequence? What could it really mean for Beckert to be "nothing more than a peaceful image seen through a shop window" (49)? An image for whom, and by what means? The question might be idle if it weren't forced so soon, in more aggressive terms, upon exactly this supposed optic idyll by its immediately following shots. If the look of sheer looking comes across as a poetic node resistant to the chase and quarry plot, our seeing of it transpires in context with a perhaps less serene poetic license. From what covert vantage, for instance, are we meant to see "through the window"? And if only, of course, by the invisible affordance of a camera stationed somewhere behind the toys, as if from a shopkeeper's absent viewpoint, what does it mean to recognize the film's own "apparatus of visibility" in this unusually salient fashion?

Then, too, why isn't the imputed poesis of the moment thwarted by diegesis in our sensing that no matter where this already and literally marked man goes (having had a chalked "M" for *Mörder* recently pressed unawares on the back of his overcoat), or whenever he stops to look, he's always being seen? The hiatus bracketed by this scene is indeed decidedly set off—though not *from* narrative so much as *by* it, and within its vise-like grip. The immediate reactivation of the film's plot drive—including both its agent's despair over detection and capture and our genre-ingrained wish for it, later if not sooner—transpires when *opsis* can no longer remain detached from *muthos* (Rancière's Aristotelian dichotomy), image from plot, but must be expressly run down and overcome by it, not just "thwarted" but terminally defeated.

Looking Espied

Like the pending crux of editing it is meant to evoke, the phrasing of this subhead goes both ways. Even just before this moment of sutured surveillance, in what Rancière sees as Beckert's temporary vacation from his own drives, and ours from the narrative's, the specular dispensation of sheer looking is not as safely barricaded from plot—least of all from its latent aggression—as it may seem. Nor, for that matter, from plot's sociopolitical context, since that commercial display of the toy store window is certainly not cleansed of a commodity fetishism over its merchandised wares within an inflationary interwar economy and its black market underbelly. Nor even suspended from plot's psychosexual violence. However much carved out from barbarity, the moment (barely more, sustained for just over ten seconds) is one in which Beckert's gaze is only triangulated, rather than directly engaged, with any supposed purity of spectacle—this, through his staring at the girl's separate delight so as either to feed off of it or actively manipulate it, or of course both.

Further, given the encroachment of the surveillance plot, it is surely no surprise that this ocular indulgence, with the killer turning his back momentarily on a world out to get him, would leave Beckert prey to the detection of his alphabetic stigma. This spying is effected by one of the army of beggars recruited by the underworld, who has now caught up with him in the near distance—as we soon realize—and is stationed (with others in relay) to track his next and every move. For plot as well as for character, then, the optic stasis of this lull in compulsion, unable to shake off its context in any wholesale way, marks little more than a temporary *repression* of the violent drive rather than its intermission. A drive whose traces, it is important to stress, have already returned in mechanical travesty—the puppetry of action—from within the graphics of the episode.

And so the importance, yet again, of that Neue Sachlichkeit motif. For framed within the reframed scenic field of the plate glass window, as we know, and nearest us, is the unrecognized double of the psychopath—jerked into violent gestures by impulses beyond his control (to say nothing of the screen actor impersonating them only by having his image yanked into action by the projector's tug on the sprocket-holed strip). The point can perhaps best be put negatively. To say that Lang here isolates a motif from the New Objectivity (puppets, automata)—and in the process brings to it, or it to, an artificial animation—is not so far to have singled this shot out from many others before and after it in *M*. The intertext is at this point a kind of prototype. Once again Lang's film remobilizes contemporary graphic art in the cinematography of secondary (and invasive) spectation. Hence, a double intermedial analog. To the extent that this mechanically activated clownish cutout calls up still images of emptied humanoid forms from the period, it places these similitudes under cinematic redescription as motorized images. To the further extent (*pace* Rancière) that the two-dimensional marionette's manic parody of the madman disturbs the dilated respite of this episode, it prepares for the further dynamization—just seconds away in the same scene—of a fixed framed image (in mirror rather than window this time) by the whiplash suture of a disruptive answering shot.

With Lang once more marking narrative juncture with optic disjunction, this pending suture takes place, in its scopic displacement, when Beckert—looking over his shoulder into the toy store entrance mirror and seeing suddenly the effect of his branding with the letter *M*—also sees the closing in of his unrealized surveillance. Window shopping has given way, only a few feet away, to reflective scrutiny. But not without the dangled mannequin having already mocked the murderer time and again when its knees are bent by mechanical repetition into the flanking angles of an embodied mimic *M*. After such a compromised momentary spell before the transparent plane of fantasy, what follows is the opacity of self-recognition under almost immediate external siege. This is to say that the letter *M*, one of the few alphabetic characters identical with its own mirror reversal, accompanies a self-image coming to Beckert now from outside himself (but only at the near distance of the mirror at first)—as if in the reversed negative imprint of a photograph: just that mode of visual identification that the police have never had in his elusive case.

Almost in that same instant, however, Beckert not only sees himself as marked man, as pariah, but sees himself *seen* as such by an illicitly deputized vigilance at one remove from his own doubled image. For over this same shoulder, along a slightly raised line of sight, Beckert stares into and through the camera into our own (soon replaced) gaze. At stake is a look "right in the eyes" in Roland Barthes's sense, from the title of a little-discussed essay in *The Responsibilities of Form*.[14] In cinema for Barthes (as distinct always from his favored photography), chief among those titular formal "responsibilities" would seem the disavowal of the camera—and through it of my espial (both senses). Barthes: "If a single gaze from the screen came to rest on me, the whole film would be lost." When Barthes thinks to distinguish the licit look into the photographic camera from its forbidden status in cinema, he means that the film would be "lost" if the suture were not managed at a somewhat oblique angle. Lost because so directly found out. Lang's is the aggressive exception that confirms the norm, so aggressive, in fact, that the discourse on suture singles out his very practice (if without mention of *M*). In a particularly cryptic turn, having given suture first a linguistic and then a rhetorical orientation (the latter as a kind of metalepsis: the trick of putting effect before cause), Jean-Pierre Oudart, in "Cinema and Suture," adduces Lang without specific example. The signifier of the look is always retroactively determined. What we see is revealed as already having been looked at, an effect deployed by Lang "with deliberate terrorist intentions." Oudart seems to be referencing the direct rather than oblique facial exchanges mentioned earlier and in passing from Lang's Wagnerian *Kriemhild's Revenge* (1924). But seven years later, the scene before us in *M* has exactly this effect as well, and linked directly here to a convulsive invasion of privacy. In the tracking of the killer, to keep to Oudart's melodramatic terms, a cinema of terror is intersected by a cinematics of terrorism. We are not so much hailed by the returned gaze as nailed by it.

What Oudart ultimately attempts at the end of his influential position paper, and again with Lang as indistinct example, is to traverse one more time the fall from the initial *jouissance* of the image—in the "hypothetical" time before its screening *from* as well as *before* us—to the moment it is inhibited by narrative, again by plotting's optical "prohibitions." These contribute to a subliminal "eroticism" that is itself not so much strictly filmic (zeroing in on some manifest object of fascination) but cinematic (luring us in and zeroing us out by reversible turns). Hence his essay's closing sentence: "The discovery that the cinema, in speaking itself, speaks of eroticism, and is the privileged space where eroticism can always be signified, should probably be credited to Lang; and although all the consequences are far from being drawn yet, this discovery engages the whole cinema." Eroticism: under the sign of the apparatus in its voyeuristic facilitations. Again, no example—except the one we have at hand. If we take that scene of intercepted toy shop desire in *M* as concerned not primarily with a murderous pedophilia in abeyance but by association, a moment later, with the violence of the deviant body's own recognition as such—not as agent of lust but as focal point of narrative desire—then Oudart's claim gains traction.

For here is certainly a scene whose broader consequences have continued to be further drawn, or at least drawn out implicitly by screen narratives, in the half century—and across the exponential media transformations—since Oudart first wrote. In terms of suture, it is one point of this book to note that the signified space (rather than object) of surveillance, its axis often coextensive with screening itself, "engages the whole of cinema" down to the present—and indeed all the more so in the recent stages of the medium's postfilmic evolution, where electronic imaging now permeates a human field of vision, including its remote spatial inspection, far wider than the rectangles of commercial cinema. The eros (and ethics) of the covert shot and its absent one have become part of a ubiquitous discourse of surveillance that only includes—but can't be reduced to—the cinematic, let alone some unplotted innocence of the image.

In any case, it seems fair to say that no look into our eyes has ever been harder on-screen to disavow than Beckert's at this optical swivel of plot. Sutured-in as the collective absent one of a yet undisclosed reverse shot, we (you, I) return the horror of Beckert's recoil by disappearing into his glimpse, by countershot, of the underworld spy ducking behind a truck. Such is the anchoring look of a reseamed fissure performed by a looking (on the spy's part) that is there for only a split second longer than our look, in instantaneous erasure, had seemed to be.[15] So has this pivotal moment in the chase plot pivoted in turn around its own 180-degree sight line, splicing in our avid narrative curiosity as one kind of assault on Beckert's already sundered specular autonomy before displacing us by another—and this time diegetic—threat. The displacement is never complete, however. As if pointedly to despoil in ironic retrospect the apparently benign context of that earlier storefront looking, spectator and spy now pose (and, in cinematographic terms, posit) an equivalent danger to Beckert as character: the localized paranoia of being seen.

Nor is the fact of our seeing, in turn, free of a lurking perturbation. An otherwise compromising chain of associations, once appeasingly delinked, would go like this: concerning Beckert's world, this isn't life, isn't even theater; it's film. We're not spies, not even ordinary live spectators; we're viewers. This isn't our surveillance; it's our strictly narrative apprehension of the prerecorded scene. But in these subliminal disclaimers, we would, according to the ideological critique typically implicit in suture theory, be protesting too much, denying in this case the very close thematic connection between our mass reaction to the child killer on screen and the modes of detection employed, within the plot, against the lone sociopath, both by bureaucracy and by the criminal mob alike. Imbricated in the eyeline stare, we are implicated perforce in its manhunt politics, whose juridical and dramaturgical satisfactions are not as easy to keep separate as a viewer might want to assume.

With Beckert now on one side of a framing transparent plane where he doesn't notice us, now at the focal point of a framed mirror image in which he momentarily (phantasmatically) does, this narratographic slippage allows no clean distinction at the level of plot between cinematic visibility and narrative's depicted invigilation. Precisely because of what Rancière notices but deflects by celebration at the opening of this episode—call it, instead, *opsis* isolated in crisis rather than arrived to alleviate it—all imaging in this sequence feels not just contrived but part of an unsettling media connivance. And there is yet another way to put this, perhaps more telling yet. Before he notices me looking through the middle-distance eyes of the spy, I see Beckert, in fixed frame, looking over his shoulder at his own newly signified double, with no big Other there to render his identity otherwise. But no suture is thereby transcended. In the coils of so totalized a surveillance, this brief "interface" shot in Žižek's specialized (often mirror-image) sense is, true to form, bilateral rather than reciprocal, self-refracted rather than mutualized by any third vantage point outside of exchanged recognition. But it is no sooner wrested from enchainment in the shot nexus than yanked back into it, offering not a break with continuity editing (in its surveillant valence) but only a self-mirroring figure, before worse coming, for the implacable *internalization* of this momentum.

With the result that invisibility emerges for the protagonist at a new premium. After hiding out over the course of the prolonged coming scene of illegal search and seizure in the urban office building, hounded down by the gang, caged like a trapped animal in an attic cubicle scanned by a flashlight as if it were the forensic equivalent of a projector's beam, Beckert is finally carried off in a body bag. His capital punishment seems already, by association, a foregone conclusion—as well the sign of a war casualty deferred. Yet he is still to be exposed again to the melodramatic frame-up of mass derision in his underworld (and underground) show trial. Here is where the eventually convergent lines of parallel montage—Beckert on the sexual hunt and then the run, the cops in full dragnet mode, the mob closing in—must necessarily come to a head, according to Deleuze (with *M* his detailed test case), in the closural energies of a showdown.[16] This is the "duel" that, borrowed with other genre overtones, is the required resolution of all prewar films of the movement-image, where parallel timelines (not released to the pure cerebration of the time-image) must be roped in and tethered together by plot. This is the case even in a threefold montage like that in *M*, where Deleuze's SAS' formula (Situation transformed by Action into new Situation) finds police pitted against mob even while each force is directed as well against Beckert.

But in *M* the final duel is in a sense abrogated, despite Deleuze's claim, when its inevitable loser is dispatched from the screen frame at the moment of his capture. The true showdown is not shown.[17] Though Deleuze never articulates a revised formula of the duel for the modernist time-image, we can nevertheless see a version of its reflexive modernism in the curtailed (and optically reencompassed) movement-image of *M.* Given the supervening role of image over action, image whether actual or virtual, in the post–WWII cinema of mentalized temporality, Deleuze notes throughout (one of his central determinants) the conversion of narrative agents to spectators in and of their own lives: the movement-image of a previous social commerce or adventure inverted, in anomie, to the sheer imaging of actions not even necessarily one's own. With Lang as prewar benchmark, this later development might well be seen as the internalization of surveillance in the form of hermetic vigil. In any case, no clear distinction between duel and self-enclosed ocular circuit can be maintained in Lang when the drastically altered situation (S' of the former paradigm) is displaced off-site and out of view in Beckert's case. Here in Lang's prewar experiment, and as inflected by his inter-art Weimar allusions, is a case of action—in and beyond the parameters of a surveillance plot—rendered inseparable from its prosecution as framed views. This is an action whose remorseless narrative drive is put at last into remission not by *opsis* but by a total release from it. What "remains to be seen" is how completely this suspended sighting brought about by closure has been prepared for by an explicit escalation of forensic picturing.

Stop-Action Impact: Intertext as Subtext

Well before that dispersion of the final duel, the mob has cornered Beckert not in a defunct industrial setting but in that bastion of modern capitalism, the office building, the space of public exchange and its commercial archives—on whose precincts these two manners of criminal, the thief and the child-murderer, are equal trespassers. And to whose settings the photography of the period has been repeatedly drawn. Preoccupied not just with factory locales (exterior and interior)—including the dynamos and turbine halls that anticipate the mise-en-scène of films from Lang's own *Metropolis* (1926) to Charlie Chaplin's *Modern Times* (1936)—the period's photography was as much concerned with industrial effects as with causes. Especially in the prolific work from the 1920s of Walter A. Peterhans, we see numerous imprint reproductions of (other) industrial copies, as for instance the frequent still lifes of mass-produced glassware, aluminum pots, hand tools, shoe trees, and the like.

At the same time, the New Sobriety gravitates as well to depopulated bureaucratic spaces in the new moderne mode of hard-edged architectural symmetry, explicitly Bauhaus and otherwise, as for instance in Hans Finsler's *Central Corridor,* from 1929. These are clean-lined and well-scrubbed impersonal spaces of an emptied, disinfected workplace that anticipate the kind of orderly image evoked first in *M* at a curious transitional moment of official alphabetic inscription. This passing two-word lettering represents an aspect of urban signage beyond the wall of wanted posters and assorted advertising pillars featured in earlier scenes (and also familiar from Neue Sachlichkeit painting as well as photography—as in Georg Scholz's 1926 oil work *Self-Portrait in Front of an Advertising Column*). This later moment of stripped-down institutional signage, however, is one that the narrative lingers over as a quasi-official direct address, a grammatical imperative, that puts the name Lang back into the command to "Drive Slowly" (*Langsam Fahren*) as it appears prominently over the symmetrically framed and sleekly gated office garage to which the mob has tracked Beckert. This inscription might seem to generate an immediate if oblique fallout for the impetus of the cinematic strip itself. For the whole prolonged sequence to follow puts the brakes on full animation and—after Beckert has been hounded down and found, bagged like animal prey, and hauled away—concludes with various shots of the aftermath like a litany of damage and casualties in photographic war reportage.

Here begins a three-stage pattern of photogrammatic disclosure that taps the narrative's deepest sense, at exactly the building climax of its surveillance and manhunt plot, of its own narrative function as a discretely articulated filmic nexus. In the first of these unexpectedly piecemeal sequences, after five quick-cut still images in a row (among them, the shots of dead or unconscious bodies [the building's security officers] involving apparent freeze-frames), we catch the slightest hint of motion in a lock still swinging in the immediate wake of forced entry and evacuation; and then, finally, a presumed still shot is gradually animated by the beam not of a projector but of a flashlight as one abandoned criminal is brought literally to the surface of his underworld. All in silence: that constitutive silence of photography before film, of Lang's cinema before sound. Moreover, as if to remind us of the quasi-forensic images that have built up in this way toward the discovered thug's retrieval and arrest, when he arrives at the police station he himself is transfixed by the office directory, including major billing for the in-house police photographer.

Just before this arrest, in stage two of the terraced photogrammatic parable, Inspector Lohmann has been handed a "protocol"—which is perused in an equally silent sequence. It is a typed report on the attack whose pages are presided over in superimposition—in a trumping of police lab by film lab—by the precinematic spooling of a ticker-tape that has either fed the information to them or will soon disseminate it further. These are pages Lohmann turns over as if they were private intertitles for a silent film being threaded through in his mind—or indeed an optical allusion to the protocinematic flip-book of photo stills turned into a miniature thumbed movie and evoked here as such by the ongoing series of lap dissolves. Call it one version of modernist stream-of-consciousness, cinema-style. What happens is that we too leaf again through the images we've just seen, and then some, seventeen fixed frames in all, several in their architectural rigidity and balance calling up a further aura of the Neue Sachlichkeit manner. And all of them fused this time by the dovetailed bridgework of lap dissolve. This amounts to a pagelike overfolding or shuffling of cinematic planes rather than the jump cuts of the previous and in some cases identical series, which the first time through was presented as sheer narration—without, now, the diegetic embedding of a read text and the associative links presumed by the investigative mind in examining it.

I say "mind" deliberately. According to Deleuze, in his unacknowledged updating of Hugo Münsterberg's mentalist thesis about cinema, the point-cut and the relinkage, as Deleuze calls them—or, in other words, the overt edit and the marked bridge—when detached from the rational montage of a sheer sensorimotor continuum, are, along with the wholly blank screen, the three indices of cinema as thought.[18] Together, cuts and ligatures collaborate in the noetic image, or what Deleuze calls the noosign: the sign in this case of a character's own mental imaging. My added point is that these spliced single frames, many of them freeze-frames, and borrowing all the more in this way as well from the analytic stasis and symmetry of the Neue Sachlichkeit, can best be said, in the Deleuzian sense, to take thought only by revealing at the same time the unthought of cinema so wholly elided in Deleuze's own phenomenology: namely, the single frame in fragmentary or blurred transition, either one.

This run of images in *M* gives thought, therefore, not to the sensorimotor image, yet not just to the association of ideas either, but to the motor of all images in the rotated spool. Further, to single out the image in the eye of police inspection in this case is to associate the photo-frame, however decoupled from its typical, split-second sequence, with the spectatorial logic of evidentiary data rather than pure imaging—with detection, with spying, with the prying rather than privatized eye, with systems of image management and ocular control. It is linked thereby, in other words, to a society of surveillance in a culture of the instrumentalized rather than the disinterested view: to modernity. Narrative film seems acknowledging here, yet again, its descent from the lost utopia of unframed visibility before either the embodied or the openly equipmental look.

But back to the inspector's mental inspection of his teletext. Despite all the bodies discovered there by typescript, and envisioned as one reads—their virtual images soon to be accompanied (we can only assume) by forensic photos eventually incorporated into the report—it is only the missing body of Beckert that concerns Inspector Lohmann. And when, pursuing its whereabouts, he moves to interrogate that one apprehended mobster hauled up to justice, the same subliminal mode of fixed-frame, quasi-photographic illustration (stage three in this sequence of foregrounded mediation) accompanies the man's coerced confession of Beckert's whereabouts. In an immediately visualized mention of the old brewery that went "belly-up" in the Depression, it is as if the photo inserts representing what the criminal describes serve so fully to visualize the site disclosed by his voiceover that they inherit and eclipse the latter's authority by uncurtaining the cinematic scene itself.[19]

With no typescript intervening this time in the crook's oral admission, what we get is a sliding transition from an overvoiced subjective insert to an actual establishing shot, the snitch's vocal signifiers replaced in process by photographic signifieds. This is an optical-free indirect discourse representing not just what's in the speaker's own mind's eye, or what is transferred from it through Lohmann's recognition of the hideout, but what is realized for us as well in transition from the photo-fixity of these manifestations to a fixed-frame, quasi-photographic shot, yet again in the New Objectivist manner of architectonic minimalism. It is a shot (of a spare stairway and railing) that opens upon the next and nearly final scene (when Beckert is dragged down it). But we arrive at this symbolic underground set for the underworld inquisition only after traversing those four entirely depopulated shots that seem operating as stand-ins for the blasted landmarks of national defeat.

If the mental slideshow (and photogrammatic subtext) of that decimated commercial space can't help but call up wartime photographs of bombed-out urban sites, this is the same wreckage and debris that have elsewhere, and programmatically, been won back for rationalized order by the sterile (because deliberately antiseptic and purified) forms of the New Objectivity. Here, too, is a sequence by which the movement-image is so arrested at its source that it can seem to return us, by way of Walter Benjamin's famous remark, to Eugène Atget's unpeopled photographs of urban settings as if they were evacuated crime scenes: in this case not just via desertion and forensic revisitation but by way of a strategic cover, in their neglect and obscurity, for the scapegoating violence of an underworld mob jury.[20] This is a violence that is later alleviated only by the victim's disappearance altogether from the frame—before his subsequent official sentencing (itself quickly cut away from) by a now legal tribunal. This second and equally abrogated judgment is a coda dispatched in a fixed shot whose architectural decor on the wall behind the judges recalls in the outlined scale of its molding a screen's blank rectangle—a vast empty sector of the overall image plane sparing us this time, like the shot as a whole, any last frame-up of the narrative's long-surveilled murderer. This release from view comes, however, only after Beckert has been forced on camera in the previous trial scene, in a jolting run of sutured shots across a focus-pulled display of reframed photographs, to confront serial photographic images of his serial victims.

This bears dwelling on, as the film, one might say, dared not. By the rack focus that brings the girls' images in and out of crisp representation in one spatial axis, and slides them past in another temporal one, their sequential evocation of cinematic dynamism, the very kinesis of their display—muted, blurred, euphemized—may evoke in just this respect the ultimate un-scene of the film: the child murders themselves. But there is a more contextual fine art register (yet another) for this mode of memento mori in regard to the repressed episodes of on-camera murder. For what, by being held up to view, these conventional wholesome photos hold offscreen—out of frame, by allusion only—is the spate of *Lustmord* art in Neue Sachklicheit drawing and painting: the aftermath of sex murders picturing the bloodied bodies of female victims as if in a repatriation of wartime violence in the midst of rampant domestic frustration, impotence, and displaced rage. In view (which is to say in the suppressed image) of this quarantined motif, all the other visual themes called up from contemporaneous art practice may seem piled up to protect us from the ultimate intertext and matrix of the plot: the violated child corpses wholly beyond representation, either in real time or by any trace of their evidentiary status in the files of the police station photographer.

Portraits of the living girls are almost too close for comfort to the pictures we would never be allowed to see. But well before and altogether aside from such individual photoprints in motion within this climactic site of the diegesis, what I've been suggesting, because I think Lang's editing technique suggests it, is that the ongoing stream of cross-references to the New Objectivists, channeled in turn by the narrative flow, serves in its turn to objectify something about cinema that otherwise goes unseen but not unknown by early audiences: namely, its immediate generation from, as well as its genealogical relation to, the fixed frame photographic imprint. The intertextual oscillation becomes in this way an infratextual resonance, a kind of hypomediation, not observable but nonetheless operative from frame to frame, subliminal but felt—even when there are no inset images, though there sometimes are—to set back and so show forth, by association, this undertextual basis in the fixed trace of the racing frame line.

Panopsis and Plot

And all of this comes barreling down in Lang's conclusion on the climactic shot where, with the killer cornered by the symbolic long arm of the law—though never once, if I may put it this way, *seen being seen* by the police—this outcast is finally and mercifully cast out from our own view. We recognize here, mission accomplished, the equivocated optics of cinema's very prosecution in the frame advance of its own narrative frame-ups: now you see it, now you don't. Narratively speaking, the duel goes so wholly unresolved that Lohmann never even fires off so much as a look at his bested captive. In this way, almost paradoxically, the case study of a modern surveillance network, in its own partial cinematic coalition of image and sound, has taken the pinioned criminal off camera just before the case can officially be brought. But that's just a little too fast—noticeably on the film's part, as well as on the part of analysis. Apprehended and locked down in that last close-up—his image isolated so as to be spared either two-shot or suture, yet as if imprisoned by framing alone—Beckert, in this last we see of him, is held before us in a privileged view, unshared by the lateral encroachment of the law.

But that privilege hardly spares him, or us, from something deep in the mechanics of cinema into which few films before (or even after) *M* have driven so consistent a wedge. Call it the social norms of scopophilia, in and beyond the movie house. One thing this last shot may bring to mind, before cutting to Beckert's absence from the day and place of judgment, is Foucault's insistence that the modern state, in its tacit parameters as a police state, was initially bolstered—and precisely in its biopolitics—by the removal of corporal punishment from the public sphere, from mass view.[21] Taking hangings and beheadings off the communal stage helped to secure a panoptic regime in which a civilian "vision" internalizes the interdicts of the law without having the satisfaction of the scapegoat spectacle through which to vent any anxious sense of rule and its cruelties. That anxiety becomes instead muted but pervasive under, again, the long arm of the law and its unseen impersonal gaze (Lang's tandem tropes). Not necessarily via stocks or scaffold, but in many other equally implacable ways, movies in a sense return a communal (but not expressly legislated) violence to public view, even while generalizing the spectatorial bloodlust they solicit into a more neutralized scopic pleasure not in itself party to the violence under depiction, which is to say vicarious without being sacrificial. But potentially uncomfortable, nonetheless, in its curiosities, its voyeuristic thrills.

The near miss of physical violence at the end of *M* offers in effect the proof negative (rather than proof positive) of its specular aggression. Though the verdict too goes offscreen and unread, leaving us only the mourning mothers in their call for further public vigilance—for more *over-sight,* as it were—there seems little doubt that violent retribution is to be meted out to Beckert, given the place of capital punishment in German criminal law of the period. Death literally goes without saying, let alone showing. But this is indeed, wholly offstage and ob-scene, the least of it. Even as a sacrifice to a communal order that may well have betrayed him into violence in the first place (as trench victim), the issue is not so much that Beckert dies for our sins, or, with more historical specificity, for the sins of a war-ravaged generation. It is how we are "spared" that dying that seems of interest to Lang's shot plan. His murdering protagonist would no doubt have been summarily executed by edict of the kangaroo court, but the law arrives just in time, all but invisible at point of capture, merely impinging on the culprit's cornered close-up. Here and at every earlier point of the film, Lang is at greater pains to manage how his audience responds to the images of detection than to elicit the spectacle of retributive violence, drawn more to the epistemological burdens of narrative than to the psychology of foreclosure and extermination.

In *M,* taking the marked man at last out-of-frame has its symmetrical dramatic ironies. Leaving its own frame forever, too, in the film's opening sequence, Elsie's balloon, like Elsie, is there one moment, gone the next. So, comparably, punitively, with Beckert. In between—and with that one exception Rancière is right to notice (if perhaps wrong to overvalue as the remedial counterpoint to plot)—few characters have ever been more excruciated than Beckert by their time *in* frame, on camera, under surveillance, in view. We don't just look on at the pain and panic. With that one signal exception that Rancière might have gone on to recognize as so radically disbanded later in the same scene, our being invisibly sutured in as perceptual center of Beckert's track-down—whatever we feel about it or him—stations our participation itself as a recurrent increment of the plot, there at the outer envelope of its visible (and visual) transactions.

And there, just there, is where the arrested visuals of those multiplying still images we've examined over Lohmann's shoulder, as it were—images seized up in their anticinematic stasis, and visible to begin with only by association with a teletyped account—go out of their way to break into the movement-image itself and to derail its normal storytelling. They do so, of course, by a direct optic pipeline to the more ordinarily materialized place of evidentiary photos in the surveillance operations of urban modernity. But insisted upon for once in all this, rather than taken invisibly for granted, is film's role, its rolling past, as a chain of studied images whose scrutiny—as graphic frames and as plot increments at once—entrains the constituent visual narrative beneath its manhunt scenario. At this level, one story Lang's montage has to tell is that of frame-advance modernism within a particular vision (using the term advisedly) of modern state bureaucracy and its relentless instinct for the restraint of transgression. This includes, in an unusually prominent part of the same story, those modernist visual forms from other media that have elsewhere worked to capture such institutional anonymities or satirize their sterility. By intertext as well as infratext, then, *M* is a film about the participation of its own surveillance ethos in the wider field of modernist visual culture, including that culture's imperatives, its addictions, its queasy depletions. In one of its furthest-reaching cognates, *M* stands not only for Murderer, Marked Man, Manhunt, or even Montage, but rather for Modern itself under the sign of the seen.

Prognostic Optics

Again, the year is 1931; Lang's venture: the tactical (rather than blanket) use of dialogue and ambient sound in a mostly (and ominously) silent film bent on maximizing its optic melodrama while minimizing production expenses in sound recording. By the necessitated shortcuts that mother invention, Lang works out an unprecedented balancing act between silent tracking and explosive capture, inaudible spying and raucous accusation, capped by the eloquent agony of a final confessional monologue. And followed again by soundless disappearance from the scene of legal arraignment. The film doesn't go silent between major events. Via contrapuntal montage, silence is the shared medium of its surveillance plot—a medium incurring in the process, as noted, a strange kind of secondary visibility. As if edging to the margin the aesthetics of recorded voice and noise, together with the realist expectations this technology further induces, Lang's first half-talkie, on the cusp of the new, adverts (in this way as well) to his medium's photomechanical underlay (and origins)—and does so by the analogical route of other contemporary image systems.

Beyond financial expedience, what emerges from Lang's industrial ingenuity is a kind of optico-cortical thought experiment. The effect isn't estranging or inveigling, either one. It is more like cross-medial and leveling. When scenes come to us, at key turns, more like shots than like envisaged locales, are we then seeing the world the way the plastic arts of the period tend to present it, not only as inert and arrested but as already seen? As pictures, not places? Already as if cataloged? An intuition like this would have, in the case of *M*, its full plot charge—and ethical fallout. In a movie whose entire narrative arc depends on spying, determinant events take place only when their sites are already sighted. Everything passes under ocular—often figured as optical—mediation: figured that way, in crucial part, by the invoked cellular increment of the still-frame track itself, whatever sonic or phonic supplements may also enhance the telling from within the showing. Thus, in sum, the extraordinary historical match of technique to plot in Lang's half-step into the talking era. The sensory economy of the surveillance theme—in precisely its media valence—is stretched to complementary limits in a parceling out of turning points across Lang's detection plot. His first sound film makes the first definitive siting of the protagonist (by anyone but the privileged and soon compromised viewer) a recognition of Beckert's unseen whistling body by the blind balloon vendor. Then, as if to honor the independence of audio from visual data on the composite track, narrative isolates the further sighting of the now-visibly marked man as an entirely silent extrusion of markedly aggressive camerawork.

But we've neither seen nor heard the half of it yet, back in 1931. In the protracted legacy of Lang's surveillance logic, the inhabited worlds of film will one day come—in our day, that is—to be optically mediated (often audially bugged as well) even before seen by certain characters themselves as well as by us: secondary traces in already screened (reframed) form, not unfolded first-hand by storytelling but yielding to scrutiny only as transmitted, stored, disembodied. Much of the time in recent cinema, certainly in the surveillance scenarios owing most to Lang's melodrama—a cinema not of the Deleuzian time-image but of the timed, or time-coded, image—we are viewing retrieved or even simultaneous closed-circuit footage (or, more to the point, digital data) on surveillance monitors or laptops: a second-order drama of the virtual. Watching quasi-photographic frames as plotted sites in Lang is one beginning of this medial end, the time-stamped video file now dominant.

So where did we leave *opsis* vs. *muthos* in regard to this obsessive scopic webwork of Lang's cinema? It isn't just that Rancière has looked the monster of plot straight in the eye and chosen, with *M*'s juggernaut of detection, one of the hardest nuts to crack for his claim. This alone might have seemed strategic. If some fleeting distilled *opsis* can get a foothold even within this one film's forced march of diegesis, then where couldn't it? The potential must indeed be medium-deep. Point taken, up to a point. But the stakes are larger yet for this revisionary philosophy of film in Rancière. Without mentioning Deleuze's treatment of *M* as a prototypical deployment of the movement-image in the mode of action montage and its mandatory resolutions, Rancière's effort at large is nonetheless to soften the overschematization of Deleuze's dyad, with its WWII watershed, and to find the "empty time" of "photogénie" inherent in the medium rather than just providing its late-modernist telos. Again, fair enough—and important. But there is another metahistorical tendency, if not a telos, that the pivotal wrench of suture we've examined via Rancière in *M* has a way of foreseeing, precisely when the same scene's initial shot, in all its momentarily isolated looking, is only a transient (and in some sense delusory) interlude: part of plot's suspense more than its suspension.

The sustained effect in question, and especially at its breaking point, puts our very role as spectators on edge. For all we know, the whole time Beckert is looking at leisure, as well as at those leisure goods, those playthings for the eye, he is being looked at from across the street. Moments later and just a few feet away, having shifted position from the outside of the window to the *inside* of the mirror's interface, so to say, he sees as much, recognizes that possibility by time-lag. Plot has co-opted *opsis* itself under the rule of surveillance. Entailed in the ensuing crux of camerawork and its crucial irony are the closed circuits not of suture alone but, in prefiguation, of CCTV as well—and of that cycle of films whose related digital interventions derive from the same electronic moment in our contemporary culture: a moment where the video game as intertext is as common as any intermedial allusion to fixed frame graphic art in Lang.

After that momentous peripety in *M*'s shot sequence and its plot alike—hinged around the storefront mirror and turning as it does on the rearview gaze at an unwanted but answering look—Lang's montage later proceeds toward its somewhat forestalled finale. It does so by disarticulating itself into sheer picture planes at moments of forensic advance—in a kind of photographic free indirection. Plot and visual evidence have become indistinguishable. It is a matter at once of mediation and theme to which Lang, five years after Rancière's postwar examples of broadcast TV in *While the City Sleeps*, returns in his last film, *The Thousand Eyes of Dr. Mabuse*, through the explicit use of those closed-circuit TV feeds coterminous at times with the story's own narration. Three decades earlier in *M*, the edited strip, under new scrutiny for its mesh with an intermittently synchronized sound track, has also told its own tale in the dismemberment of montage by serial collage. After which, justice is dealt out—and a certain narrative mercy with it—only when diegesis spares *opsis* and, taking Beckert off-frame, retains to the end that coveted invisibility to the law that, of course, the frame-bound rules of our own looking have violated.

In this regard, one may conceive of the film's rehearsed trajectory of mediations diachronically as well as synchronically. Realist painting and its arriving competitor in photography emphasized first of all, in the mid-nineteenth century, the looks of the world rather than a looking. But insofar as the automatism of photography introduced the element of relative simultaneity, it did implicate more directly than painting (in fact, indexed) the vantage point along with the vista, sighting as well as sitter, the presence of the taker and the taken-down alike. Cinema further motivated (as well as motorized) photography—yet only, with the gradual coming of narrative, so as to minimize the index of the automated look in sutured deference to a simulated scenic immediacy and the internal gazing of its portrayed agents. This is all the more obvious, with Lang's *M*, when staged in immediate correlation with a new order of "realist" paintings and photographs executed under the mandate of objectivism. Over against this associated tissue of mediated still views in Lang, even while mounted upon their photogrammatic counterparts, the mechanism of unseen cinematographic viewing—the camera as incipient spyware—seems calling itself out as the acknowledged return of an ocular (and archaeological) repressed: disclosing not just the image but its optic capture. From Lang's cinema on, and such is the boomerang of its politics as well as its "erotics" (Oudart), the moving-image apparatus is, in effect, a universal index of *potentially being watched.*

It is by such routes of photogen(et)ic reflex that Lang's motion picture as confessed machinic image file—or, in other words, as divulged engine for scopic tracking—closes the thematized gap between police work and plot. So does it end up anticipating as well the collapsed distinction between telling and showing in the hypermediations of the next century's cinema, in everything from enforced self-surveillance in Michael Haneke's *Caché* through films of helmet cams and drone scans in the new "wired war" to the electronic retrieval systems of both global espionage and Homeland Security thrillers. This, again, is the "timed image" (postphotographic, post-Deleuzian)—the image of simultaneous record and instant replay—where the otherwise "empty time" of pure optics seems to swallow up diegesis altogether in the mediacy of the virtual.

The abbreviation of Lang's title may initialize the Modern, as suggested, but its endemic ocular paranoia—outlasting any narrowly modernist textual play with the materiality of the frame line as photofile—finds a new technological register in the pervasive video tracing and transmit of our very-late-modernity of the image. So that, in the last but most prescient of all the film's pre-electronic cognates, *M* stands for—and looks dubiously forward to—all things exponentially Monitored.

2 TELESCREEN PROSE

The career-long videography of surveillance in Fritz Lang's films is what can only be called epochal, from the two-way audiovisual monitoring of the proletarian depths in *Metropolis* in 1926 through the CCTV snares of *The Thousand Eyes of Dr. Mabuse* in 1960. But the screen topic of such secretive observation and inspection has scarcely been confined to Lang's narratives, having instead consolidated its variants almost into a genre of their own, certainly a mode. Time and again the imprinted and projected visual artifact that we've paid to see features forth, within its film narrative, the real-time transmit of closed-circuit video imagery, with its transfer from site to (over)sight operating through the questionable channels of spycraft and covert motive as what we might call a "secondary omniscience." Vision itself disappears into *supervision*. Our cinematic viewing is disinterested and impassive by comparison—or so we are regularly allowed to think—even when ironically contaminated around the edges by the voyeuristic or aggressive framework of many screen episodes in this vein.

Having established a prototype with *M*, the rest of this book now separates, along Lang's own divide, between the technologies of specular vantage and, ultimately inextricable, the psychological or political damage such oversight may produce. A structural interplay regularly operates, that is, between various bureaucracies, or sheer perversities, of surveillance and the potential brutalities of audiovisual capture—and sometimes of mental imprisonment—thereby entailed. The present chapter begins by tracking the paranoia of oversight, characteristic of all Lang's films, through to its literary counterpart in George Orwell's *1984*, pointing as that novel does, in turn, to a legacy of the invasive "telescreen" in contemporary technoculture. This is a line of descent marked by films (in the next chapter) that typically indulge in, even while critiquing, the effects of such optic machination. From there forward, two subsequent chapters pursue the fine line between spectacle and inspection that gets deliberated in screen narratives directly preoccupied with the distinction between voyeurism and surveillance, eroticism and epistemophilia. Any such chapter breakdown can offer no more than an arbitrary demarcation—across film history's various genre oscillations—of a technological as well as a narratological continuum. It is nonetheless useful in assessing this trajectory to consider, early on, its syntax of subjectivity not just in cinematic editing but in those narrative prose styles—and their own "surveillant enunciation" (Levin again)—most directly intent on grasping this audiovisual dynamic, from Orwell's channeled omniscience to the tech-savvy narrative indirection of spy novelist John le Carré—each with his separate evocations of cinematic and video grammar.

Novelistic Suture: From Spectacle to Inspection

But first, the methodological crossroads at which this path forward is laid out—beginning with a word on the difference between words and pictures in a given plot's narrative sights. The difference, but also the common ground: the ground of depiction as inspection, verbal as well as visual. Under the influence of Michel Foucault on the cultural paradigm of Jeremy Bentham's panopticon, literary theory has been quick to see behind the strategies of narrative overview the logic of police-state surveillance and punishment (Foucault's *Surveiller et punir*, flattened in translation to *Discipline and Punish*). Analysis has been pursued especially in relation to received conventions of omniscient narrative and the manifestation, subsumed to it, of a character's inner thoughts when extruded and reframed by free indirect discourse.[1] The genre of the novel comes forward under this stress as an apparatus—and ultimately an institution—of epistemological license and power, if not overt discipline (other than formal) or punishment (other than of character by plot). And so the early protorealist novel down through Victorian fiction might well, as the claims have run, tend in its cultural function to acclimate the social subject as reader to a state (and implicit state apparatus) of undue visibility and always potential exposure—and thus to an internalized practice of self-monitoring constraint. One result: interpellation as the novel's version of suture, "hailing" us into cultural premises in the way cinema stitches us into (pro)visional spaces.

On the heels of Victorian fiction, film readily takes up its station in this social pedagogy and internal discipline. In its widely recognized derivation from the Victorian rhetoric of storytelling, cinema's own conventions induce responses from the spectator similar to those elicited by narrative fiction—the new medium doing so, of course, not just by analogy with optics and panoptics but in the very mode of such visual systems. And this in continuous sync with an evolution of the same optical technology that once made possible, first, the recorded serial image, then its frame line projection, and now, since the outmoding of photochemistry, the linear scan of digital registration. Yet this last phase, the digital turn, has a dominant and entirely non-narrative ubiquity outside the screen fictions it helps generate. And this real-world digital panoptic, as the flip side of digital display and computer-generated imagery, has gone so far as to collapse the very difference not just between private and public, action and transmission, but—on a sliding scale of technological intervention—between two cultural predicates turned martial in their latest brand of mediation. In wired war, that is, the infinitives *surveiller* and *punir* converge as if in the very crosshairs of geopolitical aggression. This happens (in a technological conjuncture to which chapter 6 is devoted) when electronics are deployed to scope out a target by the same medium of digital aiming by which it can then be taken out.

Short of this, however, and within one contemporary strain of screen narrative in particular, there is still—even for noncombatant surveillance tales—a decided edge of belligerence, and always a potential whiff of ballistics, in many a mediated and relayed view. This is because such manifold narrative omniscience, well after the advent of its earliest cinematographic variants, has so entirely left behind by now the model of third-person prose that it has become automated in everything from the aerial shot to the free indirect discourse of POV framing from covert camera emplacements. At the very least—in a remark that might be used to sum up those valences of narrative theory derived from Foucault—John le Carré's proposition that all novelists "are spies" meets its cinematic equivalent, for many films lately, in the thought that all cinematography gravitates ineluctably either toward the look of surveillance or of target practice—or both.[2] Which means that audience reaction, to whatever degree distanced from images thus seized and sized up, ranges (and even more narrowly wavers) between vicarious paranoia and voyeurism—and does so, as in the case of realist fiction too, as a direct function of medium rather than just theme.

What Lang's Overlord Frederson in *Metropolis* has in common with the novelistic Big Brother is more, therefore, than their equivalent stigma as oppressive and brutal figureheads. The issue of panoptic control is in both texts spectatorial as well as dictatorial, even while differently mediated by prose and screen. Differently mediated, but available for related analysis. Narratography is one way of bridging the gap. For the resistant readings of literary omniscience have, in fact, much in common with the agenda of suture theory in marking the fall from an image-in-itself to the image-for-the-other under the tyranny of the gaze. What invaded privacy is for the Foucauldian view of free indirect discourse, scopophilia (whether in the mode of desire or detection) is for the ideological critique of classic montage. One purpose of this chapter is to note certain ways in which explicit scenes of surveillance can sometimes bring these independent media critiques not just to a head but genuinely together.

Writing in "Recess"

One turns, almost inevitably, from Mabuse to Big Brother, great uncle of all surveillance masterminds in the years since Orwell's conception—and turns especially to the integral connection in his numerically anagrammatic 1948 novel (published 1949) between cinema and surveillance. This connection is manifest well before the bleakly faithful British screen adaptation by Michael Radford was released in the eponymous year 1984, with its canny opening travesty of Soviet montage for the film propaganda used to fuel the ritual Two Minutes Hate, that recurrent screening by which the Party congregates and whips into a mindless frenzy the bloodthirsty public (as mass audience). Although this technical rhetoric of sepia-burnished workers in superimposed collectivity—with its clear evocation of Sergei Eisenstein's principles getting watered down and turned poisonously Stalinist—is not explicitly developed in the novel's equivalent scene, there is an oblique precedent for it early in the novel.

The episode in question, while orienting us toward the reversible logic of the telescreen from there out—with its ocular and phonic indoctrinations as well as surveillance—also contrasts such a steady machinic gaze with the cheapjack visceral montage of cinematic propaganda. It is almost as if the standard melodrama of cinematic editing in genre narratives, in this case the war film—manipulating the spectator in its coded ways—must be anatomized and dispensed with before giving the novel's plot over to the more invasive manipulation, overt and covert at once, of the two-way telescreen. Filtering sound as well as image, and itself a caustic lampoon of the postwar television apparatus still in its rudimentary marketing, Orwell's closed-circuit teleprompter—its electronic ideology prod—operates with no mention of recording capacity. Entirely real-time, like "live TV" (although in this case intermittently two-way), the telescreen thus comes into relief as a malign exaggeration of visual commerce in the novel's own contemporaneous media scene.

In an attempt to dodge the power of the optical spyware, Winston Smith sits alone in the "recess" of the wall where once there was, he guesses, a bookcase: a sequestered space perfect for reading—and writing—when he turns illicitly to it, backed away from the sightlines of the wall-cam in a wholly *recessive* gesture of nostalgia for a now outlawed self-expression. Although the "thought police" will soon and inevitably find him out—spying on his thought as you, the reader, do by following along in the citations from his diary—Winston has nonetheless momentarily evaded the surveillant gaze. He has situated himself in the blind spot of power, taking advantage of the fact—as phrased in a striking technological pun cutting to the core of the surveillance motif—that a hard-wired prying eye like the telescreen cannot in fact "command the whole room."[3] The state's power is diminished, one might like to think at this point, in exact proportion to its evaded purview. One wants to believe that there is a way to "cheat the telescreen" (11). One soon learns better.

As if racing to use what's left of his English before Newspeak scours him clean of it, Winston lets his pen spit out—in what amounts to free-associational recall—a volley of fragmentary images from the war film he's seen the night before, its depicted carnage instinctively appreciated via the rhetoric of its camera angles. Forbidden to read in private, encouraged only to watch the talking screen, his own manic punctuation in this novice diarizing seems to have inherited a cinematographic rather than lexigraphic sense of succession. And so, with this treasonous inscription, is marked the beginning of his end: "April 4th, 1984. Last night to the flicks. All war films." A day of reckoning, or at this stage more like sheer ciphering, in a curious rebus sense: 4/4/84, the vicious circle of history standing still as if in an image of its permanent falsification. All he can do is begin to recover the immediate past, as it comes back to him—almost like a bad meal: "All war films." How many such (plural) can the state manage to program in a single evening? Are these short fictions? Or actual documentaries from the front—a dubious battleground that there is no reason to believe actually exists in this dystopian ethos of permanent and total war? So in this sense fiction anyway, whatever political subterfuge might be involved in their filming?

No matter. The violence of technique is what compels Winston in recollection. When a civilian vessel under helicopter attack is blown to smithereens, Orwell puts his hero's diary entry about this episode in italics. He does so, it would seem, to evoke both the cursive of handwriting and the frenetic emphasis of the theatrical effect—how *"the boat went all to matchwood"* (9). What is the scale of this depicted shattering? Splintered to fragments now suitable only for the milling of miniature sticklike forms—and with the overtones of explosive ignition in the synecdochal "match"? Or effect reverting to cause: a wooden model exposed (by explosion) as the mock-up that it is, further marking this sea battle as a screen fiction? One may well suspect the latter, with its clue to fictionalized violence—at least from the emphasis on an artistry in camerawork more complicated than anything resembling contemporaneous WWII combat footage in its recent (late-40s) documentary forms.

To begin with, Winston's no doubt involuntarily mimetic prose bloats in adjectival description of the opening, with "*shots of a great huge fat man*" (9), after which there is an explicit change of camera angles, for "*then you saw him through the helicopters* [sic] *gunsights*"—one helicopter, so we presume—in a sequence continued after Winston's mere breathless comma: "*then he was full of holes and the sea round him turned pink and he sank*" (8). The near phonetic miss of an echoic *pink sinking* comes by way of a comma splice operating like a quick cut to close-up. After which Winston's analysis becomes yet more explicitly cinematographic. A period after "sank" has caught the diarist's breath for him—before an uncapitalized new cluster of clauses targets the remaining passengers: "*then the helicopter planted a 20 kilo bomb in among them terrific flash.*" No time for grammar at all in the vanishing split second between "*them*" and what's left of them a moment later, when the disintegrated boat—followed by more hackwork splicing in the manner of jump cuts—"*went all to matchwood. then there was a wonderful shot of a child's arm going up up up right up into the air a helicopter with a camera in its nose must have followed it up and there was a lot of applause from the party seats*" (9). Formalist film analysis, spewed forth in this transgressive free writing, becomes ideological critique on the spot. As Orwell would be the first to insist in his famous essay "Politics and the English Language,"[4] there is a politics to the butchering of the English language that goes, in this case, beyond mimetic vividness to indoctrination—and its dawning resistance. Winston seems to be working the suturing and interpellatory bloodlust of propaganda film out of his system by getting it—and so facing it—down.

Writing is one thing, one proscribed thing, even when journaling about the routine visual narcotics that stream past and through you. Reading subversive text is quite another. At its later turning point, *1984* indulges in an anachronistic dead metaphor for surveillance at just the point when Winston is embarking on his fatal transgression, namely, devouring the seditious manuscript exposé of state coercion by Emmanuel Goldstein—this, while temporarily lulled into incautious confidence, letting down the usual guard: "He was alone; no telescreen, *no ear at the keyhole*, no nervous impulse to glance over his shoulder or cover the page with his hand" (184; emphasis added). This is when he still thinks he's safe in the illicit rented room he shares with his new lover Julia. No telescreen, he believes, "commands" any part of the room this time. The optical decor is instead, so it seems, motionless and one-way, comfortingly old-fashioned, consisting mostly of a single faded engraving of a now-ruined church—not (for some reason) hung from, but instead directly affixed to, their bedroom wall.

From listening at keyholes, that dated trope, to remote audition under conditions of technological surveillance—this is precisely the historical distance Winston wants temporarily to forget his culture has traveled. But Julia seems almost intuitively to know better when looking at the antique framed image: "'I bet that picture's got bugs behind it,' said Julia. 'I'll take it down and give it a good clean some day'" (147). The engraving is at least two hundred years old, Winston has surmised. In contrast, only two years old by the time of Orwell's writing—and thus a technological fact (and nomenclature) he probably wouldn't have known about—was the Soviet surveillance device known alternately as "The Thing," the "Buran," and (more lastingly) "the bug," invented by sound engineer Léon Theremin (for which he eventually won the Stalin Prize) and first used as a secret plant in a ceremonial seal, as wall plaque, given by the Soviets to Moscow's American ambassador in 1945.[5] With its little feeler-antenna that no doubt gave the device its insectile nickname, this "passive" listening device—transmitter-free, activated only by remote signal—was the predecessor of modern day RFID ("remote-frequency identification devices") for global tracking (later ubiquitous in films).

If the hovering pun on "got bugs behind it" (for infestation and invaded privacy at once) were available to Orwell, rather than a mere accident of linguistic history, he certainly would have wanted it, since behind this fixed engraving is indeed a hidden telescreen by which the traitorous couple is eventually exposed, their worst fears echoed back to them with a transferred epithet ("iron voice" for "steely" sound in the metaphoric sense, rather than just metallic resonance in the literal). "We are the dead," Julia has echoed to Winston's despair after reading Goldstein, and immediately: "'You are the dead,' said an iron voice behind them" (221). The picture is suddenly detached by a release latch, falls crashing to the floor, and "'Now they can see us,' said Julia" is answered at once by the shift in grammatical person—as if automatically generated by mechanical permutation: "'Now we can see you,' said the voice" (222). By the most tried and tested reflexes of interpellation, they know of their guilt, their doom, have already internalized its fatality, well before the state troubles to name it.

Beyond "Private Life"

Quite apart from the philological accident, or up-to-the-minute irony, of the bug pun, the audiovisual collision here is exactly as predicted in the reading of the manuscript that precipitated it, with Goldstein's history of mass control through mediation. Even the Catholic heresy-hunting that culminated in the Inquisition, Goldstein implies, was "tolerant" by comparison with present regimes, since "in the past no government had the power to keep its citizens under constant surveillance" (205–06). Technological reproduction began to change all that forever. Goldstein's polemic (Orwell's by ventriloquism) is directed against the endemic deceits and connivances of mass media: "The invention of print . . . made it easier to manipulate public opinion, and the film and the radio carried the process further." The point seems for a moment to have shifted entirely away from "surveillance" to propaganda. But television and its refinement offer, next, a further decisive turning point, a literal swivel between received and delivered signals. Goldstein thus anticipates, by several decades, the technological determinism of a posthumanist theorist like Friedrich Kittler when the former writes: "With the development of television, and the technical advance which made it possible to receive and transmit simultaneously on the same instrument, private life came to an end" (205–06).

The upshot is that every citizen "worth watching" can now be seen in the very process of indoctrination; in other words (strangely contorted and disorienting words at that), can "be kept for twenty-four hours a day under the eyes of the police and in the sound of official propaganda, with all other channels of communication closed" (206). The odd disjuncture (not quite parallel) of that compound prepositional phrase "in the eyes . . . and in the sound"—pointing two ways at once along a shared axis—is as disorienting as the system it excoriates. One doesn't know whether one is coming or going, in syntax or in scanned space. Or say that the two-way traffic of audiovisual signaling founders in expression on its own nefarious conflation of seeing and being seen, voiced imperatives and reciprocal eavesdropping. As if this strained grammatical manifestation of closed-circuit relay were a variant of "in the eyes as well as earshot of Big Brother," phrasal structure is under duress from the overarching template imposed here: nonindividuation via total interpenetration.

What rhetoric might call the broken syllepsis (or zeugma) in that phrasing achieves its cinematic equivalent in the film version of the novel.[6] This we find in the unstable juxtapositions of speech (often hallucinatory or offscreen) and its audition—and more often yet in the vanished difference between eyeing and being spied upon, whether collapsed by superimposition or by other forms of suspended suture. And these are only some of the ways in which the ironic disjunctures of Orwell's prose achieve their cinematographic equivalents in Radford's treatment. The film is so steeped in the focalization techniques of the novel, including its free indirect access to the thought patterns of its hero—making him a kind of narrative delegate for the storytelling libido itself—that editing subsumes Orwell's own syntactic ironies. When the narrative traps Winston in the tile-lined holding chamber before consignment to Room 101, its technique of double lap dissolve—showing the hero's head slumped in two different positions, fading then to the inconsequential difference between two more such angles of abjection—has perfectly transliterated Orwell's verbal ellipsis to an optical one: "A long time passed. If it had been midnight when the skull-faced man was taken away, it was morning; if morning, it was afternoon" (237). The second phrasing there carries a hint of the enforced paradoxes to come in Winston's torture, where 2 plus 2 is anything the Party says it is—or where, under coercion in this case, morning might well be afternoon. At work is a Deleuzian "postwar" time-image in a uniquely disturbing form: the "any-space-whatever" of aimless waiting become a virtual *space of time*—locating a duration figured without diurnal calibration. And through it all in the film version of this sequence, given the exhaustive surveillance system, what we see—in seeing Winston—is an immobilized subject reduced even beyond the "spectator" of his own agency to the merely *spectated*.

At the end of this same episode on-screen, tense structure is further distorted. Surveillance photos—separate black-and-white images—of Winston's and Julia's illicit sexual pleasure, as the Party functionary O'Brien explains when passing them in front of the beaten man, "will be recycled" (as in the novel as well) "for proletarian use." Voyeurism has been entirely subsumed to a joyless and clinical surveillance before being returned into the circuit of seedy pleasures—as evoked now by film montage in the immediately following cascade of overlays. Winston's head is being aggressively shaved, as if in a kind of emasculation, while, over his demeaned image, we see in lap dissolves (as if he remembers) a shifting series of black-and-white stills recording in close-up Julia's frozen ecstasies. Documents from the police archive, even as they evoke a lover's own POV, are thus shuffled through in approximate match cuts with the real-time humiliation of his upper body. If his own shorn cranium is mentally internalizing these last traces of their pleasure, they too will soon be excavated by torture—and finally extirpated by betrayal.

For under Big Brother, the past—including first and foremost any clutched sense of joy and defiance—does not, and never did, exist. Winston's job in the Ministry of Truth has in fact been to administer just this erasing of the record. The last time we see him at work, he has discovered and then incinerated a piece of photographic proof that contradicts one of the Party's foundational lies about the rooting out of notorious traitors. As his thoughts about this are laid open to us, including the subvocal inflection of Orwell's free indirect discourse, grammatical time seems to suffer obfuscation along with time past. For even the emphasis carried by italics doesn't fully remove the insidious ambiguity of tense from Winston's meditation on the falsified preterits and pluperfects of Party history: "Was the Party's hold upon the past less strong, he wondered, because a piece of evidence which existed no longer *had once* existed?" (79; Orwell's emphasis). The effort at clarity seems at one level obvious: evidence that existed exists no longer. But with a paradoxical syntactic undertow, confirming the juggernaut of erasure: evidence that actually existed (until destroyed) "no longer" (attached forward) had even *once* existed, stricken from being as well as from record and mind. If so, a case of syntactic lap dissolve.

Where the human subject is defined over time as the accumulation of its memories, to control and erase those mental traces is to remake that self from within, not as obedient to power but as indistinguishable from its mere emptied vessel and channel. As O'Brien explains to Winston in the course of his brutally dehumanizing interrogation and torture, Big Brother has transformed the logic of the "old despotisms" as well as the modern "totalitarianisms." While the quasi-religious commandments of such past regimes amounted to "thou shalt" and "thou shalt not," with their authoritarian appeal to belief or to constraint, by contrast "Our command is 'Thou art'": a yet more quasi-religious usurpation of divine fiat ("Let there be"). This of course means the evacuation of the human being into sheer social subject, subject (to) only in the political rather than the psychological sense. All one's instincts must be voided and inverted, so that what you are is the negation constituted by a love for your own oppression and annihilation. And this is exactly the point, at a tantalizing slant from each other, that the novel and the film bear down on in closing, but only by recalling the coercions of the telescreen and its iconic figuration of power developed from Orwell's first chapter forward.

Oculi and Foci: "So contrived that the eyes follow you when you move"

Indeed, Goldstein's nonidiomatic generalization, at narrative midpoint, about a society not only "in the sound" of its numbing ideology but in "the eyes" of its police-state implementation takes us back to the personification of power in the first description of Big Brother, which we may well remember when we have arrived at the deflected sightlines of his panoptic gaze in the film version's last shot. One notes an almost transgeneric irony in the way this "figurehead" is unfolded across the web of Orwell's rhetoric. Certainly the novel's sci-fi elements are swamped, along with any element of the fantastic, in its uniquely poised genre of futurist social satire. But it is still as if Tzvetan Todorov's principle, in his study of "the fantastic"—that many of the genre's monstrous extrapolations derive from taking a metaphor "literally"—would apply to the novel as well.[7] Think in particular of Goldstein's subversive manuscript, read *en abyme* in a different typeface by Winston, where the oligarchic logic of the state is described as a decentralized structure with "no capital" (no "capit") and, following along this same etymological groove in the next sentence, whose "titular head is a person whose whereabouts nobody knows" (208). The best way to read Orwell is always to hold tight to the historicity of words that the Party would efface, including the lines of descent sketched by etymology itself.

Moreover, that "titular head" is literalized by the giant headshot of Big Brother plastered and broadcast everywhere, yet symbolizing finally, as we see most decisively in the last scene—though differently in both novel and film—not an embodied comrade among comrades but just an "ideological state apparatus" for signaling the pervasive nature of corrupt power rather than incarnating its focal point. This leitmotif of the Big Brother icon is emphasized in the novel, on first appearance, for the way its fixed-image dissemination on posters and telescreens seems almost to come alive in its life-denying insistence, phrased here in an initial transferred predication (the poster rather than the face glaring down at the viewer) and then followed by a snaring second person: "The poster with the enormous face gazed from the wall . . . one of those pictures which are so contrived that the eyes follow you when you move" (1–2). The prose of narration, by free indirection, has thus already internalized the interpellatory grammar of the panoptic icon a moment before spelling it out: "BIG BROTHER IS WATCHING YOU, the caption beneath it ran" (2). The difference between "follow one when one moves" and "follow you" is an idiomatic realization of the iconic (and hegemonic) suture itself.

Radford's intuition about the metafilmic dimensions of the state gaze is very sure-handed, and helps explain what may seem in the last shot like its major departure—but is it?—from the novel. The first time we see Winston in his apartment, the image comes to us through a scrim of pale horizontal striations, like a low-resolution video. This is before the reverse shot—with nothing yet anticipated to this effect—serves to reveal the telescreen through which, rather than upon which, we track his actions. The oculus of domination is entirely machinic in its audiovisual constraints—and fixed-frame to boot, its eye not moving, just harvesting the always potentially incriminating evidence passing before it. The film's setup forces the reader, in a sense, to internalize the surveillance in place of the apartment set's otherwise disavowed "fourth wall"—even if (the novel makes clear) the closed-circuit link might at any given moment not be electronically activated. In this early establishing shot, then, we're reminded that diegesis is always a filmed space—but further, in this dystopian case, a space under mediation for the protagonist himself, not just for the audience.

Whenever Big Brother is beamed into domestic or public space, the eyes are upon you—even if only by optical allusion in the roving gaze. In the image's more ubiquitous dissemination as broadcast totem, Big Brother oversees the hero in the last scene as well, when finally Winston "gazed up at the enormous face. Forty years it had taken him to learn what kind of smile was hidden beneath the dark moustache" (297–98). The learning curve meets its asymptote in the very disappearance of the subject. In more immediately psychoanalytic terms, Winston's early dreams of his lost mother, drowned symbolically in slipping beyond his grasp, return—implicitly, in desperate reversion—from beneath the hirsute mask of power, so that all Winston can do is regret, all these years, his "self-willed exile from the loving breast" (298). The perversity of this final unwilled and passive "victory over himself" is there in the anatomical paradox of that clinching trope. This renaming of *victimage* as "victory," a rout of resistance whose negation is now wholly internalized, is slammed home in the last four-word sentence of fatally imprisoned free indirect: "He loved Big Brother."

In the film, by contrast, the indirect discourse gets voiced in first person, but only after John Hurt as Winston has turned away from the giant telescreen. His eyes are looking straight into the camera (or perhaps through the filthy window of the café) out of a tear-streaked face as he mumbles dimly the words "I love you." Without any explicit vocative of "Big Brother," and whispered rather than merely thought, this deviant wrinkle in the otherwise scrupulous adaptation often confuses students, who, grasping at straws, think perhaps there's some vestigial gesture (wholly improbable) in the direction of the just-departed (and equally brainwashed) Julia, somewhere beyond the widnow. They're right to notice something's off here, though, since it *is* surprising that we don't get the expected shot/countershot between the telescreen and Winston, rendering visible to the face of power (as if it were ever there to receive such an image) the subject's final capitulation to that power. Given the crushing out of the lovers' affect in the film as well, with no credible ambiguity leaving the shot ajar to a final flicker of sentiment, why this marked (180-degree) departure from the book? One way to think of it is that, by holding Winston's wasted gaze (off into nowhere) within the same frame as Big Brother's (at us and everywhere), something like Žižek's "interface effect" is realized in a flattening of the distance between subject and object, all now in the same leveled field of emptied reality.[8] The forgone edit between self and the icon of mastery could, in this sense, well imply that looking away from the telescreen is the final proof of the wholly self-embodied surveillance that finds its equivalent in the novel's searingly translucent free indirect treatment. It's not just that *anywhere* Winston looks there might well be a live telecam and resultant video feed, so that all protestations are confessions, nor just that he might finally be relaxing into the fact that we at least, invisibly reciprocating his blind gaze before our own screen, have been with him all along in the form of a displaced panopticon, studying his life as a tragic experiment in doomed human hope. Beyond either inference, or both together, if the film really knows what it's doing—knows what, in other words, this turning of himself over to Big Brother, even in turning from his image, would ultimately suggest—then perhaps cinematography, in its phonic counterpoint, has found its own mode of narrative capitulation and breakdown. For the shot plan has suspended the cognitive dynamic of shot/countershot at exactly the moment when the death grip of power has been so wholly personified (hence the iconic image), but personified as internalized (hence the averted stare), that any speech act resonates only in the echo chamber of total surrender.

There is a methodological framework at stake in this measure of difference between film and novel, and not just for "translation studies." Illustrating here again an intermedial narratography tested at greater length in the introduction to my last book on film, a method directed there at the closing moments of Henry James's *The Golden Bowl* in its screen adaptation, it would be fair to say that Orwell's novel—to establish the sight lines that orient its free indirect apostrophe to the telescreened visage of Big Brother—exploits the logic of spatial suture and dials out speech. It does both in a manner inverted by the audiovisual medium of Radford's film, where, if not handled by voice-over, the speech of submission is as necessary as its ocular axis is not. What's so revealing here is that such necessities of the photomechanical medium do not betray the novel but reinterpret it. Under the regime of totalized omniscience, anything said is heard; any thought crime, even silent, can seem overheard.

When the damage is done, one might as well speak one's defeat as think it, enunciate it into the bugged vacuum of one's finally voided identity. But no explicit suture is needed—or even relevant any longer. Given not just the omnipresence of Big Brother but his embrace by the self as a quasi-maternal origin, almost an ontological ground, such totalized power can never again fill the dialectical slot of the absent one. There is no longer any being-seen from outside a self that cannot see itself as such, as separate entity. Paranoia is turned inside out, into an abjected desire: an urge never to be weaned from the breast of absolute and decentered authority. Suspending the very epistemology of suture with the most mordant of ironies, cinema cedes its own classic apparatus to the closed circuitry of the televised and the surveilled at once. Paraphrasing Goldstein, private life does indeed meet its end. The new despotism appears in its true negative valence: omniscience as the always "present one." Without Big Brother, "thou aren't."

"Muddied footage"/"Cross-cut comparisons": Prose in Upload

It is perhaps endemic to their shared themes of duplicity and secret policing that one of the great masters of free indirect discourse and internal monologue after Orwell is David Cornwell (code name John le Carré). In his explicitly post–9/11 novel of covert electronic surveillance, *A Most Wanted Man* (2008)—building on a career-long interest in the narrative indirections and bypasses afforded by electronic eavesdropping, wiretapping, and hidden body mics—le Carré has taken on, in his prose as well as his plot, the discontinuous nature of visual rather than audio surveillance, its discrepant barrage of images caught in the process of being sorted into evidentiary montage.

German intelligence, seen tracking down (solely by visual image track at first) a suspected jihadist immigrant, boasts a "hacker" named Maximilian who "had a near-total stammer, a memory like a twelve-volume lexicon and an intuition for cobbling together extraneous scraps of information"[9]—a pastiche of information rendered toxic when taken as knowledge under the rule of the covert informant. Language itself is all but discounted here in being displaced onto mere simile ("like a lexicon")—as if in deference to the new visual discourse of the secret dossier. Verbally impaired but with a memory like language's itself, this electronics wizard is an incarnate data bank; the "scraps" he aggregates are in this case security cam files tapped into from the surveillance backlog of several different national intelligence agencies.

In light of his surveillance multitasking, the hacker's irrelevant stammer seems transferred instead to an optic staccato, with prose for several pages breaking up into grammatical fragments timed to visual juxtapositions that, as it were, speak for themselves. In what comes across like a computer-sourced update of Orwell's parodied cinematic montage, syntax operates as the rhetorical equivalent of a jump cut and automatic refocus. Noun phrases alone feature forth images found rather than asserted, needing no verbs for their nearly instantaneous access, no predication for the sheer fact of their storage and potential incrimination. Grammar itself begins to feel complicit with a network of racial profiling rather than a narrative of actual treachery. First a police mug shot. And in a subsequent paragraph, no grammar either: "A ten-line text in thick type describing him as an escaped Muslim militant" (47). Next, a moment of visual assessment, as if closing in on the photograph: "Lips pressed tight together. No smile offered or permitted" (47). A further, separate paragraph: "Eyes stretched wide open in pain . . . . Unshaven, emaciated, desperate" (47), where the physical attributes blend across the echoic internal link of *sha/acia*—prose doing its own version of graphic (or graphophonemic) matching—until punctuated by psychological inference.

At which point an investigative and increasingly invested prose is ready, in transcribing the next stutter of images, to turn more fully mimetic—not just clocked to the shunting and doubling-back of optical data but responsive to the images themselves in their internal visual disposition, here with a double phrasal triad built up of elongating modification for the lanky suspect under review: "Muddied footage of *thin bearded man* in *long dark overcoat*" (48; emphasis added). With another transit camera picking up his exit from a border-crossing truck, full clausal grammar momentarily kicks in, but only in the technological present tense (rather than a classic historical present) of keypadded upload: one paragraph each for "Lorry driver waves" and "Departing passenger does not wave" (48). More mimetic distension follows concerning a verbally transliterated image from the Hamburg train station's security cams: "Same thin figure stretched horizontal on station bench," where the more likely adverb "horizontally" is replaced in making this descriptor even less a function of some real predicate, more like an optical epithet in its variant of yet another triad like "thin horizontal figure." Next, an implicit cinematic metaphor: "Cross-cut comparisons between Issa's mug shot and enhanced still of thin bearded man on station bench," with (in electronic upgrade again) a "virtual measuring stick" soon superimposed over the image to gauge the figure's height. All this visual data mining and its calibration operates ultimately as a threatening armature of the otherwise leaden bureaucracy, the "entrenched espiocracy" (44), of the punning "Holy See" (59), lending it new eyes to accompany the ears of rumor.

Without the phonetic and rhythmic effects of both diction and syntax in le Carré, much of the earlier passage of optical cross-check would read like the storyboard for some typical found-footage prestidigitation at a spy game-like console anchoring the shot exchanges of a routine film thriller. In this same vein of hypertrophic technology, as prepared for here with the groundwork of dramatic irony, the novel ends in the double-cross of a catastrophic international stakeout whose audiovisual feeds are further "enhanced" by helicopter and satellite surveillance. This blanket of co-opted privacy for a supposed confidential transaction includes the paramilitary upgrade of an already videowired bank vault, amplifying its normal security cameras with wide-angle adjuncts, the images channeled for transmit both to nearby wired vehicles and to Berlin central. As such, the on-site installations of an embedded panoptic technology are focused on the very action that their adjustable points of view serve, in effect, to narrate for the reader as well—once mediated, that is, by le Carré's hypertuned prose: a prose tracking plot, as it does, toward its final disaster in US intervention and extreme rendition.

Before this climactic implosion of a more genuine local surveillance program—in other words, short of that last-minute peremptory onslaught by the Americans—there is a further parallel with Orwell. It is part of the massing irony of le Carré's novel that he may seem to have borrowed the function of a typographic inset (and epistemological offset) from the structure of *1984*. Recall that when we read over Winston's shoulder the seditious text by Goldstein, with the hero caught in a false euphoria about no one else watching, we might know better simply from the graphic coding of his transgression—since, available at even a superficial glance, the discourse shifts to sans serif typeface in moving, so to speak, from Orwell's prose to Goldstein's. The anathematized book is not absorbed by internal monologue or folded seamlessly into narration; its forbidden text is instead *visible* as such in its deviance, to any prying eye (the masked telescreen all along, as we discover). So, too, does le Carré deploy a suspicious typographic regress for the secret surveillance memos reviewed by higher authorities in *A Most Wanted Man*. In another stripped-down font for these embedded, filed reports (101–09), we read about the likely misrecognition of the same video imagery previously used for positive identification of the novel's chief Muslim suspect and sacrificial victim: "Possible retrospective sighting date: seventeen days ago. . . . Security video images unclear" (107)—followed by separately appended annotations of uncertainty from a field agent and his desk officer. The omniscience that earlier disappeared into the autofocused jump cuts of video evocation in prose has been sieved and sorted this time through a textual medium that equivocates it.

The effect is prototypical. For novels and narrative films alike, a recurrent taut binary in surveillance plotting is just the one anticipated here: between filtered data (often ambiguous) and active infiltration, between those who have "invigilated" (101, Carré's ironic word for it) and the frequent violence in which their work issues. The pattern continues in his latest novel, *A Delicate Truth*, from 2013, whose conspiracy plot revolves around masked "facts on the ground" in Gibraltar—about the failed kidnapping of a terrorist suspect—and lethal collateral damage in its wake. The not just aborted but murderous operation is carried out by high-tech paramilitary mercenaries whose "operational budget" provides "full American-style coverage . . . sophisticated equipment . . . plus a Predator drone for observational purposes."[10] In the opening chapter detailing the mission in the present tense, grammatical fragments toggle in and out of electronically screened contact as prose itself seems activating the very equipment, in stylistic rather then electronic upgrade, of a visual discourse. The point of focus is a hilltop "hide" in which a civil servant is sequestered with a small group of off-the-books British soldiers. "Alternating aerial and ground shots" (27), period: the plural sighting detached, freestanding, unattributable, omniscient—even while "surveillance resources" (35) still need backup by "eyes-on" ratification in between (36).

The optical automatisms of the prose continue to mount with the suspense. A trivial piece of evidence is magnified, as it were, out of all proportion: "The camera has closed on it. The camera enlarges it. Enlarges it again" (37)—with that final elliptical syntax itself telescoping the described optical effect as if by push-button imprint. Indeed, from different vantage points, "cameras were vying with each other to get at it. Aerial shots follow ground-level close-ups and wide-angle shots . . . at dizzying speed" (36–37). Enhanced by "night-vision glasses" (43) and other optical prosthetics, such is the very grain of the remediated storytelling in this set-piece opening chapter—so that there is no surprise when the new range and angle of a subsequent screen shot "takes up the narrative" (45) by real-time montage. Even the verbal picture of images that "*stole* into the camera's lens and disappeared" (44; emphasis added) may seem borrowing its diction from the electronic stealth that surveys the scene—and that elsewhere steals such moments for forensic storage and transmission.

Later in *A Delicate Truth*, by way of countersurveillance in an anachronistic mode, the hero's secret taping in the office of the corrupt cabinet minister responsible for the criminal mission is achieved with a "Cold War-era, pre-digital, industrial-sized tape recorder" left abandoned in a lower desk drawer—"an apparatus so ancient and lumbering, so redundant in our age of miniaturized technology as to be an offence to the contemporary soul" (103). The dated prosthetics of spycraft, though wholly outstripped by the computerized arsenal of the new mercenaries, retains its utility in some vestigially less corrupted form than the new profiteering in wired warfare. For here is an ideologically repurposed "apparatus" (turned against the government's own machinations) whose creaky rotations are personified (thus marginally humanized) in their "grunting and whimpering" (108) before they even take down their first incriminating human words. Perhaps in another somewhat dated analogy—to cinema itself rather than digital streams—the playback's abrupt lurch into narrative seems analogized to the work of a cinematic track thrown up without introductory formalities and visualized in progress from mere sonic traces—and their satire of ill-gotten gain: "No titles, no credits. No soothing introductory music. Just the minister's unopposed, complacent assertion, delivered to the beat of his bespoke suede boots by Lobb at a thousand pounds a foot, as he advances across the Private Office" (108).

But sonic traces are one thing, and phonic another. And in the latter case what can't be pictured is the tacit alphabetic character of the minister's later allusion to Gibraltar. In the dark as to the opening scene of high technology and below-the-radar carnage, the recording hero is also in the dark as to an imagined visual form for an arbitrary, case-sensitive signifier. He is impelled to replay one crucial phrase on the tape, with his own interrogative inflection: "'British *rock*?' He whispered aloud," the prose passing from there into free indirect: "With a capital R or a small one, please?" (117). The whole plot turns on it being the former, site of an illegal American-backed covert operation on high-profile British soil. Turns—and then drives forward, from there out, under continuous homicidal surveillance dodged where possible by the hero's aliases, disposable cell phones, memory-stick duplications of scanned traitorous documents, and other low-rent inventiveness. Until, at its climax, the pervasive optical substrate of the paranoia plot surfaces in another filmic analogy. For the world has, for the hero, "gone into slow motion" (294) just after his defiant confrontation with the mercenary kingpin—its quasi-cinematic time-out-of-joint never to be set right until the closing sacrificial (perhaps even suicidal) moment of electronic whistle-blowing to the mainstream press from an Internet cafe.

All told, the narratographic texture of le Carré's discursive remediations—from vocal through cinematic to digital transcriptions, and whether at close audial range or from hilltop, helicopter, drone, or satellite relay—do as much as Orwell's equally clean yet deftly deflected prose calibrations to render free indirect discourse itself technological and cautionary. Hearing a character's thoughts, say, as if they were continuous with her reported actions—the paradigm of *style indirect libre*—has begun seeing through a machinic optic what technology alone can make of a scene whose narration it has momentarily usurped. Telescreened prose—together with its tape deck complement—thus inherits omniscience from on high and shunts it, through the filter of cybernetic linkage or its mechanical precursors, into the grain of syntax and metaphor.

Five years before *A Delicate Truth*, at the even bleaker conclusion of *A Most Wanted Man*—where there is no hope of exposing the covert American involvement in German counterterrorism—it is bitterly appropriate that the cleric Abdullah, eventual victim of the US-German sting operation, has announced earlier in the plot: "With the Internet and TV there are no secrets anymore. Information is not knowledge, mind you. Information is dead meat. Only God can turn information into knowledge" (266). Nonetheless, as the novel's last scene implies, those who merely play God with information can turn men like himself into the "dead meat" of an expendable human datum. Building toward just such a point of no return is the inexorable work of plotting in that new millennial sense not just of narrative schema and political complot but of tracked coordinates under the electronics of global positioning—as in *A Delicate Truth* as well, that novel being five years farther along in the escalated technology of what Deleuze calls (as explored in the Postface) a post-Foucauldian "society of control" rather than of discipline.

In each book, le Carré's "surveillant enunciation" offers its own kind of spyware in capturing this tension between the invigilated and the violated, a tension always laced—on the ground of narrative, as it were—with paranoia about the never Wholly Seen. The tension is all the clearer in film's optical storytelling. There, too, it's not just that vision has been widely compromised by the logistics of supravision. It's also that narration itself has taken an ingrained taint, ironically or not, from the same devices of surveillance its heroes resist. The audiovisual rather than prose narratives to which we now return, though potentially all-seeing, circumscribe themselves in related ways according to dispensations (and resistances) technological, psychological, and political—often all at once.

3 FEEDBACK LOOPS OF THE TECHNOPTICON

Within the framed field of surveillance, what prose can only approximate, cinema reduplicates: the audiovisual sightlines of overseen action. Reduplicates, and then multiplies, often allusively, from plot to plot. In the most culturally revealing intertextual nexus on the subject of surveillance and power since Fritz Lang's *Mabuse* films were stretched out over four decades down through 1960, film history has since seen a related thread of paranoia (with all its associated threats) continued—and knotted off at intervals by allusion and mutation—across four later decades of epistemological thrillers from Michelangelo Antonioni's *Blow-Up* (1966) through Francis Ford Coppola's *The Conversation* (1974) to Brian De Palma's *Blow Out* (1981) and on to Tony Scott's *Enemy of the State* (1998). These are the major film examples to pace our discussion in this chapter, before moving in the next two into psychological terrain less explicitly staked out in advance by Lang's cinema and its scopic drives—though very much within that fold-over of terrorism into erotics spoken of so abstractly in Oudart's suture essay.

There is a single tossed-off remark, and perhaps genealogical in-joke, in Scott's 2006 *Déjà Vu* that cuts through the film's incredible battery of computerized surveillance optics. "I won't even ask how you got the audio" seems self-consciously meant to rework the shared medial (and thus audiovisual) ironies of its interlinked predecessors. All told, the historical momentum of these films, pivoting around the switch from visual to audio surveillance for *The Conversation,* is aimed toward what might be dubbed a remote technopticon of electronic overlook (and frequent eavesdropping) in closed-circuit espionage, a predominantly scopic system seen outstripping even current scientific bounds. And whenever narrative advance per se, within a given plot, is carried on the back of such a wired and remediated omniscience, we have—in terms of a discourse theory of the cinematic text—a case, once again, of what Thomas Levin identifies as "surveillant enunciation."

The archetypal film of this thematic sequence, however, Antonioni's *Blow-Up,* had no new technology to speak of. Nor does that film's photographer hero ask about the audio either when it makes no diegetic sense; we're not even sure, at a crucial moment, if the phantom soundtrack—leaves rustling through the trees of a London park—is his at all for subjective listening (remembering), or whether only we are hearing it. Apart from this scene, it may be that the photographer's playing of jazz records in between fashion shoots also leads, if only by an incidental subtext, to *The Conversation*, where the audio engineer seems so used to a setting of stolen sound that his own private saxophone playing in off-hours is laid over prerecorded jazz. More central to its own plot is that undecidably subjective moment in Antonioni, with off-frame audio as the symptom (and symbol) of epistemophilic overkill. Certainly the ur-scene of *Blow-Up* for the legacy of surveillance narratives it spawns comes when separate wall-elevated photo blow-ups are closely coupled enough in their sequence to fill in the quick-cut links of action and its sightlines and thereby evoke in the process the photogrammatic chain of cinema itself. This is at least one unmistakable title scene not only for Antonioni's film but for the study of mine that takes it up, *Between Film and Screen*. For we are caught on the cusp at that moment, or say on the generative threshold, between photochemical index and photomechanical motion. Yet that same sequence also stretches the boundary between representation and its world in an imaginative recovery of the absent past sounded by sound itself.

Optical montage, then, is only half the issue at this dramatic as well as medial turning point in *Blow-Up*, with its inferred conversion from random snaps to the coherence of a forensic frame line approximated by a serial, wall-mounted collage. The separate enlargements are studied so closely for the evidence of an attempted murder—and then, in growing anxiety, for its result in the form of a discovered corpse—that immersion in these photos returns perception to the scene of the crime (even before the hero drives back there in person): the site where he was interrupted in the attempt to capture the necessary last shots for his book of art (rather than commercial) photos. It is the scene itself that is recaptured. For we hear again in his studio (together, or not, with the obsessed photographer) the sound of wind through trees and bushes, undisturbed by the gunshot he no doubt would have heard if he had been there in time, just a few "frames" earlier. Plot aside, contemporary art photography rehearses its emergence here, in the form of contemporary art film, through precisely the non-naturalistic and presynchronous—the cognitively contrapuntal—supplement of found sound. Fidelity is no longer the measure in the art still either, but instead, among other gestures, disjunction and irony.

De Palma's *Blow Out* goes one step further and puts that hidden gunfire from the bushes back on the soundtrack—as otherwise masked by the blowout of an automobile tire leading to the "accidental" death by drowning of a presidential hopeful. By sheer happenstance, but of course intertextual determination, De Palma's technician protagonist has found himself there at the scene of the crime, there in fact to record wind sounds, only to watch the car plummet into the river—and able to rescue only a female escort as it sinks. When he hears on TV the dubious story of a cameraman coincidentally present as well, conspiracy rears its head—and he goes to work. Instead of Antonioni's photographer searching the enlarged benday dot array of his images for the increasingly pointillist evidence of a crime, in De Palma's narrative we have a slasher-film sound engineer (versus *Blow-Up*'s high-gloss fashion photographer) piecing together, off-hours, the tabloid images published from that fortuitous (and suspicious) video into a makeshift film strip, including a gun flare from the roadside bushes, and then aligning these with the found soundscape he had been accidentally recording for other purposes. Working back from effect to cause, he thus synchronizes the punctual image strip with the noise of a fired weapon as well as the answering burst of tire puncture in which it instantaneously results. For the purpose of criminal exposure, only sound cinema is fully "realistic," credibly evidentiary—though as in *Blow-Up*, the evidence is soon stolen by the conspirators. Exactly halfway between *Blow-Up*'s imaginary and incidental sound in 1966 and *Blow Out*'s audial point of departure in 1981 comes the interplay in Coppola's 1974 film of sound recording and B&W photos in an audio/visual rather than fully audiovisual surveillance dossier.

In the closing chapter of his first cinema book, "The Crisis of the Action-Image," Gilles Deleuze locates the genesis and most striking manifestations of this postwar reduction of action to anxious and two-way spectation in, by turns, the neorealism of the 1950s, the New Waves of the 1960s, and the New American Cinema of the next decade—the last with its rampant paranoid narratives. But Deleuze further situates the prehistory of this "crisis" in the evolving technological ironies of Lang's *Mabuse* sequence, where, as managed by Lang's eponymous archvillain, the exercise of power "no longer passes through a production of secret actions, but rather through a monopoly of reproduction. Occult power is confused with its effects, its supports, its media, its radios, its television, its microphones)."[1] From there to Sidney Lumet and other initiators of the New American Cinema, where "conspiracy" takes shape in precisely "the system of reception, surveillance and transmission" (210)—as in films by Lumet with the prototypical titles *The Anderson Tapes* (1971) or

Network (1976). Between these 1970s touchstones, for Deleuze, of action undermined by its recording or transmission—movement subsumed to view—falls Coppola's homage to the previous photo/motor crisis of *Blow-Up*.

Listening In: *The Conversation* in Cinematic Dialogue

As Coppola no doubt recognized, even Antonioni's closing trope in *Blow-Up* sustains the priority of image to sound, despite their latent collaboration. For it is the motion of an invisible tennis ball, suboptic prop in a fantastic match played by a mime troupe in the film's last scene, that gradually induces for the hero (this time for sure)—and on our soundtrack as well—the sound of that imaginary ball hitting both rackets and court. The analogy between their game and film's fuller mirage verges on a technological allegory. Cinema, too, is a simulated event (to some extent a participatory visualization) to which the overlay of sound may elicit further credence, though with no guarantee of something's presence. So it is that Coppola's film begins quite literally where *Blow-Up* leaves off, with a pantomime in a public space: a solitary mime wandering through San Francisco's crowded Union Square in an overhead telephoto view that gradually closes in on the busy scene. What is revealed to begin with is the mime's own fanciful performance at bothersome odds with the concentration of a lone man circling the sunny midday space in a thin plastic raincoat. The latter is already recognized, in the person of Gene Hackman, as the film's star and main protagonist, soon revealed as an uptight surveillance expert, Harry Caul, who will sheathe himself in that prophylactic wrapper through much of the film, come rain or shine. Caul, we learn, got the call for the high-paid stakeout with which the film has begun from a powerful corporate boss, an operation funded to include a full battery of directional mics and converted telescopic rifles retooled for sonic targeting. These last are instruments whose results, he ends up fearing, might be just as lethal, in effect, as if they were unmodified and loaded. This is because the couple he's taped, and brought into focus through their crosshairs, is likely to be murdered, it would seem, by the woman's jealous husband, the powerful CEO of the unnamed corporation who has commissioned Caul's spycraft.

This kind of disaster has happened before to (or through) Caul. Radical formalist that he is, interested only in the quality, not the content, of his tapes, he has discovered only after the fact, in a previous job, that their incriminating evidence led to the torture and murder of three people. Guilt-ridden Catholic that he also is, he now tries to disburden himself of this past (and of his anxiety about another pending bloodbath) to a priest in the confessional, after building up his courage in trivial admissions like "impure thoughts," "taking the Lord's name in vain," and—almost inevitable for a man who's reimbursed for information, rather than expected to purchase it—"taking newspapers off the racks without paying." As if in cinematographic free association, a rack focus blurs his close-up profile, moving lips included, just when the confession heats up—with camerawork now bringing the priest's silhouette into compensatory focus instead from behind the screen of clerical anonymity, yet leaving this mediator with nothing to say before Caul has suddenly exited the confessional. Of course even if the Father Confessor had gathered more information, it would, true to his privileged "client" relationship, be morally (and legally) unactionable. What seems suggested here, more importantly, is the parodic relation of spy to vicar, each equally vicarious, devoted to the work of processing sin, deviance, criminality even, without internalization or judgment. Along this ironic axis of comparison, confession is its own kind of inert surveillance: the one-way conduit of invaded privacy by elective disclosure. It is perhaps the deep strain (both senses) of Catholicism in Caul that we are to think explains his quasi-priestly calling, his taste for intermediation disengaged from any desire for personal human contact.

Even sex must be kept from intimacy. Leaving his mistress when she wants to know something more about him, he soon succumbs to the come-on of a party girl (and, as it turns out, conspiracy plant) joining others for drinks in Caul's loft workroom. She tells him "the whole story of my life up to now" in pretending an interest in his. Backed up against a pillar, slowly, haltingly, he lets go of a narrative, though only in third person, that amounts to "What would you do if you knew a man who loved you but wouldn't say so or tell you anything about himself?" As she presses drunkenly against him to draw his story out, the camera pans left, in an almost semicircular arc, from his tensed face in close-up profile—another confession scene—to her intent look. Left, then left again, then left once more—arcing away each time from the starting point of loosened privacy. What narratography would register, in response to this iterated accent of cinematography, and even in advance of a coming plot twist, is the coerced nature of this thinly disguised personal story, twisted out of him in resistant stages—as if he were having to rev up all over again, with each new clenched sentence or two, for this uncharacteristic self-exposure. When the camera describes its marked semicircular arc not just once but three separate times, in slightly enhanced—which is to say invasive, claustrophobic—close-ups, our special access to this awkwardly private moment is thus stressed as a medium-facilitated eavesdropping.

But more so even than it seems at the time. For only later, in the next scene, do we realize that this conversation wheedled from him has in fact been internally mediated: taped as a prank by a competitor technician there for the party (with a hidden-mic pen given to Caul as a promotional souvenir). The sex to follow—when everyone but the girl is kicked out in his rage—is followed in turn by a postcoital dream in which Caul tries to open up in turn to the young woman he's been surveilling, warning her of danger, and then further telling her the story of his sickly childhood. But all this has given his seductive bedmate time to steal the tapes (like the photographs in *Blow-Up* and the audiovisual strip in *Blow Out*) and turn them over to the corporate boss. This has happened, we soon find, under orders either from the Director himself or his ubiquitous front man (and apparent henchman) Stett, who, tailing Caul earlier, has been spotted by him through the accidental convenience of a demo spycam at the stalls of a downtown surveillance convention.

The commissioned tapes have been prematurely retrieved to ensure, given Caul's reluctance, that they do in fact fall into the hands of the Director, who wants proof of the infidelity. When they're finally paid for in person, with Caul counting out his tainted bills, the Director, listening to Stett play the tapes in the background, accuses him of "being glad it's true." Is it perhaps that Stett, Iago-like, has planted the seed of doubt in the first place? Could well be. Yet that line of conjecture is at odds with other threads in what now rapidly unravels. It is as if two separate trick endings trip each other up. So far, calling the Director nothing but "the Director" may seem to refer his power away to the omniscience of narration itself, as channeled through Caul's technology from the first God's-eye shot onward—though with the difference that Caul feels incrementally guilty for the plot that is quickly thickening around him. But it turns out, by dramatic irony and narrative reversal, that the Director himself ends up being the dupe of the plot, the complot, when his presumed homicidal revenge to come (in a hotel room mentioned on tape) turns out to be his own premeditated murder by the very couple for whom Caul is mistakenly anxious (the Director wrapped and stabbed in a plastic shower curtain reminiscent of Caul's own thin outerwear).

Vocal Inflection, Narrative Deflection

Delegated to the panoptic of surveillance expertise, the locus of omniscience is indeed faulty—either that or subject to a cheat. Here we confront a famous crux in the film, a fudging of its own recycled clue: the multiple playback of "He'd *kill* us if he got the chance." Rewound and re-audited time and again as if it were the index of sheer paranoia, the line is finally reheard as enunciating a justification instead for the couple's preemptive move of murder: "He'd kill *us* if he got the chance." If that is the real audial dynamic of the seized and resifted dialogue—escaping all electronic enhancement and fine-tuning on the tapes—its truth is recognized only outside of mediation. It occurs to Caul only after the fact, in the absence of his recordings, in an involuntary reversion to the visualized scene of the couple's dialogue in his mind's-eye view, a close-up lifted from the original surveillance scene that, this time around, cuts through all the subsequent finessing of the evidentiary apparatus to a fatally belated reconstruction of the lost inflection, a mere matter of differential volume all along: He'd KILL us / He'd kill US. So, in a once-uncertain playback, it may be thought to have wavered—though reheard now only in corrective flashback.

And it isn't just the Director who is ensnared by falling short of the omniscience his name might suggest, but in the end the protagonist as well. Just moments before the revelatory adjusted flashback, we realize that the assistant, Stett, is in cahoots with the couple, since he's looking on blandly while they refuse to meet the press in the aftermath of the murder, covered up now in the form a car crash—as if they were withdrawn into shock and grief. How does one trick ending square with the other? Assuming that the Director was the prime mover, wanting to call in a private eye as well as ear (not just the tapes but the covert photographs he insists on), with Stett merely expediting the demand, then what about Stett's obvious complicity in the later killing? As an accomplice all along, was he simply relieved to find that the incriminating counterinference of "kill *us*" was not picked up in the recording, but that a hotel room number was? Or did Stett stage the whole thing, arranging for the couple to leak the room number, as a planted lure, so as to deliberately steer the Director toward a suspected tryst that was in fact an ambush? In which case Caul was a further pawn, transmitting a message whose danger he didn't recognize from his place within an imagined antithetical scenario he thought he had uncovered.

Either Caul played into the hands of contingency and the forces of power that capitalize on it or he was actually meant to deliver the bait—the room number—that would be fatal in an unexpected way (in which case the very mention of murder seems woefully unguarded on the couple's part). Surely the murk of motive isn't meant to come clear. This very indetermination is the film's truest Watergate-era paranoia. Whether or not Caul has failed as a perfectionist technician, missing the beat of an emphasis, he ends up, misled by his tape, listening-in next door to the hotel slaughter, conjuring in subjective shots the wrongly fantasized murder—yet still only surveilling, not intervening. And if in fact he's been set up, rather than just willfully embroiled, then his exacting procedures were counted on to turn up the planted lead to a lethal rendezvous in the first place, one whose darker (perhaps literally unspoken) intonation is no more than a guilty (and self-clarifying) rerun in his mind's ear—rather than the decisive trump card it is usually taken to be in commentary. Who's to know? Such a narrative blind spot is the epistemological vanishing point of the film's whole surveillance nightmare.

Either way, his craft, however obsessive, has failed him. As the logic of the plot demands, he must now divest entirely of his equipmental prosthetics, especially when realizing that such technology has been turned against him by corporate interests. In the final sequence, the bugger has become the bugged. There is a more specific narratographic circle closed here as well. In describing the threefold pan of what amounts to the film's second abortive confession scene—"What would you think of a man who . . . ?"—I mentioned how it is only later, in graduated stages, that this cinematographic gesture makes some formal and thematic sense. Only later, that is, do we realize the corresponding audial manipulation (the disguised mic) as a delayed equivalent to that disembodied visual surveillance: a rotating camera brought up too close for comfort and repeated as if it were strapping the unwilling speaker to the pillar (as well as to the female body) he is pressed against. But then only later yet, much later—in the film's last shot—does the convex equivalent of that same panning motion return to define the film's final irony. The camera is found not half-circling its target this time but, rotated on an opposite axis, sweeping back and forth past it.

The effect is a famous one. In closure, we are watching the hero watched, worked away at, as if he is being *seen to death*. One further detail from religious iconography also serves to carry us back to that generic silhouette of the Father Confessor behind the scrim of impersonality, a lent ear ultimately heedless. For, barricaded in his apartment, after a call warning him that "we know you know" and "we'll be watching you," Caul tears the place apart, literally ripping out its floorboards, looking for any hidden recorders, audial or visual. With hesitation at first, then desperately, after checking everything else for bugs, he smashes open in sacrilege his statue of the Blessed Virgin. Empty—as if among the things not to be heard by it are prayers as well as compromising phone calls to the police. At which point, from an imaginary position above and beyond him in every sense, the narrative camera swivels back and forth in two slow arcs like the motorized sweep of a spycam taking in Caul's lone saxophone playing. With the ceiling operating here as the proverbial fourth wall, technology has been returned, once plot is over, to the regime of a spectral and oppressive omniscience. All that is now happening in this narrative, but then all that ever was, with or without the permission of character, is its filming for us. Via "surveillant enunciation" yet again, paranoia's worst fear cuts to an ontological quick: the fear that one might become a character in someone else's movie. If Winston Smith in the film version of *1984* had anything left of himself to protect, such would have been the immanent threat to his autonomy when he is found looking straight into the camera at the end: backed rather than faced by Big Brother, and so framed invisibly by viewers beyond him.

From *The Conversation*, we move forward now a quarter century to the already contested Orwellian surveillance options proliferated by new media in recent years, and in particular to a single film of prognostic angst in these matters (*Enemy of the State*) from the turn of the millennium, on the very eve of 9/11 and Homeland Security. In doing so we pass over the dystopian sci-fi more directly indebted to the telescreen ethos of *1984* and circumscribed within the same genre of futurist fiction. This includes films I've discussed elsewhere, from François Truffaut's *Fahrenheit 451* (1967) and Stanley Kubrick's *2001: A Space Odyssey* through George Lucas's *THX-1138* (1981) to Andrew Niccol's *Gattaca* (1997), narratives in which every closed-circuit monitor is likely to be not just predictive but monitory—and, beyond that, an audiovisual flashpoint for my contention that movies of the future tend to be about the future of movies.[2] Such systems of transmission mutate everywhere into instrumentalities of control, often taking the form of a narcotic distraction—but in any case repeatedly taking their place in cautionary plots about dehumanization and surrogate presence. This phobic strand of narrative is abundantly represented in the genre of sci-fi down through the century's end with *The Matrix* (Andy and Lana Wachowski, 1999)—and well beyond. Of course, the mental drama of *1984* has another and important legacy that minimizes the sci-fi gadgetry of technofuturism in deference to the psychosocial and political traumas of violated privacy. So it is that the state-sponsored terrorism of such rescinded rights—when held to contemporaneous rather than invented machines of surveillance—

can still seldom avoid its manifest debts to the archetype of Big Brother. The Director in *The Conversation*—even when scapegoated to the corporate system itself, whose thought police "know that you know"—is no exception.

Security Cams, Detective Playback

Ahead for discussion waits the 1998 film *Enemy of the State* that, along with *The Matrix* of the next year, so differently closes out the cinematic century in the midst of its last decade's wholehearted turn to the digital. But before considering the former in detail, a film that takes *The Conversation* as its clear sounding-board and prototype in the mode of paranoid thriller, we pause in the mid-1990s over a particularly schematic intersection of violence and surveillance under the title *Tesis*. This is a Spanish film of wholly justified paranoia that seems to review and permute the full range of options sampled by our comparison of European modernism in the late 1960s (Antonioni) with 1970s New Hollywood (Coppola). Along this whole spectrum, the checkpoints are complex and interlinked. There is the audiovisual spying that detects violence. There is the audiovisual spying that leads to violence. There is the audiovisual spying that is in itself a violence. And then there is the violence spied upon for its own sake, a documentary prurience. The ratio of emphasis among these nodes of mediation determines the thematic parameters as well as the plot arc of many a film concerned with the condition of being filmed.

In this sense, Alejandro Amenábar's *Tesis* (*Thesis*, 1996) looks both forward and back—as one can see in anticipating its successors in a certain line of forensic image scrutiny when pitted against sociopathic brutality. Over a decade later, in *The Girl with the Dragon Tattoo* (Niels Arden Oplev, 2009; David Fincher, 2011), the serial killer is foiled by detective work whose early turning point, very much in the manner of *Blow Out*'s update of *Blow-Up*, involves the laptop sequencing and step-time video manipulation of separate newspaper photos of a local parade crowd years before. This incidental archive is turned from a feature story into a forensic dossier (and electronic decoupage) in which the static equivalent of a shot/countershot axis is worked out to reveal the focal point of fear for a woman subsequently gone missing and presumed murdered. Suture is itself fabricated to recover the real spatial disposition of a past moment. In this way, the police photo record of the slain women the killer has left behind is complemented by an image file that eventually helps to curtail that serial slaughter. The pattern is familiar: remediation to the rescue, abetted later in the plot by the killer caught for playback by the lens of a home security cam.

Some films are more completely centered on the contrast of real-time violence and preventive mediation than others, of course. Eschewing the director's previous emphasis on privately recorded murder in counterpoint with routine street surveillance in *Benny's Video* (1992), Michael Haneke's savage *Funny Games* (1997)—in direct assault on the contemporary audience's interest in screen violence—restricts diegetic mediation to channel-surfed TV thrills and displaces its own filmic reflex to the reverse-action and freeze-frame ironies of screen rhetoric itself. The year before saw Amenábar's less relentless polemic—almost a gothic satire in the guise of metacinematic slasher film. The unabashed (if partly tongue-in-cheek) cultural thesis of *Tesis* is in fact that commercial film production feels increasingly obliged to pander—as the film's highly effective thriller plot decidedly does in its own right—to a mass audience's interest in violent images: even images witnessing to real rather than fictional violence in the snuff-film mode.

The coils of the plot delineate a veritable template for the recent equivocation between voyeurism and aggression in unbidden imaging. *Tesis* opens with a girl trying to break through a police barricade—flouting the injunction to "look the other way"—in order to see the severed body of a subway-track suicide. She is accused of "morbid interest" by the cops and is shoved back from the platform, denied (as we are) the gruesome countershot. In the next scene, as if this were momentarily mitigating, we discover that she is in film school working on the early stages of her graduate thesis on "audiovisual violence," requesting her professor to access some hard-core footage under lock and key in the college vaults—and insisting that she has no personal, only a professional, interest in the genre. He does so, then screens the film for himself out of curiosity in an empty classroom, and is found dead of an asthma attack and heart failure the next day. Coming upon his corpse, the heroine, Ángela, ejects the tape (this later-denied act having been recorded, unbeknownst to her—and to us at the time—by overhead security) and, after being able at first only to listen to its horrific screams on the audiotrack, finally watches the full mayhem of an anonymous young woman's beating and chainsaw dismemberment. She watches it, in fact, with a male classmate and aficionado, Chema, a student filmmaker and an addict of extreme screen violence who mocks her for the pretended clinical nature of her scholarly interest.

In studying this tape that "killed" their teacher, he realizes that the single-shot vérité "aesthetic" of the snuff film has been violated by cuts whenever the victim seems about to name the killer-cameraman, thus proving that the victim (recognized by Chema as a long-missing former classmate) must have known her murderer. In its form/content loop, this episode is all but a narratographic parable. The revealed anomaly of disjunct cuts turns the fiendish brutality of filmed hacking and slicing into its own surveillance file for the eventual tracking down of the killer; spoiled by redaction, the indexical integrity of the snuff film indirectly indexes its own perpetrator. Clues accumulate in this vein, including the fact that the use of a digital zoom from two years before—when the girl went missing—confirms that the hideous images must have been recorded by the only camera then marketed with that feature. Which, as Chema the insider knows, was purchased in multiple copies for the student production unit at the university. Evidence quickly mounts, and it turns out that the grotesque footage is the work of a snuff-film ring spearheaded by Ángela's new faculty advisor and thesis director, who urges his students in lecture to "save Spanish cinema" by bucking American popularity and "giving the audience just what they want." Criminal violence, in its degradation of image and narrative both, here allegorizes a surrender to mass popular craving in its less punishable forms.

But at this point the ubiquitous culture of the image and its inuring (rather than directly injurious) effects—whether for the watcher or the watched, the thriller-film addict or the social subject under surveillance—is turned back on itself once again. This comes to pass only when the film has reached its own twofold and violent (if visually restrained and deflected) climax. After many twists of the thriller plot—where Ángela's initial repulsion, turned voyeuristic despite herself, has yet again (true to genre format) become evidentiary and detective-driven—the professor and his student henchman are, one after the other, killed on camera in separate sites (and camcorder sights): first by Chema, then by Ángela herself, in the process of their separate attempts to film her slaughter at their hands. But the real media twist is that the professor's role in their complicity is first confirmed by his being spotted through surveillance cameras in the off-limits film vaults: this data-banked documentary footage accessed by Chema from his friend at the security desk in exchange for rare video porn.

But as for the immediate plot, the cautionary fable is circular and complete, the threat vitiated. Only through the film professor's being automatically filmed (by motion-triggered video) is his own deliberate and vicious filming brought to light—at which point the scenes of his death and, next, of his student accomplice are seen for the most part through the viewfinder of digital cameras no longer under their homicidal control. Further victims are thus spared by an inverted videology of everyday life, one kind of "documentary" camera (for the protection of the vaults) securitizing against another (the slasher-film apparatus). For the victims past and potential: die by the image, but sometimes find yourself saved by it. For the videographer: kill on film, till you're caught by it—and then yourself executed on it. Here is a cultural environment, a festered media ecology, in which, with everything already on camera—including a security-checked populace in continuous passive registration—there is next to nothing that the same populace, as commercial public, isn't inclined to see, just as there is almost no place where they can demur from being seen. So that criminal prevention falls within the same closed video circuit as sadistic witness. On a final mordant and all but parodic note to this effect, the film ends with Ángela and Chema (the latter recovering from his attack by the student killer) exiting his hospital ward past rows of bedridden patients staring avidly at a TV broadcast—with all mandatory on-screen caveats ironically in place about images to come that a viewer might find shocking or repellent. For what is to be screened-within-the-screen, just as the narrative breaks off, is one of the uncovered snuff ring's heinous tapes served up for afternoon consumption by way of a public service news show.

In the decade and a half of surveillance-inflected thrillers since Amenábar's 1996 release, the overall format of this irony has lost nothing of its timeliness. In a culture of passive specularity and digital vigilance, an acquiescence in universal exposure continues to find narrative manifestation as the flipside of perverse, coercive, or lethal imaging, with commercial cinema negotiating the genre space between. What results is a kind of alternating current in the surveillance thematic. For every film like *Southland Tales* (Richard Kelly, 2006) indulging in the phobic turn—with its Grand Guignol (or Terry Gilliamesque) conjuring of universal video penetration into private space, according to a post–WWIII extension of the Patriot Act under control of the corrupt and privatized USI-Dent Corporation—there are such compensatory fantasies, regarding optical data banks, as *Contagion* (Steven Soderbergh, 2011). Apart from its own paranoid and punning subplot about a malicious blogger "gone viral," the regime of panoptic electronics is recruited there, with momentary success, to address a global pandemic. This happens when security disks from a Hong Kong casino—recalling Martin Scorsese's *Casino* (1995) or Soderbergh's own ironic reversal in *Ocean's Eleven* (2001)—are digitally enhanced and improbably maneuvered in order to detect (as epidemiological clue) a first fatal contact with the infection. Yet, however editorialized, the recent proliferation (including international web and satellite linkage) of such spycam technology only exaggerates and ramifies the alternating ethical force fields inherent in the surveillance mode. To be sure, in the scores of films since *Tesis* whose narratives pivot on surveillance, there persists an implied cultural thesis that, almost without fail, keeps the erotics of scopophilia in the same orbit with the politics of epistemophobia. This is the case even when—short of the psychodramas that will concern us in the next two chapters—the polar issues, as in *Enemy of the State*, are linked only at the periphery of plot and spun off like a deflationary joke.

The State of the Enemy: From Cell to Satellite

So back to the Hollywood lineage more directly descending from Coppola's surveillance masterwork. Everything in *The Conversation*—including even a multiple open-air surveillance relay across several disguised security agents eavesdropping on a central couple in an urban park—leads directly, and by the route of open allusion, to *Enemy of the State* (Tony Scott, 1998), though the couple is in this case the hero and heroine. This includes the casting of Gene Hackman again as a paranoid loner (and renegade surveillance expert) going under the pseudonym Brill after being twenty years out of circulation as a dumped National Security agent (as he has been twenty-five years removed from his Harry Caul role). Despite his extreme and electronically fortified "retirement," Brill is unwillingly smoked out into the open as part of a countersurveillance intrigue. The backstory is his to tell at one point: about having been involved in a coup attempt in Iran and being cut loose by the NSA, hung out to dry after a regime change in mid-complot. Since then he's been doing only undercover private-"eye" work with his sophisticated if somewhat makeshift equipment.

He belatedly tells all this to the hero, a high-paid lawyer named Robert Dean (Will Smith) who has contracted (through a former girlfriend working with Brill) for an incriminating surveillance tape of a Mafia boss fraternizing with other mob leaders in a violation of his parole. Dean needs this tape to pressure the thug into lightening up on his clients, the union leaders he's been strong-arming. To redouble the surveillance motif, it turns out that the eventual meeting of the law and the outlaw—Dean and the criminal he's trying to intimidate—has transpired under the very eye of FBI agents in a permanent, low-tech telephoto stakeout on the Mafia headquarters—so blatant that the mobsters salute the cameras as they come and go, indifferent to their recorded identification.

To this site of forensic technology and potential criminal evidence the plot later returns. But for now it is another tape that is at issue—and for which Dean is being tracked. Yet he is quite unaware of its having been passed off to him in a shopping bag by a conspiracy-minded journalist before the latter was killed for it. When Dean's young children stumble upon its playback apparatus amid their dad's packages, thinking it's a video game of some sort, they make off with it, can't play it, and then forget about it. We don't need to see it played ourselves either, since we've already watched its events unfold in the precredit sequence, not realizing at the time—any more than do the characters involved—that the action is being filmed (within the film). What is recorded there is the lakeside murder (via lethal injection as simulated heart attack) of an aging senator by an ambitious would-be deputy director of the National Security Agency and his thug operatives: a senator who was militating against a vote for the villain's pet project, the oxymoronic "Telecommunications Security and Privacy Act," sneeringly enunciated in vocal scare quotes by the lawmaker and dismissed contemptuously as a rank violation of Constitutionally guaranteed rights of privacy—and all this, with weird prescience, three years before 9/11 and the Patriot Act.

But filmed how? In the rogue NSA agent's lethal rush to securitize the state, no external threats are mentioned, no terrorist plots, no foreign enemies. As we soon learn, the only invasion of our borders at stake is, ironically, that of migrating Canadian geese, which might or might not, depending on their flight patterns, set off a motion-sensitive camera installed for a government-sponsored study funded by an arm of the Washington bureaucracy obviously more benign than the NSA. This is the digital camera that happens to be triggered into filming the senator's murder from the other side of the lake. When word of this tape leaks, sight unseen, the NSA's entire battery of global surveillance is surreptitiously brought to bear on eliminating Dean, who supposedly has it. Every time the NSA culprit, Reynolds, orders up satellite surveillance, and before in each case we cut to a sci-fi-like image of an orbiting antenna dish, he's told by his flunkies: "We're already on it." The terrestrial panoptic is a fait accompli. And every other conceivable device of telescopic sighting and directional miking, hidden cameras and global positioning chips, helicopter spotting and the like, closes the dragnet around the still-clueless Dean. As a suspected secondhand witness to treason and murder, he is soon framed for a murder of his own so as to increase routine police surveillance. Yet the NSA is even more thorough than that. Half a dozen separate tracking bugs are sewn into his coat and slacks, as well as embedded in the sole of his shoe, in the same commando raid that wires his home for audiovisual relay. The result is that—in a perverse reversal of a norm—he must at one point strip almost naked to avoid *exposure.*

At which turn, another reversal redirects the plot. Teamed up with Brill, Dean joins him in a plan based on the "lesson learned" from guerrilla tactics in Vietnam. If you're battling a huge superpower, your advantage is mostly that of flexibility and swiftness compared to its lumbering assault. So the idea is to go mobile and pick up any debris from the assailers, using it against its source. From within a single genre plot, here is launched the paradigm for almost a decade-and-a-half's worth of surveillance films down to the present: the fantasy that the "little guy" can fight back, turn discarded (or otherwise found) tech to his own advantage, beat the technopticon at its own gaze. Hence Brill gathers up all the ripped-free surveillance bugs from Dean's house and clothes and, partly through his deftness with laptop hacking, repurposes them so that the spies can be spied upon, discomfited, thrown off their game and the track at once.

Rearguard Techno-Guerillas

The first stage of this counteroffensive involves bugging the house of the villain, Reynolds, and leading him to discover it by finding himself imaged on his own TV. Later, the pressure is increased by installing hidden cameras in the hotel room of a senator mobilizing for the Telecommunications Security Act and recording him in flagrante with a female staffer about to perform oral sex. Brill jokes about this as if it were live-feed porn, saying to Dean: "You're too young to see this part." Dean responds as if in a double entendre (bodily rather than narrative "part"): "So is she." What seems like a comic throwaway, this whole episode is actually an epistemological boomerang, since this fine line between surveillance and erotic voyeurism will return, as if curatively reconfigured, at the end of the film.

Until then, the irony of the buggers bugged amounts mostly to a dilatory tactic. Dean's only real hope at the end is to trick Reynolds, in search of the video that shows him murdering the senator, into confronting the mob boss for it—as if Reynolds were pressing (unaware of it) for the earlier video about parole-busting contact with the other mobsters. Not since Lang have parallel plotlines converged in a more evenly matched and reciprocally cathartic duel between forensic overlords and a criminal underworld. For what ensues is the two ideologically antithetical but in fact equally vicious cartels—a global surveillance bureaucracy and a brutal Mafia culture—shooting it out in an internecine bloodbath, leaving over a dozen dead. (Here the debt to Coppola may well be sensed to extend beyond *The Conversation* to his first *Godfather* film two years before.) The system purges itself—the rogue protective agency and the homegrown criminal threat—under the recording eyes of the old-fashioned, search warrant-responsible, statically entrenched FBI stakeout, discovering the violence too late for interception but in time to call in the police for cleanup. The institutional dialectic is entirely meliorative, which is to say genre-consolatory: if one part of our government turns criminal and homicidal, checks and balances will straighten things out.

Notable—in this new ecology of invaded privacy—is that, given the tech advantage of the NSA, the standard FBI villains of paranoia thrillers have become as benign as bird-watchers. Moreover, even the narrative catalyst of countersurveillance, Brill, disappears in the chain reaction he has helped precipitate. He slips away after the shoot-out, going undercover again in the literal disguise of a police uniform. In turn, Reynolds's geek henchmen admit, under FBI interrogation—relayed to us, in fact, via the real-time enunciation of interrogation-booth surveillance cams—that they thought it was all only a "training op," no more real in the long run, though with live actors, than the video game Dean's kids were hoping for. All is normalized in the rapid scramble for closure. Dean himself goes back both to work and to his home life. His wife is still as feisty as ever, and just as counterestablishment, mocking the compromised senator who had pushed the Telecommunications Security Bill when, in a TV interview, he admits, about the NSA debacle, that we do seem to need someone to "monitor the monitors." Sarcastically, from the family-room couch, the wife's rhetorical question: "Oh, and who's gonna monitor the monitors of the monitors?" One more notch of normalization is required for a less-anxious finish. Moving to wrest this "epilogue" away from politics to domestic harmony, and to recover suspended conjugal relations for a rom-com genre closure now that the paranoia plot has run its course, Dean quips: "I wouldn't mind doing some monitoring of my own." And fully accepting this rerouting of surveillance paranoia back to the light-hearted scopophilia of sexual desire, she plays along: "Yes, you've got a lot of monitoring to make up for." Asks their preteen son: "Are you talking about sex?" All covert operations, even the byways of euphemistic dialogue, are likely to be intercepted, it would seem, but the real threat has clearly abated.

And as the son is hustled off to bed, Dean kills time until the promised erotic monitoring by flicking on the TV, only to discover his own face grinning back at him by way of a bug left behind by Brill in the overhead smoke detector, intercut with live images of the surveillance genius escaped incognito to the proverbial desert island, sending back a video postcard with "Wish you were here" written in the surf-washed sand. Quickly, however, the normal channels of TV transmission take over, reassert themselves, and the last line of the film comes in a TV interview conducted by Larry King, in cameo, with the duplicitous senator—as we cut away again, via reverse cosmic zoom, from the antenna-heavy suburban rooftops to the familiar wheeling satellite vantage point. King's lingering overvoice: "You have no right to come into my home." No, that right is reserved only for broadcast TV, either cabled or satellite-beamed, but elective and one-way in any case—not for the tentacles of closed-circuit entrapment. Just as illegal eyewitnessing is domesticated in the end to the intimate erotic and consensual gaze, so is televisual transmission to the leisure intake of exactly that spectatorship it shares with Hollywood film: a return to a seeing without being seen.

In this jokey ending, however, there is a glitch or a technical trick that, in either case, seems so continuous with the reparative tone of the close that it could almost be intentional. When Dean sees himself on the screen as a beaming Will Smith, he is treated to an impossible full suture, a frontal view, when in fact the hidden ceiling camera would make "eye contact" with its subject only if he were looking up—so that his face would appear on TV as it does only to us, not to him. Looking at the suddenly closed circuit of his home monitor, he would see only the *over*head shot of himself, still *under* surveillance. The decision to "correct" this tilt—for a cleaner and quite unironic symmetry—is probably all that has happened here. Yet the filmmakers couldn't have been sure we wouldn't notice, since everyone has experienced the convenience-store disorientation of seeing oneself on an overhead monitor as if from an unsuspecting angle in the eyes of another. (In fact, this angular displacement of sightlines plays an actual plot role in the surveillance-convention episode of *The Conversation*, that predecessor narrative so much on this later film's mind—where, as mentioned above, in an optically torqued over-the-shoulder shot, Caul sees himself being tailed.)

But whether or not we are meant to notice this ruse of the shot/reverse shot at the end of *Enemy of the State*, its stumbling block to plausibility does fit the whole loosening effort at resolution. The residual aura of surveillance, both in dialogue (the marital monitoring metaphor) and framing, gets sidetracked from threat to pleasure—relaxed into when deployed to resemble the reverse conduit of invited electronics via tuned-in TV. After all the nefarious being-seen by which our hero has been victimized, including the computer-induced equivalents of identity theft (leading to his defiant "I want my life back"), he is returned to an image of himself facilitated by surveillance under the aegis of poetic license. Until then, anything like telecommunications security has been, of course, murderously betrayed in its protective logic and co-opted for the ends of private ambition. Despite the NSA's rationale for such infringed liberties, the ideological overview behind its technological oversight—including unmentioned but presumably numberless threats to American life and sovereignty from untold directions—the film's title remains tellingly singular. Internal as well as foreign enemies there may be, but something else is characterized here as well. Technological excess has made an enemy of the state itself.

In Michel Foucault's terms, related to Louis Althusser's, and since taken up by Giorgio Agamben (in *What Is an Apparatus?*)—as well as in terms related to the politics of ideological critique behind apparatus theory at large in cinema studies—the human agent subjugated by the remote control-apparatus of the state *becomes* a subject thereby. True freedom, according to Agamben, can in this sense come only from a "profanation of apparatuses."[3] Seizing the leavings of power and converting them to insurgent weaponry, as Brill demonstrates, is one way (in genre fantasy) to effect what Agamben sees as this necessary sacrilege: a defiance of the mystified and quasi-theological power of a system everywhere lording it over the individual agent. Say that the apparatus is figured in *Enemy of the State* by satellite positioning devices as channeled through subsidiary surveillance techniques, a kind of divine omniscience writ small in implemented computer code. In this case, required for defiance—for profanation—is either a breaking into and ransacking of the temples of control or, somewhat more feasibly, the remote blasphemy of interception and disruption. But even in the genre-sponsored turning of the tables for its tech revenge plot, Scott's paranoid thriller takes the conservative final route—via a deflating comic turn—of domesticating the apparatus after all, befriending it. Genre is strained to its (not unfamiliar) inner limit in burying its own axiomatic anxiety.

Given Agamben's interest elsewhere in avant-garde filmmaking, with no subterfuge of mimesis or immersion, it is to be expected, perhaps, that his thoughts don't run, even in a book so titled, to the ideological critique of classic cinema developed under the umbrella of "apparatus theory" and its subject-stationing suture. But certainly the insistence on self-suture in the shot/countershot comedy of self-recognition at the end of *Enemy of the State*, in clear violation of its own technologic, suggests the urge, on the hero's part, to accept legal as well as lawyerly subjecthood under the eye of a media culture—at least once it can be supposed purged, at least momentarily, of traitorous potential. TV thus plays its ideological part (and with it, on it—via synecdoche and *mise en abyme*—the spectacle of film stardom, complete with the marquee face in intercut close-ups). Talk shows like Larry King's included, the televised image becomes a half-hearted and last-ditch case of the apparatus reconsecrated. The absence of on-screen TV broadcast (or mention) in the two films on which the next chapter concentrates (*Rear Window* and *Peeping Tom*) is among several measures of the psychic claustrophobia that less anodyne entertainments than Scott's, films more deeply entangled in the psychomachia of surveillance, regularly diagnose. But we stay here, for a while longer, with genre films that continue the fantasy of the techno-bricoleur who, even when cornered by the state panopticon, can still succeed in fighting back. Which is to say:

Sighting Back

Genres tend to be problem-solvents; they wash away difficulties, dissolve rather than resolve them. In making the intractable seem actionable, their closures gravitate to fantasy. How so with low-boil anxieties about paramilitary surveillance in the Homeland Security mode under the reign of anti-Terror? After the repeated inmixing of detective-genre elements and surveillance phobia in many of the films we've revisited, in two of the latest and most involuted examples, *The Bourne Legacy* (Tony Gilroy, 2012) and *Total Recall* (Len Wiseman, 2012), detection is reserved mainly for the hero's efforts to find out not who done it, but who he himself is—and why so many people want him in their mediated weapon sights.[4]

Right from the first segment of the original trilogy, in *The Bourne Identity* (counterfactual pun already in play), Jason Bourne can't remember who he is—because he isn't. Born David Webb instead, he has been retooled as a CIA spy and hit man under the eponymous alias. But "psychogenic amnesia" after gunshot wounds has erased this false identity—almost as if the bullets had killed him. Nor is it he (Matt Damon)—merely played by a different actor (James Bond–style)—who comes back in 2012's *Legacy*. It's another mind-warped and interchangeable operative from a new iteration not just of the same franchise but of the same covert initiative (Jeremy Renner as Aaron Cross).

Next door in the multiplex, *Total Recall* (remake of the 1990 film by Paul Verhoeven), parades another self-estranged hero, his own true identity firewalled by a computerized surveillance regime of autocratic state control. A delayed recognition may well set in for the viewer, too, as well as for the character at a different level. Our screen hero as someone he isn't: What could in fact be more cinematic? Every actor is in role rather than in earnest. Spy plots have always tapped into the theatricality of human performance, where all is scripted, programmed, now even digitally modified. But even when the hero, in both films, hasn't quite grown back into his role yet, there he is on the remote screens of those who actually recognize him—as their target.

In the first *Bourne* film, the inaugural moment of digital surveillance is entirely routine: a lone security installation in Zurich's American Consulate, from which the still clueless hero tries to naively avert his face (sent immediately into mass dissemination as forensic image). From there out, the trilogy continually ramps up its surveillance tech across a frenetic gamut of electronic spyware and computerized mapping, including automatic digital cameras in power-drive sequence, magnetic remote trackers, co-opted TSA footage, high-speed passport cross-checks from international customs sites, and weather-satellite images combed for clues. The chief CIA overseer in the latest *Bourne* film barks out (by metonymy): "Give me every camera you've got." This finally includes—in the ultimate remote mode for mandatory car-chase climaxes—the computer upload of all urban toll and traffic cams.

Ever since the implicitly punning surveillance bugs (or "spyders"?) scurrying for information across floors and walls in 2002's *Minority Report* (Steven Spielberg), the ingenuities of optical data gathering know no limit. Hence another link between the genealogy of *Legacy* and *Total Recall.* In the third and most tech-heavy of the trilogy (*The Bourne Ultimatum*), a transmitted image, coruscated with digital breakups on the CIA screen, is being sent from a viewfinder attached to an automatic handgun targeting Bourne. The sci-fi license of *Total Recall,* during a similar attack on the cornered hero, takes this optical tooling of weaponry several steps further in one wild leap. "Get eyes in there" is the command, and one of the robot police fires off a presumed machine gun, but instead a whole rotary cartridge of mini webcams punctures the walls and thus rims the room's perimeter with tiny oculi designed to triangulate the kill by remote transmission. In a marked conflation of cinematic technique and futurist technology, the resulting shoot-out is indistinguishable from the montage shot plan of its own execution. If only the criminal mastermind in Lang's *The Thousand Eyes of Doctor Mabuse* had had this device at hand, he wouldn't have needed all that closed-circuit TV for Cold War espionage. In the conflation of optics and ballistics at the heart of the surveillance plot, vision is a weapon.

Vision—and its associated wireless channels. As if extrapolated from a current unease about data mining and identity theft, the hero of the new *Total Recall* realizes at one point that he must remove the cell phone filaments surgically embedded in his hand to prevent remote tracking by its signal—a "palm pilot" turned from "handy" tool to weapons-guidance system. Bourne, likewise, has a laser implant removed in the trilogy's first segment. And in the new sequel, an early montage episode cuts between a drone control center in Virginia and the Alaskan wilderness where Cross is being double-crossed by his own agency. The attempt to take him out is foiled only when, in a rather bravura conception, he transfers his cyborg status onto another animal killer by removing the tracker chip from his thigh and, with the "predator" drone closing in, feeding the miniature GPS to an attacking wolf as decoy prey.

Then, too, the good spy will know how to track his own spymasters. In *The Bourne Supremacy*, speaking on a wiretapped line to a female official at the CIA, the recorded hero has her twice in his sights from adjacent office buildings, first in the crosshairs of an assault rifle, later with the naked eye—and stuns her both times by admitting as much. In a blend of *Rear Window* and *The Conversation*, old-fashioned surveillance—his eyes-on stakeout versus the CIA wiretapping—is dropped like a still-operable fossil into the new ricochet of remote electronic transmits. Thrown into relief in this way, the computerized video saturation of these plots is part of their dystopian selling point in the vague War on Terror aura they, like *Total Recall* in a futurist variant, mean to evoke. Yet where surveillance serves in this way to resuscitate the detective genre, it has, as chapter 6 will show, suffocated the actual Mideast war picture. What fails so miserably with audiences in the hypermediated desert films of Mideast intelligence gathering and counterinsurgency, with all its helmet-cam imagery and laptop video intercut with drone scans, pays off here instead when the technology is hyped into rogue threat rather than the vérité treatment of a military morass. Threat, plus the fantasy of its overcoming in kind.

To begin with, political topicalities in the *Bourne* films are off-loaded onto the broad phobic specter of electronic search and weaponized seizure. The trilogy was concerned with real rather than electronically induced amnesia and its flashes of recovery, a pattern continued in *Legacy* through a series of repressed memories and their flashbacks, traumatic returns of supposedly patriotic violence. Enemies of the state are never specified, but Abu Ghraib and Guantanamo hang heavily in the air. In *The Bourne Ultimatum*, we've seen the hero hooded and waterboarded by CIA operatives. In the last and definitive flashback to this ambiguous scene, we learn that he has finally been "broken down" and "remade." Amnesia, his original and instigating affliction, turns out, in the rounding off of the trilogy, to have been a self-protective resource: blocking memories he can't bear. For only in the end is he goaded into recalling that he once proved his willingness to "give [himself] to the program" by reluctantly executing a hooded double for himself. This is a man who looks, when the blindfold is removed, like one of the "American citizens" who Bourne has later discovered, to his horror, are among the assassinated victims of the program—as if this were worse than the foreign nationals or the African head of state also targeted by armed espionage.

That was the trilogy. The *Legacy* plugs indirectly into a new topical anxiety: not just the erosion of private will by surveillance and brutality but of organic autonomy by biogenetic tampering. Yet, in the process, this latest film's slowly disclosed backstory may seem in retrospect to exonerate a sustained improbability in the preceding three. Bourne, when impersonated by the mild-mannered Damon, was all along a rather unlikely superhero—too fast, tough, and adept, too smart, altogether too quick on his feet. As character as well as actor, his prowess seemed fabricated. It was. He had been, as he ultimately learns, refashioned by torture, brainwashing, and homicidal calisthenics. Even so, the results remain implausible. The *Legacy*—named in part for the inherited ruthlessness of this human engineering—goes one clarifying step further. Bourne's successors in the "Outcome" program are in another way too good to be true, like doped Olympians, where aggression itself is chemically supplemented (like the pharmaceutically induced "primal violence" of the experimental Vietnam squad in *Jacob's Ladder* [1990]). Here, too, the programmatic doping is in its own right aggressive: first with the enforced regimen of body- and mind-altering pills, then with the toxic virus used to kill off the agents when the program goes sour.

Even when meant to be enabling rather than lethal, the approach is a kind of biological warfare in its own right. This we learn in an unusually telegraphic exposition from a female neurologist whose metaphors, like so much else in these films, shunt between communications technology and ballistic assault. A virus, when not fatal, is the best "delivery system," she explains, in "reprogramming" human genetics, but one has to know where to strike in this campaign of "genomic targeting." With the opening sequence of failed aerial takeout behind us, it's hard not to think that drone sighting through computer technology is being replicated in its logic at the level of neurobiology and its top-secret interventions. Hearing all this, Cross gets her to accompany him to the Manila lab where, with an injection of a live culture, he can "viral off" the drugs for good by way of a permanent genetic boost.

After a last grinding motorcycle chase through congested Manila streets, they escape with their lives into the open sea on a friendly junk. Doctored hero and virologist heroine have obviously consummated below deck their so far merely expedient pairing (in this typically sex-starved franchise). For they are now topside in a laconic post-coital haze, their borrowed fishing boat floating out past the atolls in the South China Sea as the hero begins charting their uncertain course on a weather-worn map. The film's last line is hers, with a sly smile: "I was sort of hoping we were lost." Not so, just freed for a moment and left floating, their vehicle well-stocked with sequel bait. Yet their receding image within a panoramic wide-angle shot is tied back to the film's whole contrapuntal aesthetic. Cinematography has alternated between the hyperlong shot (like the hero's chances) and the gargantuan close-up, which involves at times an intimacy, in car or rented room, that regularly seems a kind of dramatic respite, suggesting no threat from the off-frame space of surveillance. But not always—and never for long. In extreme narrative close-up in the neurology lab for his earlier checkup, pressing the doctor for answers about "behavioral design," Cross is rebuffed with "Enough information . . . don't you know we're on camera?" No mere cinematic in-joke here. The remark has done what the films in this surveillance genre always do: deflect any twinge of voyeurism onto the diegetic paranoia of invaded privacy. All Cross does is glance upward knowingly. No reverse shot locates the hidden camera. It's as ubiquitous as narrative omniscience itself. And as flexible.

Certainly the energy of *Legacy* comes mainly—across one dilated and equally flamboyant chase sequence after another—from the rub not just of past against present but of event against its mediation. At the film's emotional turning point, we watch Cross looking on at a superseded former self in a laptop upload of his army enlistment photograph. He does so by way of explaining to the neurologist why he is so attached to his "cognitive enhancement" pills. When the blank stare of this photo was first recorded, his IQ had to be faked by the recruiter to make the army minimum. Better a killing machine, Cross implies, than a dysfunctional reject.

This retrospect falls into place within a franchise-familiar series of flashbacks that pace the film by inserted memory bursts—though without the fuller justification of clinical amnesia and its breakthroughs from the trilogy. The present time frame of the *Legacy* plot is soon interrupted by a close-up of Cross, under interrogation and his former name, battered and addled, in what amounts to his second (this time CIA) recruitment. That flashback, linked to another in which his handler talks him out of moral qualms after a killing, then become an electronic playback on the handler's own monitor during the Internet manhunt. In its third and final recurrence (and functional exorcism), this grilling humiliation is next replayed as Cross's own feverish nightmare after his viral injection in Manila, from which he does in fact actually awake—once and for all, his juiced-up powers now permanent. Yet privacy must still be won back. Trapped in the live channels and searchable files of the new technopticon, all one can ever hope to do is to block access.

Beyond the counterpoint of such recursive scenes, remembered or recorded, there is a yet more dominant pattern, synchronic rather than diachronic—playing not between present and past, through memory or upload, but across parallel streams of time present. In the vehicular mayhem that peaks at the end of *Legacy*, everything "on the ground," burned rubber and all, is contrasted with the high-tech monitoring of the intended escape route. The film is constantly cutting away from the desktop and full-screen surveillance panels at command central to the satellite-relayed frenzy. (Says the CIA special unit director as the escape plot thickens and he uproots to higher-tech quarters: "I need a crisis suite with fully integrated grids.") The typically underlit and cinema-like space to which we remove, a kind of off-site "theater of operations," is complete with so many viewing screens that it looks like an overloaded editing room out of which separate fixed camera shots might conceivably be pieced together into an action sequence. But not quite, and only in grainy B&W at best.

Alternating montage has become a structuring alternation between two entirely different image protocols, one the manhunt's own hyperkinetic montage chase, the other a mutating rectilinear collage at the receiving end of simultaneous transmission in the command hub. Yet more is at stake than just making us grateful, even in the face of the zingy video banks of command central, for old-fashioned, full-screen movie action when we are released back into it. This is partly because the action sequences themselves are shot—and digitally edited—so much in the handheld, multicam mode of fractured continuity that they, even though in full color, might almost have been hi-def surveillance composites from multiple tracking angles. And, more importantly, because the hero has so fiercely refused to keep to his vulnerable place in the scene under surveillance—and has consistently fought back, co-opted rather than just defied the network that would snare him, refused passivity under its gaze.

Despite the magic virus immunizing the hero in *Legacy* against normal human vulnerabilities, the deepest genre fantasy ends up feeling more technological than biomedical. One laconic turn of dialogue serves indirectly to flag this. Admitting his fears of cognitive degradation from hunk genius back to lunkhead—as hinted in a couple of dead-eyed regressive close-ups as the meds wear off—Cross admits: "It would be real hard to go back." Who are we to doubt it, by analogy with our own kinds of prosthetic enablements and affordances, the infogadgetry of our everyday computer interfaces—in each case a putative mode of "cognitive enhancement"?

Never "Off-Grid"

Here, then, the motif of doping fades into a larger tech horizon of cyborgian prosthetics. Equipment nostalgia has no place in current films—or filming—like this, any more than in the everyday planned obsolescence of each new digital "enhancement" to hit the market. Every artificial increase in "behavioral design" and "sensory function" (in the vocabulary of *Bourne* neurology), every time-saving gizmo or big-screen dazzlement they throw at us, addicts us further. This is our digital fix. The fantasy here isn't that there's someplace in Pacific waters where one can float both at peace and "off-grid"—as the inevitable next installment in this tireless franchise is sure to remind us. Nor, more broadly, that private space may still somehow be made safe from invasion. The fantasy, rather, is simply that you can't lose by winning; that the very system that "remakes you," and in the process makes you electronically deft and surveillance-savvy, thus gives you the wherewithal to hold your own, even when such prowess is pitted, in a given dystopian narrative, against a full-bore paramilitary assault.

The latest James Bond, *Skyfall* (Sam Mendes, 2012), makes this point as if upside down, so that self-defense against electronic manipulation reverts to low-grade anachronistic weaponry. In this respect *Skyfall* is a departure that underscores the current action-film norm. It also follows a pattern in the triad of Daniel Craig's Bonds: a descending technological trajectory in which the hero is progressively less "equipped" in his own right for the new technopticon. *Casino Royale* (Martin Campbell, 2006) was threaded together by confiscated cell-phone clues based on numbers last called. This motif includes a scene in which Bond breaks into the security control room of a casino and rifles through the time-coded DVDs for the date spread by which, when replaying it on the monitor, he is able to match the exact time of a killer's message to an arriving guest, who is caught on camera taking the call just as the valet takes his car. In *Quantum of Solace* (Marc Forster, 2008), with Bond stripped even further of ancillary gadgets, the surveillance potential is reserved for M (Judi Dench) in London and the electronic mapping of covert operatives at various international sites. Projected in wall-sized reframings and overlaps in the reconnaissance chamber, this global-access apparatus is debuted for her at her command to "Astonish me" (with the same intricate touchpad graphics available for the DVD paratext as we search again for our favorite action locales chapter by chapter).

Skyfall completes the picture of a denuded tech hero by having the whole spectrum of electronic gadgetry almost entirely confined to rogue villainy, not national defense. Its former machinic flourishes are replaced for the hero by a lone instrument of low-tech predigital transmission: a miniature hidden radio for signaling help. This is the case for Bond himself—even while M, from command central in London, is now able to monitor and coach the action at almost every turn—in real time—by audio implants: rather like a second-unit director of stuntmen in an action sequence. But narrative privilege splits down the middle. As the spectacle of the opening action sequence plays out before our eyes, it reaches M's ears only like a voiceover. Even as we alone see what's going on, it is up to her to decide what will happen next. Whereas M's refrain in *Casino Royale* was to keep Bond's eyes on the prize, on the "big picture," which never quite materializes for the spectator, at the start of *Skyfall* her decision to risk his life by a fellow agent's sniper bullet seems less a sign of heartless decisiveness than of her directorial obligation, long-distance, to call all the shots.

Remote intelligence of this sort is the metropole's only hope. It's clear that globetrotting, preemptive violence in souped-up armed sports cars (once dear to this franchise) has by now taken second seat to the global threat of cyberterrorism and contravened surveillance. The archvillain this time, a turncoat agent bent on revenge, is a superhacker able to commandeer the full surveillance capacity of the British Secret Service and expose its embedded covert agents on international websites—as well as programming his own escape route even before capture. His defeat comes only when the London computer team leaves an encrypted trail of evidence, in Bond's sequestering of M, so arcane that only the brilliant villain could pride himself on decoding it. By this lure Bond then proceeds to entrap him—and improbably foil his armored helicopter attack—with an old-fashioned hunting rifle, construction dynamite, and knife. Our hero has thus taken one step further back from that simple radio transmitter to which, except for a personalized handgun, his arsenal of electronics has been reduced in the mandatory scene of Q's provisioning: exactly the retro-tech that had saved the day when he signaled for helicopter backup in a first showdown with the villain. At the film's climax, however, he is without even this dated supplement to hand-to-hand combat. If you can't beat the cybergenius at his own game, you can at least seduce him—by his very strengths at the keypad—into a primitive ambush and a classic movement-image duel (Deleuze again: his emphasis on montage convergence in *M*).

In its suspension—rather than mere downsizing—of the hero's surveillance capability, *Skyfall* remains a clarifying exception to routine celebrations of techno-revenge. In film after film, *The Bourne Legacy* and *Total Recall* most recently, it is instead the cornered loner hero who hacks back into the technopolitical structure that has spawned, trained, and victimized him. The localized revenge fantasy at the end of *Total Recall* is, more specifically, that a double agent killer, converted to true revolutionary, could escape federated surveillance—in one grid-tracked chase after another—and bring down the entire system. No accident that this imagined defiance involves a flashy weapon of countersurveillance: a digital face mask almost good enough to fool airport security. Although such genre-derived subterfuge is neutralized almost as soon as contrived, disintegrated in a bitmap breakup, it harbors something more ingrained. These narratives are a far cry from the downbeat post-Watergate paranoia films about illicit government surveillance—and not least because their freakish technological sophistication, verging at times into sci-fi, seem to be playing into the digital hands of an audience still bothering to dam up their web streams for an occasional night at the movies.

The real structuring fantasy of *The Bourne Legacy* isn't, in that throwaway closing vista of the couple adrift in the South China Sea, that there might be a way to "securitize" some removed realm of our own on which no oversight can home in. It is, rather, that with ever-improved manual and cognitive skills, there could be a pushing back: that the digital fix (as quandary) we're in—including the fix that they may have on us (as targets, even if only commercial)—has some potential fix of its own, some inbuilt, protective mastery waiting to be implemented.[5] Or at the very least, an ingenuity sufficient to *detourn* the system, as when remote surveillance, finally tracking in on the Manila room from which Bourne has absconded reborn, finds his message—instead of his image—on the mirror, descriptive and imperative both: "No More."

As the video-game ad tucked into the supplemental material on the DVD release of the second *Bourne* film promises: with controls in hand "You become Bourne"—which is to say, as at the movies too, you forget yourself in the image of the superhero. (You may well forget, too, that this was originally and most famously a cautionary line, and later tagline, in Robert Weine's *The Cabinet of Dr. Caligari* [1920], the obsessive "You must become Caligari," suggesting the perverse lines of identification between moviegoer and the spell cast by an on-screen mesmerist and "medium.") Becoming the image one sees, transferring agency to one's avatar, is a trope all the more recognizable these days when replete, in sci-fi film, with biometric downloads and sensory upgrades, prosthetic apps, memory-extensions, laser and cellular implants, and so on. Indeed, with computer games and feature films increasingly indistinguishable in their first-person vectors of hyperkinetic identification, such a tagline formula abets the genre myth of audiovisual "enhancement" as empowerment. In regard to the only audience demographic that finally counts, the commercial loop, like the surveillance feed, has become a closed-circuit mechanism in its own right. The expertise you practice at home is what you go to the multiplex to celebrate. And when your heroes fight back against exacerbated forms of networked existence, what Agamben celebrates as an insurgent technique of resisted panoptic imposition—again, the "profanation" of the "apparatuses"—comes through, however extravagant its bravado, in a superficially profane and trivialized form.

Pitched more fully into the realm of the techno fantastic for another recent thriller sequel, there is, in this logic, a further turn of the screw, one where "moviemaking" itself becomes a defensive weapon. The digital inversion of face recognition as facial mirage in *Total Recall* has its self-conscious precedent, no doubt, in the plastic masks of the *Mission Impossible* series. But in *Mission Impossible: Ghost Protocol* (Brad Bird, 2011), the most ingenious devices—accompanying this signature trick—are now enhanced visual prostheses in a computerized rather than cosmetic mode. These involve such optical gadgets as the video electronics of contact lenses facilitating remotely transmitted facial matchups in a crowd. But they also include what can only be called optical countersurveillance: duped images. The franchise toolkit includes this time a toy red balloon with a remote camera relay and encryption device that, when dropped into a Kremlin air vent, recodes the Soviet's own optical-recognition technology. Once inside the building with this assistance, the misrecognized (and again face-masked) hero and his sidekick momentarily disable a CCTV camera in order to unpack, out of wired sight, a weirdly sophisticated optical technology that confounds the armed guard stationed in a wholly unobstructed space open to his direct surveillance while backed by several closed-circuit monitors for more remote oversight.

The effect is as hard to beat as it is to detail. This new byzantine device of the intruders involves a self-extending Mylar-like movie screen, behind which the US operatives edge forward toward the top-security door they seek. Rather than letting Soviet video tools make them into a screen image for detection, they remake the enemy's inhabited space into a rectangular optical illusion, screening out their mission. What has transpired is as much a piece of avant-garde video-installation art as it is a surveillance decoy. The rapidly mobile camera attached to this portable scrim photographs the lengthening space behind it and immediately rear-projects that image, cued and rescaled to the perspectival sightlines of the now suspicious guard moving back and forth at his post. The result is that the screen remains invisible to him in (as) the natural recession of the hall's geometry. In this way is the medium fully instrumentalized within diegetic space. The movie that notoriously missed being made in 3-D, because of production disputes with the director, has made its own 3-D movie inside it.

As one more version of the beat-them-at-their-own-game syndrome, the auto-allegory here is suitably circular. Not just random electronic props but an entire movie apparatus in digital upgrade, with its own version of CGI (computer-generated imagery), has come to the aid of invincible (because here invisible) movie heroes in this ad hoc spectacle of digital camouflage, this true ghostly protocol. Again, it takes a new kind of secret camerawork to defeat the security cam on its own terms. Both with and without such a sci-fi extension of technology's current optical arsenal, two films remain for discussion in which—by closed circuit and apocalyptic short-out, respectively—surveillance camerawork operates as if to remake the whole notion of a "world viewed," in Stanley Cavell's title, inducing new versions of what his subtitle calls "reflections on the ontology of film."[6]

The previous genre fictions should have prepared us for any attempt at taking the complementary measure of the medial ironies pushed to a new limit by these films. In narrative terms, what we have seen, often secondhand—through telephoto lenses, security cams, surveillance photo dossiers, and so forth, including what we've overheard via the "sound thief" (John le Carré's recurrent term) of covert micing—is a litany of human agency compromised by spectation and related modes of stolen privacy: a trail of movement-images (in Deleuze's baseline sense) framed and potentially curtailed by time-coded ones. In Antonioni, Coppola, and

De Palma, photographers and audio engineers—resisting their status as the mere implements of mediation, hoping to act upon what they've tracked—are foiled by the theft of their evidence. In contrast, as spelled out most explicitly in *Enemy of the State*, the victims of surveillance in more recent films are marginally empowered to resist—even from their place at its attenuated focal point—the audiovisual network that would entrammel them. We might say that their techno castration meets its revenge fantasy in a tactical e-masculation. But along such an axis of reversible electronic vigilance—when taken either to narratological or to ontological limits—all that is left to hypothesize for screen imaging is the total despotism or the total eclipse of its surveillant trace, either the turning of all human stories into a sampled digital archive or the turning of all life, so posited, off.

Look Out

The two indie films operating to these related ends, American and British, respectively, do so by carrying surveillance beyond theme to medial precondition: one by formalist constraint, one by doomsday satire. In *Look* (Adam Rifkin, 2007, mutated into a short-lived TV series, a kind of meta-"reality show," in 2011), there is no narrative image that is not under explicit and delimited surveillance—or rather, that isn't the residuum of that surveillance. In fact, its DVD reissue inscribes its paratextual irony onto the surface of the disk, which images the oculus of a surveillance lens rimmed with magnification ratios. In *The Nine Lives of Tomas Katz* (Ben Hopkins, 2000), there is, in a related but bizarrely different way, no protective distance between secondary transmission within the narrative and the projection of our own film: the cancellation of the one is the effacement of the other. Rifkin's title plays between *look* as noun (whether tacitly objective or subjective in grammatical terms: the look of, the look by) and its activation by imperative (look at the way they look at themselves, for instance, in the two-way dressing room mirror). Within this tacit oscillation we are invited to see images that would otherwise waste away in security-cam storage, unengaged by narrative (that is, forensic) motive, indeed theoretically inactivated as image at all. In *Tomas Katz*, by contrast, we are made to look on at the disengagement of the very cameras that securitize, in effect, the existence of our world. Holding off on the latter ontological ironies for a moment, we can consider first the epistemological intricacies of *Look*.

Department store security cams privy to teenage shoplifting as well as to staff members' sexual peccadillos in the storeroom; video surveillance in high school corridors and parking lots revealing the buildup to a teacher's statutory rape of a sexually aggressive student; a double security installation at a convenience store capturing the cell-phone picture taken by the clerk of the cop killers' license plate previously caught on the dashboard cam of a squad car and then broadcast as part of the police manhunt—just some of the randomized footage pulled together, with or without police investigation, so as to turn "looking" (optical targeting) into plot. What is so remarkable about the experience of watching this film, even though it never releases the viewer from a permeating self-consciousness about its mostly fixed camera angles, is the way its piecemeal narrative folds the arbitrary mélange of these sightings into the felt texture of everyday filmmaking. And not just in an era when it's likely that at least some part of any screen narrative is likely to be relayed via remediated surveillance images. (These include the now-familiar ATM shot—the machine's own POV—that records, in this case, a robbery and abduction, with only the mechanically requested receipt floating past the camera in the wind after the kidnapping of the account holder.) But what comes through in *Look*—above and beyond the motivated internal views of the surveillance subtext—is something instead about narrative pastiche at large and the radical depersonification of the narratorial function in even standard moviemaking.

Here, too, with this interlocking assemblage, as with most narrative—although in ways we can't help asking ourselves about this time—we don't know who's reviewing the footage or juxtaposing it, nor even how much of it is meant to have been diegetically accessed at all, whether by authorities, lawyers, police. It exists simply *in transmission* to us as anthology plot, wholly unsutured, but dramatically involving and consequential nonetheless. And more than that, its piecing together exercises the same license, and operates under the same aegis, as mainstream narrative. Even the biggest cheat (the audible soundtrack) in the film's supposed narrative recuperation of a passive surveillance archive—at first disorienting, if not infuriating—ends up, in a roundabout way, serving the purposes of the film's remediated impersonal purview. For sound recording is the unashamed wild card dealt out improbably by one episode after another. Restricted point of view from one camera, limited zoom function, reverse and fast-forward, jump cuts: these credibly anchor the plot to the surveillance apparatus that delivers its every increment. Yet, by contrast, even the egregious "fiction" of sound, of audible dialogue, in each narrative module—the suspended disbelief required to accept an audial as well as a merely visual record in this security-cam mode—operates with a broader metafilmic inference. Straining credibility, the film actually serves to lay bare (especially in the overhead—and artificially overheard—long shots of department stores or malls or parking lots) the artifice of direct dialogue in the similar shots of typical movie fare. For these moments are regularly a function, instead, of overdubbing or postsynchronization: a kind of routine audio telescoping to bring distant figures into narrative intimacy.

"Look" is what we do in the presence of on-screen narrative, and listen is what else we do. In their melded contribution to the cognitive parameters of narrative duration, surveillance signals come to seem no less arbitrary an ingredient in the configured fictive space than more traditional (and typically disavowed) operations of the cinematic machine. A robocam as part of a bomb-defusion operation on a passenger bus; a nanny cam that allows a dimension of interior domesticity in one plot strand; interrogation room surveillance that records the upshot of the rape charge, after presenting the accuser with previous surveillances tapes of her eager stalking: all this, woven together in separate strands with other elapsed events in technological regress, is nothing more than a parable of traditional film's own contrapuntal premise—under the more than ordinarily blown cover, that is, of omniscience.

The interest sustained by this nondiegetic motivation of the security footage, this emergence of narrative(s) without any but mechanically focalized narration, can be contrasted, in a less innovative vein of commercial storytelling, with the sci-fi surveillance thriller *Eagle Eye* (2008). This is a film made by the same director, D. J. Caruso, who remade *Rear Window* in 2007 as *Disturbia*, replacing the Greenwich Village courtyard with a suburban setting, Jeffries's tormenting cast with an itchy electronic ankle monitor on the teenage hero under house arrest, and the equally "incapacitated" recording device of the telephoto lens with an active camcorder. In *Eagle Eye* a year later—reversing a surveillance axis running from civilian snooping to state oversight—a relentless array of panoptic images comparable to the various anchored sightings of *Look* (from TSA emplacements to bank surveillance cams to the overhead zoom-in reading, from federal office security, of a secret fax communiqué, including at least a dozen more reframed images as well) is entirely motived, at the narrative level, by the work of a self-reprogramming supercomputer assigned to orchestrate all US mainland surveillance as well as all international input. But the computer is blocked by human meddling in an attempt to abort a Mideast drone assassination in the precredit sequence, a strike based on insufficient biometric recognition of a suspected jihadist (a mere mourner at a Muslim funeral, as it turns out). When the algorithmic assessment is overridden by the president from Air Force One, the computer deduces that the US leader (together with the passive acquiescence of Congress) is the greatest threat in rendering us vulnerable to terrorist reprisal—and thus schemes to take him out by bomb blast, along with House and Senate members, at his State of the Union address. This programming must be resisted, of course, by the bravery and local ingenuity of the far-flung, spied-upon subjects the computer moves to use as tools: prosthetic agents of its own multiplied but immobilized eye.

Seen to Be

Sci-fi physics, in tackling the surveillance question, can wax more metaphysical as well, as promised in the British indie satire *The Nine Lives of Tomas Katz.* Once positing a pervasively recorded present, with all duration turned to image, surveillance sci-fi can also imagine the sheer erasure of time. Alien invasion is the opening trope in the aggression of the eponymous Tomas Katz, whose nine lives name the serial incarnations he achieves by vampirizing (and vaporizing) the human bodies whose visible outer shell he assumes. The film begins with a precredit surveillance montage of satellite disks and traffic cams as if the pending supernatural threat—of both solar and species eclipse—could ever be monitored or averted. In fact, surveillance is the final medium of earth's violation, rather than a defense against it. The last two of Katz's nine transformations are a direct assault on optical media, the terrestrial interloper becoming first—via female im-"personation"—a TV commentator whose opinions, as well as whose ventriloquized looks, he takes on as if simply by watching. The next and last body-snatching operates not through broadcast but closed-circuit TV. A security cam at London's surveillance center, showing a lone male figure approaching the main control room, reveals his digital morphing into Katz, having come there to attack national security at its source.

As it turns out, the ordinary soapbox crazies we've seen earlier are right: the world is coming to an end with the total eclipse of the sun, and Katz is the emissary of this cosmic blackout. On the same TV talk show sabotaged by his telepathic gender switch, we later see a rabbi pundit exhumed, after being dead for two years, so as to be interviewed about divine purview and the course of messianic history. The gods have always looked over us, from the time of the Olympians, he opines, even as narrative cuts away, as earlier, to yet more CCTV shots of people bound for glory in the pending death cars of the Tube. Trouble is, admits the rabbi, the gods themselves have degenerated into what we have now:

namely, "Dave." This, at the London surveillance hub, is the cretinous functionary sitting at the controls of several hundred surveillance monitors and making minor decisions about the world under inspection, there at the helm alongside his boorish, snack-munching coworker.

Dave wants his counterpart to guess which POV is his favorite. One fixed-framed console shows a crack in some distant pavement supposedly "getting bigger." Another, inert smokestacks. And so on, with dull variety, some four hundred or more such transmissions—each numbered for easy recognition, including the monitor that displays for the technicians an apparently familiar sight ("not again!"): a guy starting to masturbate in front of his TV screen, porn perhaps in progress. They phone him and he stops in panic. "I love the interactive part," says Dave. No suture, just the remote invasion of privacy. But with that final on-camera metamorphosis of Katz replacing none other than Dave's sidekick in the process of returning to the control board, the incognito alien now tempts Dave, as if pandering to the fantasy of his Olympian omnipotence, to simply obliterate London by taking it off-line—starting with the suburbs. Whereas the 1965 paranoid surveillance allegory by Samuel Beckett, *Film,* borrows Bishop Berkeley's notion that "to be is to be perceived" (*esse est percipi*), the trauma of such objectifying (rather than subjective) "sightedness" is quite explicitly worked out half a century later in *Tomas Katz*. Not to be seen is not just to be invisible, but indeed to be wholly nonexistent. Such is the scopic regime over which Dave presides as minor functionary. And the simple monosyllable "No" triggers the erasure. As soon as he's alone, Dave's off-camera voice commands, true to his boorish scopophilia, "No skirts," but he soon gets into the negative ontological groove with "No legs," "No cars," and finally—as the last London buildings disappear from the monitored skyline at his behest—"No substance," leaving just a full-frame image of a sky on one of his remaining monitors, followed by "No light," "No clouds," "No sounds," "No birds," and in the final eradication, "No Dave."

Surveillance is so total, so definitive of contemporary social circulation, so *constitutive,* that its serial erasure cancels the very objects of its gaze, including the presumed mediatory function of its own operator, effaced here—sans suture—by some mode of voice recognition technology, perhaps, installed in the throne room of his abrogated power. In any case, with a further flick of the wrist or not, Dave speaks forth his own eradication. Godhead in travesty, fiat in reverse, he is the idiot scapegoat for the system he has betrayed only by exposing. The closed circuit has become a true vicious circle. In an ontology of sheer surveillance, one corrosive question remains, answered in the negative by just this concluding sequence of shots: Are you really there when no one is looking?

Alternately: Is there any proof of innocence, let alone of existence, if one leads one's life untraced, unperceived, unrecorded? The ingenious British thriller *Freeze Frame* (John Simpson, 2004) seems named for the hero's fear that his video self-surveillance might fail him in its continuous record and latent playback, seizing up before the needed event is captured—as well as named for a technique used only in the "imaginary" reconstruction (in narrative flashback) of the multiple killings of which he has previously been accused. Simpson's film takes the proliferation of UK surveillance, satirized in *Tomas Katz,* and turns it sardonically on its head—so that one is potentially victimized only by going unrecorded. After being acquitted on grounds of "police entrapment," the hero spends the next ten years (and all of his time on camera in our film) taping himself in fixed but not frozen frames encoded in their four corners with telltale abbreviations—first of his punning name, Sean Veil (SV), then of camera placement, date, and (bottom right) the running spin of hour, minute, second, and frame.

The premise (and display format) is oddly close to a Hollywood film of the same year, *The Final Cut* (Omar Naim) in which a kind of inverted self-surveillance is achieved by a prenatal digital implant that records everything in the subject's field of vision from the birth canal to death, edited for "rememory" screenings at one's funeral.[7] This is the elective internalization (and reversal) of a trope of aggressive surveillance explored years before by Alain Tanner in his film *Death Watch* (1982), where a predatory journalist sacrifices one eye for a hidden camera implant in order to record the last days of a dying woman for live-TV broadcast (a sci-fi fantasy in advance of "reality TV").[8] With a more pointed motive in *Freeze Frame,* Veil cannot bear life without an alibi if he is ever accused again of one of London's many unsolved murders. Caught in a triple conspiracy and a further entrapment scheme, with his exculpating tapes stolen (the *Blow-Up* paradigm again) and his ensconced network of embedded cameras smashed or unplugged, his final exoneration comes only from a laptop webcam he manages to activate in the course of a final shoot-out, its images replayed for the arriving police detective as evidence—and, following a temporal ellipsis, as our retroactive full-screen climax. In a coda, the last of Veil's running internal monologues of "things to remember" is again over-voiced on the film track as we watch through the viewfinder of a prosthetic "selfcam" that he wears awkwardly strapped to his body whenever he leaves his wired lair: "Off camera is off guard." In the continuous loop of self-record, the titular freezing of frame is one's only nemesis, with its dated overtones of photomechanical process before the affordances of uninterrupted electronic tracing.

Keeping this in mind and himself in view, Veil—refusing the privacy he might have claimed by birthright, but which is mocked now by his name—enters the recent "action-image" roster in Deleuze's sense (crossed with the time-image of retraced and datelined spectation) as yet another version of the loner hero turning the electronic implements of incrimination to his own defensive benefit. The price of success in this desperation is as extreme as the film makes it look. And even when the fantasy of pushback, if not exactly quick fix, is far less exorbitant, the feedback loops meant to disengage from the chokehold of the technopticon's closed circuitry—whether mordant here or black comic in *Tomas Katz* or pure digital slapstick at the end of *Enemy of the State*—can scarcely avoid underscoring the electronic entanglements of contemporary life.

4 IN PLANE SIGHT

Some events transpire in plain view; some are submitted, by acknowledgment or not, to the planar record of an optic imprint, whether material or electronic, filmic or digital. On this matter of live sighting versus storage, certain screen narratives hover, more than others even in the same genre, between plots of the former (espial) and admissions—not always openly narrated—of the latter (indexical record). For many of these films, surveillance is one name, explicit or not, for just that indeterminate and often shifting zone marked out between these poles: the narratively separable but complementary modes of private eyeing and preserved visual trace. Separable, at least, when not too fully recognized *as* film to begin with, where the distinction may begin to evanesce—whether into the forgettable given of visibility or a deliberate irony of looking, recorded or not.

The scopic function is, of course, somatic as well as medial, biological and affective as well as machinic. Accordingly, this chapter and the next shift from a technoptic to a psychosocial emphasis in the screen treatment of covert or coercive viewing. So far, discussion has traversed one line of technological sleuthing from telescreen to satellite imaging. From opposite genre directions, discussion bore down on both a quasi-documentary pastiche (*Look*) and a satiric sci-fi apocalypse (*The Nine Lives of Tomas Katz*) that serve in contrary ways to refigure the electronics of today's replete visual archive as a totalized narrative matrix. We turned then to a film phobically entitled *Freeze Frame*: named for the worst fear of a character who has so wholly internalized the disciplinary routine of time-coded panoptic monitoring that he exists in terror of its seizing up—and thus leaving his life led, however briefly, in desperate separation from its evidentiary video trace.

The paired films under consideration next, along with those gathered in the subsequent chapter, follow a similar postwar trajectory through and beyond the last century's millennial (and digital) tipping point. *Rear Window* and *Peeping Tom* bring sexual psychology into close tow across the wake of a surveillance mentality. And they do so, in the process, through moments of filmic disclosure or distortion over which narratography continues to stand watch. Later films in this lineage work ultimately to subordinate the technology of remote vision, even when centering on it, to the psychology of unseen looking. Yet any such chapter division between techne and psyche reflects—as may already be obvious—nothing more than two sides of the same coin: a coin that narrative film tries to cash in on thematically from its knowing exposé of more perverse specularities than its own.

All by itself the title of Alfred Hitchcock's *Rear Window* (1954) suggests, of course, the rectangular optic field necessary for any screen plot, thriller or otherwise. The phrase also invites an approach to such optics through the rear-view framework of a later decade's film theory. We have looked back on *M* from the vantage of apparatus theory to focus a more coherent retrospective account of Fritz Lang's optical manipulations, and the effort continues with Hitchcock. In the current atmosphere of screen studies, the attempt to rescan a former horizon of late-1960s analytic work under the aspect of applied theory—and through it certain historical landmarks in cinema's narration of the surveillant frame—can, even under the leveling steamroller of a post-theory indifference, still seem uniquely instructive.

A comparison of two position papers from the same French theorist, at the top of his bent and the peak of a theoretical moment, can show at least one decisive common denominator between apparatus theory and the poststructuralist narratology also newly formulated at the time. From which comparison, in turn, there develops a further triangulation: a third term that in a sense unites the other two at the level of the medium's material base—and that is continually pertinent in audiovisual narratives concerned with remediated technological surveillance and the psychic dislocation it may induce. At any level of "projection," optical or cortical, this third term is the unnamed and separately unseen photogram—the sprocketed fixity—that underlies, wholly suppressed or not, photography's rapid-file transformation into film. And to which the two major films compared in this chapter, *Peeping Tom* (Michael Powell, 1960) along with *Rear Window*, gravitate at pivotal moments, middle and late: moments that seem explicitly staged to extrude the relation of frame line to its underlying photoframes.

The years and theoretical papers in question mark the turn of a decade. For Jean-Pierre Oudart, "The System of the Suture" (1969) might well have been glossed by the same vocabulary that, a year later—when crossbred with the terminology of Roland Barthes and stamped by a formulation of Louis Althusser's—was associated with the collective commentary Oudart himself initiated at *Cahiers du Cinéma* (1970) on John Ford's film

Young Mr. Lincoln (1939).[1] This is an approach to narrative film as a textual system, as distinct from an "interpretation" of a particular cinematic artifact, that seeks—rather than the "reading" of a classic work—instead to track the exclusions by which the film, any film, does its work. Such an approach doesn't set about second-guessing a narrative by dredging for repressed content. Rather, it follows the logic of a "structuring absence" (like that, as it happens, of the camera elided from shot to shot in the suture system). It does so in order to take a given film at the face value of its own intentional reticences and deflections, whether technological or ideological. It decodes the film as "inscription"—both photomechanical and dramaturgic—for "what it has to say in what it leaves unsaid" (447), with Oudart explicitly alluding (in the narratological essay on Ford rather than the broader apparatus essay) to Althusser's image of "the internal shadows of an exclusion" (447).

But Althusser's evocative phrase bleeds back into the conceptual paradigm of Oudart's suture theory as well. At the level of shot/countershot, the shadow of a gap (making room for a camera whose presence is no sooner obvious than it is disavowed) is precisely what must be masked. That rupture gets stitched over (and usually bound back into narrative), though never quite erased. Mutatis mutandis, at the broader level of narrative causation, contradictions must be subsumed rather than resolved in the advance of action (Lincoln, in Ford's treatment, as embodiment of a law that violently suppresses all violence, for instance). Together, these two shadowings by the antithetical (freestanding image by the apparatus of its making, thematic emphasis by its cancelling opposite) amount—at different, incremental scales—to comparable ghostings by the unseen, the unspoken.

Together, too, they point to that third term beneath each exclusionary "suture"—each repaired surgical excision—of shot and plot respectively. For at the minimal end of any such scalar filmic spectrum, before the strip as frame line ever generates the edited difference of replaced camera positions rather than just displaced frame cells, there is the shadow of another shadow. This is that primary exclusion so openly manifested to early audiences—yet soon and increasingly "masked" (and here in the technical sense, by the calibrated rotation of the Maltese cross) by gradual sophistications of the apparatus. Over time, what results is a muting of that "flicker effect" derived from the dark spectral bar between frames—a shadow whose pulsive recurrence marks the exclusion of one by the next in order to generate the composite present image in the continuous wake, the afterimage, of preceding serialized disappearances. From strip to cut to narratological continuity, from the material ground up through syntactic articulations to the fuller stage of diegesis and plot—at every level gaps of this sort are available to narrative incorporation and reinflection, for exposure and recuperation. Aside from such narrative reinvestment, however, what in these elisions "goes without saying" (in the otherwise said) is partly the message of the medium itself as a tacitly acknowledged fact.

What further goes without saying from a contemporary vantage is the way this "third"—in fact, originary—term is no longer operable in a postfilmic cinema whose shot increments and ocular shifts undergo no displacement in the frame line but only a recompositing from within their bitmap digital grid. This we'll come to. But for now we are attuned to the second-order audiovisual structure in films that are not just photomechanically activated but that tap into the very relation of spectacle to photo or phonic imprint—often, like *M*, the relation of mobile surveillance to forensic picturing. And in particular, in this chapter, to films whose manifest (whose immanent) capture of the human image and voice for narrative deployment seems inseparable at times, as much psychologically as technically, from the othering of lives by techniques of surveillance within the plot.

As we've seen, the fact of photomechanics, and of its consequences, is given a unique stress—in tension with the pressure toward sonic and phonic continuities—in Lang's first sound film. What invites examination next is the way the whole spectrum of structuring exclusions, from strip on up to narrative and thematic discrepancies, is traversed by the plot of a later classic film—and another variant of surveillance cinema—in *Rear Window*. This is a film that falls just on the far side from *M* in the postwar divide marked by Gilles Deleuze's tendentious cinema history. Indeed, *Rear Window* is a film that Deleuze instances as one of the earliest landmarks of the time-image, a typifying case in point for him (though narratively overdetermined by its injured hero). On this understanding, the former protagonist of the movement-image in the form of action cinema is now reduced from agent to mere "spectator" of his own life (anticipating the stalled action and anomie of later films in the European modernist tradition by Michelangelo Antonioni or Ingmar Bergman).[2]

Jacques Rancière takes sensible objection to this characterization (indeed this extrapolation from character to medium) of a film in which the image itself is not immobilized, but only a narrative agent: amid entirely conventional filming, a single injured and wheelchair-bound protagonist. Rancière thus queries the link in Deleuze between the enforced stasis of *Rear Window*'s photographer hero, former "chaser after images" (115), his leg now in a cast, and the paralysis by vertigo of the explicit detective (also played by James Stewart) in Hitchcock's next film, *Vertigo* (1958). Though the hero is again in an emasculating cast, a body "corset" this time, Rancière still finds it "strange" to suggest that the image itself, rather than just the character in each case, has lost its "motor extension," or that "psychomotor problems" operate so as to "hinder the linear arrangement of the images and the action from moving forward."[3] Certainly the Hitchcock examples (what we might call overthematized by Deleuze) don't work as well for his philosophical taxonomy as the later *L'Avventura* (1960), where in Antonioni's film, for instance, the real adventure left to screen narrative is that of camerawork and editing in circumscribing the constrained field of human impulse. Yet it is precisely on Rancière's own founding antipodal grounds of *opsis* versus *muthos*, visibility versus narrative force, that Deleuze's position is most suggestive. One can indeed come to see the stationary plight of Hitchcock's voyeuristic heroes, especially *Rear Window*'s L. B. Jeffries, erstwhile photojournalist and worldwide image sleuth, as probing to something other than sheer plot premise. The hero all but incarnates the very notion—contingent, literally accidental—of a fixed-point gaze and its scopic drives.

In *Rear Window*, certainly, dialogue—with its jokes about seedy peeping—abets the system of images in keeping an optics of the apparatus in mind. If character-as-spectator is the very premise of the surveillance film—fashioning a narrative mode (or quasi-genre) out of a certain modernist visual reflexivity in variant form—then the delay in a viewer's identifying *Rear Window* with this modal category, a delay facilitated by the film's slow comic start, may in itself have developed other lines of inference in the interval. For it comes to seem that the character denied *muthos* or action, reduced to sheer *opsis*, is the narrative conduit by which a spectatorial ethics (rather than just a plot format) gets only gradually—and thus all the more instructively—transformed from voyeurism to eventual surveillance, from unexcused watching to purposeful lookout.

This happens across a path cleared by the marginalizations and unexpected partial returns of optical (photographic) technology itself. What we find at key turns is thus the recursive advent of the photo apparatus from within the narrative of its suspended use: an *opsis* by prosthesis that falls far short of a metafilmic parable until it obliquely adds up to one after all. This takes awhile to see, its accretions being those of plot itself. And it is certainly revealing to notice, in respect to a fungible underlying template, the chiastic inversion of this plot in relation to Hitchcock's subsequent masterwork *Vertigo* four years later. *Vertigo*: where what begins as paid surveillance, with never a picture taken, no recording technology of any sort in requisition, is scripted in advance—by the villain's complot—to fester for the hero into voyeuristic obsession. The overarching generic patterns of psychological melodrama and detection pivot around the same scopic drive in these inverse classics, differently pursued or recuperated in each.

Windowed Pictures: Tele-Visioning and the Fourth Wall

Rear Window: one of the essential film titles. Even the timing of its initial commercial distribution confirms the logic of internal framing by which its encompassing irony is developed. In its day, it was a summer thriller. I saw it first—or, say better, I stared intensely at it—in downtown Fort Lauderdale, then my home town, in the first month of its national release in a sweltering August (they all were), escaping with the rest of a theater-going populace into an "air-cooled" space from a routine heat and humidity at least as bad as that with which the film so topically (and tropically) opens in a New York City summer. Most anywhere in its August screenings, in fact, the spectator would have known rather intimately what it means to distract oneself from body heat by ocular fascination. But then or now—whether seated before the *Window*'s widescreen purview, or sharing the video with students by way of a miserable overhead projector, or watching it on home monitors—in every case a strange sense of optic recession always sets in, quite beyond the first rectangular threshold of its "interior courtyard" view on which Jeff's own curtain goes up with the titles.

I don't imagine I'm alone in this. How long does a viewer have to stare through the frame-coincident big-screen rear window, as if at (and into) a projected world not so much of occupied cubicles as of framed rectangles crowded with visible human motion—how long does one have to stare through the eyes of a chair-bound media-savvy commercial imagemaker, our incapacitated photographer-hero, often with a secondary lens in front of his eye, before beginning to suspect those frustratingly distanced subsidiary spaces as stand-ins for inset mediations in their own right? This isn't a directly metafilmic effect, as if we (and Jeff in our stead) were watching an overstrained parallel montage distributed instead across a collage of separate movie-like portals (like a stacking of outdoor though not exactly drive-in movies). Rather, with or without the hero's *tele*-vision lens in hand (his huge telephoto supplement to a broken camera), these facing rectangulated scenarios, each with its own "broadcast" if muted sound, come to resemble just the sort of smaller screens not only that one leaves behind for a night at the magnified movies but (the more interesting inference) that so many of these 1954 apartment-dwellers would themselves have had, and had visibly turned on—Jeff not least, in his long weeks of recuperation.

To the gathering dismay of Hollywood in the face of its New York electronic competitors, already in 1954 there were weekly broadcasts of *The Jack Benny Show, Burns and Allen, I Love Lucy,* the debut of *Disneyland* a year before the amusement park (the first Hollywood studio crossover, in fact, to the small screen), not to mention (in light of our current theme) the aptly titled sitcom *Mr. Peepers*. These are the shows (including, a year later, *Alfred Hitchcock Presents*) that would have varied the lives of an apartment block like the one we see in the movie: that would have amused a lonely woman, kept bickering couples from each other's throats, provided distraction even for newlyweds, and certainly kept an invalid photographer's eyes, at least intermittently, away from his windows. The cinema repeatedly "dreams its rivals," as Paul Young puts it (with no emphasis on *Rear Window*), but often dreams them in repression, in displacement.[4] Cinema—including its constituent relation to photography—is here the visual mode of choice, Hollywood-studio cinema in particular, with the statistical likelihood of televisual captivation sacrificed to it. Indeed, thirty years before *Indiana Jones and the Temple of Doom* (1984) begins by match cut between the Paramountain and the scene of action (launching a now decades-long trend in the "narrativization" of the logo), the wide-angle view afforded by Hitchcock's film is itself tacitly celebrated when the Paramount imprimatur appears inch by inch, revealed by descending stages in the self-lowered window curtain of the film's last shot: the paratext as metatext for a framed experience quintessentially cinematic to begin with.[5]

Pursuing his sense of a televisual unconscious in postwar film, Young notes that the mid-1940s marketing of TV advances its appeal as "a household technology that functioned like a picture window, allowing the private viewer to enjoy the public world from a distance" (167)—but that also, in a kind of cultural inversion, "put the very notion of the private sphere as privileged safe haven on display" (167). In the abstract, such privacies enjoy a reciprocal remove from each other, viewer's from the viewed. And beyond that, even in the early days of video broadcast, TV material—apart from the materialities of its transmission as private-home reception—gravitated in comic and dramatic formats to domestic settings that tended to fetishize the home life that the new audiovisual appliance was proffered to enhance. Given his setting a decade further along in the mass-marketing of the home screen, but, like his neighbors, markedly without TV, Jeffries resorts (reverts) instead to the actual "picture window" of marketing tropology, peering from his housebound domesticity into other scenes like it. But, unmediated, he finds he cannot *keep the distance* the spectatorial gaze would seem at first to provide. In a movie named for this default of privacy in one-way windowed access, the general shift from theatrical cinema to domestic TV—a transformation of subjectivity, as Young chiastically sums it up, from "private-in-public to public-in-private" (167)—has carried the voyeurism of such privacy one magnifying lens too far.

Nonetheless, the evocation of TV—as "structuring absence" within (as well as the figure for) each rectangle opposite Jeff's optically enhanced perch—by no means overrules the cinematic reflexivity it miniaturizes. For another repression looms as well, of an "excluded shadow" (varying Althusser) substantial enough to shade an entire square-block neighborhood when the sun is at the proper angle. And the narrative necessity of this exclusion is continuous, moreover, with a technological premise of the medium that operates in ways tied directly to the surveillance theme of Hitchcock's film and to its mechanical implementation, both as and within the screen plot. Michel Chion's brief essay on *Rear Window* makes much of this—for him, the film's central, or say focal, repression.[6] By this he means the denial of the entire apartment wall (and its analogous windows) from which Jeff looks *out*: the whole bank of other apartments, that is, those on his side of the building, into which his room-with-a-view is slotted. Presumably, inevitably, there are open windows above and below him that might have revealed similar incriminating angles, or clarifications, on the murderer's apartment in particular, perhaps better epistemological vantages. To mark the view we share as privileged, however, there can be no competition with other such angles of vision.

Narrative mandate thus finds its optical match. The boxed-off neighborhood is reduced to a "cone" of vision with only one private "apex" (112) in the eye of the hero. The other points of prospect are kept off-frame, effaced, surrendered to functional nonexistence. Chion speaks of them in the title of his essay—with a clear reference to a standard idiom for the space of the camera in an ordinary interior shot—as the "fourth side" (rather than "fourth wall"). The implication is synecdochal. In this case the term doesn't primarily call up the frequently invisible interior wall opposite Jeff's window, invisible whenever we see out over his shoulder or through his optical aids (and filled with his photographs, as it happens, whenever we look back into the apartment from the outside of that same window). The term summons up unseen, instead, the whole vertical and horizontal extension that houses him in the diegesis.

That's as far as Chion goes with his sense of this larger "repression" before turning to the similarly focalized sound mix of the film, adding only, in a short paragraph of transitional afterthought: "We would, moreover, ask if an exclusion so radical, and so essential to the function of the film, is not without a relation to what Jean-Pierre Oudart . . . said of the conjuring away of the space of the Absent one" (114). The asking is rhetorical. But it deserves pursuit. For the "relation" between general narrative camerawork subsumed first to point-of-view and then getting narrowed in the process to a single line of sight, a relation that this film is "not without," can be further specified as exactly the relation between suture and narrative that films about surveillance tend to educe and elucidate. What is "essential to the function of the film" is certainly the optical even before ocular exclusion adduced by Chion, medial even before narratival. What the same critic stops just short of saying is *why*: in this case, because disinfecting (by deleting) the ancillary voyeurism that Jeff's unseen neighbors might be positioned to indulge in serves to relegate and subsume every other potential site of spying to Jeff's central rectangular window and its self-conditioning inference. Why, then, more precisely, is there only this one window on the fourth wall? Because all by itself—however many inset screens-within-the-screen are offered up to view across from it, or presumed flanking it—only one window can open upon such an undisguisedly fictional scene: the cinematic aperture per se, nudged into parable by precisely the erasure of its lateral or otherwise adjacent competition. In this film, there is only the single rear window of cinema itself—where each spectator-voyeur is alone in the tether of identification, "private-in-public" by optical constitution.

But more than that. Or less: another structuring lacuna. No visual recording on Jeff's part—I mean no *visible* moment of photography—takes place in this film about a once avid, now frustrated photographer. It is as if this absence is designed to narrow the distance, for plot's duration at least, between his experience and ours, each equally visual, neither actively recorded: say passive, submissive—until we later learn that he had in fact, at least a couple of weeks earlier, been taking voyeuristic photos after all, which he cops to, under his breath at one point, as "leg art." Still, and at the very least until then, the absence of the on-camera photographic act operates alongside Chion's stress on how the film must repress other optical conditions more favorable perhaps than its own, other angles on the crime scene. And there is, as noted above, a social—as well as a narratological and technical—repression at play in this as well. In the movie house we watch the housebound hero, and watch with him, wanting always—in our terraced seating or perhaps from our own sill-like balcony view—to forget the neighbors to the left and right of us, "below" and "above" in the rows. Such is the primal repression that leads to immersion in what we are intent on seeing. This is the repression to which suture contributes, with its effacement of filming, and which this one plot highlights in part by its peripheral hints of a photographic mediation explicitly, rather than just tacitly, suspended: held off, that is, in the thick of a spectacle that is figured as an unmediated private theater of ocular fascination and surveillance.

For most of *Rear Window*, the human gaze is denied mimetic simulations, except for the glamour photographs doted on unseen by Jeff's fashionable girlfriend Lisa (Grace Kelly) in the film's last shot. Here we see her reading on the sly an issue of *Harper's Bazaar* while Jeff sleeps (Orientalized exoticism domesticated by a single titular allusion, as far from Jeff's globe-trotting wanderlust as ever)—this, instead of the Tibet travel book she's taken up as proof of her suitedness for the adventuresome Girl Friday he would require in a wife. After the plot has moved us from heterosexual voyeurism through spousal murder to objective surveillance and detection, voyeurism itself seems "cured" in the end by being subsumed to the same-sex identificatory projections of the fashion industry upon which a postwar image culture comes increasingly to feed. But within the diegesis, with the heroine's pages averted from us, our viewing is spared this reduction. We have Grace Kelly, in casual (rather than high) chic this time, to look at instead. With her rapt immersion in the legible "Beauty Issue," we find rehearsed under compression the entire Hitchcock aesthetic: the interplay between adventure and beauty in the tangible thrill of each.

Moreover, the very occlusion of photography in this cinematic scene of reading may throw us back on the marginalized photo images earlier thrown into relief by plot. The only reproduced images rendered visible to us, the only photos we linger on—with the one exception whose force we must approach, as the film does, slowly—are hovered over for us by the camera rather than the characters. This happens in the second phase of the opening bravura traveling shot that has slowly panned through the courtyard and then, after spotting the latent protagonist in a sweat-drenched sleep next to his window, drifts past him over relics of the former life he may be dreaming of: to begin with, thrilling B&W location photos hung above a pile of damaged camera parts. Incapacitated twice over, as we soon discover, the photojournalist is immobilized before a neighborhood panorama that has no marketable interest. He is an injured professional out of luck and work at once, who hears on the phone from his editor later that, because of his injury, he's being denied a trip to the next "hot spot" he had predicted. Kashmir is about "to go up in smoke" like the billowing aftermath of a military explosion we saw on the wall in that early slow pan of both the effects (framed) and the debris (smashed camera) of his craft, the remains of a better day. The narrative camera has glided—in this implicit backstory—across dramatic shots of adventurous locales, incendiary accidents, combat zones, explosions, including the most recent race car catastrophe, or one like it, to which Jeff got too close. Further to the left, Hitchcock's panning camera has next brought into its moving frame not a victimized body from some such violent scene but, no less gruesome at first glance, the backlit toothy negative, skeletal in its inversion, of a stylish blonde's close-up: an image visible (a normalizing moment later) in positive multiples on the stack of glossy magazines coming quickly into view next to it—our chance to look at the kind of image that the heroine will only at the very end be given the privacy to enjoy. This evidence of the print multiple is topped with a 35mm photostrip, sign of the progress from capture to lab—but also a reminder of the process still going forward (from frame to frame) in the projection of our movie.

Narrative Foreplay

Within this ongoing visual narrative, the photographer himself is going nowhere. The documentarian is reduced to an immobile optic stalker, his telephoto lens being eventually taken up only to replace—with the iris mask of its POV—the earlier paired peepholes of his more modest binocular sightings. "We've become a race of Peeping Toms," quips his smart-aleck nurse Stella when first walking in on him, his spyglasses at the ready. Only two things might redeem this inert scopophilia: either image-making or honest detective work. In other words: either medium or genre. Yet stressed in his case again and again—as precisely what ails him—is the detachment of optics from professional recording, of looking from journalistic picturing: in particular, of vagrant pleasure from photographic work.

Laura Mulvey's interest in this film as an exhibit for her claims of visual pleasure via the phallic camera would find additional fuel in a particularly loaded line of dialogue from the irrepressible Stella.[7] She has reminded Jeffries of an earlier era in which "they used to put your eyes out with a hot poker" for a crime that's now, at worst, only a misdemeanor. Not until the film actually called *Peeping Tom*, six years later, will the phallic gaze be more explicitly realized in the double entendres of screen dialogue than when Stella asks rhetorically if "any of those bikini bombshells you've been watching are worth a hot poker"—where the word "worth" jabs both ways at once, erotic and punitive: worthy of (in vicarious desire); worth the price of (in reprisal). When we later find out that he has in fact been photographing their leggy antics from the immobile vantage resulting from his plaster-cast lower limb, the medieval interdict has achieved its full technological update. But all this is still only pending.

Until the unusually delayed moment of Hitchcock's cameo in the role of a suited figure (an upscale clocksmith?) winding the timepiece on a mantel—a kind of displaced metronome belonging to the struggling composer in one of the apartments opposite—the film has been relatively plotless. The Master's reputed suspense has been held almost entirely in a suspension of its own signature effects, with the narrative seemingly as stalled as both the hero and the blocked composer. It is as if Hitchcock must arrive in propria persona to adjust the very pace of event, to wind up the plot itself with his fabled touch. From here out, to borrow from other Hitchcock titles, it is suspicion alone that holds the viewer-hero spellbound until he is ready to dial, if not *M* for murder, at least his friend the detective with a report of suspected homicide. And it is important to remember that what has deferred action, delayed any real suspense even, until this point in the film is all the sexual banter about inaction, about passive viewing. Yet even while postponing the lurid events to come, such dialogue has been their immediate preparation.

And it continues to be. Helping to ferry the larger contradictions of the film in maneuvering from dubious peeping to the kind of keen-eyed witness the hero's ordinary photographic work has amounted to, the idiomatic ramblings of the voluble nurse continue to include telling figures of speech. The "hot poker" admonition is soon replaced by her contempt for Jeff's "intelligent approach" to the question of marriage. For her, mating should be determined—in an unspoken ocular matrix of the entire film—by the street-smart equivalent of "love at first sight." In her version of courtship, love is an instinctual violence triggered by unmediated eye contact. "Two people see each other, they like each other," they should come together like "two taxis" colliding on Broadway. And when she is made aware of the pitiful neurotic solitude of Miss Lonely Hearts on the first floor opposite, she asks—in an ocular metaphor, as if forgetting her contempt for her patient's spying in the first place—whether there isn't "someone who could cast an eye on her?"

Jeff has in fact done so, but only in the literal sense—and in a revealing cinematographic tug on this early thread of verbal irony. Narrative camerawork again substitutes for the hero's own, his reduction to the unmediated gaze. Framed by one of the three windows in Miss Lonely Heart's apartment, as seen from one of the matching three panes of his own oversized window, she toasts to her imaginary date, screen left. In response, with wine Lisa has just poured, but while she is off camera in the kitchen, Jeff the bachelor-loner raises his glass in solidarity. He toasts Miss Lonely Hearts, that is, rather than Lisa, along an axis, a sightline, perpendicular to that of the solitary woman's fantasy exchange—his wistful recognition sutured in by way of an impossible countershot. The very mismatch in sightlines, or say the split seam of the suture, makes for the irony, the poignancy, of this intercut sequence. For a moment the hero's voyeurism has, along with ours, passed over into sympathetic identification, only to snap back again when the imaginary ocular relay is broken.

Throughout, distance is always kept—or reasserted—in this way. Early on, with Jeff's fever registering on the thermometer only a few degrees above the urban temperature outside, his nurse diagnoses a "hormone deficiency." How can she tell? "All the bathing beauties you've been staring at this past month haven't raised your temperature one degree." The true "hotspots" (political, distant, escapable) that excite him, instead, are those he can flatten to two photochemical dimensions. In a sense he gets his druthers when the languid sexuality of his purview turns to violence: which is to say, when cheesecake vistas of the dancer he refers to with the dismembering sexism of "Miss Torso" are transferred to the telltale traces of an actual decapitated wife in another visible apartment. Yet this is a violence that eventually turns back on him—along the same 180-degree axis he has previously exploited.

From Oculust to Documentation: A Return of the Photoscopic Repressed

Only as plot thickens (along with the magnifying lenses he uses to follow it) does Jeff's surveillance finally revert to a lone remnant of his normal professional practice. For the most part he is *homo mimeticus* without a medium. There is, yes, the telescopic sight that brings light in, and, in the end, the flashbulb attachment that spreads light out. But in between these prosthetic supplements to the camera, his ocular stakeout, in narrative time, leaves no diegetic trace on film of any kind. The only recording precedes our looking, as with any film, of course—but in a way that gets particularized here in certain of his slides that he tactically recalls at one impasse in his detective work. Returned from the near past, this transient minor exception to the lack of any glimpsed technological intervention, even in an avocational mode, keeps the photographic subtext alive on the way to its ironic climax. One result is that the full force of this photographic episode can be felt only within the spectrum of exclusions that brackets it. Our sense of the photographic subtext may function in this way to encrypt the film's own photomechanical undertext.

Whereas Jeff has previously brought the murderer Thorwald up close through incriminating telephoto sightings, not shots, what happens at the end, in contrast, requires that Jeff fend him back off with four reloaded camera flashes that stun the killer's vision in his threatening approach across the invalid's own apartment. Even there, no forensic photos are taken, just blinding flares given in a reverse POV. Four times the bulb goes off at close range. Suture is in this case an ocular assault, a stinging rather than implicit blind spot. The inherent "shadow of exclusion" has replaced the absented camera by a blood-red scotoma, with the hero's face in the murderer's countershot POV going momentarily absent. What we see is a circular red flare answering to the earlier iris masks around the killer's own image from Jeff's optically aided POV. It is from such a distance that Thorwald was denied, until the last stage of discovered surveillance, any countershot of his own out past the window of his exposure. It is only after the reconnoitering of his apartment by Lisa that the killer stares across the courtyard to see Jeff looking back. To reverse the lines of power yet again in this axis of reciprocal sighting, even when its distance is closed to the point of homicidal threat, we move to Jeff's frantic ingenuity with the flashbulbs. Mere vestiges of his former photographic work, they mark the fact that our incapacitated voyeur—slowly turned into amateur detective after the suspected murder—is defended only by a partial return to the materials of his visual craft, which in their current repurposing call up a cinematographic effect as well. Stopping the killer dead in his tracks with the source of photographic light, it is as if, to stave off fatality, Jeff has effected four approximate and dilatory freeze-frames within his own lived film.

A circle is hereby closed, within which photographic process—rather than the function of its accessories—has been mostly hollowed out, rendered inoperable. Initiating the long, slow arc of this medial irony, the narrative's initial panning shot had paced us through various aspects of imaging—light-boxed negative, individual photo prints, mass-magazine imprint along with the equipment of its generation—all locked into the near past of the film's own photo record along with the snippet of processed strip. After that, bookending the detective plot that emerges, we have a subdivision between the two mechanical enhancements of vision in photographic work, magnifying lens (the telephoto spyglass) and lumen-booster (the flash apparatus). The ironies of this sidelined photomechanical motif are built up, nonetheless, around a brief scene of actual photographic decoding as unexpected as it is pivotal.

The buildup has been hard to miss. The first sign that voyeurism could be linked to something more urgent (and supposedly more justified) comes, though in mostly comic form, when Jeff is on the phone with his editor about his missed geopolitical assignment while watching an ad hoc helicopter "surveillance" of two topless girls just below his own line of sight on the roof opposite. With TV-news helicopters not introduced to L.A. broadcasting till later in the decade, the inference seems to be that even the military-industrial complex has succumbed to the Peeping Tom fever. Something must give. It is only after a couple's dog across the courtyard is found dead, and the wife wails accusation at the whole neighborhood for not caring, that the hero's specular distraction grows fully justified in his concern for Thorwald's presumed previous victim, the missing (and, it turns out, butchered) wife. Ocular proof positive—the closest we get to it, and in the photographic sense of positive—even if a transparent slide is retrieved at last from the archive of mediation amid the flurry of mere spectation.

The scene in question is studious, verging on laborious, in delivering its point. Jeff is finally able to convince Stella and Lisa that something is decidedly wrong when he gets them to hold up to the light a slide that, before the film even begins, he has taken of the courtyard flower bed. Spurred by a hunch, he has asked Lisa to fetch for him from the shelf a "viewer" along with a box of slides taken "about two weeks ago." Rifling through them, he mumbles to himself that he hopes he "took something else besides leg art." Soon he finds what he's hoping for, as a yardstick of the present evidentiary setting. But he needs to teach his secondary witnesses how to read it. He asks Lisa and Stella to alternate the slide in question with the unaided view of the current garden from the same angle: "Now take it down; look again; now take it down." Each woman complies. What results, filling the narrative screen in the process, is that the recorded image (of time past) enters into a heuristic oscillation with the seen present—as if in the minimal differential of a filmstrip, one frame edged away by its seemingly real-time successor—so as to reveal that certain flowers appear to shrink rather than grow over time, the garden plot therefore having been obviously disturbed by digging and rebedding. The surveillance plot is directly affected as well. But so is the mechanism of framed sighting at large—and its substrate of photograms.

Lifted from narrative burial for the first time—and associated indirectly with the photographer-hero's stock in trade—is the underlying unit of cinema itself in the single optic frame. For what we see in these alternating (but presutured) POV shots, in the frame/blank/frame of both Stella's and Lisa's delegated roles as forensic spectators, is the very difference that makes for cinematic change—a difference parsed for once into circumstantial evidence within the screen world. The disabled professional photographer and avocational sleuth has found satisfaction, after all, in this remnant of his own reporting medium, as if it were a piece of otherwise inconsequential evidence retrieved from an arbitrary surveillance file. But the satisfaction comes (to the on-screen viewers in our place) only if there is a "narrating" character, or, more generally, a genre narrative, to tell the likes of us what to look for. Otherwise, the differential is as minimal as those on a film strip itself, all but subliminal, negligible in immediate sequence, in isolation barely discernible: in short, photomechanical film degree zero. And here, too, a rhetorical emphasis in the script seems probing to a medial emphasis one level down. This happens—through an undertone of mechanical recurrence built into the very rhythm of dialogue—when, with only the slightest inflectional variation on precisely the telltale differential of any film frame from what succeeds and so animates it, Jeff insists to his trial audience, about the slide's measure of temporal alteration: "There's one important change, one important change"—as if he were unconsciously miming the very frame advance by which it is made visible.

On view here, in the bar-like blur between images indistinguishably recorded and real, is that shadow of an internal exclusion in cinema called mechanical timing itself, rather than real time. In the vertical shuttle performed on command with the slide by Lisa and Stella, the recorded shot gives way in full-screen POV to a present reality which, despite its paradoxical reversal of vegetal time, captures in circumscribed form nothing less than the notion of "becoming" in the phenomenology of cinematic duration from André Bazin to Deleuze, where the fixity of the strip disappears into its eventuation as moving image. In the smallest compass of these tandem "transparencies" (one on the narrative film strip as "live shot," one refiguring it in remediated portable isolation)—or, in other words, in this glide from a backlit (sunlit) single slide to the daylight squint of a diegetic eye—Hitchcock has mounted a thematized epitome of his own narrative apparatus. Rather than mere voyeurism, surveillance in screen narrative seems almost defined by this sequence as the moment when looking is itself not just motivated but denaturalized, all but motorized, stored for review and scrutiny—in short, instrumentalized at one remove from the medium we're watching, even if in some sense doubling it. Doubling it—while at the same time inverting its "organic" logic. If in normal cinema, by the frame line's infinitesimal progressions, motion comes into being before our eyes, it is only the same means that would allow for its mechanical reversal—a reversal (*un*growing flowers) matched for once by a clue in the real.

This curious epistemological episode, in its photomechanical basis, clearly exceeds the necessities of plot. Yet the wavering between then and now, full-frame photo transparency and full-frame screenshot, is a definitive balancing act at the plot's true filmic turning point. Apart from establishing shots of the women's gazes as they peer at and past the slide, what we see more prominently, and dramatically, in the POV framing of the garden is more like a filmmaker himself running a sequence back and forth through an editing machine looking for continuity errors, whether of lighting, framing, or mise-en-scène. With this moment explicitly motivated as optic decipherment, put it that close reading may become, as D. A. Miller demonstrates elsewhere and otherwise with Hitchcock, indeed "too close"—so close that, in this case, plot dissolves into its own undertext, the photochemistry of its own serial imprints.[8] That's Hitchcock for you. Such is the mastery of a suspension, rather than merely a suspense, that remains hovering between process and product, filming and telling, medium and narrative turn.

Plot's Double Game

We began with an effort to align the logic of elision in a psychoanalytic suture theory with the repressed contradictions taken up by narrative theory. We can go further now, in the case of *Rear Window*. We may say that screen narrative *is* suture—at least the kind of classic narrative that Hitchcock not only brought to such a high polish but pushed, in that episode just examined, to a kind of granular inner limit. Short of that allegorized nub of sheer frame advance, narrative is constituted by suture because the point of view must often be dissimulated as other than the camera's—taken up instead by a character in whose motion, in whose travels and travails, we become not just invested and immersed but at times inserted. And never more schematically than in the scene just reviewed. In the exhumation of a single photograph in proof of an exhumed garden plot (and complot), the foundational transfer between recorded world and its populated gazing in distilled to an on-camera, rather than typically in-camera, splitting of the difference. Narrowed to the same ocular scale and shuffled as if to the point of a rudimentary animation effect, the two-frame view undergoes a radical back-and-forth not just between frames but between narrative space and medium. There, screen-wide before us, a photochemical image made visible; there, now, the world being seen by participant witnesses. Narrative cinema in embryo. Suture has been put on exhibit from within an otherwise inconsequential shot and its reverse shot (staring women, external view and its previous trace). Such a displacement of camerawork by enacted gaze is exactly the fiction of immediacy that this one interactive moment of mediated spectation in *Rear Window*—slide trace versus immanent vision—drags back by association to the action of the track rather than the mere tracking of a villainous action.

And with the pulsive intermittence of that embedded binary slide show, we find fulfilled, even in its momentary hiatus (with a retrieved image from before the time of plot), the narrative's whole double game. This is the game that Hitchcock's screen narrative, founded in the image track of an optical medium, has played with its photographer hero in his training of our gaze: a hero with whom we identify precisely because of his impeded identity as the recording "I." For here is a film that goes explicitly out of its way—first with the bashed camera and its former wall-hung effects, then with magnifying lens and flashbulb weaponry in the absence of any "loaded" film—to hold optical mimesis in suspension by the concerted search for ocular proof. Although *Rear Window* keeps filming its narrative events, at the same time it keeps narrated filming—that is, on-screen recording of any kind—at bay, in abeyance. It does so even while—dead center in the plot, at the minimalist turning point we've been considering—it catches a glimpse, catches us up in a glimpse, of the differentials on which such filming always depends: inscribed change distributed over a calibrated temporal succession in the vertical toggle of now, then down, now again, then down. As the past frame is brought forward to make sense of the reframed present, what we're further reminded of at this turn may well be that all photomechanical screen presence, what we used to know as filmic cinema, operates always—as mediation—in medias res: dependent twenty-four times per second on an act of protensive retention, of vanishing displaced by arrival.

It is in the nature of classic narrative that the incidental detail is swallowed up in the overdetermined one. It happens at every turn of *Rear Window*. Lisa might well have brought Jeff a TV set, if for no other reason than to keep his eyes inside until she arrived each evening. More to the point, Jeff might have looked in his closet or cupboard for some other, undamaged camera—perhaps the same one with which, before the film started, he seems to have photographed the garden in an idle moment between bouts of a more voyeuristic "art." But true to screen form, such elective exclusions from the narrational, and hence optical, field are made to disappear into the manifest and axiomatic one: the excluded mobility of his injured body. One forestalled capacity (action) covers for another forsworn one (the act of secondary imaging). One constraint on motor skill is a sign for the other—until we finally discover otherwise. The implications of the latter (image-making kept in check along with mediated viewing) are subsumed, as if their abrogation were normal and routine, to the former setback (body in arrest). These comparable disempowerments are associated only by a loose and dubious metonymy. Only one scene calls the bluff of this evicted mediation amid the optical adjuncts of its camerawork strewn about. This is the scene, complete with an audience of two (Stella and Lisa), that installs photo mediation as surveillance's own cure for voyeurism. Otherwise, apart from that reversible slide "advance," any optical movement, any image capture, is narrative's own—always dependent on the motor flow we do not in itself see. In momentarily overcoming such an unmediated voyeurism at the level of plot, that pivotal fleeting upsurge of technological forensics—there with that lone slide lifted repeatedly to the eye—has found, as so often with this surveillance motif in filmic cinema, the baseline, the medial point of departure, for its machinated optics.

I don't mean to be magnifying the otherwise inconsequential into a looming centrality. What's so important about this episode is how minor it actually remains, how strained and dilated it feels in the moment—and how easily forgotten as a plot turn. The cinema not only "dreams its rivals"—as if made visible in the viewer's own waking dream—but at times, for the viewer once more, dreams its own unconscious as such. In *M*, the interart checkpoints of fixed framings as well as actual still shots, in their Neue Sachlichkeit overtones, serve to recover from sound synchronization the very increments of such alignment in the single cellular unit of photomorphology (within the grammar of montage). In a related way, this is what the intermedia allusions to the photo cell within the moving-image system of film do in the long run, and with comparable indirection, in *Rear Window*. The true title shot of the film in this respect is not just the opening pan from the window (arriving at what I have called elsewhere, in such a recursive scooping up of single serial photographs, a "photopan"): a shot that reveals our framed view as a character's own private outlook (once his feverishness begins to clear). This eponymous scenic paradigm is completed only at the film's end, with the lowering of the triptych window's bamboo shade—divided logically into three panels when lifted in sequence at the film's start, but substituted now with an uninterrupted "wide-screen" occlusion stretched to render irrelevant, perhaps, any comparisons with three-panel Cinerama (which debuted two years before). Closing in as visual frame on an isolated rectangle within the diegesis is here figurative for the diegesis all told—at its point of industrial production. For out of this single width of descending panel (not just over it)—in a trick superimposition as internal unfurling—rolls down the Paramount logo, imprimatur of the "production values" that have made possible our own Technicolor viewing. What unfolds there (as if to remind us of the scroll that constitutes all film) is a semitransparent scrim that would in fact occlude or curtain the narrative view—yet which, as its touted source and productive engine, is otherwise responsible, millimeter by descending millimeter across its surface, second by projected second, for what we serially see and accept as narratively seen.

And in between these opening and closing phases of the title shot, a photomechanical primal scene: a backlit image in search, as it were, of genre transparency. Not, perhaps, since Lang's serial collage of lap-dissolved fixed frames—in realization of a teletyped spool of eyewitness documentation—has the undertext of cinema been more fully unearthed in connection with surveillant optics and the wider media landscape of its own historical moment. From the hero's own ocular vantage in *Rear Window*, undistracted by the new broadcast medium, the comparable subtraction of televisual access from each framed sector of action across the way turns every offered room to a view of its own, at least as much like a movie, whatever the topical irony, as like a TV screen. And it is this nonrivalrous dreamscape (if you will) of isomorphic reframing that is carried, by further inferential homology, all the way down to the single cellular rectangle of the photostrip (and frame line): not just a unit of narrative evidence but the fundament of pure optic difference in search of plot.

If *Rear Window* looks back just over two decades to *M* and forward, just under two decades, to a tacit commonality between apparatus theory and screen narratology, it also looks a half-century forward to an ever-lengthening roster of surveillance films. In flight from intimacy with the embodied glamour of Grace Kelly's Lisa, the incapacitated hero would, turning aside to a world of impersonal action, and even without photographing it, rather look than touch. But then escapism, turned gradually to paranoia and external commitment, evolves into justified police action. There was something there worth seeing all along. He wasn't just sexually skittish in being tempted to look away from Lisa's allure; some instincts were firing properly. No unusual false consciousness gnaws away at this logic (his looking being unauthorized and kinky; yours in the audience paid for and thus justified up front). There is only the double game of genre: the sublimation of characterological deviance by plot itself, whereby scopophilia (like any hyperattentiveness in a preoccupied hero, paranoid or not) is made to pay off—at least when, in this case, mutating from voyeurism through vigilance to motivated surveillance. The plot stalls long enough to make us feel complicit in idle fascination, perhaps, but then barrels ahead in full-bore narrative vindication.

But we also find in Hitchcock's film a further crucial rudiment of the surveillance mode so much still, and increasingly, with us. This is the recurrent fantasy that when the tables are turned, when the protagonist is himself the object of a lethal stare (whether in the sudden countersurveillance of *Rear Window*'s last plot crisis or across a longer stretch of narrative in other films), victory can nevertheless be seized from the raw technological matter of threatened defeat. This is as true today of the electronic everyman versus a high-tech military-industrial cyclops as it was in 1954 with Hitchcock's double reversal. No matter how outmanned the protagonist (typically male) may seem (in this case wheelchaired shut-in rather than on-the-job photographer), it is often a makeshift audiovisual technology (flashbulbs here, a hacker's cell phone and its inbuilt digital cameras more recently) that serves to rejoin the uncontaminated aura of the screening all told, rather than the perverse spying it narrates, and to win technically assisted resolution for hero and plot at once.

There are exceptions to this rule—but operating still within the abstract outlines of its paradigm. A famous example follows. According to genre convention, surveillance must regularly be punished by more of the same—the same-but-different—cleansing narrative cinema of any indirect contamination in the process. As in *Rear Window*, the equipmental dimension of imaging, however co-opted or retooled, needs revalidation in defense of that less aggressive sighting known as cinema. In one grotesque case, however, cinematography itself must be forsworn within the plot, in precisely its links to surveillance, in order for the criminal perpetrator to direct his lethal gaze back at himself. Where Jeffries is an incapacitated still photographer working in the thematic service of a tolerable cinematic voyeurism and epistemophilia—or, in other words, on behalf of viewing's restored norms—Mark Lewis in Michael Powell's *Peeping Tom* alternates active employment as movie cameraman and still photographer. He does so even while turning his off-hours camerawork (together with its voyeuristic knife-murdering and simultaneous filmic record) against his own surrendered body in the long run. In her sustained psychoanalytic commentary on the 1999 Criterion DVD release of the film, Laura Mulvey stresses its debt to Lang's *M* both in its serial killer theme and in Powell's general homage to the aesthetic of German Expressionism.[9] Then, too, in its climactic sequence, *Peeping Tom* becomes, like *M*, a manhunt film. Childhood victim of sadistic surveillance and current focal point of a police dragnet, Powell's protagonist—unlike Lang's Beckert, who was removed from view entirely for a judgment not the film's to mete out—goes so far in self-abjection in the last scene as, in effect, to record for the police his own fatal "capture," at once alive and dead, on film. And not just on film, but in a stroboscopic burst of serial photos that serve to refigure that filming—and that death.

In view of all such sociopathic viewing, the approximate span of a single postwar decade rehearses (which is to say historically anticipates) a curious dialectic at stake in so many of our preceding examples. In 1949, 1954, 1960: by roughly even increments across related narrative media, the tables are turned, not once but twice, at exactly the swivel point (in both fiction and film) between the optic libido and a blanketing web of coercive surveillance, or say between voyeuristic impulse and compulsory recording. In the novel *1984*, state surveillance is so total and crushing that scopophilia—in fact any *philia*, including proletarian pornography—constitutes a redemptive drive, revolutionary in itself. By contrast, in a contemporary social fable (rather than socialist dystopia) like *Rear Window*, scopophilia must be cured of voyeurism en route to detective surveillance—and this in the name of a vigilantism we now, decades later, call "neighborhood watch."

With the oculocenteric Grand Guignol of 1960's *Peeping Tom*, however, there is a kind of dialectical implosion of these two poles. We have certainly moved beyond the social satire in Hitchcock voiced by the nurse's passing diagnosis: "We've become a race of Peeping Toms." As if alluding to her remark by way of a structuring intertext, even while narrowing her anthropology to the violence of patriarchal nurture rather than evolutionary nature, Powell's film offers a lacerating exposure of surveillance as the very cause of voyeurism. But not in one and the same subject. Indeed, when the filmically spied-upon boy (under his father's photomechanical surveillance regimen) becomes the adult and titular "scoptophiliac" (the film's pronunciation of a term more often known now without the *t*), the son has murderously supplemented his voyeurism not just with his own camera but with its erectile knife blade. Being surveilled has turned him hungry for image, if only in revenge. The closed psychic circuitry of this is at least as perverse as it sounds.

The Primal Seen

Peeping Tom "exposes" its protagonist as a kind of *photagonist*, tortured by the need not only to see but to record: to do unto others, we discover, what was done unto him in a childhood violated at every moment by his father's invasive camerawork. Before the credits of this expertly shot 35mm color film, we see—at first in color, through the gridded viewfinder of a literally tracking camera—the shaky handheld optic of an on-site filming: a prostitute followed to her room and terrorized in a truncated POV sequence that ends in the close-up frenzy of her death scream. We shift immediately to the scene's own reprojection as already developed footage in silent black-and-white, and this behind Powell's own credits: the snuff film as processed and screened by the psychopathic photographer in his own dark room, where the blood-dyed color that's drained from the image on-screen fills his lab instead with the lurid glow of his infrared developing lights. This narrative rerun is now followed by projected images, also in black-and-white, of the crime scene, to which the killer has returned as supposed documentarian, and where he pretends, when asked, to be a reporter from "The Observer."

Crucial explanatory blanks are gradually filled in. A professional cinematographer by day, currently at work on a mainstream film production, Mark Lewis moonlights as a soft-core pornographer who takes risqué (and for them highly risky) photos of models whom, like the prostitute we begin with, he kills whenever possible with the third leg of a camera tripod, lethally unsheathed as a thin-bladed knife. That's how he does it; we soon learn why. But not before the film's opening has mercilessly retraced—from his first "pure" (prenarrative) image forward, already wholly contaminated (and in fact cross-gridded in the viewfinder)—the fall into invested framing rather than unadulterated viewing. This is that myth of the originary screen vision—of the view truly "found" rather than made—whose attempted illusory restoration one main thrust of suture theory in effect tends to ironize. And would certainly find decimated in this case.

In the process, the two-stage opening sequence, in its seamless ellipsis from cause to effect (from color viewfinder sighting to projected black-and-white stock) is actually three-staged—since, before it all, we see Mark framed as he moves down the deserted street toward the woman he will soon reframe by his own camera lens. This layered logic returns us to a vexing of Christian Metz's twofold format of identification (first with the filming, then with the filmed). If in *M*, in front of the toy shop, Beckert's look back, behind his own back, at the prying camera is not just a strain on suture but a collapse of primary upon secondary identification—so that our own virtual look is what terrorizes the character—such a collapse is all the clearer by being redoubled, as it is, from the opening of *Peeping Tom* forward. If we identify with the camera that follows Mark down an alley and then transfers its color POV to his own viewfinder, we are thus identifying with a barely differentiated field of vision made obvious later when we identify with (that is, try imagining for ourselves) Mark's affect when he again becomes visible on screen, once more from the back—behind the credits this time—watching his own "rushes" in their full libidinal charge. What the rest of the film continues to imply is that identifying with a camera is no different, in this one dysfunctional case, from identifying with a character whose entire manhood could be subsumed to the admission that "I am a camera." But the continuity of this implication moves through carefully timed layers of explication.

What unites Mark's professional cinematography with his homicidal obsessions and thus binds the dramaturgic disjunction of the film's two plotlines—divided as the narrative is between commercial cinema and perverse camerawork, light comic satire regarding the film whose crew he anchors and gothic claustrophobia in the film he stars in—receives the hint of an early if resisted disclosure. This results when Helen, a young woman renting an apartment for her and her mother in Mark's former family home, and intrigued by the handsome and laconic young landlord, asks to see his darkroom, then some of the films processed and stored there. As in the credits, the lab becomes again an exhibition venue, cause and effect telescoped as symptoms of the same derangement. With obvious trepidation on his part, Mark shows her "home movies" of what might be called his surveillant bildungsroman. For he was reared as a kind of "human subject" in his scientist father's clinical experiments about childhood responses to fear. The short film episodes that picture these induced traumas include, for instance, the shot of a lizard dropped by metonymy into the crotch of the sleeping boy's pajamas.

And more than that: the scene of sexuality itself is turned fearful when Mark's titillated peek at a couple kissing on a park bench is unmanned by the prying eye of his father's camera, recording not the couple but the boy's reactions to being seen staring. These dubious early shots in Mark's cinematographic history set the tone, and the neurotic stage, for the even more psychoanalytically fraught nexus to come in this 16mm archive of his upbringing, all of it projected for Helen's increasingly repulsed inspection. And this before she can quite fathom its full consequences for the man she is drawn to. For viewers of Helen's viewing, however, knowing already (as we do) of Mark's opening sex murder, more may seem clear at this point. In this unreeling 16mm sequence—by which erotic curiosity is misrouted from desire toward fear (voyeurized couple to nighttime genital phobia)—the groundwork is certainly laid for the later sublimation of sex by violence in his impotent killing spree.

After the photographed phallic trauma of the lizard, there follows a less aggressive but no less brutal stage of the father's experiment. The virtual primal scene of Mark's childhood—variant of the boy child in Freud being exposed to the sight of parental sex as a potentially castrating violence—emerges as a scenario symbolically split and refracted, even as it is displaced into less naked forms of confronted paternal desire. Not allowed to spy upon eroticism in voyeuristic privacy, but kept instead under the lens of behavioral surveillance—to see if there might be (just might be) some visible fear latent there, as well, in adolescent sexual curiosity—Mark is later filmed as he watches his own father's new couplehood (if not coupling). And not just watches, but records: through the camera gifted to him as a coming-of-age present just after the loss of his mother. It is the son's looking wanly down on her corpse—one of her hands demurely covering her lower lap, the other laid open for a valedictory grasp—that is the penultimate image of him we see recorded by the father's camera. In it, the mother's body is photographed only from the neck down before being eulogized and interred—on camera, but not as shown to us. It is, we come to suspect, that missing face of the frame-decapitated maternal corpse that must be replaced, again and again, insatiably, by the castrated son in his serial murders, all requiring—as we eventually learn—the headshot in close-up (of a female body not quite dead) that his father's footage has in fact so strikingly elided in photographing the boy at his mother's bier.

With Helen horrified and incredulous at the images so far, Mark speeds through the record of his mother's funeral, her ritual removal from view, as if fast-forwarding his father's footage (though it is only the nondiegetic piano soundtrack that accelerates, not the visible projector reels). The elision thus seems a purely subjective gesture on Mark's part. We are not this time privy to the image projected for Helen. We have only Mark's rushed words for what he is sweeping past and under at once, "her funeral and then her burial," before arriving at a bathing-suit pose of her young blond replacement, married "six weeks later" by his father in a collapse of generational transference and a caving-in of the Oedipal triangle (father rather than son replacing the mother with a younger object of desire). As if to emphasize the barely repressed psychic scars left by this rapid chain of past events, the adult Mark bridges over those last rites—once reeled past—in what thereby registers as suppressed mourning for his mother. He refers to the loss with clenched neutrality as merely "the previous sequence" in his father's filmic record, as if the son's whole biography, including the trauma of the buried mother, is subsumed to the patriarch's scientific cinematography.

Opening the Wound of Suture

What immediately follows carries a further and compressed explanatory power in Freudian terms. With the mother gone from the circuit of eroticized affection, the son, instead of carrying over his own desire to a new object (at least in prospect), has been usurped in this role by the father and is given instead a compensatory camera, a phallic substitute, a fetish (all these terms kept in rigorous circulation by Mulvey in her audio commentary), while the father, in effect, marries his way into the next generation and, by association, the son's place. Castration is complete, its prosthesis obvious. So that after all the psychosexual humiliations caught on surveillance camera in Mark's (de)formative years, it will eventually be *his* turn to inflict the same by way of substitute phallic gratification. This is what the virtually adulterous haste of the patriarchal remarriage, when submitted to further optical figuration in the pivotal disclosure scene with Helen, goes on, in a sense, to predict.

This foreboding showdown of apertures and focal distances happens with extreme technological overdetermination. It is pivotal in every sense, especially in regard to the reciprocal axis of optical recording. Once the father has helped Mark's new mother adjust the focus of her POV shot, it is she, the incarnation of step-maternal sexuality, who is photographing this whole ritual initiation of the boy in the fumbling manipulation of his first 16mm camera. She does so from exactly that position off camera, and on our side of it, that she shares with Mark's father, recording the boy's novice efforts to film *them*, or, say, to bear them in view. If his lens were large and clear enough to be zeroed in on by their (and thus the narrative's) camera, reflecting as it would the monocular eye of his father's supervening lens, the screen frame would be caught up in a telltale hall of optic mirrors at the doubly receding horizons of the scene's already metafilmic irony. For as we watch now with Helen in her recoil, along the same sightline, it is only what the father's camera has recorded (even by an erotically vested operator) that we are seeing, not what Mark's initial efforts at recording might have traced in the quintessential voyeurism entailed here: the displaced primal scene of the new paternal couple giving themselves over to his aided gaze. In the present, by contrast, Helen—in watching this retrieved footage—has in view nothing other than Mark pointing a camera, in perspectival effect, at her. And since she has discovered enough by now to recognize the latent horror (if not quite the murderous threat) of that, she forces him to turn off the projector after having refused to let him actually photograph her reactions with a present-tense camera.

Two systems of exchange intercept and upend each other here. In the shunt between internally projected screen image and Helen in pained close-up, an alternation of shots: the past scene versus its present interpretation, back and forth. On that internal screen, however, with no narrational give-and-take, there is only the simultaneity of filming and being filmed. Funneling through as we do to that dizzying regress of scopic obsession—stitched in by the encompassing rhythm of shot and countershot there in the darkroom, where projection is aimed at introjection—the optical ethics of the footage spiral out of control (ours included). At one level, defenses may seem to hold. Helen is there in our place, drawing the fire of Mark's gaze (both of the boy on-screen and his present self next to her, studying her fear). As we watch her watching the image of Mark's being watched and filmed, while finally filming in his own right, we at least go unwatched. Or so we may at first think. So, to be sure, the general institution of cinema encourages us to assume—above and beyond the apparatus of its suture. We are the appointed absent ones, untainted, detached. Which is of course the final myth that the prurient scopic fascination of this film fable is bent on exploding. And I allude deliberately to Rancière's utopian premise of *photogénie* freed from plot. Instead, in the ricochet (or duel) of camera lenses screened in this scene (and focused by the POV of the paternal camera), what transpires is an eliding of any breathing room between site and its sighting as well as between vision and its record—all absorbed into the filming of filming across the interface and face-off of the generations.

In our being made privy to this, wedged into its interplay, Helen is our delegate, our surrogate, our double. Once she forbids Mark's present filming of her fear in front of the screen, she is in one sense safe; certainly the on-screen camera of the initiated boy is powerless to see her. She must know this, insisting now on a suspension of its image not for its threat to her freedom from capture but for the withering bleakness that the prolonged shot has already captured. This is its appalling nature as diagnostic spectacle rather than surveillance mechanism, the retailed misery of its biographical narrative, where the clinical ambitions of the father are so unsparingly visited upon the son. That horror might be our motive too, if we were to decide we'd had enough and turned off the DVD player. Instead we keep on looking from the edge of our seats. So who's to say that the film isn't, in fact, filming us, photographing our own scopic desires, the interlaced pleasure principle of our own acquiescence in the fearful?

Even at the plot level, the Freudian undertow never lets up from here out. When Mark is next seen back on duty with the film crew, a psychiatrist is brought on the set to help the traumatized lead actress after she has seen a corpse hidden in a trunk (dumped there, as only we know, by the camera operator after his late-night rendezvous with his victim on set). Feeling the doctor out for possible therapeutic advice on his voyeurism, Mark introduces himself as a "focus puller," and the German psychiatrist says cryptically, "So am I, in a way"—as if to suggest that psychoanalysis is meant to bring the underside of consciousness into various levels of conceptual close-up. In the immediately preceding scene, explaining how she knows that something is wrong with him, Helen's blind mother puts it this way: "Instinct, Mark; it's a wonderful thing. It's a pity you can't photograph that." Yet this is exactly what the father tried to do, the behaviorist researcher wanting to record the outer signs of the instinct of fear. The real fears are invisible, however, and often impenetrable. Only a narrative film can photograph them—and only through the secondary implications of its tracked action, in this case its slasher psychodrama and the focus-pulled moments of its own most arresting disclosures.

Mark's whole trajectory has been asphyxiating—even before the knife goes into his own throat. Photographed by his father in a way that invaded his privacy in the very years of his sexual awakening, shot looking on at his mother's corpse and at the woman who replaces her—not for him, in the normative line of descent, but for his father instead—Mark, his life foreclosed in this direction, goes on (inherited camera in hand) to kill any number of other blondes of roughly the new mother's age. He does so while filming their fear at the moment of ultimate male penetration, repeating the father's cruelty—until finally able to stab to death the phallic father in himself. His last murder, offscreen, was of a self-styled pinup model. On screen, he pinions himself. Mark's last words are an apology to Helen: not for what he's put her through, but for not being able to provide still shots for her children's book about a magic camera: "Sorry I couldn't photograph the faces for you, Helen."

But this is said at exactly the moment when his pretimed still cameras have set off their flashbulbs in recording his own face in the staggered moments just before death. For the last few scenes, his doom pending, he's been filming a 16mm "documentary" of his final days and hours, as if completing his father's work. This includes repeated shots of the police dragnet closing in: his own criminal rather than psychological surveillance this time. But just at the point of no return he gives up moving-image footage and reverts to flashbulb-lit stills. These serial ignitions are designed to capture his last line of movement toward his own sacrificial blade, like a deconstructed filmstrip. Moreover, the bulbs are backed as usual by the curved reflective surface that, in its anomalous mutation until now, enlarged to the scale of a portable mirror, he has deployed in his previous murders—we've belatedly discovered—so as to return the female look of terror upon her recoiling gaze in an anamorphic distortion. With his own pubescent fears and desires never off camera, it is as if his transition to manhood requires the displacement and mastery of all residual fear, including all anxious eros, by foisting it onto his serial objects of desire in the form of mortal panic. A subjection to surveillance, too deeply internalized, finds relief only in the violent othering of such self-inspection. These pages have begun to estimate the implications for the reversible axis of detected violence and its violent detection in the next half century of social and cinematic practice, given its exponential dependence on invasive technology.

But this closed circuit of violence, including its warped libidinal syndrome in *Peeping Tom*, is now normalized on the way to the film's closure. For the most conventional surveillance dimension in the plot, in counterpoint with the police reconnaissance, has been reserved for introduction in this final sequence. Long after Helen has been exposed to the father's silent-film footage, monitoring the boy's experimentally induced fears, Mark now plays audiotapes for her of his own weeping and screaming at various moments of his early life, age five, age eight, and so on, revealing that every room in the house was "wired for sound." And "still is," he admits—as he plays back sounds of her earlier birthday party and of another lodger's private advances to her that we haven't heard before. These tapes of eavesdropping—of sonic voyeurism—run on during the rest of the scene until his death, after which they arrive at the voice of the father, enunciated by the director himself (who played the father in the earlier episode with the birthday camera). He comes on mic there as a terrorizing *acousmêtre* (Chion) speaking the film's obituary line: "Don't be a silly boy, dry your eyes." Don't blur your vision; it's all you have. Offscreen, unanchored, omnipotent, uncastrated (in Chion's terms), this is the voice of the Other—and here of the Author as well, narratival and biographic—operating as interdict.

But the eyes, dry or otherwise, are no longer necessary by then, for Mark has fulfilled what Mulvey stresses as the inherent turn from sadism to masochism and thus lies dead on his darkroom floor, with the projector spooling off the last of its enchained single frames. Mulvey, who will go on to write a book in part about the liminal difference between photography and film as obliquely recuperated in the pause function of home-theater digital viewing—and this in light of Bazin and Barthes on photographic "embalming" over against the "mummified" duration of cinema's serial frame line[10]—is certainly a critic poised to note (and does so in her Criterion commentary) the thematization of this difference as a trope of closure at the end of Powell's film. Photography, as she will later expand the notion, is the figured death of film, just as, within the diegesis of this one film, cinematography threatens the death of those it corners.

In contrast, then, those motion-timed photo flares that pace Mark's death (those snapshots timed to "wave goodbye," as he puts it) now call up, for Mulvey, "the earliest experiments that prefigured the invention of the cinema. The Muybridge analysis of movement is reversed in a movement toward stillness . . . a metaphor for the stillness at the end of all narrative"—while also (in fact rather than figure) being an actual rather than metaphoric remission, finally, from the all-too-literally invasive record of the lived body in time, to whose mental vulnerability the father's original recording had been devoted. Raised on camera, Mark dies on and by it. If the differential garden slide in *Rear Window* was the first of the two moments mentioned early on that gravitate—in this chapter's two chief narrative exhibits—to the "relation of frame line to its underlying photoframes," this gauntlet of flash cameras clocking Mark to his fatal finish line is the second. Each smokes out the evidentiary libido into plain sight, planar sighting.

As the projector in *Peeping Tom,* running in the background through this whole suicide scene, finally winds down in figured entropy, it is clear that only a thereby suspended gaze—with imaging itself stopped dead in its track(s)—can break the murderous cycle. And it is deeply right that—with sprocket noise no longer audible from the inert projector, and with the audiotapes of terror wound off as well—the return of cinema's constitutively repressed and silent fixed-frame imaging should take this form. Repressed by necessity within the lifelike simulacrum of screen motion, filming reverts in closure to the explicit, quasi-forensic purposes of precinematic chronophotography—and this in symbolic arrest of a constrained life violated at origin by the "biograph" of ongoing surveillance. It is as if, in the end, Mark has taken the police's crime scene photos for them, "analyzing" (rather than reanimating) his own last lunge upon the apparatus of his execution. Mark's fate at the end of *Peeping Tom* all but refigures in this way the flashbulb aggression at the climax of *Rear Window,* though inverted now to the protagonist's exorcizing self-exposure to his own tools. If we've stayed through to this perverse finish, fascinated, riveted—as if pinned down by the film's own camera and its grotesque revelations—it's worth asking again whether the film hasn't surveilled something in our own visual urges, our own indulged fears, in fact: something less superficial than the outward signs in which Mark's professor father would have been interested.

After *Peeping Tom*, film history waits just over half a century to top this sickly pitch of erotic impasse concerning the gaze of desire, the surfaces its scans, the flesh it punctures. For if, even conceivably, there is a more perverse stage beyond the biographical (and erotic) gap wedged open by *Peeping Tom* between surveillance and voyeurism, it would have to be the gradations of security-cam imaging and CCTV sampling on the way to a sadistic scopophilia—and beyond—in Pedro Almodóvar's 2011 *The Skin I Live In*. Here is a film in which the surveillance tech remains mostly routine even as it ironizes the muted sci-fi elements of a remade rather than just monitored human form. To abstract the film's complicated flashback structure of family melodrama to the mere outline of its erotic plot—and its electronic relays—is to offer the most immediate way of assessing its fierce ironic logic. Following the accidental disfigurement and suicide of his wife, a transgenics surgeon has his license revoked for testing versions of a new protective skin not on mice but on humans. His one remaining (and entirely illegal) female patient, Vera, is imprisoned, for years thereafter, under round-the-clock surveillance in his combined mansion and operating theater, watched over from kitchen consoles by the housekeeper, who also recognizes—through another surveillance camera—the arrival of her criminal son at the back door. His image appears there just after she has seen him on TV news: reported as caught by a commercial security cam (though not as yet legally apprehended) in the progress of an attempted robbery.

This nested set of optical transmits gives way now to the son's attempted rape of Vera, whom he recognizes as the double of his former lover, wife of the doctor, with whom he had tried to elope. The sexual rivalry persists still—until the doctor kills him. And rivalry it certainly still is, since we have seen the doctor in his bedroom, stretched on a settee and staring at a nearly life-sized video projection—a special feed from one among his several closed-circuit hookups—offering a high-definition digital image of Vera. Her comparably reclined body, odalisque-like, is lingered over in salacious delectation: surveillance turned erotic in a close-up exchange of glances, hers unwitting, that travesties classic suture as much as it violates human privacy—and its surgical aftermath. For, as we know by now, an unsutured gaze doesn't encompass the full extent of the doctor's more than skin-deep fascination with his patient's remodeled image. We have learned in flashback that Vera, untrue to the etymology of her name, has been radically altered to resemble his wife, not just by multiple plastic surgeries using variants of his epidermal technique—as seen in a transitional montage—but by a more decisive intervention yet. There is nothing veracious about Vera's desired body, including the skin s/he has been made to hide in and call living.

For the doctor, as we come to learn through another delayed flashback—in a castrating revenge against a young man named Vicente whom he suspects of raping his daughter—has performed gender reassignment on the culprit, a vaginoplasty, only to find himself erotically drawn to, and hence eager to enhance, the boy's resemblance not just to his victim but to her look-alike mother. Not just the victim's privacy has been lost by surveillance, then, but his privates too—by the crime that necessitates his monitored imprisonment. In an inversion of the Oedipal triangle (rather than its mere collapse in *Peeping Tom*), the male agent who would steal the daughter from the father—the daughter taking the displaced role of the eclipsed (in this case dead) mother—must become again not the usurper but, in surrogate form, the original sexual object. Having, in the mad-scientist tradition, made a woman this time, not a man, the surgeon makes the further effort to turn her into the bride of Doctor Frankenstein himself. But when intercourse is finally attempted, Vera (through her inner Vicente, as it were, or as it was), pretending to look for lubricant to reduce the pain, asserts a former phallic power of instinctive penetration and shoots the doctor dead in his bed. In a pattern familiar to us from the self-stabbing of *Peeping Tom,* the superfice of image and its displayed fears—whether photomechanically surveilled or voyeurized, whether for behaviorist science, genetic engineering, or pornographic gratification—can be resisted only by the asserted *third* dimension of the terminal puncture wound.

Lines of sight become angles of attack and penetration. In the narrative economy of surveillance and reprisal, the tension between event and its record, between three inhabited and two traced dimensions—as focused by lethal puncture (as a travesty of the focal point itself)—emerges as a shared turning point in the films just considered. The pattern of violent reversal was set by Hitchcock, even though the formerly knife-wielding villain of *Rear Window* breaks unarmed into the hero's space. The intrusion is no less violent for that, no less a 3-D penetration. It is as if the safely flattened field of photography in its typical form has been invaded, the image of the murderous Thor*wald* not at this point securely "walled" off as spectacle for inspection, violence no longer held apart under comfortable scrutiny in photo-like planar sight. With neither plate glass window nor photo plate intervening between the media agent and an immediate lethal threat, all that Hitchcock's protagonist can do is to recruit the ancillary equipment of his craft to keep the lit if unrecorded danger at more than arm's length for as long as possible—at a photograph*able* if not in fact captured distance.

Such is the maintained distance of surveillance, until collapsed after all into the arena of a physical duel (that Deleuzean format) sending the hero himself, rather than just his gaze, back out the open window and into another immobilizing leg cast. To move from the screening out of reality by its bracketed representations (or their associated distancing) to the skin one lives (and dies) in—each emphasis a comment on the visible surface of desire and aggression—is to trace one optic common denominator of surveillance cinema in that mode of psychodrama on which the following chapter will also be trained. If Oudart's sense that Lang's technique discovered something essential about the "erotics" of the apparatus in precisely the "terrorist" deployment of its eyeline probes—something whose consequences for film history could scarcely have been fully developed in Lang's own work—then this chapter and the next offer a continuing gloss on the psychodynamic of suture in just this regard. But compared to the gender savagery on which Almodóvar's plot turns, the othering of lives to come falls (as with Hitchcock and Powell) wholly within the domain of ethical (and now by extension political) fable rather than gothic sci-fi.

5 THE OTHERING OF LIVES

The Lives of Others: a quintessential surveillance title. This 2006 German film (Florian Henckel von Donnersmarck) looks back two decades on Stasi espionage in Cold War East Berlin. But the title has its positive valence as well. To such lives there are many routes of access other than cinematic—including theatrical and literary, as the film suggests in the unrolling of its plot—as well as by voyeurism and surveillance, which its narrative also puts into sustained contrast with those more aesthetic channels of empathy. In the process, *The Lives of Others* takes its place in an ongoing audio/visual dialectic. Cinematic manifestation reduced at one point from moving image to discrete photo dossier in Lang's first sound film; photographs matched to merely fantasized sound in *Blow-Up*; covert photographic proof contracted for along with evidentiary sound in *The Conversation*; image wedded to found sound in *Blow Out*, turning random audial capture into unwitting surveillance; electronic bugging devised not just for the seizing of image and sound together but for remote GPS tracking in the abstract bitmap grids of *Enemy of the State*: this image/sound nexus delineates in its own right an evolving historical interplay of optical, sonic, and digital informatics. Against such a backdrop in the lineage of surveillance cinema, a contemporary electronic mastery of traced motion and invaded space throws into relief the deliberate limitations of dated and purely audial monitoring in *The Lives of Others*.

The uncertain genre ground of the surveillance motif is familiar to us from its extreme melodramatic hybrids. In Hitchcock and Powell, a morally suspect or psychologically brutal surveillance is given over to active detection (if only of the protagonist himself in *Peeping Tom*) across the building drama of the film's slasher plot. As crossed most recently with sci-fi gothic in the case of Pedro Almódovar, the genre (as well as plot) tension turns on bodily mutilation and murder either abetted, ferreted out, or further eroticized by filmic or video camerawork. The genre admixtures persist with comparable but deferred eruptions in films where voyeurism and violence continue to shadow the sightlines of objective surveillance. Of the narratives paired in this chapter, one is a spy "procedural" about state surveillance; the other, *Caché* (Michael Haneke, 2005), the psychological study of a life braced against any internalized vigilance, where the technology of clandestine filming is refigured almost entirely as the threat of self-recognition. Two films we might fairly call psychopolitical thrillers, though oppositely weighted: one toward the defiance of authoritarian control by the softening route of psychological identification, one toward the onset of the political in assault upon a resolutely closed psyche. In each case, the deployment of dated, low-tech surveillance (noncomputerized spyware in a mid-1980s setting; analog video twenty years later) disappears almost entirely into an extended metaphor for ethical cognizance. To realize how a film of Stasi espionage behind the Berlin Wall can cross-examine a parable of the walled-off bourgeois self is one goal of this comparison, pursued in each case via the narratography of a thematized (and then gradually vaporized) technical machination.

Secret Policing

There are no opening credits to *The Lives of Others*, just two frames of brief text explaining how 100,000 members of the secret police in the so-called German Democratic Republic before glasnost, supported by 200,000 informants, served in implementing the state's announced goal "to know everything." This brief prologue is followed by the opening caption "November 1984," introducing an episode of relentless interrogation that eventually cracks its victim and forces out of him the name of a Western collaborator. Yet the year 1984 has, this time, its light at the end of the tunnel, its chink in the Wall. Nothing in this first sequence, however, would kindle such hope. The interrogator takes handwritten notes, with no hint, yet, of other recording technology. But the fact of covert recording soon comes clear with a cut that seems directly borrowed from a famous segue in Lang's *Testament of Dr. Mabuse*. Inspector Lohmann in Lang's opening sequence, having just heard the mad ramblings of one of the arch-criminal's victims, remarks, "He must have gone out of his mind with fear"—and we cut to Dr. Baum (Mabuse's double and soon posthumous avatar) in a lecture hall finishing the sentence by linguistic match cut: "It's not as uncommon as you might think." It would seem that the film whose opening scene we've been watching is subsumed wholesale to a pedagogic object lesson in someone else's suspicious discourse. Same with *The Lives of Others* when, about halfway through the gloomily lit interrogation scene, we flash forward to its playback on a (previously hidden) tape deck before a brightly lit class taught by the master interrogator himself, Gerd Wiesler, who explains each cruel nuance of the system while noting the name of a student who naively (treasonously) finds it "inhuman." When Wiesler then "rewinds the tape" to make a further point, we flash back again to the scene unfolding before us—full-frame and in what we had previously taken to be "real time." The movie we just started watching has already been recycled from someone else's interrogation archive.

Almost at once, in the next sequence, we drop this plot and interrogated character altogether and join Wiesler and a Stasi coworker in the balcony of a theatrical performance preceded at last by the film's deferred title, as if naming the theater itself as the eponymous staged microcosm for the inspection of others' motives and desires. The playwright Georg Dreyman, there looking on from a box—a true "patriot," we're told (despite his dissident sympathies)—is in no way "subversive," as his factory-set, Soviet-realist staging would seem to confirm. Yet a move is made by the party boss to put him under arbitrary suspicion and surveillance nonetheless. Wiesler is assigned to wire the apartment with a full team of agents, leaving them at one point to inspect the secret hideout upstairs in the attic that will provide his command center. As he exits Dreyman's apartment we see him through an iris mask that, upon his return moments later, is revealed to be the POV of a woman across the hall spying through the peephole on the squad of uninvited guests. Yet again, the movie we are watching is subordinated after the fact to the particularized surveillance mechanism (albeit low-tech) of a character within the film.

As if put on alert by this transition, we are now readied for the vicarious plot to unroll in double-tracked montage between the target site and the scene of inspection—a "spying" all but misnamed in that it is entirely audial, with the exception of a lone and routine surveillance cam positioned over the apartment's front door. Whereas the sound engineer in *The Conversation* replays in his mind the tacit "footage" of the couple his surveillance team once stalked (and secretly photographed), even while he is later merely listening to their doctored voices on reel-to-reel tape; and whereas the sound engineer of *Blow Out* is able to fabricate in more than imagination, from discovered photos, a virtual film of what he had missed registering in person (sound included)—by contrast, Wiesler in *The Lives of Others*, with his stakeout in a deserted space above the apartment of the playwright and his actress-mistress, has only wiretapping and audial bugs to go by in putting together an actionable case against the artist. He suffers from a default in the full sensory complement of surveillance technology. In pallid compensation, the agent sketches out a chalk diagram of the apartment, with figures placed in typical position for the writer and his mistress—more like police markers of fallen bodies within the perimeters of a crime scene than a horizontal picture plane of visual representation. Image, however impoverished, must try defraying the visual deficit of the wiretap. Later, Wiesler takes up a position, headphones in place, matched to the spatial coordinates of Dreyman and his partner as extrapolated from his audial feed. His attempt is ultimately to map their trespass with, and upon, his own body.

This is only the beginning of an intense, perverse, but ultimately redemptive identification developed with the more vivid lives he documents. But it takes time. Bureacracy only slowly gives way to quasi-textual intimacy. Typed transcripts are produced on a daily basis by Wiesler and his prurient assistant, the latter functionary serving to emphasize the audially displaced voyeurism of their task by showing an interest only in the overheard sex. In contrast, Wiesler—who, as if repeating the protagonist's affectless sex life in *The Conversation*, finds at one point some impassive relief with a prostitute—is more intimately caught in the human drama below, shedding tears at one point when Dreyman plays a memorial piece at the piano, titled "Sonata for an Honest Man," after the suicide of his friend, a blacklisted director. The very sound of free expression, in or out of bed, is what slowly opens the Stasi spy to a more perilous empathy yet.

The purely auditory transference between apartment and surveillance aerie is marked in the sonata sequence, as well as less dramatically at other times, by a panning camera movement made continuous, by match cut in motion, between, in this case, the keyboard memorial downstairs and the scene of eavesdropping (and its otherwise joyless "keyboard" input of typescript) above—as if the sound bridge were in fact an emotional as well as cinematographic ligature between the two spaces. So important is this turning point, as stressed by the matched swivel of camerawork (circling Wiesler from behind until his tear-stained face is visible), that even its preparation sets us slightly on edge in setting up the affective relay. The sonata is first heard nondiegetically, as if the hero has it already in mind as he approaches the piano—where, implausibly, he picks up the melodic line in midstream. Until then, the sound is nothing that could have been overheard, either in the apartment itself or within earshot of its bugging. Only when entered upon as elegiac performance is its internal memory ready for covert recording, to say nothing of an almost telepathic (though in fact technologized) empathy.

From such lowered defenses on the spy's part, it is only one more (and treasonous) step to a direct abetting by Wiesler of his enemy's love life—and, finally, of his political transgression. Fully invested in the gathering intrigue around the couple, he intervenes personally (though anonymously, as one of the actress's fans) to prevent their breakup, and later pictures (in subjective superimposition over the text his colleague has prepared) the "vigorous acts of intimacy" that followed her return—not in voyeurist gratification but in cloaked fellow-feeling. Whatever erotic fixations may be pandered to here, however close such compassion may verge on sexual titillation as well as sedition, the film is unabashedly and resolutely sentimental about this turn from surveillance through voyeurism to quasi-theatrical identification.

The renowned playwright has ended up, unawares, in the equivalent of his own radio play. And when he incriminates himself with his liberal comrades, Wiesler, instead of closing in for the kill, covers for him with his Stasi boss, who grows increasingly suspicious of Wiesler's withheld information and suspected sympathy. Finally, Dreyman is about to be caught quite literally red-handed. After drafting an exposé of East German suicide statistics on a portable typewriter—with a red ribbon, no less (a machine subsequently hidden away so that the font pressures and wear can't be traced to him)—he gets the article published anonymously in West Berlin. Especially in view of that earlier typescript overrun by images of the couple's reunited sex, an irony of blocked mediation is entailed by this plot turn. However telltale the material keystroke traces might be to later forensic detection, the initial act of text production has generated, in the moment, a wiretapped stream of evidence that no sound engineer would be able decode, let alone transcribe for the typescript of his own nightly report. The sheer sound of alphabetic impress delivers nothing of the text itself. In this direction, surveillance has reached its dead end.

But Wiesler has in any case lost interest in exposing Dreyman. When a forced search of the apartment is certain to turn up the incriminating machine under loose floorboards, we discover that a further intervention on Wiesler's part (hiding the typewriter elsewhere) has prevented the playwright's arrest. All this is, as before, entirely unrecognized by Dreyman, who has never laid eyes on this one-way secret sharer—but not unguessed by Weisler's Stasi commander. Once the stakeout has been aborted, Wiesler is demoted to the lowest rung of the surveillance bureaucracy, consigned to the steaming open of private letters at a forlorn basement desk, where this time an incoming radio broadcast (rather than closed-circuit tap) announces the fall of the Wall through the shared earphones of a colleague. The next time we see Wiesler, swept up into the new commercial economy of East Berlin, his unskilled work is to deliver not (even unopened) mail but mere commercial publicity fliers. It is there, making the rounds, that he is finally recognized in the flesh by Dreyman, who, learning belatedly that he had long been under surveillance during the Communist regime, has just discovered Wiesler's photo and code number, as his "case officer," in the Stasi files (made public after 1989), attached to the falsified (exculpating) report on his political resistance.

The previously unsuspecting playwright knows now that his life has been saved by this act of suppressed surveillance data, and he immediately seeks out the man in a spirit of acknowledgment, gratitude, or whatever else it is he might find to say. He thinks better of it, however, as he sees the lone figure in the distance making his quasi-postal deliveries. Sometime later, Wiesler, still delivering leaflets door to door, notices a giant publicity photo of Dreyman, answering at a vastly different scale to the snapshot of Wiesler uncovered in the previous sequence. Two images are thus found facing each other off only as such, as public-record photos, across an indeterminate narrative gap; two sundered players in an espionage game coming to deferred recognition only through the secondary mediation of visual imprint. The publicity poster hangs in the window of a bookstore stacked with copies of Dreyman's new novel, *Sonata for an Honest Man*—dedicated, Wiesler sees when opening it, to his anonymous Stasi code number, HGWXX7. We don't need to assume unequivocally that the novel is written about Wiesler in the first place, that it is in fact the novelization of the film we've just watched, to feel the force of this dedication as a communicative gesture across time: the meeting of minds that never took place in person. When the clerk asks if he wants the book giftwrapped, the answer—"No, it's for me"—so clearly resonates beyond the commercial transaction to the whole psychological interaction of the plot that, at the very word "me," a freeze-frame on Wiesler's satisfied look of recognition offers, in close-up, its own version of the screen-sized poster of his alter ego we've just seen facing the street. In this way two giant close-ups, one photographic, one cinematographic (the latter a digital evocation of classic film's original photogrammatic freeze), summon the very work of cinema in the staging, the framing, of this one narrative's probed psychological mutuality.

In his book *In Defense of Lost Causes*, Slavoj Žižek emphasizes the "obvious" homosexual subtext brought to a resolution toward the end, the "libidinal" fixation with Dreyman on Wiesler's part being reversed along the same voyeuristic axis when Dreyman tracks Wiesler on his menial rounds.[1] The film seems too sentimental, too humanist, for that. Certainly Žižek is right to note the upending of surveillance in the penultimate scene: "The situation is thus effectively reversed; the observed victim is now the observer" (63). But this requires no further erotic ironies of the bugger bugged. It does not mean that Dreyman, with his female partner removed from the triangle by her suicide, having discovered Wiesler's sacrifice for him, "reciprocates in amorous terms" (63) by briefly tailing the former agent. The vector toward any meeting whatever is deflected by personal as well as historical reticence, certainly not by homosexual panic. In sum, the reciprocation has been textual, not sexual. What is indeed, first and foremost, "effectively reversed" by the inset novel is the invaded privacy of a surveillance dossier when turned to the impersonality—and suspended actionability—of fictional narrative, first in Wiesler's tampering with the facts of a seditious writing act, later in the full music of a written fiction. Illegal search and seizure is rectified, we are to think, by poetic license. Or put it another way: the movie is given over to us, in closure, having cleansed itself of the compromised parallel montage by which, right from the start, our reception of a particular scene couldn't be cleanly extricated from its recording by an intermediate state apparatus. Only by this narrative restitution, in the peeling away of espionage from montage, do the lives of others become, as in literary fiction, fair game again.

Hidden Agendas, Sequestered Lives

One comparable genius of Haneke's *Caché* is to take the topical issue of surveillance, empty it of its ordinary motive, and turn it not so much upside down as inside out. Haneke does so by sustaining the topos in the abstract for as long as possible, drained of apparent motive, goal, or specific human target, before converting its very medium into a snare for the media celebrity it is turned against—and then sweeping the whole question of spycams under the rug of moral and political allegory. This ironic variant of the mode derives in part from that imbrication of surveillance with detection worked out so differently in films including *Rear Window*, *The Conversation*, and *Enemy of the State*. But whereas the playwright in *The Lives of Others* discovers after the fact that he has been surveilled, and turns the coda into a brief detection plot, in *Caché* the TV star begins by trying to detect the source of his surveillance until the whole technology of the hidden camera dissipates from mystery into trope.

As marked by its title, Haneke's earlier film, *Benny's Video* (1992), is, by contrast, openly and centrally about a teenage videographer who has wired his parents' home for surveillance (as if willing the kinds of transgression he might thus capture): a boy so inured to violent media that he needs eventually to experience real violence, and kills to achieve this immediacy, only in turn to record it (the murder of his new girlfriend) as a means of renewable media witness. *Caché* is, instead, about unsourced videotapes stationed to record, at first, only the most mundane and neutral of images, which are upsetting not for what they show, but for just the opposite—for how there's nothing to see but the fact that the recipients are being watched. And this from the film's first shot forward, retroactively disclosed as surveillance video. From there out, we're often unsure, at least at first, about whether what we're viewing is being invisibly viewed and recorded, and by whom, from just beyond our frame.

Film history can be illuminating here in tracing a split legacy in Haneke's work from a single perverse classic in deviant filial psychology. One line of descent from *Peeping Tom* can be noted in *Benny's Video*, if only on second viewing, when a man standing to one side of the pig slaughter in Benny's handheld, pretitle taping, is recognized as his father—as if directing the "shoot" with hand signals: the parent who, in every other aspect of the child's warped psychology as well, is a clear source of the problem, contributing to his son's calculating and affectless will to power. After the slain animal and the murdered girl logged on Benny's camcorder, the third violence it records is in fact the cruel cover-up of her murder schemed by his parents off-frame in the next room: a tape whose incriminating audio is ultimately turned over to the police, with the last shot of the arrested parents coming through to us on a station-house security cam. Silent video has finally caught up with the optically blank audio track. In *Caché*, it is the figure of the willful and unfeeling father who is again placed under surveillance, this time for the damaging legacy wrought by his own unregretted childhood selfishness and his cold-eyed denial of responsibility, or even sympathy, ever since. Patriarchy is everywhere under suspicion of an ethical collapse—and subject to violent counterreaction. By his father's surveillance, Mark Lewis in *Peeping Tom* is doomed from the start, his cinematography merely the long deferral of a suicidal drive; Benny, himself emotionally ruined, at least gets fiercely even by means of his camcorder audio; more ambiguously in *Caché*, the estranged son, in association with the surveillance video, may have begun to fight back—and this only by looking straight in the eye, at one generational and political remove, those childhood ghosts his father so rigidly evades.

With its past-participial title, *Caché* (*Hidden* in British release) may refer as well—by loose French wordplay—to the cultural *cachet* of a TV talk-show host, a literary impresario, whose self-confidence is eroded by the hidden cameras that slowly prod him to disclose his own equally hidden past. Here another curious loop in the film history of voyeurism and surveillance may be detected. For it is as if the whole conceit of Haneke's reversed domestic surveillance has taken its cue from the advice of the feisty nurse Stella in *Rear Window,* with her proposed corrective for the "race of Peeping Toms" we've become: "What people oughta do is get outside their own house and look in for a change." Resisting this logic even when confronted with its video manifestation, Georges Laurent is already in denial when telling friends at a dinner party that the tapings of his home, night and day, are just meant to "show us that we're under surveillance." In fact, they've already shown him something else as well—though unadmitted as yet to his wife: the link of these videos, somehow, back to his childhood and the Algerian son of his family's servants who, when orphaned and about to become his stepbrother, Georges lied about to get him sent away. It's as if, in reviewing the tapes of his domestic facade, the axis of registration has gone interior, become that of his own unconscious—as a disruptive flashback, triggered by the second of the videos, makes inescapable.

But that's too fast, as one so often goes in replaying this film in one's mind. More revealing, instead, is to rescan the serial tapes as patiently as plot dispenses them, and in their exact order, rather than selectively and for their aggregate charge. If the net effect of the surveillance is at first to force Georges into seeing his own life from the outside, rather than from within his protective cocoon of privilege, the building irony of this coercion passes through a measured reverse of surveillance logic from passive targeting to the bait and lure of a detective plot. But where surveillance also mutates into detection in films like *Rear Window* or *The Conversation,* here it passes through and beyond that second stage as well to discover the present scene of one's own past crime. And in the long run, the incriminated subject, so the film may finally suggest, can at that point only revert to a paranoid sense of ongoing surveillance and exposure—even if no longer technological—in the foreseen aftermath of a long-suppressed guilt brought suddenly to light. To this inference of the much-debated last shot we will need to come back—armed by the formal ironies of framing and reframing that prepare it.

For now, the inexorable buildup. Not being able to imagine where the camera could have been hidden on the punning rue des Iris, the street running perpendicular to his townhouse—since the shot is so crisp that it couldn't have been photographed through a car window—Georges says of the first surveillance episode: "It will remain a mystery." On subsequent viewings of the film, this line of dialogue becomes more a global caveat than a local bafflement. Stand warned: we are never to learn for sure. Galling, at least nagging, might sum up a certain kind of viewer frustration at the unsolved mystery. Yet the ambiguities of *Caché* are not a thicket of loose ends. They are the braided strands of explicitly truncated genre expectations that are all leading ultimately in the same direction—beyond genre. *Caché* is certainly not a standard whodunit—blatantly not. In mid-detection, the victim (Majid, the Algerian boy now in middle age) kills *himself* in Georges's presence. The mystery of agency concerns only that sequence of videotapes whose long-mounting relevance will now seem to have disappeared at exactly this apogee of violence, even if the very scene is (as it would appear from the camera angle) still being internally recorded. Refusing to answer, as the film does, the question of who exactly made the surveillance videos, let alone how, we are left only with: Why would one? Or, in other words, what could have motivated such a scheme? And to this question—only when there is no satisfaction to be had on other counts—we realize that we have long known the answer. Plot itself, which, tied inextricably to complot, disappears into this knowledge, this metanarrative recognition, well before the end.

Trying to piece together the imponderables of hidden camera position into some form of plausibility is an exercise whose very impasse may thus help solve, by indirection, its own residual puzzle. But only if the viewer is able to trade—or cash in—one level of uncertainty for another. To see how this might work, a flat-footed stepping off of the plot's sheer sequence—even before any attempt to sort out its logic—can gain unexpected traction. The premise, once established, is quickly ramified. VHS tapes are anonymously home-delivered that show nothing but an outside view of the home itself, first in daylight, then at night. Round-the-clock surveillance: rather like the sort a wealthy urban homeowner, like our protagonist Georges, might have provided for himself as a further defensive perimeter in addition to his gated entry. But tension gathers with the continuing video installments. The second tape arrives with a supplement, a clue: the primitive drawing of a face dripping blood from its mouth. And suddenly Georges flashes on an episode from the past in his boyhood home—so suddenly that the memory must have been lurking there all along, carefully policed into repression.

The next tape is a POV shot of that former home, eliciting (by jump cut) his real-time return (in an almost Pavlovian reflex) to his mother's sickbed to find out what she knows about the ailing Algerian boy she and Georges's father sent away to the sanitorium and never heard from since. She doesn't want to talk about it: "too painful." The closer Georges gets to recovering the past, the more details seem to be pointing straight at it, even if in figurative form. At the dinner party previously interrupted by the delivery of that homestead tape, for instance, its arrival followed a guest's absurd shaggy-dog story about how he himself is, in fact (with a barking lunge at the hostess to prove it), the reincarnation of a woman's dead dog. What the family home is soon materialized on the TV screen to envisage (together with the other suspicions Georges harbors unmentioned) is therefore a less supernatural way in which the past may *come back to bite you*. A few scenes later, the next tape shows the neighborhood and apartment complex, not of Georges and his wife Anne this time, but of the orphaned boy grown up—though we realize that this, too, is a taped image (not an autonomous new film "scene") only when it is run backward by Georges to clarify a street name as part of that preprogrammed detective work in which this video has ensnared him.

With trepidation, he accepts this second hook as well, retracing the steps of the mediation to the now unknown (rather than past and familiar) scene itself. The surveillant target has gone searching, the stalked turned stalker. In this way have the tapes fulfilled their task in snapping him out of his complacency, his passivity. He answers the call, follows the lead, and knocks on the door of 047. Mission accomplished (even if we're still asking whose): that is, confrontation achieved, the past met again face-to-face. Except that, with no shred of sympathy, Georges faces it down rather than up to it, accusing the Algerian man of "terrorism" against his family and thus reinscribing the colonial stereotype that led, in the first place, to the police slaughter of the boy's parents in a Paris demonstration. The last tape recorded in the film (at least as far as we know) is here—from a vantage point at the far side of Majid's kitchen—capturing Georges's threats against him, despite the man's denying all knowledge of the video aggression. Again, we learn about this filming-within-the-film only retrospectively. We are kept from suspecting it at the time by the dynamic crisscross of camera angles before their face-off is later re-seen on monitors (by Anne at home, by Georges's boss at the TV studio) in a fixed-frame medium long shot.

Remaining a Mystery

Given that each and every viewing of the preceding neutral videologs that have led us (and Georges) to this point of no return has been taken in by the viewer full-screen, with all diegetic reaction in off-frame voice-over, it may be easy enough to imagine the whole screen narrative so far without their intermediation as such, but just the scenes so filmed.[2] Such an act of imagination would constitute a thought experiment that seems hardwired into the film's own self-unraveling in its knotty mode as a surveillance and detection plot. In which case, the film's allegory of itself would run this way. First, we get establishing shots of Georges and Anne's well-to-do apartment, into whose interior the reminder of a bloody past (metonymic for Majid's tubercular childhood, metaphoric for colonial repression) intrudes. Then POV shots of motoring into the countryside to question the ailing mother. Next, with no satisfaction from his mother, a POV shot of driving, in consequence, to the outlying Paris neighborhood in search of Majid's address, followed by Georges's nervous walk, via handheld camera, down the long barren hall to apartment 047.[3]

Rounding out this rendezvous with the past in Majid's kitchen, on Georges's second and final appearance there, we then lock down on the scene of suicide in one of the director's signature fixed-frame exposés of human noncommunication. How has all this been filmed? How else? By narration itself.[4] For this is a narration that has kept us discomfited and on our toes precisely by toeing a slyly fine line between the two strata of identification in Christian Metz's psychoanalytic semiology: the difference, so potently equivocated here, between primary and secondary identification. For Metz, respectively and in order: an identification first with the camera and then with a character, the latter sometimes through a POV shot that borrows back some force of primary alignment as well. In Haneke's ironically vexed case, however, the secondary angle of surveillant identification is with an always-elided cameraman character who (never to be discovered) simply vanishes into the apparatus of narrative spectation. Mainly, what the narrative supplement of the tapes accomplishes, in the movie as we have it, is to intervene between a "media personality" and his own worst fears of finding his sequestered subjectivity on camera. And to do so while luring him into contact with the past on which his cultured facade has been erected. Secondary imaging is decidedly irrelevant when interface yields to face-to-face encounter, lending a further irony to Majid's last words: "I just wanted you to be present." That's the very motto of the film's ethic of retribution. Georges must be dislodged from his complacency by being made, first, to see the same picture of his life that we do—from the outside looking on, then in—and finally, in consequence, by being made to face something wholly other, yet from which that complacent surface cannot be disassociated.

It is a perfect touch that when Georges lies to Anne about having had no first encounter with Majid, the pathetic fib he reaches for is that 047 wasn't a residence at all, just a "storage room of some kind" (with its tacit biographical cache?). Certainly what has been on hold for years is soon to erupt. When his prevarication is exposed and Anne ends up replaying the video of Georges's first meeting in Majid's apartment, from the same camera angle that will later record the suicide, she is immediately convinced—as we may well be—that the accused man knows nothing about the surveillance campaign, and that he is entirely surprised to see his old nemesis at his door, with only the lens of its everyday spyhole to forewarn him. What she doesn't see, because what the camera wouldn't have been able to record from its fixed position somewhere at the far side of the kitchen, is the initial confrontation in the hall. This is Majid's muted burst of recognition (from his having previously recognized Georges on TV, he soon explains) couched in the mere idiom of instructed viewing: "Look who it is!" (as if he was in unlikely control of a voice-activated videotape).

Many scenes later, just before Majid slits his throat in front of Georges—after an intervening arrest and humiliation at the latter's instigation (Georges suspecting Majid of abducting his own briefly missing son Pierrot and calling in the cops)—there is an ambiguity in Majid's renewed disavowal of the hidden camcorder. His passing insistence that "I knew nothing about the tapes," cast into the past tense, may suggest that he has heard all the details since—from his son, the now-suspected perpetrator. By process of elimination, one is certainly drawn to the idea that the son—though not feasibly having executed the filming from unseen tripod-stable positions and their "fourth-wall" violations—does show, nonetheless, exactly the bottled-up resentment sufficient to have motivated this effort. So that maybe Georges was onto something when, though Anne dismissed it as pointless speculation, he surmised that the cartoonish sketch of a bloody chicken looked like "a child's drawing." A *grown* child's, perhaps, and on his parent's behalf? As much as the viewer is no doubt still being "had"—amid deliberately cultivated imponderables—in gravitating to such a barely coherent explanation, still this gives us a way to read the yet more cryptic conclusion of the film.

Part of the closing inference goes markedly unspoken, processed only by indirection. One moral and psychological likelihood, if occurring to us only on subsequent reflection: how guilty the Algerian's son would (must) feel, how miserably responsible, if it was in fact his high-handed moralistic prank that had backfired in the face of Georges's unyielding defense mechanisms and thus had pushed his father over the edge. And despite this, how implacable he remains. Which means he couldn't have done it? Or that only someone so embittered could override his own share in a guilt that, of course less accidental in Georges's case, goes farther back for the onetime childhood competitor to a less mitigable source? As usual, however, the closer one gets to psychological nuance in Haneke, the further from assurance. But certainly a paranoia about this nameless son of the next generation is allowed to persist—and perhaps to swallow up the film's closing shot.

Would this be Georges's assumption too, that the son's meddling has brought on the tragedy? Is that why, beyond his inveterate defensiveness, he remains so unyielding? Who knows what he thinks? He never tells anyone, and seems to admit little to himself. Nor can we be sure what is being processed in his unconscious. But we can guess. Again camera angles have offered in their symmetry a clear line of inference: even camera angles with no risk of implying video mediation, yet in their fixed-frame shots entailing a deep continuity with initial procedures of mediation as surveillance—and this, yet again, in the mode of surveillance as self-exposure. Interrupting his visit to his mother, a flashback to Majid killing the family rooster at Georges's behest (when pretending his parents had commanded it) ends with the boy stalking Georges with his threatening hatchet in a prolonged POV shot from the back of the barn—from which a jump cut takes us to the adult Georges, there again in his former home, waking in a cold sweat from this nightmare.

The narrative pumps are by this point fully primed. As if by the unfolding of an answering chiastic pattern at the end, one-half of the two-shot coda will seem immediately legible in light of this earlier nightmare assault. That retroactively disclosed dream insert in the homestead episode—first the aggressive mirage, then Georges writhing on his pillow—is reversed at the end by the transition from bed as shelter to an undefended onslaught of another oneiric image. After Majid's throat-cutting echo of the original barnyard treachery, Georges takes sleeping pills before crawling naked into bed in broad daylight, followed by—the cinematographic cues seem inescapable—another dreamscape from the same childhood POV. There, in extreme long shot, we see how the unwanted and betrayed stepbrother is, after agonized resistance, finally driven away from his adopted home by hospital authorities—either as this scene of exile is actually remembered from Georges's former stakeout at the back of the barn or as it is reconstructed in the unconscious of the drugged sleeper so as to match the earlier traumatic POV: a nightmare this time, in the film's penultimate shot, of guilty witness stripped of fantasized physical threat.

Yet the underlying nightmare of true vulnerability may in fact be what comes next and last with the prolonged closing frame, a different threat materialized. In Georges's last words on the phone to Anne, before a routine "I love you too," he asks her to tell their son, quite out of the blue, "not to be too hard on his old man" (not to wake him up when he comes home? not to resent him forever?). It's this seemingly undermotivated, if in its own way overdetermined, line of dialogue that we may remember as the film's last, and famously ambiguous, shot displaces the flashback image of exile with—what? another dream scenario?—this time not of a separation but of a bond forged. It is a shot notoriously hard to decipher just at the visual level, though still in the unflinching, fixed-frame geometry associated with the (now internalized?) surveillance cam. But there they are in any case, a little hard to spot at first: the nameless son and Georges's own Pierrot, talking together and then separating on the high school steps. A first meeting? A conspiratorial debriefing? In any case, the patriarch's worst fear, as almost half-expressed to his wife on the phone moments before, may seem immediately to have come true. Is this indeed a case of the sins of the father revenged by the sons? Have they been in cahoots all along? Or, that aside, is this the sure sign that Pierrot will, at the very least, be learning by hearsay about his father's inglorious past—even if he doesn't know yet? Asked otherwise: Is this meeting of the next generation happening in real time, in parallel montage, in the same late afternoon in which Georges lies asleep? Or is the interracial rapport forged or recommitted to here meant, alternately, to represent Georges's entirely subjective nightmare of the future, any day now, where a new hybrid society, racially leveled, will hold him forever responsible, have him always in the contemptuous sights of its ethical mind's eye?

Our being made to ask such questions in ways like this is what the film has accomplished in its swerve from surveillance to detection and back again. It is just this epistemological arc that has been by now wholly subjectivized, demediated—especially when its final, probable, and most horrific spycam shot (of the kitchen bloodbath) has been left to dissipate without plot uptake. No one mentions or seems to suspect the possibility that the sickening scene was, yet again, like the last one at the same site, caught on tape—with its image of Georges doing nothing, neglecting even to report the corpse to the police. Even when our lone eyewitness later suggests that the violent deed was done so as to legally (rather than just ethically) implicate him, no mention is made of the likely hidden camera—even to rule it out so as, in his paranoia, to leave him the deliberately incriminated victim of mere circumstantial evidence. All in all, technical mediation is no longer of concern. Maybe never was. In any case, the game is over, the jig up, the genre device suspended. It is, again, as if the filming has just been Haneke's all along. All that has happened in the narrative denouement—in the time between a father's death and the convergence of the next generation at the scene of institutional instruction—is one final confrontation at Georges's office, where the suspected videographer has become a real-time stalker, Majid's son wanting "only to know how it feels to have a man's death on your conscience." The son has come for firsthand evidence, and gets only continued denial, no expression even of regret—which is proof enough, as the boy implies with some satisfaction, of how this one man's conscience does operate.

In this final exposure, video record is no longer of use, just as it was never of central import. The plot-long pattern of electronic surveillance (without real spying)—turned en route, via reverse detection, to bait and entrapment—has exhausted itself in Georges's resolute refusal to *see himself*. Yet it is a refusal optically figured one last time after all. The elevator carrying Georges and his accuser up to his office is full of people, with every unoccluded face recorded by the camera in real space—except the implacable face of Georges. He alone, wedged in just behind and to the side of the unseen camera, is visible to us only as a mirror image reframed at the other side of the crowded, indeed claustrophobic, optic field. It is an image that never catches its own eye in the mirror, with Georges looking nervously askance at the blankly threatening son who, by contrast, is seen from the front and back at once: head on, that is, as well as in the opposite mirror he is pressed up against. He is not so much split or doubled as rounded in his resentment, making a three-dimensional claim on that mere image of himself behind which Georges, the erstwhile TV image, insists on retreating. In this emblematic collapse of any sutured interchange, the only absent one is Georges himself.

Such planarity is the empty refuge of the man's cloaked and starved depth: the persona, once again, hidden in plane sight. In Haneke's plotting—its intrigue of mediation finally lifted, if only by default of all empirical solution—the guiding design remains clear enough. The cinematic act of filming narrative surveillance has come down to no more, and no less, than film narrative itself in the present form of its relentless diagnostic optic. What might have been a story of techno-empowerment—the little guy strikes back, in the thriller turn of Hollywood cinema—is instead a disembodied parable to the same effect. As media personality, Georges is at the controls of the videosphere, a power broker of the "apparatus" in Agamben's generalized terms. Indeed, the one time we are fooled by a full-screen image that we think is meant to have advanced plot to a new diegetic scene on his television show's stage set (and that is not, yet again, a surprise surveillance tape), what we have entered upon instead is a digital editing session of the show's prerecorded duration, filling our screen as it submits to rewind and ellipsis. We hear Georges's voice, off-frame, instructing the technicians to elide material in the full-frame image before us, a discourse that has gotten too "theoretical" for mass consumption. Elsewhere, he is himself his own best censor of the difficult. In command of the image, he can be shaken loose from his nervous grip on power only by what Agamben designates as a "profanation of the apparatuses": the media personality "remediatized" in his privacy by the invasive tapes, in precisely their function as figures both for *being seen*—it hardly matters by whom—and (as plot drivers) for needing *to look back* (in present social space as well as in biographical and political time), to recognize the other whose observation you elicit.[5] The buffer zone between Georges and the world must be converted to a weapon against him. Broadcast must be turned to exposure, the apparatus defamed from outside the temples of its power, a media hegemony profaned.

Produced at the height of contemporary surveillance discourse, the two quite different films here paired against each other—one sentimental, one acerbic, one the historical narrative of the recent national past, the other the story of a repressed personal history in its ethical overtones—arrange in different ways to turn the very logic of surveillance inside out. In these two films about the radical other, political and sociological, respectively, the technology of surveillance is itself othered, derealized, rendered metaphoric. Spyware mutates first to a prosthetics of empathy in the one case, then to a final aesthetic transference through literary narrative, while in the other surveillance confronts in reverse the refusal of both self-recognition and the empathy to which it might open. Secondary surveillant identification—through his earphones in Wiesler's mind's eye—achieves en route theater's moral force in *The Lives of Others*, so that menace is turned to clemency. In *Caché,* with Georges fortified against all such lives, the elisions of surveillance anxiety disappear altogether into narrative sequence on the path to a final refusal of sutured recognition.

It is no incidental realism of mise en scène in *Caché* that part of the diagnosis of media's pervasive (if superficial) power has included in the background—unattended on the home TV screen, unrecognized by Georges in its oblique relevance—images of the Iraq war (or, more to the point, of anti-Arab violence in overreaching defense against "terrorism"). These are images that serve to import momentarily into Haneke's closed system of irony—concerning a moral and racial blind spot at the intersection of surveillance and detective plotting—the whole separate contemporary genre (with its upsurge of surveillance tech) to which we next turn, a genre increasingly defined by the equivocal politics of war's digital mediation. Where surveillance is never just metaphoric. For Georges instead, in the evacuated ethical space between his own video journalism and the assault by private videotapes, politics—together with its denials—begins at home.

6 DIGITAL RECONNAISSANCE AND WIRED WAR

When Iraq War footage on the TV monitor of the book-lined townhouse in *Caché* comes to replace surveillance videos that track a guilt by association back to the protagonist's own gradually flayed past, it is a racialized aggression that binds together each phase of home screening—in precisely the eye of political indifference turned to private anxiety. This chapter brings just such grainy video images of Mideast tension and anti-Arab violence forward to full-screen remediation at the site of their own handheld recording, often in surveillance mode. The narratographic investigation that results will be followed by two chapters parceled out—beyond realist counterinsurgency—to post–9/11 time-travel fantasies of antiterrorist intercession in the sci-fi mode of teleportation and its magic audiovisual apparatuses. But even in the Mideast combat films taken up here, the life-and-death stakes of military assault are often attenuated by remote telepresence and its buffering video relays, operational on site, vicarious after the fact: from helmet cam to YouTube.

When pitched, even implicitly, as the critique of an indifferent or inured mass audience, this cinematic gesture has a recognizable political lineage in the history of related visual arts. Take, for example, another monitory "M," six years after Fritz Lang. Before turning to the new image-dominant rather than scene-setting montage that sustains the contemporary war film, consider a photocollage *about* war on film, from 1937, by the famous anti-Nazi polemicist John Heartfield. With its double-ply title, *Mahnung* ("Warning"), this piece (of discrepant fused pieces) is named both for the film image pictured within it and for its captioned setting in the passive ambience of a commercial movie theater, where reception may come without provocation. If the one warning isn't enough, a further polemic reframes it. Heartfield's pastiche layers in several rows of faceless male heads, backs toward us, beneath the frontal stare of an onscreen victim in the violent newsreel footage at which they are staring: a Chinese mother holding a bloodied child in giant close-up, with a toppled bridge and corpse-strewn railroad tracks in the Japanese-ravaged distance. Its German legend, spelled out at the bottom, would translate to:

"Today you still see the war in other countries on film. But know this: if you don't unite to defend yourselves, tomorrow it will kill you too." Recorded violence is no less real for being absent.

In Heartfield's recessional image, the relevant community is already gathered there, as audience, awaiting transformation into a resistant body politic. Until that should happen, however, war on film risks being only a medial distraction, not a call to arms—as much dissociated from felt reality as are the collaged laminates from each other, slamming Asian victims up against inert Western witness. Too often such dissociation is the fate of war on-screen in its nondocumentary modes, shielded from us as spectacle, channeled by the protocols of fictional narrative. Or, failing that in war films of the last decade, decentered by a skittish authenticity of technique into slice-of-death vignettes resembling the daily fodder of broadcast TV and web videos. These are images in which the so-called surgical strike (where the patient dies so that the "operation" may be successful) is hardly as antiseptic as its name might suggest, with "collateral damage" a kind of secondary infection in this nonmedical "theater of operations." And at this writing, the electronic fallout from our wars in Iraq and Afghanistan, concerning unmanned assassination flights, drones on in Capitol Hill debate.

To assess the recent spate of anti-epics in the antiwar mode is, first of all, to reflect on the screen's audiovisual technique in precisely its fit (or ironic misfit) with the military technology of optical surveillance whose aim (in both senses) the films regularly refuse to heroize. War pictures: a category newly equivocated. In the Mideast war film, there is an implicit tension between what, on the one hand, contemporary warfare increasingly does—with the electronic enhancement of its lethal optics—and, on the other, the Hollywood genre into which its latest representations are uncomfortably slotted. Other anomalies call out for a querying of the lexicon, but the genre tag is certainly among them. War pictures: a clause as well as a phrase. Regardless of national politics, war's true regime is scopic (but in this regard always partly phantasmatic, assuming a scope that cannot be summoned to unitary view).[1] Concentrated in the half decade since *Jarhead* in 2005, with its backcast on the first Gulf War, screen narratives of the Iraq and Afghanistan wars down through their depoliticized epitome in 2011's *The Hurt Locker*—films from *Home of the Brave* (2006) to *The Green Zone* (2010)—usually have in common, including their lack of mass appeal, the layered electronic relays of secondary imaging in the place of narrative immediacy. They are often less war movies than movies of combat imaging, less about military spectacle than about the specular apparatus of battlefield surveillance.

War Pictures

In the typically remediated look of US war efforts, the battery of enhanced optical technology does nothing to sustain the classic visual iconography of the war-film genre. There are few panoramic scenes in these narratives of the last decade, no martial choreography, no geometric symmetries of spectacle, few wide-screen needs—or satisfactions—whatsoever. Battle, usually renamed "firefight"—a function more of ad hoc counterinsurgency than grand design—has fragmented into the extreme contingencies of sniping and roadside bomb blasts. War is so total that it is nowhere and everywhere at once. So that what the War on Terror film serves to picture is for the most part a soldiery without a genre. Even when decisively specular in its aerial execution, such warfare has little compelling spectacle. And on the ground, the troops sharing images from their cell phones and camcorders catch no glimpse of a grand *plan* (itself, in French, the term for the scale of a shot). Although the philosopher Paul Virilio has repeatedly linked cinema at large to a battlefield's "logistics of perception," these new films—with their depleted plots of intermittent skirmishes, roadside sabotage by improvised explosive devices (IEDs), recurrent panic, mayhem, and localized reprisal—have lost almost all narrative (as well as martial) *logic* while surrendering perception to the flash of image and its random capture.[2]

"Don't look at the camera! Just go by like you're fighting," barks Francis Ford Coppola in a cameo role as a TV journalist in *Apocalypse Now* (1979). Announces Marlon Brando as Kurtz later in the film: "Horror and mortal terror are your friends. If they are not then they are enemies to be feared." We've come a long way from the cinematic ironies of the Vietnam War's greatest film treatment. En route to the latest Iraq War narratives, we've in fact passed recently through a scene in *Jarhead* (Sam Mendes, 2005) in which marine recruits are whipped into a frenzy for the first Gulf War by a screening of the helicopter juggernaut from Coppola's epic. The allusion is rounded out later in Kuwait—in the period before digital camcorders or cell-phone video—when, no longer pretending not to be televised, some of the soldiers give cautious on-camera interviews to a network journalist about their feelings for the mission.

The next irreversible stage in this development is again technological as well as political. In screen narratives of the second Desert Storm, where American military power comes down on both sides of Kurtz's alternative, a personified Terror is now the stated US enemy. And it is the military that is busy filming itself at every turn, from high-altitude surveillance transmits to those video diaries and cell-phone souvenirs that associate the journals of violence (or its R&R interludes) with what we might call weapons of mass distraction in media culture at large. While seizing on these linked aspects of current Mideast violence, ideological and optical, American films about Iraq and Afghanistan kept failing at the box office. We were told in the press it's too close for comfort, too soon for analysis, too much like free TV to warrant ticket prices. The real problem is that it's too shapeless for plot. Fighting terror with terror is one thing; finding narrative drive or closure for the confrontation, let alone some modicum of catharsis, is another. To say nothing of a formal coherence taut enough to secure a cogent oppositional stance. Instead of some fresh and persuasive emphasis, the frequent antiwar burden of these films feels like stress only in the other sense, disorienting and demoralized—especially when the most salient formal feature, the blanketing of plot by a thick quilt of digital mediation, seems part of a diagnosed syndrome to begin with, where every tour of duty comes equipped with tourist cams and every other move is shot from above in someone else's movie. Battle fatigue has grown stylistic, afflicting the picturing as well as its scene.

The original "shock and awe" was a war-film idea, the imperialist vestige of a genre fantasy, where part of the US arsenal was the very spectacle of its unleashed power. What remains, and for the US troops as well now, is a paranoid setting without a vivid scenario, a genre template left begging for the energies of plot. With no clear demarcation between the good guys and the bad, narrative itself seems stalled, balked. We found no weapons of mass destruction (WMDs) in Iraq, just IEDs detonating everywhere. Strong storytelling is among the casualties of such "improvised" devices. Gone, it bears repeating, are scenographic staples of the combat genre, beachheads to be won, fortresses held. We get instead random checkpoint suicides, grenade and mortar ambushes in blind alleys, frantic house searches, impromptu firefights—all of it saturated by video: not only secondhand embedded footage but the ubiquitous remote control of drone predator surveillance in the high-tech fantasy of an ultimately unmanned victory.

To register the difference between this and the classic war film, even a film made more recently about a "classic" war, we can look to a recent study of the genre over the course of American film history. A stress on collective and national memory runs throughout Elisabeth Bronfen's *Specters of War: Hollywood's Engagement with Military Conflict.*[3] One among many formal markers of this effect appears in her treatment of *Saving Private Ryan* (Steven Spielberg, 1998), whose bookended structure works to circumscribe the nature of epic cinema's place in the shared memory of modern conflict. This structure emerges only after the fact when we realize that the film's cemetery prologue has involved the title character—across a sound bridge of crashing waves—in an apparently subjective flashback to footage of the Omaha Beach landing at which, as a captured paratrooper, he wasn't in fact present (140–41). The war picture is here picturing its own reconstituted iconography. Or put it that the "specter" of mass battle, as envisioned rather than lived, takes shape always and already in the form of screen spectacle, which the latest films have reduced, for the most part, to surveillance video.

In Harm's Sway: Plot Under Siege

To think of this in the more openly paradoxical terms of an unmanned heroics in recent war films is to see the genre problem at once, where the damage is inflicted not just on characters but on plot. Narrative agency is subsumed to technology at every level, from aerial tracking, where characters are just faceless pawns on a monitoring grid, to eye-level confrontations, where any human posture toward an encroaching violence—from suspense to panic—often feels as virtual, as permeated by mediation, as computer interactivity in some low-resolution video game. For the soldier to see action in this context is more like an ocular than a military idiom. In a vocabulary equally familiar to aerial reconnaissance and such high-tech video transmissions, the very programming of a genre, even an antiwar genre, may seem to have crashed—and in part from electronic overload at the plot level itself.

The visible features of this collapse are rampant in the mandatory but hackneyed techniques of digital intervention, where the crisis, decidedly macro as well as micro, shows itself now in tactical surveillance views, now in private camcorder files, each disembodied and impassive—with the space between, in this asymmetric warfare, filled mostly by death. If Vietnam was the "TV war," the occupation of Iraq and Afghanistan is instead a digital-video and laptop war, not only logged but at times waged by electronic relays, with cell phones as well as infrared predator screens helping to trigger the same bombs whose carnage they may also record. In film versions of this conflict, narrative stalemate is thus matched, rather than overcome, by the inevitable and increasingly stale kinetics of its visual treatment. Not just a stylistic tic but a political symptom, these vérité effects are a common denominator easy to lose sight of in the more obvious deadlocks of plotting, even though much of the blockage to narrative drive is in fact regularly located, framed, and diagnosed by just this compulsive optical—rather than ideological—mediation. With no genre formats to count on, these narratives can project only a visual "look," where the graininess of the image, infrared or video, must stand in for the true grittiness of the mission. Without clear lines drawn in the sand, there is only dust on the nervous handheld lens.

Alongside plots openly concerned with capturing enemy images as often as combatants (*Battle for Haditha, Redacted, The Situation*), there are storylines turning on CIA operatives at their keypads, monitors, and cell phones in rapid alternation with agents in the field (*Body of Lies, The Kingdom, Rendition*). Regular intercutting from strategic control centers to war zones is stretched at times, beyond the immediate span of telecommunication, to full-blown parallel editing across hemispheric distances (*Lions for Lambs, Syriana*) in what amounts to a geopolitics of montage. In this obsessive nest of mediations, top-down but also bottom-up, one mode of digital registration is strategic, offensive, potentially ballistic, keeping a latent victim in its remote crosshairs; the other implements a psychic defense mechanism. One is coolly removed by default in aerial surveillance; the other tries to impose a related degree of separation, up-close but impersonal, between bodily violence and its recorded impact. The line between reconnaissance and cognition itself can become as blurred as the images that would sometimes seek to cross it.

Both modes of mediation, stratospheric and atmospheric, from bombs on automatic pilot to videocam headsets, have direct consequences for the main functions of narrative in plot and character, omniscience and subjectivity. Where we expect an encompassing narrative overview, the proverbial big picture, we get only robot scans, objective, uneditorialized. Where we expect the raw drama of combat and its private tolls, we get violence, suffering, and its counterassaults, buffered everywhere by autofocus viewfinders. These Iraq plots can thus be seen struggling to cohere within the intersecting spheres of two broader cinematic kinds: the traditional war (or antiwar) film and the new Hollywood plots of surveillance paranoia, in overseas and homeland settings alike. This dubious overlap is the gray area, and increasingly the no-man's-land, between military action and the deeply mixed message of high-tech technophobia. And the overlap can become in itself a double bind, formal as well as geopolitical, so that a considered recoil from strategic disaster or human atrocity is hard to sustain. Critique dissipates into technique. In the new digital milieu, anything approaching oppositional cinema in a realist combat mode risks being thwarted by the requisite authenticities of its own visualization.

The genuine antiwar film requires of cinema some special work of witness. *Apocalypse Now* wanted to suggest that although you think you've seen it on TV, you've never seen it like this. You had to have been there, and 70mm is the next best thing. That's the gesture of epic reconstruction that survives even the baroque allegorical hyperbole of the Kurtz plot. Nearly half a decade after the Indochina cease-fire, film could at last give us new eyes for the unthinkable. Retrospection is invaluable, but also needed is another kind of distance, technical rather than historical: a stylistic distance lately telescoped or vanished altogether in the new Iraq regime of participant record.

The fact that the United States was still in the thick of the Mideast killing when these films appeared isn't all that prevented a clear ethical and political perspective, then. On top of this, indeed layered directly over it, the continuous video traces of such violence within plot leave next to no space for the visual rhetoric of exposé. In analytic as well as digital terms, there's no exposure time, no lag for ironic or polemical reframing. There's only the electronic tracking of terror moment by moment. The legacy of oppositional cinema, and its leverage, is in large part forfeited by just this relentless instantaneous videography. Here, then, is where ethics and media ethos, politics and style, are impossible to separate. Sure, you may think you've seen it all on YouTube and cable networks, and this time you'd be right, you have: seen it the way the military itself has, at both ends of a lethal stealth—aerial hits and surface ambushes alike—each recorded in the real time of pending annihilation, zoom versus pan, impersonal targeting over against the jittery focus of patrol.

Moreover, it is through just this convergent battery of imaging that the war is subsequently "brought home"—for deliberate video replay as "war porn" on veteran laptops and TV monitors as well as in the shattering form of unwanted memory traces. As part two of an opening desert scenario, or alternately as an attempted genre all its own, the returning-vet film, even without the surveillance cutaways of combat plots, still borrows the contrapuntal techniques of war-zone intercutting: no longer between command central and life (or death) on the ground, but now between lethal intensities in the desert and their brain-injured return, via post-traumatic stress disorder, from the midst of emotional desertion back home. And if this brand of montage is no longer exactly geopolitical in an overt disjunction between center and periphery, or between satellite omniscience and personal agency, it remains the marker of an ethical as well as psychic dissociation. In this vein there are films whose editing disjunctively crosses the emotional fissures of stress disorder between traumatic flashbacks (often via replayed combat video) and a failed acclimation (let alone heroic acclaim) in stateside homecoming (*In the Valley of Elah*, *Badland*), as well as those plots that further alternate (via camcorder flashbacks) between separate ordeals of reassimilation among a loosely knit cast of returning soldiers (*Home of the Brave*, *Stop-Loss*), thus widening the national map of no return. But before any such overview of domestic disintegration, an implacable surveillance overseas. Before the perils of introspection, the war machine as mediated spectacle—where action is repeatedly trapped, and plot curtailed, in the lenses of a power whose flip side is the impotence of being all-seen.

Robomniscience

It is easy to see why the panoptic model—which derives from the idea of a central point of view circumscribing all visible space under a mobile and pinioning gaze—can become a paradigm for omniscient narrative itself. By contrast, the new global technopticon—with its electromechanics of spycams, orbital or otherwise mobile—lets the peopled world roll past under its totalized purview even while arranging for the local vantage of electronic targeting. Establishing the broad model of panoptic control, Foucault's original French title hadn't yet been generalized to the English "discipline" that may in fact preclude the need for punitive intervention: *Surveiller et punir*. In wired war, the same "control panel" regularly—and regulatively—operates both functions.

This pattern is evident again in one of the most recent commercial disappointments among these frequently combined war and espionage films, Ridley Scott's *Body of Lies* (2008). For all its star ammunition, there is no heroic narrative to load. The film's Mideast plot ends where it began, with blurry satellite images of the espied. In a prologue located by intertitle in "Manchester, England," the first shot is of an incendiary videotape playing on the TV screen of a terrorist cell: a Muslim cleric inciting the jihadist cadre to "revenge the American war on the Muslim world." As they do moments later, by exploding themselves along with half a residential block when the counterterror forces are heard moving in. In a sudden shift of perspective from shaky action footage to a delayed establishing shot, this is a blast now captured through an aerial surveillance image remediated on broadcast TV. The circle of violence is self-perpetuating. The cleric's harangue (full-frame, ambiguously live at first), once it is disclosed (by reverse tracking shot) as a video playback on a TV monitor, triggers a real-time violence later disseminated as a TV image.

From there we cut, via intertitle again, to "Samarra, Iraq"—for another urban aerial shot—before zeroing in on the hero at the onset of an espionage plot that returns finally, but with no real finish, to this remote omniscience. In between, and tracked at every turn by cell-phone transmissions between the CIA strategist, Hoffman (Russell Crowe), and his field operative, Ferris (Leonardo DiCaprio), what transpires is a counterinsurgency scheme of such weird ingenuity that it begins to feel more like a metaphor for business as usual than a tactical strike against it. What comes to pass is another endangering of narrative itself, so that the extreme complications of the plot seem to collapse under their own weight as a foregone conclusion. US military presence in the Mideast spawns rather than quells anti-American violence. Preemptive measures serve only to escalate what they would placate. Sound familiar? It's certainly a premise that has found narrative manifestation before. But what if the CIA did more than passively accept the disaster of America's counterproductive presence in Iraq by actually staging its fallout in the breeding ground of jihadist cells? What, that is, if counterinsurgency took the form of counterfeit terrorism in a fabricated parallel universe designed to draw from hiding a leading Al-Qaeda figure jealous of his fictive counterpart? When this coded version of America's self-inflicted setbacks in the region actually succeeds in smoking out the ruthless Al-Qaeda mastermind, his apprehension is rushed and anticlimactic. He's simply whisked away in an unmarked car. Cornering one more bloodthirsty zealot doesn't much matter anymore, at least for narrative design.

As if to confirm that "spying" has no endgame in this new theater of war, the movie whose Iraq segment began in transition from the overhead sighting of the Manchester blast to a panoptic scan of the Samarra cityscape—with its own brewing violence—now closes with the truncation of a continuing electronic reconnaissance directed again at its own agent. More than once before, Ferris has strained skyward to catch a glint of sunlight off the otherwise invisible predator drones. Toward the end, too, our star well knows he's still "on screen." Scott's long final shot borrows much of its unsettling effect by allusion to an earlier film of CIA treachery. In *Syriana*, it is another renegade US agent who is sacrificed in the end as collateral damage in the robot-controlled bombing of an upstart Saudi prince willing to negotiate oil deals with the Chinese, where the assassination is both registered and executed on the targeting grid of a video relay at CIA headquarters. The comparable last satellite perspective of *Body of Lies* seems meant to make us equally nervous for its defecting hero—until it dismisses him as expendable only in the everyday bureaucratic sense. Sick of CIA double-dealing, taken with the Mideast and a local nurse to boot, Ferris has refused his promotion to a Washington desk job and resigned from the agency. The last image peters out while tracking him by remote control as he wanders between the tents of a Jordanian bazaar, until Hoffman answers an offscreen technician's "Are we staying with him?" in the negative: "Buddy's alone—he's all by himself." Privacy can be won only by a flight from the corporate eye. "Copy that . . . Clearing off target." To have been seen is admittedly to have been locked all along in the gunsights of power.

With our dropout hero fallen beneath the radar, cancelled voyeurism is the closest thing to narrative resolution—at least when there's no fuller picture to be had, no rectifying new perspective as well as no further "agency" for any protagonist to serve. Or even embody. Yet it is our own full-frame, 35mm image that now suffers a last digital fritz and breakdown on exit, film devolved in passing to the digital. This ocular conceit is not only an obvious technical deceit, but a further rhetorical turn. There's nothing left to see if the technopticon has lost interest; by the same token, what we've therefore been watching until now has been privileged material. To compensate for any lack of satisfying climax, at least we've supposedly been privy to some top-secret CIA feeds, allowing us for once to see the world the way the secret service does. And not, of course, just visually. For at a certain level of geopolitical oversight—to whose plotting our hero (any hero) is no longer instrumental—all monitored enemy activity, whether or not we foment or even fabricate it, can be made to serve our militarist purposes. A film doesn't have to be even half good to be fleetingly brilliant, which is not to say popular, when it lets American imperialist logic declare itself so nakedly.

Lions for Lambs (Robert Redford, 2007), otherwise talky and obvious, has one gripping visual moment in the same surveillance vein. In the overseas sector of its multiplot structure, two idealistic army recruits are downed and surrounded on an Afghan mountaintop in an aborted helicopter strike. By a sustained irony of scale, the encircling Taliban are kept at bay for as long as possible by the strafings of smart bombs monitored from command central. But not smart enough. When time runs out, the doomed soldiers must at last face the enemy gunmen across real rather than mediated space. At this point we cut away—to remote transmits on the mission-control screens—for the guttering infrared glow of the two fallen bodies in the cessation of all movement. In retrospect, and beyond its grueling exposure of war's new asymmetric destruction, the fatal time lag of those remote-controlled bombings seems, once again, all but allegorical. It is already too late for decisive high-tech (and high-altitude) interventions in this war of ideologies. There is no position left that stands above it all, none that can call all the shots.

Scoped Out

In the absence of any decisive political rather than optic overview, we also have, besides the self-inspection by continuous video imaging among soldiers on the ground, the ad hoc tactics of low-level digital surveillance by antiterrorist bureaucrats at their Mideast desks. The disjointed perspective that results can skew whole plots, as with counterterror films like *Rendition* (Gavin Hood, 2007) or even the more traditional action thriller *Vantage Point* (Pete Travis, 2007), where in each case temporal replay, despite its more or less obvious electronic models, is ultimately a narrative figure rather than a technological function.

In *Rendition,* after an opening suicide bombing in a North African square, the CIA orders the "extreme rendition" of a suspected collaborator. He is soon subjected to waterboarding by the local chief of police, whose investigation of the attack has so far gone nowhere. A tourist camcorder recovered from the blast has shown a woman approaching the bomb-strapped terrorist, but, even after repeated scannings of the video, she can't be identified—and offers no clues. A week later, the police chief's daughter, who had eloped in the meantime with a young jihadist, discovers a plot to kill her father in revenge for his brutal methods. When she races to intercept this vendetta, she enters upon the same scene the film began with, where our sudden flash of recognition (literalized by a brief transitional whiteout of the full-screen image) reveals her as the already-recorded first victim of the blast. With this drastic time loop, the pace of the trick ending goes into mordant slow motion just before her lover's detonation. In this slowed shot/reverse shot of horrified recognition, the Deleuzian movement-image duel has become a time-image *liebestod* in a suture that converts each to the instantaneous absent one. The film's temporal (turned historical) irony compounds itself. If all such violence is a continuous repetition anyway, witnessing has no purchase. And yet what we do see by narrative's own structural emblem is that the sins of the father have already been visited upon the next generation.

Usually digital surveillance and image manipulation are represented within the plot rather than, as with the temporal rewind of *Rendition,* foisted upon it by blunt narrative license (in sliding association there with that forensic camcorder replay). As if intuiting this, most of the Iraq movies are preoccupied with low-altitude and hands-on imaging, even when enhanced by telephoto or night-vision lenses. Brian De Palma's 2007 "docudrama" of a particularly brutal Iraq incident, *Redacted,* exploits this technique of optical processing almost to the point of manic travesty, where the only mission with any focus has become transmission itself.[4] The narrative begins with live video footage at an Iraq checkpoint, overvoiced on the camcorder of a recruit, Salazar, hoping to parlay his harrowing images into film-school admission after his tour of duty. His recurrent digital diary alternates from there on with an interpolated French documentary, embedded journalistic footage, Internet posts on both jihadist and American protest websites, Al Jazeera news broadcasts, incriminating surveillance videos from fixed camera positions on the base, and then, after one of his buddies is blown apart by an IED, more of his camcorder views of the squad's rape-and-murder revenge spree, the victims' bodies finally burned beyond recognition off camera. From there we move to a twin-screen laptop video chat between the tormented officer who didn't try hard enough to stop the violence and his lawyer father back home, urging him to keep a lid on it.

In this cross fire of total visual transcription, Salazar alludes at one point to Jean-Luc Godard by promising on camera that his digital diary will guarantee "truth 24 times a second, 24/7," a boast made just before he is kidnapped from in front of his own tripod by masked Al-Qaeda henchmen and soon executed on (another) camera: the talking head become a severed one. All that can impede this voracious mediation is, in the narrative's very last shot, the digital freeze on the victim's former squad leader fighting back tears as he reluctantly has his picture taken at a homecoming party. His own metaphors for an ineradicable guilt have in fact just rehearsed the very evolution of optical media from photochemical to digital imprint, those searing "snapshots" of rape, murder, and immolation being forever "burned into my brain."

The escalating violence of *Redacted*, barely aspiring to a plot at all, brakes to a halt where many of the homecoming films begin, even as they get no further by way of story than the lingering diagnosis of mental lesions and emotional paralysis. One film promises otherwise for much of its length. *Stop-Loss* (Kimberly Peirce, 2008) tracks a discharged vet, King (Ryan Phillippe), whose justified legal outrage over enforced reenlistment (the "Stop-Loss" program) forces him to go AWOL. At the end, under cover of darkness, he is about to become a "ghost" by crossing illegally into Mexico—a Homeland Security paranoia in reverse—but recommits instead to the ongoing transgression of another foreign border. For we suddenly cut (a shock cut in every sense) to a roll call of the enlisted in broad daylight—as if he's seen the light at last in filing silently onto the army bus for a return to Iraq. Better a corpse than a living ghost. Optical technique is now left, all on its own, to round off the plot as a vicious circle.

The film began, just before a last deadly mission in Iraq, with King's buddies toasting their pending discharge with a handmade video of the sort frequently posted on YouTube and said by the director to have inspired the visual design of the film. These images are soon followed by a grim funeral montage in memory of the subsequently fallen. This is just the sort of personal videolog that the returned vets gather drunkenly to rescreen on a laptop after they've aimlessly resumed their civilian lives. They can't get the war movie out of their heads. Even earlier, the transition from the last round of Iraq violence to a homecoming parade in Texas is negotiated in King's mind by full-screen memories of those obituary videos hastily edited together in the desert, whose silent images drown out at first the patriotic cheers of welcome. Here we see again that recurrent device of traumatic recurrence itself: flashback as digital playback.[5] An encircling irony is painfully clear, in this and many other films shunting between combat record and stateside reprise. The electronic eye inherent in optical surveillance in prosecuting the war is a technology that haunts any attempted extrication from its killing fields.

And if film's own medium can deliver in this ironic way at least some measure of oppositional energy, so, too, is the political capitulation of this one film's ending at least somewhat mitigated. Despite its ethics of renewed duty, the whole closing sequence, with families tearfully waving goodbye, floats past in slightly slowed motion. The film seems sleepwalking through its own worst nightmare of redeployment—again, as in *Rendition*, the pace of ceaseless repetition, no end in sight. The almost subliminal retardation of this last sequence hints less at a ritual solemnity than at a mechanical treadmill of recycled bodies, elegiac before the fact: the true loss that there is no stopping. When mourning is involved at this scale, visual effects don't need to be full-blown ideas, let alone subversive intentions, to help in thinking things through.

Looking with Other Eyes

This much is certainly evident in another multiplot diagnosis of crosswired intrigue in Iraq, *The Situation* (Philip Haas, 2006), which arrives at its climax in a moment of bleak optical, rather than diplomatic, mediation. After he is gunned down by accident in an anti-insurgent raid, the last act of an Iraqi photojournalist smitten with the American reporter heroine is to snap off—almost by a pun on reflex action—a half-dozen spasmodic shots of her, marked by shutter clicks on the soundtrack, as she bends over his mangled body. She notices these stored images only in the LCD preview screen in the film's last scene: a series of increasing close-ups—as if in a decomposed strip of live motion—as she once knelt toward his virtual corpse along a truncated vector of contact. Stressed by this ironic deferral of standard filmic intercutting, so that she has become in effect his posthumous reverse shot, what we sense is that the best any American—or any reporter—could do in an occupied Iraq is to see one's presence in the eyes of the other.

The Situation activates in that closing moment yet another conversion of unexpected plotting into political irony, as we saw at a more inclusive narrative scale with the CIA-generated terror cell in *Body of Lies*. There, anti-American violence came to be simulated by the Americans themselves. A similar vein of displaced aggression is evident in the narrative false lead of another and stronger film. US soldiers perpetrate a collective act of violent reprisal in a bleak border zone between military and civilian authority: the stabbing and burning of a defenseless victim and the butchering of the body before its hasty burial in the desert sands (where it is later unearthed only as dismembered, charred bones). No, this isn't a version of the real-life and real-death events in Iraq that triggered De Palma's *Redacted*, with the repeated penetration of the innocent victim before slaying her and burning her corpse. As the withheld, shocking, and in fact dislocated revelation of *In the Valley of Elah* (Paul Haggis, 2007), it is not a case of interracial rape and mayhem this time, but another kind of pent-up violence: the pointless homeland murder, by repeated knife wounds, of a returning vet by a drunken member of his squad, followed by its starkly literal "cover-up" in the New Mexico dirt, just on the invisible dividing line between military property and the beat of the local police. In every sense, the dream of repatriation is dead on arrival.

When Deerfield (Tommy Lee Jones), father of the missing soldier, a vet and former military police detective himself, first goes into action, however, we for once, with the facts still held back from us, seem caught up in a real genre plot. But when this detective thriller has its mounting suspicions of criminal US behavior in the Mideast confirmed instead in the American West, it is again an uprush of mediated images that keys the shift from factual disclosure to deflected recognition. At the outset, Deerfield thinks he'll find clues on the cell phone he confiscates from his son's barrack room, but what he retrieves are for the most part "unstable" and "degraded" shots of violence, torture, and panic in Iraq, often recorded from inside his son's armored vehicle, including one lingering, inexplicable roadside image of a young boy's body, which the investigating father prints off at one point, without explanation, on a commercial photocopier. It is only later, when he has uncovered the implausible and macabre facts of his own boy's stateside murder, that this proud veteran must own up to the causal connection between it and the contagious overseas violence.

He does so only by letting the truth be driven home to him (at the now-shared controls of abusive force). This unfolds when, leaving the scene of one mindless crime, he takes the wheel of his own truck only to hallucinate his way back into his son's previous violence. Suddenly the screen jumps—across flashbacks from the cell-phone images that have previously riveted him—to an inset and subjective 35mm realization of the culminating Iraq incident in his now-unclouded mind's eye: the deliberate running down of someone else's innocent son in the road. You don't have to have been there. You only have to be willing to envision it, to internalize the optical record as your own inherited flashback. Deerfield becomes the ideal viewer of the movie he's in. The whiplash exchange between then and now, us and them, is the immediate political charge of this climactic montage. Digital surveillance via optical data mining, here on a one-to-one basis, breaking as it does with the system of suture, has brought the trauma into focus from another space and time. The film that opens with a logo pretending to be a video image recovering from its digital glitches and breakups has, two hours later, closed instead by foregrounding its inherent cinematographic power to figure an ethics of clarified vision.

Same with a stunning moment near the climax of *Battle for Haditha* (2007) by the British documentarian Nick Broomfield, who this time fictionalizes US military violence in Iraq even while using real ex-marines to improvise most of the dialogue. The high-profile news story from November of 2005: US troops erupt in mass murder as revenge for a roadside bombing. The invented backstory: Al-Qaeda's role in the international videotape exposé of these American war crimes. When a bomb detonated by cell phone destroys a Marine Humvee, within minutes the incensed squad launches an arbitrary counterattack on the adjacent neighborhood, killing two dozen Iraqis, many of them noncombatants, including women and children. The savagery comes to light only in the end because the insurgents who trigger the explosion and inadvertently precipitate the neighborhood rampage are instructed to "film everything" in the mass reprisal so that "the world will see what America is doing" (the obverse and complement to the jihadists' routine use of successful bombings caught on video as a terrorist recruitment tool).

And a further media twist, which torques round to a point before the bombing plot has even gotten underway. For one of the two Al-Qaeda conscripts is first introduced in the act of dispensing rather than recording images at a video store, slipping DVD porn to US soldiers making their rounds at gunpoint. The truly obscene footage of this image vendor, however, will come only later: first the house-by-house camcorder record of bullet-riddled families, then his filming of their mass funeral, and finally a videotaped interview with the lone surviving child of a slain family. When jihadists leak this videolog of war crimes to *Time* magazine, for broadcast in turn on American TV ("Student Footage Reveals Marine Cover-Up"), the loop of secondary mediation is fully closed. Yet there is one visual sequence that has achieved its chilling schematic power by breaking free from all the familiar optical layering dutifully remobilized here by Broomfield, everything from crosshaired rifle sightings, or the digital grids of drone scans in command-post relays, to President Bush rebroadcasted in a flak jacket on Arab TV as if to inflame anti-American sentiment.

Burrowing through all this at the film's violent apogee, Broomfield's ordinarily handheld camera locks in on an arresting—because eerily arrested—point of vision without audition. The buildup to this bravura shot is traced in clear cinematographic stages. The so-called "360-degree war"—where, without a real front, death can come at you from any direction—is reversed here, in the film's orgy of house-by-house retaliation, by the rotary swish pans that take in, and take out, whole rooms at a time in a single sweep of surveillance and annihilation. But at one turn in the mounting violence, the point of view is exchanged—as it so rarely is in these films—for that of an Iraqi subject at the receiving end of this line of fire. At the sound of approaching gunshots, an elderly man goes to his protective front-door peephole to "see what's happening." Through a blurry iris shot, we watch the US soldiers blast open an outer gate with grenades—before cutting back to an interior side view of this incidental victim shredded through the door by machine-gun fire and blown halfway across the room.

From this result of a sutured countershot through the useless miniature lens of domestic "surveillance," the filming has every reason to withdraw. So it is that the narrative POV suddenly cuts—and drops—to the empty space under a still-occupied bed, where only the camera has had time to hide. In this fixed, prolonged, abject shot, during which all sound but the lugubrious orchestral score has been dialed out, we are trapped in a fixed-frame view of a pair of marine feet (the US "boots on the ground") around which a rain of empty shells pelts the floor—until all motion subsides on the mattress above them, above us. In this visualized multiple discharge of a self-defeating revenge, the true American footprint is indelibly left on the region. Probing well beyond the preceding style of faux documentary, here is a devastating optical metaphor that pits reciprocally faceless cultures against each other over the unseen middle space—and void—of death.

To get such an irony down in a single framed image is about all one can ask of any antiterror film, as with the mediated flashback montage that closes *In the Valley of Elah*. Since the violence in Iraq has been repeatedly laid open to video transcript, a screen narrative true to the fabric of digital record and surveillance—to the regime change in media as well as military control—can't pretend to show us something otherwise unseen. But as cinema rather than webcam upload or cell-phone file or posted Internet image or infrared satellite feed, narrative film, even in default of plot solutions, can nonetheless work to show us some aspect of this bloodshed seen otherwise. And this even if, after all the violence, what we are further made to see in Broomfield's averted shot is the need at times, a need human enough, to look aside from the often-mutual brutalities of killers and killed in this pervasive reign of terror. Though film may try taking on a collective nightmare, and taking up an oppositional stance toward it, there is still only so much we can bear having the camera take in for us.

Battleground Zero: "Duel" as Genre Throwback

The asymmetry of that last framing has a way of reframing a larger issue: the rarity of the "shoot-out" in the current dramaturgy of war. One recalls again Gilles Deleuze's account of *M* and the underlying narratological transformation—pivoted on the duel format—from an establishing "situation" into its revised state (S'). There is actually one plot from the overseas War on Terror that manages to stabilize (or bracket) the conflict long enough to evoke this more prototypical movement-image format of SAS'—where the transformative action, in this case, is that of heroic deactivation itself. *The Hurt Locker* (Kathryn Bigelow, 2008) does arrange for that climactic duel with the enemy necessary in classic cinema to stage the resolution of opposed (whether or not separately montaged) forces. Here the duel is between man and mechanics, American soldier and the delegated violence of a faceless enemy in time-bomb form, and the victory is indeed for once over terror itself in a defusing of an imminent IED blast. This film's reversion from those refracted, hypermediated narratives more characteristic of Mideast war pictures to the monolithic (if jagged-edged) pace of the movement-image explains, no doubt, a good part of its success with the critics, if not (yet again) with a mass ticket-buying public. This, plus the fact that the main narrative action is in the service, via a lone American hero, of preventing violence and death for a change, rather than perpetrating it. Not uplifting, the film has at least—within its suspended political critique—a satisfying sense of dramatic form.

On top of that, and helping to explain its unique succès d'estime, its cinematographic treatment avoids the stylistic pitfalls of the other Iraq and Afghanistan films, their vérité deference to embedded and shakily relayed points of technologically aided view, dizzying and dispersive, splintering all sense of unmediated agency. *The Hurt Locker* does so by making these signature conditions of the conflict *entirely* stylistic: the rack focus, the broken 180-degree rules, the swish pans, even the most unorthodox jump cuts—the last instancing, for montage theorist Jacques Aumont, a clear case of the digital "image," touchstone of a postfilmic aesthetic, in ascendancy over "vision" (in anything like its classical narrative articulation via suture).[6] These tics of the unsourced image, tethered to no sightlines, are no longer the diegetic interplay of prosthetically enabled character perspectives in a lethally contested space. They are the inherited gestures of narrative camerawork per se, absorbing discrepancies and fissures into a handheld aesthetic reminiscent of—though not anchored directly to—an otherwise ubiquitous and wearying cross fire of electronic sightings and surveillance elsewhere in Mideast visual representations. Far more than the adept and tension-addicted hero whose concentrated labors we linger over, the film seems itself jittery on his behalf. The one extended exception, in a protracted firefight wedged between the bomb defusing operations of the main narrative line, may in fact be designed to orient the rest of the technique in combat optics, as the hero alternates between portable telescopic sight and rifle barrel in aligning his assault against a bunkered and unseen enemy. Through the very prolongation of the episode, the sustained facelessness of the human enemy is symbolically acknowledged. But the real duel remains.

Working toward the film's overall desubjectivization of cinematic optics, where the manic becomes largerly machinic (or psychological only by contagion and displacement), the first extended scene of Bigelow's narrative isolates, foregrounds, and then purges from its melodramatic system—even while dispersing them into sheer unmotivated camerawork—the distancing devices of explicit electronic sighting in connection with embattled human sight. The film opens, that is, with the disorienting jump-cut footage, including digital skids and breakups, of low-angle traveling shots. Only gradually do we understand these views as the POV of a flimsy ground-level robot caught in the process of defusing a makeshift bomb. The bot (subbing for a human body) soon suffers mechanical failure (loses the first of all tools, its wheel) and is never seen—nor seen *via*—again. From there on it's mano a nitro, in a duel to be humanly identified with. Though the soldier's enterprise is largely depoliticized in *The Hurt Locker*, the anthropocentrism of the film's unmediated vision—once the camera-fitted robot malfunctions its way to the sidelines—does, I think, shed a clearer-than-ever light on what goes wrong, dramaturgically, with so many other films of this cycle, this subgenre. Except in outbreaks of nonmilitary violence, many of their protagonists are never quite all there, but merely looking on at some degree of optic separation. By contrast, the hero's body in *The Hurt Locker* is very much on the line.

With Bigelow's film before us, further light is cast, too, on the larger problem of representing war, and not least the blanket War on Terror—a problem for which the Iraq and Afghanistan narratives are such exacerbated test cases. In this respect, visual texture and its calculated optical regress in these films point to a narratographic register for the more general point made by Fredric Jameson in an essay called "War and Representation."[7] He shows how the structural problem with the narrative treatment of war in literature (which is also, in film, a problem of mediation) is that the focusing of agency around a single hero will not serve to constellate the larger "action" (in the military sense) at stake, or the "mission," even while reliance instead on the squad, cadre, or cohort, to say nothing of the battalion, offers too amorphous a narrative vector to carry the plot if not the day. Jameson rightly sees a failed resolution between, one might say, the abstraction of the "cause" and the sense data of its prosecuted "effects" in action. But he stops short of mapping this in the dialectical terms of his familiar semiotic square so as to determine the "cognitive horizons" (and potential "political unconscious") of the battle plot and its representational breakdowns.[8] As a foursquare diagram of this sort would make clear, the evaporation of heroic agency that Jameson notes is all the more obvious in the hypermediated optics of War on Terror films. The analytic gesture invited, in his typical use of the semiotic grid, would be to resist the initial binary as exhaustive (the finalized either/or of abstraction versus sensation) and instead to diversify a preliminary (and supposedly primal) contrast into the diagonal poles of its more absolute contradictories. Antinomy is thus ramified into a fuller semantic field. It might have looked like figure 6.01 in schematic form.

Any totalization suggested by the concept of total war still founders on the dichotomy between idea and execution, abstract "action" as conceived and strategized (say counterinsurgency) and the event(s) of its enactment on the ground. The desperate attempt (typical of most war narratives) to resolve the establishing dichotomy between abstract and

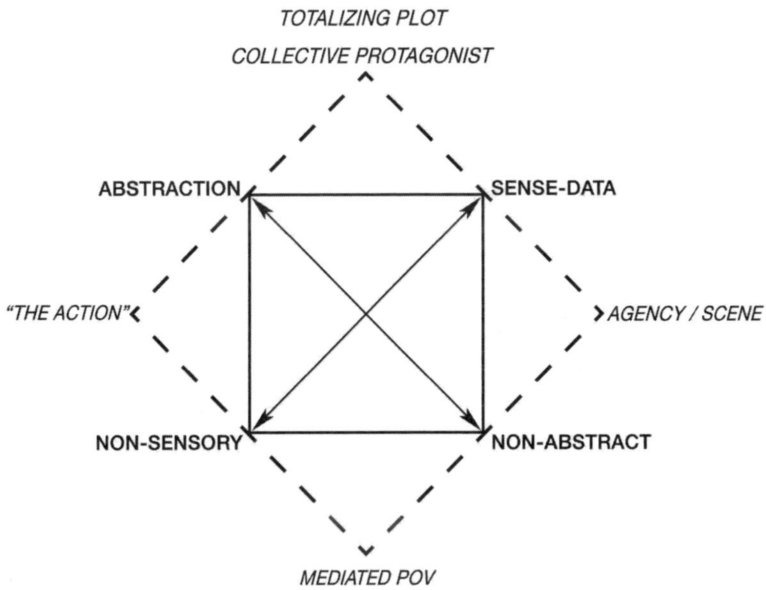

Fig. 6.01

concrete determinants of an ultimately collective protagonist (the corps, rather than the private body)—pitched between a nonsensory abstraction of the "war effort" and the nonabstract viscerality of its exertions in the "battle scene"—is all the more apparent, given the constraints of its literalized optical perspective, in the cinematic treatment of war (though this is not Jameson's particular subject in the essay). And a film like *The Hurt Locker*—all exponential suspense, little US-perpetrated violence in sight, fueling the same adrenalin rush in us that it serves to diagnose in its hero, and relating each implicitly to the video-game venting of energy that another and more neurotic squad member has a version of shell-shocked recourse to—is a film that has entirely hedged its dramatic bets. By reverting to the classic movement-image duel in a human triumph over low-tech and jerry-rigged explosives, the narrative wins its applause by losing much of the war's whole context. Deleuze would be the first to recognize that, under the sway of globalized computational forces, the time-bomb thriller—in an almost nostalgic movement-image mode—can scarcely defuse the broader militarist implications of even its own optic treatment. With the digital time-image subsumed at once to the age of disembodied electronic transmission, to the terrestrial contraction of time and space, and to the new remote scan of surveillance's killing *fields of view,* the traditional viewing act, the channel of vision itself—once surrendered to the image, to sheer interface—has a hard time refocalizing itself as an agency of the look.

Moreover, returning to our developing version of a Jamesonian semiotic gridwork, the blocked overlap—in conceptualizing war—between strategic design and local performance, martial scheme and violent contingency, would find in the very technology of computerized combat a unique version of double negation (the neutral fourth term of neither/nor in Jameson's typical graphings, submerged in the bottom quadrant). Given the cases before us, this neutered zone would locate that blinkered focus (and either abrogated or, in some cases, delayed overview—kicked up to aerial reconnaissance) that is repeatedly signaled by the nonsensory (i.e., mediated, secondarized) but also nonabstract (i.e., perceptual) nature of the electronic POV: optic, not ocular, all image, no vision. The senses of sight and audition involved at this remove are neither engaged nor afflicted in the same way as in unmediated conflict. Such a high proportion of the action in these recent screen treatments seems tied to the neo-Deleuzian agent as spectator—that is, to the solider as himself an embedded videographer of his own tedium and ordeal, hooked on (as well as up to) the laptop relays (and morbid replays) of his digital record. Such war films are hampered by the very ethos of optical recording by which the narrated events are themselves navigated. As a result, these film narratives can make little sense of the remediated senses themselves under siege by the war machine, a machine that is thoroughly computerized and, indeed, increasingly remote. For it is the work of these narratives, even when not the manifest intent, to tolerate (at their commercial peril) an implosion of form and content so complete that they replicate the nervous uncertainty of vision that their heroes both suffer in action and reproduce in their video transcripts. In this cinematographic syndrome, there is little distance, little chance of a measured and critical narrative detachment, little vision apart from an immersive wired sighting. Once war has been all but redefined as the technopticon fully loaded, all derivatives of omniscience are compromised, even while all subjectivity is displaced to the online melodrama of video witness.

Formal analysis reaches a kind of lower limit at the point of such films' own stylistic impasse, where technique and potential critique collide with, and elide, each other. When the *exposé* of digital prosthesis, including its dehumanized interface with an alien terrain and its people under high-tech assault, finds its only proper *exposition* in more of the same optical displacement, the crucial distinction between evidence and investigation grows as blurred as the handheld image or low-resolution satellite feed that must convey them both. So it is that, from issues of both narrated aerial surveillance and self-voyeurized violence in the handheld mode, any full account of such war pictures must back out (or down) one level to the stratum of their latest hybrid mix—as image systems—of both digital and celluloid representation. Where two impulses overlap and perturb each other: contemporaneous technological authenticity and narrative technique.

Even when not shot entirely in high-definition digital video (as was *Redacted*), these are films about a computerized warfare saturated in its own right by optical electronics, the fragmented kinetic textures of whose screen treatment are already standard evening-news fare. Digital war in video transmission has, therefore, a hard time being remediated by "realist" cinema into anything we don't know too well already, not just in its political and moral quagmire but in its visual style. And a hard time—even once bringing such trauma and atrocity to reframed view—of getting any cinematographic, and hence "editorial," distance on them. An aspiration toward broadcast vérité collapses into a disempowered aesthetic of the familiar.[9] One frequent result is just what we've been noticing. The leverage needed for an often-intended ethical recoil—failing a more strongly imposed (and therefore already inauthentic) narrative line in these shapeless conflicts—is short-circuited a priori by this redoubling of topic and representational mode (another case of ocular cause subsumed to its stylistic effects) within the twin ambits of amateur recording and satellite overview.

Strictly speaking, in medial terms, *filmed* wars are mostly behind us. Digital capture is increasingly the medium of record as well as of execution. War pictures are one thing; but now computerized picturing makes war. In the coils of drone predation, for instance, what is shot down is also, for the record, shot—as well as triggered by this same automatic optic recognition in the first place. And in the digital sublime of counterterrorist sci-fi, the disembodied human projectile—the broadcast body as sheer data stream—offers its own version of a surgical strike, a preemptive search and seizure, in the recursive timeline of an alternate reality. Or, say, in a parallel geopolitical universe. As confirmed by such paramilitary derivatives of the war film in sci-fi guise as *Déjà Vu* and *Source Code*—and indeed across war's treatment in each main technological phase of screen manifestation, once photomechanical, now postfilmic—an undeniable tendency has long been endemic. In sum—if never in conclusion, because war keeps happening, both on and, if you will, increasingly *in* camera—cinema, as with visual art more broadly, can in itself contemplate war as a case of the *image unto death*.

7 RETROSPECULAR EYES

One way to review the arc of discussion so far involves settling for the impurities of narrative designation once they settle out from more "stable" compounds. The "surveillance film" is no one's idea of a recognized canonical genre—and if only a subgenre, then "sub" to what: detective film? action thriller? psychodrama? Even when surveillance does end up substituting for one overriding generic expectation or another and becomes in fact the dominant narrative chord, still this doesn't make for a genre in itself—at least not yet in cinema history. Surveillance and criminal tracking have always been themes (well before Fritz Lang; think only of *The Cabinet of Dr. Caligari*), whether articulating the main spine of a plot or traversing it as a secondary motif. But what's changed over time is both the ethical and technical centrality of this thematic charge.

Further, in the last decade or more, surveillance has also become a mode—I'm almost tempted to say a style. It has grown into a means for treating narrative material of whatever sort, even established genres like the war film or sci-fi: treating it at a distance, reframed, mediated, and, because often surreptitious, bringing at times a margin of unease with it into the auditorium of theatrical viewing. Even when the surveillance motif is intermittent, the means (the mode, the style) can be pervasive. More and more often lately, we watch watching—with much of the pertinent genre action filtered through various covert relays and video captures. To borrow an odd throwaway line from the first of two films that remain for extensive discussion: "Surveillance has two *l*s"—as if one for the etymologically phantasmal *veil* it strips, the second for a root verb it nominalizes. Apart from any such incidental orthographic point, the 2006 detective hero of *Déjà Vu* is in fact correcting the misspelling committed on the spot by a cyberoptics technician. Lately, confronting such a desk jockey, it is indeed the action hero who should know. For whether he is its agent or more frequently its object, surveillance is the thriller protagonist's new métier. And in his mission there often resides as well, residually, if only fantastically, the hand-to-hand-combat action so often excluded by more realistic films in the wired-war genre. It is as if all that mere looking in the mode of the time-coded image, however riveting in the marvels of its remote control, needs to burst out into the movement-image duel after all, the time-stamped sighting now an immersive scene.

Spygame Videology

The box-office benchmark for surveillance blockbusters certainly belongs to James Cameron's 2009 CGI epic, *Avatar,* whose title in fact names the fantastic means—a method borrowed from cinema's rival in on-screen entertainment, electronic gaming—for entering vicariously, through a computer-generated virtual surrogate, into worlds otherwise unimagined and unavailable. *Avatar* is a spy thriller in which the double agent is literally doubled by a body not his own, sleeker, more agile, a biogenetic camouflage. It is the paraplegic veteran, otherwise confined to a wheelchair, who is assigned that empowering role, his job to infiltrate an alien environment as agent provocateur. Then, too, like any gamer, he is the catalyst for all action, which eventually backfires according to cinematic plan. Unlike gamers, however, he is found at his computer only when the excitement is over, assigned the further role of its keyboard scribe, logging in his adventures after the fact—rather than downloading them from their coded program. Still, this supplemental chore tasks the entire film with the obvious logic of a gamer interface, rather in the way that Cameron's *Titanic* (1997) begins with a present-day computer simulation of the sinking ship so as to offer the candid baseline for its CGI extrapolations.

In each case, the just slightly displaced medium *is* the message. Same with those two other surveillance films in the sci-fi genre, *Déjà Vu* (Tony Scott, 2006) and *Source Code* (Duncan Jones, 2011). These are films whose machinic surveillance—through the paramilitary magic of new computerized optics, and in the even more explicit mode of detection heroics—locates in fact the full weight of their sci-fi burden, trespassing as their short-term time-traveling heroes do on a past space rather than being launched into a futuristic otherworld. There are no spaceships in such cases, just computerized time transporters. In the process, several uneven techno-thematic developments are overlapped in a crossbred descent from those recent cyber-thrillers remobilized for screen treatments of the globalized War on Terror. On this understanding, Friedrich Kittler's historical model has swallowed its own tail in the synchronic ironies of technique. Electronically devised military optics do in fact precede the very media application and commercial deployment that now, in the case of this latest phase of the big-screen action genre, turn back on their own developmental conditions to dissect the video armatures of both paramilitary reconnaissance and assault.

At which point the digitization of the war film (as of war itself)—aligning that classic screen genre with a broader, if more diffuse, cycle of surveillance films—sees its mutation as well into Homeland Security sci-fi like *Déjà Vu* and *Source Code*. At the same time, the venerable narrative format of spywork detection in the manner of CIA or Interpol manhunt has been directly crossed (and even cross-wired) with a new phase of tech-excluded—yet all the more unabashedly computer-generated—fantasy. Time travel as preternatural premise, that is, has been shifted to a psychic mining of human memory banks in Christopher Nolan's *Inception* (2010), with the expected hypertech apparatuses in a story of corporate spying replaced by mechanically unaided raids on the substrata of consciousness, all cutting-edge electronic gadgetry gone into curious remission.

And since Nolan's film, this tendency, too, persists. Why this suppression, or sometimes outmaneuvering, of high-tech mediation—as in an otherworldly fantasy of defied predestination like *The Adjustment Bureau* (George Nolfi, 2011)? This is a film in which the superhuman rather than electronic premise, "We monitor the entire world," is a boast accomplished without fiber optics, just a God's-eye-view. Why this frequent downplaying of surveillance technology when it is everywhere to be seen in daily life on the way to the multiplex, and even in the theater lobby's own security cameras? Why the exclusion of keypad wizardry, given the video games one might stay home to play instead? It isn't just that the fantasy thriller as genre is now more freewheeling in its plot options than anything permitted by the technological inventions of sci-fi, whose devices are increasingly hard to render exotic. It's also that these action fantasies repeatedly imagine what amounts, even when unspoken, to a willed escape from the whole spectrum of such technology, everything from quotidian prosthetics to the logistics of a digital technopticon. It is an escape that registers as false consciousness with regard to its own production values, to say nothing of its cultural context in the era of social interface.

"We monitor the entire world." Such is the contemporary language of hidden surveillance cams, satellite tracking, or data scanning when used, instead, as mere metaphor for divine artifice in *The Adjustment Bureau*—rather than taken literally as computerized oversight in the standard paranoia fare of military-industrial espionage. Either way, though, and as we've seen in films from *Enemy of the State* through *The Bourne Legacy*, an anxiety over ubiquitous monitoring pervades the latest action-thriller trend in the fantastic genre, with its particular closural fantasy of getting out from under view. These films tend to occlude their expected sci-fi horizons for a vanishing point in erotic romance, risking all for love and its privatizing of desire. Here is a pattern not unfamiliar in the history of Hollywood's uneasy encounter with new media, from radio and TV through video games and digital surveillance. A confrontational or even crossbred aesthetic (wide-screen versus small screen, new "navigational" storylines, for instance, rather than traditional plots) tends nonetheless to mask audiovisual assimilations or enhancements with an ethics of resistance. Boosted cinematic technique often goes so far as to help show how the technology it borrows goes *too* far.

And this mix of animus and fascination, all the clearer in the age of CGI animation, is best understood against the backdrop of previous genre maneuvers. A long-standing common denominator of tech thrillers, beginning with the first 1980s wave of digitization—and Hollywood's corporate discomfort about competing image systems—consists in the various deflections of such topicality: the muting or erasure of computerization as *media* topic, its transmutation by the dodges of plot into other versions of social disquiet and technological paranoia, as, for instance, in that earlier industrial moment, into the dangers of mainframe war games or undetectable cyborgs infiltrating social space, as represented in such films as *WarGames* (1983), *Robocop* (1987), and *The Lawnmower Man* (1992).[1]

Since then, and even in their own deployment of digital technology as spectacle, screen plots are frequently arranged to distract us from the obvious by the improbable, from our technological dependence to otherwise afforded marvels. And long after the early years of countercomputer thematics, given the wholesale corporate absorption of electronic platforms and techniques into mainstream cinema production, what is now more often staved off by minimized electronics within a fictional narrative is just this new complicity, rather than any former competition, between the specular apparatus of cinema and a digitized screen technology. This avoidance, this deflected tech, tends to be negotiated by an implied politics of the digital regime, where excesses of mediation and surveillance within the narrative are checked and redirected, even when mostly unnamed as such. According to an elusive ratio of production values to moral valuation, recent film plots often appear to be forging a silent escape pact with their own medium.

Panoptic Bureaucracy

"We are the people who make sure things happen according to plan," says the squad leader of the business-suited archangelic syndicate in *The Adjustment Bureau,* followed by his claim to "monitor" all worldly activity as if to technologize the vocabulary not just of eternal oversight but of divine intercession—yet with no portable viewing devices or digital data caches involved. These overlords are instead old-fashioned telepaths whose remote-control power, entirely nonelectronic, is aimed at managing the hero's ascent to president-"elect" in a theological as well ballot-box sense, though couched in the boardroom lingo of the "chairman" and his long-term "Plan." In the radically supernatural plot of divine election in *The Adjustment Bureau,* human agency must refuse its assigned fate as a mere pawn in the overview of the Plan. Yet such a monitory politics of escaped surveillance and embraced personal contingency recruits a CGI poetics almost as if to remind us of the electronic mediation that would normally focus such concerns. When the master plot of the chairman—extraterrestrial CEO as executor of human history—is revealed to the hero as the literal book of his fate, a diary of the future, its pages are the place where, as the saying goes, everything is written. Or more like encoded. For the open surface of this divinatory volume—even before a blue lifeline (in CGI animation) snakes through the black-and-white of time's micromanaged labyrinthine turns and their red-hot flashpoints—looks in its schematic intricacy like nothing so much as a computer motherboard remediated on an iPad screen.

The lurking unease raised by *The Adjustment Bureau,* then, is a sense that corporate self-maintenance does indeed, short of a miracle, tend at least indirectly to run our lives, rule our futures, call all the shots—and reduce all supernatural surmise to a mere *faith in the new world order.* When at the end of the film, having thwarted his monitored destiny, the hero finally takes the prescribed book of fate into, as it were, his own hands, its later pages vanish into the freed-up space of the indeterminate as if with the F/X equivalent of a sorcerer's disappearing ink. This particular electronic effect is at least as much a cinematic conceit as a narrated instrumental procedure, a matter of screen poetics rather than any notable electronic turn in the plot. Here is one digital excision that has nothing to do with the kind of mind-wipe narrative of computer sci-fi, but is primarily a visual analogue—ceding to the unknown—of truncated plotting itself. And its release to the open-ended.

For the contemporary audience, it's not really the Plan that anyone worries about, but the networked capitalist system—for which the supernatural variant of digital surveillance, even when foiled in a visual conceit for resisted cosmic programming, remains both a symptom and an apt emblem. It is from an imposed extraterrestrial determinism that the proven escape in *The Adjustment Bureau* is figured, at the level of medium rather than morality play, only after a series of secret portals has been traversed by the hero, in the climactic chase sequence, like hypertext windows opening onto digitally composited alternate worlds. What comes next and last, after the expunged text of the hero's codified future, is the old-fangled, quintessentially predigital technique of slow motion in the final shot. Hero and heroine are loosed into the flux of urban street traffic—just two among the throng, the no-longer-chosen (but instead choosing) ones—as they undulate hand-in-hand toward the camera and their future. It is a future they're willing to let take (by optical metaphor) its own good time, freed from the treadmill of quasi-digital mapping into the hoary rhetoric of slow-motion romantic closure, the happily ever-so-slowly after.

A device notably dated elsewhere, like slo-mo lyricism, is meant to be redeemed here in relief against the tacit backdrop of surveillance tech in supernatural disguise. Far more typical these days is a fear of global monitoring answered in kind from the ground up, with the hero taking the system of image relay under his own implausible control. It is only in the openly sci-fi variants of this techno-action premise that no secondary credibility need be strained to achieve this turnaround. I have called *The Adjustment Bureau* a film of "defied predestination." So, in a sense, with the two sci-fi surveillance films to which we now turn, where such temporal defiance takes the ex post facto form of time travel for the purpose of prevented violence—and this in opposition not to supernatural but to geopolitical forces otherwise beyond control. The antifantastic is turned inside out. Refused predestination becomes a plot, instead, of defied diachrony itself.

Wired Manhunts and the Mind Game

Dateline: 2006/2011. The issue of domestic sabotage is raised by two schematically twinned film narratives in direct narrative contrast with military enlistment for Mideast service in the War on Terror. Planted by a malcontent civilian in each plot, a homemade bomb causes scores of deaths on a vehicle of mass transport. Top-secret paramilitary surveillance is called upon for forensic investigation, its computerized ingenuities gradually (by protracted delay) veering off into sheer sci-fi. I describe these two films interchangeably. In the process, they appear to gloss each other's fantasies. So thoroughly surveilled and scanned is this terrorist near-past that its least clue can be isolated and analyzed. But more than that. As revealed to us only by a postponed disclosure, it happens that elapsed time can be made present again, recreated, entered and reinhabited: like movies—if they were real. But only one lone hero per plot—on computerized loan to this cataclysmic past—has the will and stamina for more than audiovisual surveillance and information mining: for reversing the so-called course of history as well as its data streams; for making a preemptive strike against terrorism and actually rescuing lives rather than just assigning guilt. He defies life-threatening technological odds and, saving the world in microcosm, also gets the girl, bringing her back from a death his transported presence has forestalled. It's uncanny: they feel like they've met before. The couple, that is—but the films too, in a sense.

Yes, *Source Code* (2011) is *Déjà Vu* (2006) all over again, taking its place in the spate of post–9/11 films that constitute a kind of paranoid cycle all their own: a "Homeland Security" genre of metasurveillance fueled by the ultimate fantasy of turning back the clock on disaster. These are films of stateside trauma (including *State of Play* and *Eagle Eye*) where narrative optics, usually matched closely to automatic digital scans within the plot, are related, in turn, on the geopolitical home front, to the disparate satellite feeds and fragmented narrative omniscience in the Iraq and Afghanistan war movies themselves: films that share our queasiness not only about robotic violence but about its associated prosthetic analogues in all manner of computerized remote agency.

When not openly foregrounded, however, such machine agency may just as often suffer repression as plot device, left only to its manifestation in cinematic technique itself. This is where the electronic assists to industrial screen production may sometimes operate, upgraded, within Christian Metz's distinction between visible and invisible *trucage* (the F/X that are special enough to see, and may, in turn, be thematized as tools, versus those that pass unnoted by the eye in order to sustain other visualizations).[2] This minimization of topical (optical) techne happens not just in *Inception* and *The Adjustment Bureau* but in other films where time-travel and excavated memory (rather than just data mining) are delinked from explicit digital apparatuses and made to seem paranormal and apparitional. Many of these films are part of the cycle known as the "puzzle" or "mind-game" film, in which a trick ending forces the rescanning (sometimes in explicit flashback) of everything we've seen to that point.[3]

Such plots are thus the structural opposite, and in fact ontological negation, of what this study has left to explore as the *instrumental mon-*

tage of other sci-fi (rather than fantasy) narratives. Or call it *diegetic montage*, where reality itself can be cross cut. The greatest theorist of the fine line dividing these two forms (fantasy from sci-fi) in their literary incarnation, Tzvetan Todorov, sees the genre question disappearing in the end into the medium as a whole, when the uncanniness equivocated by the fantastic as plot type (until it is explained away as scientific "marvel") comes to be understood as the uncanniness of literature at large.[4] So, too, mutatis mutandis, with the salient mutations of screen visibility. This is apparent—by naturalized (if that can be the word in this case) mirage—whenever the uncanny virtualities on-screen are diffused into the uncanniness of all screen worlds, there by dint of machination and by grace of illusion. Certainly *Déjà Vu* and *Source Code*, films in the cyberfiction mode, are hybrid narratives (time-loop surveillance plots) in which any initial orientation toward the "instrumental marvelous" (Todorov) of electronic time travel—as genre determinant—has tapped in the process the deeper technical fundament of all film.[5]

Such conditioning mediality is often manifested (and all the more so in the age of our hybrid photomechanical and electronic image tracks) in what I am calling the in-plot instrumentalizing of montage. These are shots where a deliberative editing of the screen image—that is, the edited images that make up the constructed screen world—enter into the diegesis, by thin disguise, as a technology of the virtual, the quasi-spectral. In this way the thematized electronics of a now-pictured (rather than foundational and picturing) montage can be made over to view as an equipmental function of the "computopian" possibilities (and monitory risks) of a digitally triggered parallel universe. If, for Todorov, we might say that the genie's carpet as marvelous vehicle of spatial transport is ultimately subordinated to the magic scene changes of literary narrative itself, so, too, with films that operate now and then by ceding their vehicles of wondrous transit to the obviously phantasmatic scrim—and uncanny presencing—of a hypertrophic cinema and the edited shot exchanges of its narrative interface. And not least in films where the prosthetic tunnel vision of an implausibly enhanced surveillance appears to be shared by hero and spectator alike—and, as such, involves an unprecedented breach in suture itself that even Lang could never have foreseen. One puzzle that often needs solving is how and to what extent futurist electronic wizardry is only like present projection after all.

But this aside for a moment, another puzzle about puzzle films is their longevity across the turn of the millennium. Mostly escapist in their hermetic (and hermeneutic) satisfactions? Exhausting all interest in their internal working out? Self-consuming artifacts? Or paranoid symptoms of an increasingly unstable sense of grounding in the global present? Mind-game films may solve nothing beyond themselves, but, given their variations on the fantastic, it is important to notice what they are fantasies *of*. In the case of *Déjà Vu* and *Source Code*, 9/11 explains much. In these sci-fi forms, the fictional science of time travel is aimed, via wish-fulfillment, not just at a preternaturally empowered search and seizure but at the wholesale computer alchemy of retroactive disarming. Yet as soon as the force of epistemology in such films (the surveillance thriller plot) turns ontological (the alternate reality fable), they tip over from forensics into equipmental fantasies of a new computer sublime, whether positive or negative.

Before this post–9/11 moment, the computer was sometimes suspiciously unplugged in the time-travel plot, whose logic served to displace video gaming itself, as electronic obsession, onto psychosis instead. Again and again, encountering teen heroes lost in the throes of virtual images and alternative timelines, we were to see them as more biologically dysfunctional than prosthetically adept, schizoid more than android, manic rather than electromagnetic in both their angst and their emotional escape routes. That pattern, characteristic of Generation Xbox, has been reversed lately—for the War on Terror epoch and its Home (Security) front—by tech-heavy sci-fi versions of time-travel narratives in the same trick-ending or puzzle-film cycle. Earlier, the eponymous Donnie Darko (Richard Kelly, 2001) and the hero of *The Butterfly Effect* (Eric Bress, J. Mackye Gruber, 2004) were troubled youths with no apparent vent in computer-game surrogacy, yet whose malleable reality and its special-effects rendering spoke indirectly to the digital climate of new Hollywood production—including the big screen's growing competition from (in these cases, narratively repressed) computer video.

The earlier salience of such computer-indifferent teen heroes—anomalous even then within an audience demographic of keyboard addiction—has been supplanted in the next round of Hollywood fantasy by adult paramilitary operatives in the grips of sophisticated digital technology. Such an updated heroic testing ground—with, yet again, lethal and even posthumous consequences—draws its analogies more openly now from the escalating challenges of on-screen avatars and first-person graphics in the video playing field. Where desktop virtuality was once an unspoken trope for emotional transport and psychotic break, electronic imaging has more recently become the literalized vehicle for either reparative or escapist time travel. And in another technological feedback loop, it's all the more obvious in the closely paired films by Scott and

Jones, *Déjà Vu* and *Source Code*, that Hollywood plotting is borrowing part of its twist-finish syndrome from the "alternate ending" supplements on the DVD menu, mass-marketed versions of their narratives' own "parallel universe" logic.[6]

Then, too, there is a further twist in the mind-game cycle that has been rewired by these films into sci-fi upgrades of a psychosomatic fantasy plot. In each of these screen (and metascreen) narratives the hero enters and extends his own death moment in the key of remediation (both senses). This is the tech upgrade of the merely remedial (healing) delay in the twist endings of films like *The Sixth Sense* (M. Night Shyamalan, 1999) and *The Others* (Alejandro Amenábar, 2001). Premised, almost neurologically, on the dilated moment of death itself—as a compressed scenario of its own deferral (*An Occurrence at Owl Creek Bridge* as archetype)—the hero of *The Sixth Sense*, fatally shot in the opening episode, realizes, accepts, and gives in to that death only (along with our realization of it) at the very end—as if one prolonged moment of emotional release. Same with the mother in *The Others*, who must outlast the instant of her suicide, over the entire length of plot, to acknowledge both it and the immediately preceding murder of her children. In *Source Code*'s more recent sci-fi version of a related time-loop puzzle, however, the death-moment synapses that might once have flared up in a distended instant of consolation get "remapped" elsewhere onto a possible-world doppelganger not flickering out on the instant but given full computer-boosted dilation into a parallel universe. The remedial split second before extinction, inhabited by a plot-long fantasy, has been replaced (or allegorized) by time's own digitized remediation. Once again, as in *The Sixth Sense* or *The Others*, with the main protagonist no longer manifest in real time to the summoned interlocutors of a protensive last moment, and thus with presence equivocated by post-mortem incarnation (or, say, by the absent one radically literalized), the elision of the two-shot and the rents of suture are our truest clue.

But whether in a fantasy deferral of death by the rendering therapeutic of its distended moment or by some other fashioning of virtual reality, what—come to think of it, as we tend to do somewhere en route through these plots—what is film to begin with but a parallel universe, an artificial space opened in a time not our own? A rhetorical question like this can seem to underlie a whole narrative cycle. Puzzled out before our eyes are certain conditions and limits of projection's own medium—even when no technology gets mentioned. And this is all the more the case in *Déjà Vu* and *Source Code*, when the futurist science portrayed by the films is that of a new, computer-driven audiovisual regime and a brave new world of virtual cyberpresence, with digitally fueled time travel in each plot making preemptive terrorist interception possible even after its bomb-detonating event.

Yet the course of such cinematic disclosure isn't always immediate or continuous. In the tech contortions of these more recent sci-fi puzzlers, exposure of the medium in its digitally enhanced and manipulated form, though more inevitable in its way, is all the more readily masked by futurist electronic technology. Embedded computer necromancy is thus easy to miss at first, if not for long, as either the implicit telos or undoing—asymptote or parody—of the commercial medium we're watching. Certainly Metz's dictum—to the effect that all montage *is trucage* (i.e., "special effect," "trick")—continues to find new narrative deployment in the time-travel mode—where what is tricked, optically and otherwise, is more than the ending, yet where just such tricking of image or plot may, at moments, be openly given away en route. Such puzzle films often extrude in this way their own filmic (or postfilmic) conditions as a pertinent inflection of their central narrative paradox. Why? One thing for sure: just when the representational credibility that sustains the arc of mystery and detection is swept away by an existential game changer, the film's whole diegetic construct is put in doubt within the disclosure of a reconfigured and wholly virtual real. Gauging this broad drift in the puzzle-film cycle helps mark the way in which, beyond the sometimes quasi-magical (Todorov: supernatural) manifestations of overt ghost stories, certain surveillance films too—in their out-of-body turns—enter the rolls of the technogothic: *Source Code* most obviously, as prepared by a similar premise in *Déjà Vu*.

Déja Views: "A single trailing moment of now, in the past"

Redivi/Vu . . . . The already secreted past becomes the remediated virtual present. To begin (where *Source Code* in its own derivative turn later does) with *Déjà Vu*'s sci-fi premise, a straightforward summary of the plot is indistinguishable from a litany of its metafilmic ironies. A terrorist car bomber has found the perfect venue: a New Orleans ferry bringing returning soldiers back to their families. And in the eventual disclosure of his motives, a further violence is being brought home. The mass murderer has been rejected for Mideast service because he was deemed too gung-ho and bloodthirsty for the American ranks, a man thought to be, in his words, "overcommitted." The will-to-carnage summoned and thereby unleashed by overseas aggression comes back to haunt us stateside. But that's only the beginning of the militarist subtext. Long before the killer's apprehension, street-smart ATF detective Doug Carlin (Denzel Washington) is brought in on a secret high-tech operation called the "surveillance window." What the CIA technicians have been able to do—in a composite program using standard closed-circuit urban video as well as the image feeds from seven orbiting satellites—is generate a computer-simulated 360-degree access (at precisely the scale of wide-screen theatrical projection) to private urban space, beginning in its demonstration scene with predictable cosmic zooms and swish pans. Yet the all-but-holographic restaging of a crime site requires so much storage that the projected image, and its capacity for rotation and enlargement, lags four days behind the real time in which the electronic traces are first laid down. Explained as "a single trailing moment of now—in the past," it amounts to the braiding together of several separate data streams, "trailing" time in both senses, tracking it down.

That's the setup: the first-level explanation. The era of instantaneous transmission has become so overloaded in its detail (more like Hollywood production than everyday domestic web use, especially in the age of CGI "rendering time," which happens to be exactly the phrase used to explain the CIA apparatus) that it reverts ironically to the time lag of traditional film, which must also wait for its technical processing before it can be screened and edited. An early hint from the awed and baffled detective is dropped in a throwaway line, as if pointing up the all-too-cinematic (read: all-too-realist) nature of the equipment: "I won't even ask you how you got the audio." (It seems merely another case of poetic license, as with the relayed dialogue of *Look*.) And the remaining two twists in this time-loop plot in fact render the idea more cinematically reflexive yet—even while less credible. It turns out that the composite rotational image is so powerful that it has not just reconfigured the past, reconstructed from microsecond to microsecond, but has reenergized it, entirely to the surprise of the scientists, into an immanent duplicate of foregone event: a warp in time, "a time-fold" in their jargon, a "wormhole." Optical technology has outplayed its own hand and produced the first time machine. At this midpoint "switch" of its trick plot, well before the forking and recursive timelines upon which the film's bloggers dote, *Déjà Vu* has closed the distance between surveillance and spectacle, document and immersive environment. It has done so precisely by debuting its "window" function, in its wide-screen expanse, as a movie come true: a movie that, like all cinema, seems as we watch—and this time truly is—functioning less as a trace of some elapsed action than as an unfolding in the now of present events in their very *becoming*. Paradox technologized, Hitchcock refigured: the temporal rear-view window that is any recorded film translated to the surveillance window of present access that is any viewed film.

My allusion above to André Bazin—cinema as a death-defiant "becoming" of the world before our eyes—is not incidental. For the film incorporates, on the very underside of its explicit plot, a veritable parable of the Bazinian relation of rigor mortis to photography and film. Faced with a corpse in the morgue, the coroner takes Polaroid shots of her body for the autopsy files. In light of Bazin's metaphor for photography as time embalmed, the medium is in this case working its chemical transformation in visible development time.[7] In the next scene, other photographs of the dead girl, though not of her actual corpse, are turned over to the detective by her grieving father to make her "real" in his otherwise impersonal detective work. This explicitness about the still image is followed by the hyperreal invasion of her privacy through the supposed "replay" of the surveillance window, only for us to find out that the continuous optical becoming of cinema has found its full ontological correlative in the time-warp miracle of this screened past. Not just, in Bazin's further metaphor for film, a case of "change mummified" (here in an almost 3-D overload of triangulated audiovisual data), this is instead the "real" woman herself, electronically realized in the recovered prelude to her death.

Wanting to confirm this implication of the delayed scientific disclosure, Carlin asks if the image he's been watching is of a woman indeed still alive. In response, he gets double-talk and cover-up. The answer, he insists, should be simpler. He takes a chair and smashes one of the surveillance monitors, saying, "Now that's broken, that's dead, it hasn't"—mocking their mumbo jumbo—"transitioned into some different state of entropy." So: Is the on-screen victim already dead or in fact still alive in a separate space-time? In the more immediate terms of his own analogy, is she just a monitored image? Or—and hence worth saving—a more than virtual presence somewhere? The answer is the one we expect by time-travel convention, and the one that in this particular case draws directly on the photographic subtext of the film's metaphysical figurations. From corpse, to photo replicas of that inanimate object, to snapshots of her living form, to her temporal reconstitution as a kinetic agent on screen, all the way through to the electronic presencing of a body born again to its own previously elapsed becoming: such is the course of the film's metaphorics of cinema itself in its local narrative transition from mere optical data through visual tracking to plot's engulfing immanence in the here and now.

All such disclosure, however, has been very slowly doled out. It's only when the eventual murder victim on-screen, four days ago, acts as if she feels spied on that either we or the hero begin to suspect the truth. In following her around the inner corners of her reinscribed space, he comes upon her own inscription in her diary not only of a metafilmic sense of voyeurism but of the nation's collective unease about unwarranted surveillance: "I've got that weird I'm-being-watched feeling." The point is further italicized by a pun when male technicians justify ogling her in the shower to "see if the suspect's clean." Two paradigms from classic narratology cooperate here in ways familiar to us from the surveillance cycle we've been examining, where real-time monitoring and retroactive detection often overlap. If, for Todorov and Peter Brooks, detection fiction epitomizes narrative structure *tout court* in its explanatory retracing of elapsed event, with inquest substituting for former quest narrative, then it is further the case that the time-travel plot blasts open the model from within.[8] Scott's narrative has been hovering until now in the zone of Todorov's "fantastic" instead, where an uncanniness of the sort suggested by the film's title, and exemplified most explicitly by the heroine's "weird" second sight about being sighted—as seen inscribed in her diary by (retrospecular) spycam—is balanced against, until tipped over into, the "marvelous" explanation: beyond total surveillance, an electronically totalized past uploaded not just for review but for literal revisitation. The transitional dialogue, on the way to full narrative revelation, comes at her funeral, where the briefly sampled eulogy deploys the tropes of apocalypse and resurrection in a theological version of what science, a couple of scenes later, will turn out to have instrumentalized—as capped by this consolatory liturgical transcendence of all loss: "God calls forth the past." But if not quite in time to redeem its victims in the flesh, leave it to the equally "supernatural" technology of the sci-fi genre.

An earlier clue—uncanny at first as well, then backfilled with a more astonishing parascientific explanation—emerges when the detective discovers from his ATF colleagues that his fingerprints are all over the heroine's apartment, even though we have seen him search it in plastic gloves. Later we realize that the bloody rags and gauze he found there were his own—once his time travel has propelled him back to a time before that first visit already recorded in "real narrative time." Extrapolated here into Todorov's "instrumental marvelous," the prototypical detective of the narratological model is on the trail of his *own* unrecognized traces, having been there, as it were, before himself. In sum: if detective fiction crystallizes all emplotment as the structuring comprehension of a "previous" event, time travel allows that previousness to be reconvened for unmediated investigation, for real-time surveillance.

Anticipating just this level of confessed sci-fi logic, a crucial plot turn in *Déjà Vu,* with its own brand of supernatural twist, lies coiled in wait. Before being catapulted into the past in his own person, the detective hero must actually track down that past, by strictly vehicular means, in the space of its former traces. All the technobabble of the preparatory sequences, we realize, has been built up to grease the wheels of a metafilmic car chase. In this most spectacular of the hero's forays into the past, the very logic of Hollywood editing is submitted to reconception as electronic illusionism, where medium has become something more fully telepathic, mediumistic. In this sequence, the hero at the speeding wheel of a souped-up Hummer, wearing a headset connected to the "surveillance window," tails the villain at night on a rainy freeway, his efforts further remediated in the control room. The results are a veritable laboratory of edited filmic sequence. The enemy is kept in sight in one eye (through the optical feed of the digital transmission device) while, with the aid of the other eye, the hero is trying to dodge oncoming rush-hour traffic in broad daylight—and four days later. Finally, the time-tunneling detective comes face-to-face—but in an optical one-way street—with the killer, who stares blankly through him (across the gap of time itself) into an unnerving sense of his destiny, but with no present nemesis to anchor the eyeline match. The mass murderer of *M* could at least tether his paranoia to the lurking Other. The new homicidal terrorist is always and everywhere spied. As if internalizing the entire ethos of contemporary surveillance culture, quite apart from its current figuration as paracinematic, the world seems all eyes. Nor is time on the villain's side, either, in his confession as an optical pawn of the plot. For a second ironic temporality besides that of digital rendering time obtrudes in this scene. From the point of view (in both senses) of industrial production, the very condition of traditional cinema—its inscription of separate shots within an articulated (and fabricated) composite space—is parsed into inoperability from within this sci-fi upgrade. Far more openly than in *The Sixth Sense* or *The Others,* for instance, the foundational suture of narrative cinema has itself become what it always invisibly is, only more so here: a time-lapse effect. Then, too, with Lang and Deleuze in mind again, the climactic duel of the movement-image has become, through digital sorcery, the virtual face-off of a time-coded interface.

Earlier, and even as if by accident, Scott's film can seem to gloss (as well as gloss over) the artifice of its production. This is to say that a mere plot glitch in the time-travel "window" of *Déjà Vu* serves to palm off computer simulation inside the story onto the means of storytelling itself. When the ATF detective is beginning to sniff out the truth about the CIA surveillance apparatus being more than a mere display panel of time past, but rather an opening on the full-scale (rather than just widescreen) reconstitution of that past, he confirms his hunch by beaming a laser pointer from the computer control room into the space he is uncomfortably, voyeuristically, surveilling, where the heroine feels an uncanny sense, already, of being watched. She actually sees at this point the red laser dot on her own wall, and at the moment of her bafflement and mounting anxiety, the apparatus itself panics and crashes. In the bad English of the script, the hero has "broached" (rather than "breached") the system. But what in fact he *has* broached is its systemic relation to the surveillance window of our film as a whole. Within plot, the detail of the laser gun makes no sense. The past that has been electronically recovered by a world-heavy load of data isn't all there within the frame of the "window." The girl exists now, miraculously enough, back in her own rooms across town, in the lifeworld of four days previous. So no reason the laser beam should show up there. Unless her existence lays claim to no more ambient surround than the framed space of the moving images that convey her. Unless. As if. Aha: unless that "weird I'm-being-watched feeling" is, anagrammatically, a feeling of being "wired" from the ground up. What has been recovered by computer—so this aberrant moment suggests—is only, that is, the diegetic frame of recorded events, not their independent presence and duration. As in any movie, what you see is not just what you get, but all there is. Later scenes in *Déjà Vu* gather to suggest as much, with cinema constituting our own time travel before that of the characters. In this way is cinema also shown forth, yet again, as its own mode of mediated surveillance.

An added topical wrinkle only tucks further into this logic. In view again of Kittler's claims for military invention as the recurrent harbinger of media advance, an overt military link in *Déjà Vu* comes bearing a metafilmic irony about the disappearing fourth wall of cinema's quasi-theatrical mise-en-scène. As one of the surveillance engineers puts it, their "window" is "able to see through walls" precisely because they have access, not just to Hummers, but to the "same infrared heat-sensitive stuff they've been using in Iraq." The technological feedback loop is complete and, one guesses, supposedly consoling. The so-called War on Terror is fought at home as it is abroad, with the same vanguard electronics—but, in the present case, by way of well-intentioned individual surveillance rather than mass targeting.

Where Vietnam was the TV war, our Mideast incursions have become a more literal war of mediation, since the technologies of surveillance and targeting, and in turn prosecution and broadcast, have grown nearly identical. We have satellite imaging to thank or blame both for what we are able to do there and for what we see of it on the evening news. The only way out of this double bind, according to Hollywood genre formats—the only way to transcend the invasive video surveillance that can at any moment turn violent, the imaging technology that can store and obliterate at once—is the route into sci-fi fantasy, where in *Déjà Vu* the continuous networked present is overtaken (paradoxically, preternaturally) by the inscribed trail of a suddenly immanent past. And can it be an accident that this happens exactly in connection with a scheme of ex post facto prevention—the ultimate fantasy in this epoch of 9/11 hindsight? Typical in being strictly implicit, buried in a single allusion to Iraq-War technology, here is the unthought wish that, if we could actually turn back the clock, there would be no War on Terror, nor terrorism's assault on us. This is no doubt why, though our super-swift detective hero is twice recognized as a legendary veteran of the Oklahoma City bombing, the homebred paramilitary threat of the McVeigh-like culprit must be further crossed with his army-enlistment ambitions for Mideast service. White supremacy is thereby subsumed to the broader field of imperialist backfire.

And concerning this paramilitary dimension of Scott's film, there is a curious isolated fallout in his brother's *Body of Lies* four years later, where sci-fi is brought down to earth—to the satellite-surveilled and infrared-filtered ground of Mideast infiltration—in an early polemical monologue by the hero's CIA boss. This antijihadist polemic is dictated at first into voice-recognition software and processed on his own computer monitor before being transferred by sound bridge to a rehearsed performance of the same "text," sotto voce, to government honchos in the intelligence community. The gist of his extended, almost metaphysical, conceit: that the jihadists are not just resisting all things progressive, in some loose sense fighting against the future, but that they are actually doing battle with the future's personification in American operatives. Which means, reciprocally, that the CIA agents are fighting the past. This is a reconditioned past whose deliberately primitive means of escaping surveillance is, as the jeremiad continues, to dispense even with its agents' own cell phones and revert to oral messaging, encoded handwriting, and (in a constrained contemporaneity, let us say) to the use of one-off DVD video instructions or imprinted data files, never duplicated, and literally burned after viewing. As the CIA boss insists (and as Ridley Scott might have learned from *Déjà Vu* alone), the trouble with fighting the past from the future is that the past is "invisible" to the present: not discerned, that is, let alone intercepted, without special ontological and optical aids. Science fiction, held in abeyance as genre, offers here the very figure of speech for geopolitical challenge.

Fantasy, instead, is an easier rallying point. But even in *Déjà Vu*, the fantasy of retrospection must be generated from scratch each time out. There, as well as in *Source Code* after it, we are plunged again into the post–9/11 crisis of further mass death at the hands of terrorism—before the quantum leap (cinematographically figured) into a happy ending. In *Déjà Vu*, the technique (matched to technology) of restitution follows from those multiple timelines where the hero must die in one to save the girl, while returning in another temporal stream to claim her. All of this is explained by the technicians, with mandatory economy, according to "branching universe theory," where every return in time, altering the past, precipitates an independent and parallel graft of new reality.[9] Long after a proleptic first sequence in which the (already dead) detective is first seen in slow motion as he hears his own cell phone ringing from the body bag of his corpse, we see the explanation for this, in a parallel timeline, as he is done in by the bomb. But this only for him to end up, in another "trailing moment of now"—and after a recursive image of that same slowed motion at the start—reuniting with the girl and driving her off into the narrative closure of an especially nondramatic stop-action frame (equivalent to the crop-box freeze functions deployed earlier in scanning the wide-screen surveillance panel, but turned rhetorical rather than diegetic when gone full-frame). This particularly "dated" photomechanical (and now digitally trivial) device offers the filmic frame line's material equivalent of an arrested timeline. And it does so just in the way that slow motion—another time-image like the freeze-frame in Deleuze's sense (an *opsign* rather than a mere visual image, as for instance at the close of *The Adjustment Bureau* as well)—has already figured, early and late, the temporal manipulation of the (intervening) intervention plot. (So, too, the freeze-frame, always with its latent Bazinian overtones, awaits its own digital upgrade at the death-defying climax of *Source Code*.)

But not merely these familiar cinematic tropes are requisitioned by Scott's plot to figure, almost nostalgically, the cutting-edge new technology it depicts. Everyday digital tech, in the case of the cell phone and its normal affordances, operates as a subtext to explain the instrumental melodrama of temporal transport. Before the scientist lets the hero risk his own body in disintegrated transit through the surveillance window, a handwritten message—as an inorganic guinea pig, so to speak—is sent back into the past in an incidentally motivated effort to alert the hero himself to a surveillance suspect, before the ferry has ever blown up. But his partner gets the note instead, and is led to his murder by it. Tampering with the past is as risky as it would seem impossible, yes, but the more "normative" technological insinuation remains. Before the hero himself climbs into the electronic teleportation chamber, that is, it has already been naturalized as a kind of glorified text-messaging machine. Only after the message goes through—with the hero correcting the spelling of "surveillance" by having the technician add a second *l*, as if he had been "texting" too fast—is the routine magic ready to be extrapolated from. What happens in the next stage of the enterprise requires turning a human being into the electronic signals of a communication circuit. This passing and minor episode of misspelled text in *Déjà Vu* could almost be the source of *Source Code*'s most telling contemporaneous irony—associated precisely, and twice over, with a disembodied e-text as figure for the trauma of radical cyberpresence. This, too, will require summarizing a plot whose puzzling deferrals can't begin to camouflage their metafilmic dimensions. For *Source Code*, like all narrative film, is a film in which the projected afterlife of a hero—no longer bearing any immobile resemblance to his origin and model—operates, and in this regard more like a screen actor than a person, through the assuming of character by proxy: in this case, becoming a surveillance agent in a world not his own.

One last point about the quotidian analogs in *Déjà Vu*, including the link between real-time text messaging and transtemporal teleportation: an almost neglible idiomatic shorthand might have prepared us early on for the conflation of optical record with inhabited ocular vision. When first arriving at the crime scene, Carlin has announced, in ordering a call to police headquarters, "I want all the surveillance" associated with the blast site, by which he means, of course, the surveillance videos, not the oversight itself. Yet it is the latter that, further along in the plot, he himself, transmediated, comes to embody. But even before this, the arrested suture that brought villain and cyberhelmeted hero together across a four-day hiatus, and thus exposed the countershot logic of classic cinema as itself a temporal ruse, has been tethered back to another Deleuzian duel (this time in real-time) when the terrorist is finally caught and submitted to interrogation. While the villain is maundering on about his delusional sense of a messianic Destiny—boasting that he will live on in infamy—the wondrous high tech that has tracked him down is brought back to earth, reduced and normalized, in the form of a single surveillance camera watched in a control booth by FBI agents as our ATF hero, at first massaging the killer's ego, elicits a full confession from him.

From the sublime to the merely incriminating, one can't have too much mediation. Sci-fi returns here to the realist home ground of police procedural in order to tether its extrapolated computer machinations to standard forensic practice as well as to ordinary electronic telecommunications. Half a decade later, in its grotesque vision of computerized human prosthesis, *Source Code* has a hard time doing both, normalizing the black technomagic of detection and communication at once—but it tries. In its extreme case, e-text and the feeds of optical surveillance dissolve into each other at a narrative's withering pivot point.

8 PARALLEL WORLD EDITING

What have we seen by looking, chapter by chapter, along such covert or uncanny sightlines? One thing for certain: electronic surveillance is a sighting without a seeing subject. A subject views; surveillance records. In this sense surveillance is the ne plus ultra of the "videosphere" in Régis Debray's terms: "vision without a gaze."[1] Or, alternately, in terms from Jacques Aumont, a case of the image detached from vision. In recent cinema, another dichotomy follows on the heels of such distinctions. The so-called *subject under surveillance* (Beckert in *M*) is wholly objectified. By contrast, the subject reduced in its own right to surveillance conduit (Carlin once dematerialized and teleported in *Déjà Vu*, the coming hero of *Source Code* as computerized scanner rather than inhabited body) is an online info bank. Commentary has not been slow to take note of this recent turn. Like *M* in regard to theories of classic montage, *Source Code* (2011) has become a minor litmus test in current writing about the posthuman in cinema—not because it is better than other films in this cyborgian vein, or because it offers their compendium, but rather because, in stretching out of shape its time-travel premise by a detective trajectory, then bending it back recursively on itself, it takes any such conjoined logic both to an extreme and to pieces at once.[2]

With or without a sense of influence from such mind-game scenarios of death's distended instant as in *The Sixth Sense* or *The Others*, a plot summary of *Source Code* disappears on the spot into schematization, so contrived is the sci-fi donnée of this War on Terror fable. A critically injured US pilot from the Afghan front is now on assignment back home (complete with simulated cockpit seat), being commanded—electronically commandeered—to revisit a terrorist bombing on a Chicago commuter train. Though the disaster has happened just eight minutes ago, if he can be piloted (projected) back in time to the scene, he may be able to locate the bomber and forestall a threatened next attack. This time-travel teleportation—by recursive trial and error until he gets it right—is less cumbersome than it might have been because he has no functional somatic mass to weigh him down in these bouts of digital telepathy. He is put through space and his paces at once by a mind meld with an(other) posthumous victim whose train seat and brain he takes over, and whose bomb-blast immolation he must repeatedly endure—in its mental trauma rather than physical damage.

This is required until he masters the incremental fairy-tale-like (now video game-modeled) tests on the way to detecting the US rather than jihadist culprit, at which point he insists at all costs—in true movie-hero fashion—on "saving the girl" as well. It is then that conundrum runs rampant in discursive form. The hero struggles to work out the time-travel logistics and paradoxes that both spawn and bedevil his plans, even while orders from his superiors try countermanding this: "Don't think . . . just act." But what drives the plot forward from such abstract slumps of sci-fi exposition in the branching-universe mode to renewed "thriller" status is more like thinking than real acting: a computer-enhanced brain function. This is a performance free of all physical gesture for a body invulnerable to the terrorist's bomb because already, in previous combat, blown away—we finally (and horrifically) discover—from the chest down.

In light of a TV series from the next year, here one may contemplate two sides of the same biopolitical coin in covert surveillance. In the 2012 season of *Homeland*, cyberhacking is translated to the hands-off equivalent of physical butchering—so that the onetime CIA director responsible for the mass collateral damage of drone strikes becomes by way of revenge, as vice president, the remote electronic victim of a surgical (heart) attack by terrorist "wiretapping." In *Source Code*, by contrast, the wired heart of the eviscerated hacking agent himself is artificially kept pumping so that he can effect search and seizure operations by a cerebral circuitry so remote as to operate in two times (as well as two places) at once. In such narratives, the cyborgian body is under assault as cybernetic receiver and sender alike—the switch point of strikes both punitive and preventive on a sliding scale from biotech plausibility to full-scale sci-fi trope.

"Thank you for your service, Captain": the hero's only official reward in *Source Code*. His is an "immaterial" industry of service—rather than so-called manual labor—after all, a case of disembodied reconnaissance whose data stream has no personified line of sight: again, images of the past without incarnate vision. This is to say that the conceptual impetus of *Source Code* is clearest when, in undisguised light (or shadow) of its predecessor, *Déjà Vu*, its subsequent time-travel plot—half a decade farther along in computerized mainstream production—is understood as a perverse variant of an evolving mode of surveillance cinema. The sooner one recognizes *Source Code* as such, the sooner one comes upon what is more deeply wrong with (or troubling about) it—in just that frame of reference. Repeatedly, of course, surveillance is the screen mode where theme and technique are so triangulated that they delimit in reception (narratographic reception, at least) the medial base itself, as in *M*. Surveillance in Lang's film, straining suture to and beyond its limits, implicates a system of projection that is concomitantly "exposed" in its photo-mechanical basis—even as it is narratively laid bare at its most aggressive in the turning point of the manhunt plot. In *Source Code*, theme and technique, surveillance and suture, are again, as in *Déjà Vu* before it, pressed to medial crisis around the question of a now-digitized "screen image"—now digitized, that is, in a *wholly digitized now*. It is by this triangulation that plot becomes, as in *M* and *Déjà Vu* alike—and precisely via a technical wrench to the very maintenance of suture—an anatomy of cinema's own mediation, once photomechanical, lately electronic. Or consider all this in its broader ontological arc. Where in the modernist spirit of an artifact like *M* the medium might well petition for attention from within the plot of monitored humanity it activates, what stands revealed, by contrast, in the latest surveillance narratives—from *The Nine Lives of Tomas Katz* in 2000 down to the present—is the antithetical postmodern spirit in which (post)human agency is only a medial function to begin with.

Unmistakable in its sustained surveillance parable, *Déjà Vu* came into release just as my last book on film was going to press. Tony Scott's sci-fi manhunt plot would have found a place there otherwise. For *Framed Time* is a study that follows Gilles Deleuze's interrogative lead in the closing speculation from his second cinema volume, *The Time-Image*, about whether (writing as he did in the early 1980s) the "numeric image" at the onset of computerized visuals would operate from within, and so transfigure, the postwar time-image—or inaugurate a whole new digital regime.[3] (Deleuze's open-ended question is one more way of wondering, as many still do, whether the move from classical to modern actually cedes in turn to something unto itself that should be known as postmodern.) And since montage was a chief pressure point for a transition between the movement-image and the time-image, the computer-driven time warps of current sci-fi in a surveillance mode—depending on neither parallel nor alternate templates of a routine sort but on time differentials implausibly machinated and simultaneous—continue the stress testing of montage for a digital epoch.

The attempt in *Framed Time* to think along with—and historically beyond—Deleuze in this regard led me to concentrate on the first decade after the 1995 centenary of photomechanical film and the elusive interweaving of theme and electronic medium that characterized so many of its proliferating fantasy narratives. These are plots whose technical machination, paired with sidelined digital anxiety, often seems to traverse the very difference, material and historical both, between two dispensations of cinema, filmic and postfilmic: that is, between the integral photocell on a spooling strip and the digital scan of computer-generated images (CGI) or the more ubiquitous techniques of computer editing.

Moreover, such a difference has been recruited by a surprising number of plots to figure the on-screen manifestation (and mutation) of frame/d time. This involves—as in the phonetic "lap dissolve" of that very phrase (*d* blurred with *t* by dental elision)—the increment under disappearance by the image in frame line or binary scan: disappeared by it in the sense of disappearing into it, into its induced differential image of motion within the ongoing screen frame.[4] Such movies (no longer entirely "films"), characterized by an exponential incorporation of CGI effects, tend, nonetheless, toward an active suppression of computerization as theme, where the phenomenological image becomes instead an optic sign of the marvelous. I extend that investigation now, with *Source Code* as one recent and exacerbated case in point, into the realm of the Deleuzian *sonsign* as well (voice signifying beyond itself, denatured), whose wavelengths can also be found to operate—not unlike the visual morphing of contorted time-travel or "temportation" plots—more as a travesty of the time-image than as a philosophical widening of its parameters.

When the hero of *Source Code* achieves a computerized transcendence of the apparatus itself into an undelimited alternate reality, we learn this not by further fantastic paraphernalia but by a routine mobile transmit from his cell phone within this branching universe. Here is a film whose belated (and indeed at one level still posthumous) suppression of digital phobias—after a plot-long dystopian ordeal centered in fact on the temporal distortions of coercive computer science—arrives with a last-ditch and unconvincing cellular euphoria ("new media" degree zero) in paranormal transmission within a digitally generated parallel universe. This technically silent (but narratively "recited") text message is sent by a veritable military prisoner: one of our own, forced by his own superiors into repeated computerized salvos, then sprung at last by the very technology that has previously entrapped him as recurrent temporal projectile. The severed body of a comatose soldier, having been rewired for a secret time-travel mission of none other than remote surveillance, computer-boosted into an alternate reality of putatively limited duration, is now finally aided (by a sympathetic captor, his designated "mission dispatcher") in his miraculously successful effort at fleeing into a parallel world forever. In the process, human temporality is furiously refigured, or disfigured, by every aspect of the film's time-loop fantasy. That last disembodied cell-phone text and nondiegetic voice-over is simply the final turn of this prosthetic screw. Turning on a prolonged degradation of the time-image from philosophy to plot monstrosity, and in particular of the *sonsign* (building toward the closing e-text voice-over) from philosopheme to narrative irony, Duncan Jones's film also mobilizes most of the other topoi of the Deleuzian time-image to be traced in atrophied or equipmental form in turn-of-the-millennium cinema.

These flashpoints of temporality are divided in their effects across Deleuze's own rough-hewn but useful distinction (following Michelangelo Antonioni)—regarding certain typical earlier avatars of the time-image—between "European cinema" (the "art film") and "American science fiction," as, for instance, between *Last Year at Marienbad* and the differently fateful calendrical designation of *2001: A Space Odyssey* (1969).[5] In contrast to the doubled body as reciprocal and sutured focal point for its own death and transfiguration in the closing sequence of Stanley Kubrick's narrative, as marked by the alternate *sonsigns* of the astronaut's helmet-encased breathing, in *Source Code* the cognitive duplication of the out-of-body sensorium enters a computer-driven time loop in which the supposed body of the military agent we've been watching, as touchstone of the movement-image, is revealed to be entirely virtual in its every corporeal as well temporal aspect, including its merely "signified" rather than supposedly audited voice. In the terms of Thomas Y. Levin so germinal for this investigation, here is surveillance—in its function for screen narrative as a "rhetoric of the temporal index," the very trace of temporal event in process—undergoing second-order troping as an ontological crisis, one in which even the timed sound waves of apparent speech no longer bear any indexical relation to the lived body, but only to the computer-duped time of its postponed nescience. For this is a film whose plot grimly prevents, and then ends up bluntly finessing, the normal coincidence of image and sound in the hero as incarnate plot agent.

Deleuzian Time and Cinementation

Deleuzian semiology is at its most unique in taxonomizing the *noosigns* (thought-signs) in postwar screen narrative, those moments where cinematic mediation demands a kind of interpretive meditation on the very time of sound figure or visual image. Outside of those notable films in the modernist vein, however, that raise variously profound roadblocks to passive viewing, such a demand can remain entirely implicit. Yet with cinema conceived as a machine *for* as well as *of* thought, even a formulaic narrative and its slick twists can, if not wax philosophical, at least jog ideas never openly raised by its storytelling. In doing so it may even take the unexpected measure of its own medial basis, including the sound/image composite of traditional screen projection. To phrase this composite in the kind of linguistic fusion that in its own right keeps eye and ear, script and phonemic undertext, in reciprocal suspension, this signifying force field might be identified as the never-arrested temporal flux of *oculaurality*. How this comes into play for a final chapter in a book on surveillance concentrating now on a single film named for the "source code" of computer lingo depends in part on social context (a pervasive antiterrorist ethos), on intertextual framing (the narrative's debts to *Déjà Vu*), and on the film's own uncomfortable shunt between primary and secondary identification (Christian Metz) for a character (no longer quite a person) whose use to the present is only as a camera-like spectral relay of past onsite surveillance in telepathic reconstitution, its artificially animated and mobile eyes and ears. A film whose dialogue never mentions "surveillance" once (just the simile of a "security camera"), yet in which the "surveillance window" of transtemporal opportunity in *Déjà Vu* is its undisguised model, has contrived its plot around the structuring absence of its own rough subgeneric designation: a functional absence, including its association with CCTV prototypes, that returns with a vengeance in the midpoint "reveal" of its own ontological trick about the hero's deceptive material presence and embodied voice.

The Deleuzian inflection of digital virtuality in this one film comes clear against the backdrop of our broader view of the technopticon and its voyeuristic equivalents. From *M* through *Peeping Tom* to *Caché* and *The Skin I Live In*: the shock to consciousness of lives under inspection, the psychosomatic and sometimes even (allegorically) surgical nature of such penetrated privacy. With or without—without at first in Lang, and then increasingly with—a diegetic machine of the gaze to anchor the syndrome, narration is itself reduced at certain stress points to personified invasive camerawork, detected people to sheer targets, lives to images. Genres of detection, melodrama, the gothic, the action thriller—all may overlappingly converge on this line of depicted inspection. But another emergent genre variant now flourishes, and all the more often since being put into tacit counterpoint with the wired-war films of satellite-guided ballistics: namely, the high-tech surveillance thriller.

If, according to Deleuze's still twentieth-century chronology, the "postwar time-image" tends to reduce the actor to spectator, this new and "numeric" (digitized) War-on-Terror mode of proliferated electronic spying reduces agency again to the sheer movement-image, yet this time in the diegetic (if only machinic) eye of the other. The apex of the movement-image as duel (Deleuze on the mainstay of his prewar template) is now a displaced and mediated face-off in the register of human action. It is waged between *being seen* (or in the case of our final exhibit with *Source Code*, merely being *seen through*—as humanoid surveillance apparatus) and seeing for oneself, seeing how to act, whether in revenge or escape. In the anodyne conclusions of many such plots, the result tends toward civilian autonomy—valorized against all odds—as a heroic defiance of (if sometimes still in) the eye of the state.

This recent cycle is represented, on the one hand, by scenarios of overtly political paranoia like *Enemy of the State* or *The Bourne Legacy* and, on the other, by computer sci-fi like *Déjà Vu* and *Source Code*. Channeled by such plot formulas, three alternate and limited facets of heroic action, two of which we've already examined in detail, surface by turns to define this new pattern. Under inspection and assault, one can seize the reins of specular power from a bureaucratic enemy by going low (under the radar of high) tech. Or one can work from within a fantastic and deceptively benign computerized technology to exceed its mandate and convert specular surveillance back to redemptive action. Or, as we're now to see, one (though not really one at all anymore, but instead an agency split from within) can supposedly transcend a coercive electronic program that has turned an encorpsed self into a mere surveillance circuit. In this case, such transcendence is effected only by escaping the digital data stream of the monitored relay system and going magically off grid. Whatever the genre variant, need it be said that each manner of corrective action is a fantasy?

What, then, are those signature aspects of the Deleuzian time-image—with its "sheets of the past" in superimposition on the present—that now so often, and in *Source Code* so flagrantly, get twisted into sci-fi knots? And how might these features engender, cheapen, or encumber that shift from watching to thinking, from reception to reflection, that everywhere inflects Deleuze's account of screen temporality in its ocular and aural valences? How, in short, in the interface between screen image and mental picture, might the aberrant sound/image ratio in *Source Code* operate as *cinementation*? In his modernist paradigm, Deleuze stresses those more or less existential manifestations of time-consciousness that break with the sensorimotor continuum. These include, on half a dozen salient fronts, the (1) "forking" narrative, often involving the spatiotemporal disorientation of (2) "any-space-whatever"; the diegetic prominence of (3) "the telepath" and (4) "the double" as part of an underlying conversion of protagonists from motor agents to (5) "spectators" within and *of* their own experience; and finally the links between screen and brain modeled on the concept of cinema as (6) "spiritual automaton," the very mechanization of a cognitive being-in-the-world.[6] Extrapolated from the cinematographic experiments of high modernism and redistributed across the time-loop fictions and forking-path narratives of recent CGI-heavy cinema, as they often are, these crisis points of sensorimotor discontinuity come to a dense concentration in *Source Code*. This is a film where—in a revealing match-up with the Deleuzian breakdown above—(1) iterated "forks" in time, computer instigated, teleport the protagonist as sheer optico-auditory probe into the (2) "any-space-whatever" of variable reconnaissance targeting as both a remote-controlled (3) "pathic" medium and a (4) doppelganger worthy of Poe—inhabiting, in the film's own lingo, the "synaptic map" of a dead man; this makes for a serial séance channeled through a sheerly machinic (5) "spectator" whose near-corpse as (6) "spiritual" entity is wholly "automatized" and all but robotically maintained as a kind of quasi-somatic filtering (rather than screening) device in an out-of-body surveillance circuit.

As part of this artifice, the standard-issue synchronous voicing of the hero's speaking image is a more than ordinary illusion that gets finally disclosed—at an unforeseen peripety en route toward a further trick ending—as the utter divorce, diegetically presented, of the speaking subject from all sensorimotor continuum on-screen. Undermined in this way (despite faux close-ups) is the Deleuzian "affection-image" that offers such a crucial hinge between action and reaction, cause and effect, in the philosopher's understanding of traditional movement-image cinema. The time-image has hereby outsmarted itself in yet another baroque sci-fi form, sabotaged its own axiomatic basis (and springboard) in the credited phenomenology of human gesture, human movement. Without this realist basis, time (as exploratory image or idea) has nothing to immobilize, break with, or dilate upon. How this double bind operates in *Source Code*, and with what narrative blowback, what metaphysical repercussions, only plot can tell, even when it isn't wholly leveling with us.

And as it unfolds, another philosopher in the Deleuzian tradition may come to mind. The expendable body of the downed pilot in *Source Code*—subject now only to computer crashes in his repeated mortal expenditures—may not amount exactly to Giorgio Agamben's all-but-subhuman model of *homo sacer,* entailing as that paradigm does the defamed exile from community for a body neither ceremonially executed nor ritually sacrificed—a figure to which the abject Beckert in *M* more closely corresponds. Nonetheless, the entirely clandestine iteration of the soldier's psychosomatic suffering in *Source Code,* his generic availability for being killed and then killed again (despite our hero's protestations that "one death is enough to die for your country") offers, as with *homo sacer,* no public catharsis of any kind.[7] The top-secret computerized second sight he is made to manipulate (and endure) goes unseen, unheralded, purging nothing that the present community will even know about. But what the plot of *Source Code* does bring to mind in Agamben, as an organizing distinction, is what gets diagnosed—in the philosopher's influential view of biopolitics—as the always systemically potential degradation by state power of *bios* (biography, civic presence) to the bare animal life he evokes by the term *zoe.*

In Jones's film, without letup in its cruelty, the pattern is reversed. *Zoe* at its lower limit, the barely pulsing animate body of the hero, is rewired for a bioreceptivity not its (because not his) own. Surveillance is assigned by proxy to the last phase of a retrospective lifeline that the hero's coopted retinal and audio channels can retrace, graph, map—but only by "synaptic" links. In his borrowed death, he "relives" in extinction the truncated biography of the Other so as to scour it for clues. Such is the usurped (if also postmortem) *bios* that can be mastered only, in Deleuze's terms, by the emptying of agency into sheer perception: in this case, through the immobilized motor options of a remote (and digitally focalized) cognition—until, within the entirely virtual imaging of character as displaced spectator, time is up.

That's the purported logic. The seeming glitch, which turns out to be a sci-fi hitching point, is that the human data conduit, once borrowing the physical frame of another corpse to focalize his posthumous transmissions, has not just cognitive but (reembodied) physical capacities. The spying eye can in fact act, perform, exert virtual leverage on the space its cognitive (and anatomically borrowed) frame inhabits. Plot's logic is rewritten on the spot, though disclosed only by gradual stages. Idealizing the function of normal surveillance scans, the hero can purposefully intervene in what the metaphysical "instant replay" helps him perceptually discover. But that is true, we come to realize (or come to find unlikely) only because each return into the past (as in *Dejà Vu* also) launches a branching reality all its own. And it is just this electro-alchemy that its agent tries finally to convince his controllers of—in order to be released from computer bondage into its digitally generated virtual world.

Cyberopsis and Instru/mental Montage

Avatar is a film of displaced virtual reality, its computer-screen "exit interviews" after each fantastic transport throwing into relief the high-tech vicariousness of its paraplegic hero. Yet what if the maimed but electronically enabled war veteran were not just, as in *Avatar*, a paraplegic but a quadriplegic—and in fact a disemboweled—pilot, yet still undischarged as a corpse, kept instead on military counterterrorist assignment stateside? Such, as we know, is exactly the premise of *Source Code*, whose hero is the victim of a third and fatal Mideast posting. Haunted by flashbacks mixed with memory prompts (assorted playing cards) reminiscent of *The Manchurian Candidate* (John Frankenheimer, 1962; Jonathan Demme, 2004), he is denied a standard body bag and, after fake ashes are presented to his grieving father, secretly installed in a life-support tank as a wired torso jacked into a top-secret paramilitary computer designed for "time reassignment." It is the story of reverse castration, both for a veteran's severed body and for Homeland Security itself.

There is an auterist streak in all this. Jones began his career with a mordant short film about long-distance satellite surveillance, called *Whistle* (2002), in which a high-tech transnational hit man is taken out by his own technology behind a final blank screen and its metaphor of obliteration. So the theme of the weaponized digital image persists in Jones's work. But what's global about the premise of *Source Code* isn't simply the way Paul Virilio's "logistics of perception" linking war and cinema have become a "globallistics" of computerized targeting. At issue is a methodological crux as well as a technological one. There are dozens of other films lately in which, by persistently mediated camerawork, all difference has been elided between an aesthetics of postmillennial hyperrealism and an ethics of surveillance, whether verging on sci-fi or not. What if the question of total electronic purview were reversed and it were the victimized protagonist who had become the involuntary subject rather than object of surveillance, or not so much the subject as the apparatus? That's, again, the starting point of *Source Code*. But how to approach its global phobia about clandestine imaging even when its terrorist thematic has, as with the film's obvious 2006 prototype in *Déja Vu*, taken an entirely domestic and apolitical turn? How else but to register, within an international anxiety about secret image transmit, the way the sci-fi escalations of this one plot try in part, by a last-ditch ditching of a previous reality, to disarm such endemic fears?

So, a fourfold set of determinants renders *Source Code* paradigmatic in the current narrative climate, bringing it forward at the far historical end of a discussion beginning in comparable detail with Lang's *M*. Auteurist theme and international zeitgeist in one: surveillance. Genre: sci-fi. Cycle (prominent for well over a decade now): time-loop virtual reality. Mode: surveillance—converted to reverse paranoia, with consolatory trick ending. In *Source Code*, the techno-futurism is quite clearly projected from contemporary concerns not only about surveillance and abrogated privacy rights and the ethics of drone interventions but about the psychic tolls of repeated military deployment from a diminished volunteer army, crossed in turn with life-support and euthanasia debates. With no "living will" in either sense, the film's hero, involuntarily sent back into an antiterrorist if civilian theater of war as indeed a mediated and disembodied spectator, suffers from what might be called PMSD, postmortem stress disorder, the plot thus inverting the logic of a 2005 film called *The Jacket* (John Maybury), where a Gulf War veteran in a coffin fantasizes his sci-fi teleportation back into the world of the living, a postmortem mirage undermined by trick ending.[8] And the legacy goes back as well to one of the earliest of the mind-game war films, *Jacob's Ladder* (Adrian Lyne, 1990), in which the plot-long psychotic hallucinations of the Vietnam vet are the result of the army's own performance-enhancing drugs—still poisoning his mind on his own military deathbed instead of (as the plot detour has fooled us into assuming) in his homecoming rampage and decline. In *Source Code*, operating in reverse, the trick ending rescues the dead end of a paramilitary thriller by a heavier dose yet of sheer sci-fi.

But *Source Code* can also usefully be seen (once more the auteurist overtones) against the backdrop of Jones's previous feature, *Moon* (2009), where the hero, working for Lunar Industries, oversees the harvesting of a new and nonpolluting world fuel source, Helium 3, only to discover that, in the interest of energy efficiency, he himself is recyclable, if not biodegradable: one of an endless series of clones under constant computer surveillance after being retrieved, one by one, several years apart, from cryogenic storage. *Moon*'s revelation scene comes when the present incarnation of the hero clicks through an electronically leaked series of data-banked images of himself just before, time and again, his vaporization and replacement. In the genre terms of Tzvetan Todorov's theory of "the fantastic," the previous tease of an uncanny explanation—that cabin fever had driven him psychotic and he was seeing double in the supposed company of his accidentally discovered clone—is trumped by the delayed fuse of the sci-fi explanation in actual biometric replication. By contrast with this turn in *Moon*, the cultural angst leveraged by *Source Code* goes beyond stem cell controversy to something like the techno gothic of brain stem research: the human body repurposed as neurocognitive antenna. In the process, so-called "wired war" isn't just unmanned; it is de-manned.

In its own right, of course, the high-tech surveillance motif, often swallowing the entire genre of the detective film in one gulp, leans of late repeatedly and heavily toward sci-fi, in everything from *Déjà Vu* to the dreary *Eagle Eye*. It does so whenever the technology gets ahead of the military-industrial curve or, as in *Source Code*, drags the futurized human body with it into audiovisual obsolescence. In this light, electronic surveillance is one logical vector of sci-fi's reflexive visuality: a machinic watching unwatched by any human agency in the narrative field of view. Even in current technology, optical intake of this sort goes regularly unactivated—except on a retrospective basis when some forensic motive is engaged. In its most sophisticated forms, the optic trigger of the CCTV camera records only sudden arrests of a continuous flow or motion, or sudden lurches into motion. Normative human or vehicular traffic goes by unfiled. Cinematic epistemology in a nutshell: a looking-on selectively (our gaze channeled by editing) from an unspied space to which plot remains blind.

Like the motion-sensitive traffic cam, then, the film camera is engaged only when something potentially important is happening (i.e., made to happen). What is it exactly, via hyperbole, that turns this situation, this situated and only latent viewing, from a cultural (and narrative) given to an extended parable in *Source Code*? This effect is achieved whenever the camera's disembodied purview is executed as a literal penetration of the surveilled space: transmission as the human missile of defensive weaponry, and this from a secret Homeland Security outpost whose call sign is the quaint "Beleaguered Castle." As we cut between this computerized base of operation—indeed, this electronic baseline for the hero's remaining subjecthood and subjection at once—montage becomes instrumental (diegetic) rather than just narratival. Via a grotesque literalization of technique with respect to the hero, parallel editing is *done unto him* by cyberoptic recycling rather than simply articulating his exploits in their screen presentation. No Deleuzian duel (in the strict sense) is in fact possible across these montaged worlds of then and now. It could take place only—so the hero insists on attempting—within the evidentiary (but, he is repeatedly told, irreparable) simulation of time past, where he can, despite all cybernetic logic, face down the villain *before* disaster happens.

"Like a Convenience Store Security Camera"

The plot is sheer trope. An American pilot downed and dismembered has been given a return "tour" of duty in the morbidly specular sense, and this time only on the electronically armed home front, where his somatic remains are repurposed in the prosthetic form of a reconnaissance apparatus by which his consciousness can be projected (a tacit cinematic trope) into the residual neural traces of a terrorist victim. If this is a brutal reduction of the movement-image to the time-image for the hero's immobilized torso, it is equally a case, in its collapse of Jacques Rancière's dialectic, where the very action of the diegesis, sans movement, has become pure opsis (with derivative motor supplements—except in virtual form). In the film's first scene, the hero finds himself mentally catapulted into the body of a male passenger on a commuter train bound for Chicago (with that last adjective passing unnoticed as "computer," rather than "commuter," through several of my drafts before spotted when read aloud as a conference paper: a telltale slip about a mode of transit entirely caught up here in a circuit of electronic navigation). The new involuntary mission of Captain Colter Stevens (Jake Gyllenhaal) is to detect and identify a domestic terrorist whose next boasted move, after blowing up the train, will be to detonate a dirty bomb downtown. The protagonist is thus charged (electronically) to invade by remote control the dead man's trace memories and find the terrorist, not to prevent the disaster that has already happened but to inject himself into the serial violence and stem its ongoing tide.

Across the length of plot, we alternate in a kind of hypertrophic parallel montage—turned, I repeat, diegetic and hence instrumental—between the hero projected onto the speeding train, until yet again incinerated, and his debriefing in the podlike chamber. This locus of return is so reminiscent of his downed cockpit that he assumes at first it is a simulator (or "sim," as he calls it) in a virtual combat trainer. Slowly he ferrets out the truth: that the only death he has not yet died for his country is total brain death. Finally it is explained to him by the formulaic "mad scientist"—in the clichéd sci-fi idioms of "parabolic calculus"—that his cerebral cortex is activated as a remote wireless feed from the residual brain waves of a blast victim whose synapses have retained, for looped replay, the last minutes of cognition "like a convenience store security camera" at "closing time." The epistemology of surveillance has thus been rerouted through ontological fantasy—where, as with not only *The Jacket* but, before that, *The Sixth Sense* and *The Others* (or in a military context again, *Jacob's Ladder*), the lead character is dead from the getgo. Technically dead at least, if not technologically.

As it turns out, the morphing capsule that imprisons the hero is indeed altogether simulated, even his own body a mere digital "manifestation" as well: an internalized CGI effect to help "orient him" in his spectatorial assignment as mobile surveillance antenna, a sort of human probe or drone. The movement-image has thus gone entirely virtual when out-of-body action renders all spatiotemporal whereabouts a Deleuzian "any-space-whatever" assimilated to informatic processing by electronic tap. In lieu of real action, though, there is in part an optic (and ultimately cinematic) reflex action. In seeming to recognize his own body, the hero is only seeing things; we accept this as if knowing that, even in more normative circumstances, the movie actor only embodies a given character on-screen in a provisional way. Jake Gyllenhaal is there only, after all, to "orient" us toward the character Colter Stevens, who in this case, this anomalous diegetic case, has survived his own proper body.

But not without vampirizing—or say turning to computerized zombie—the physical person, instead, of the dead man from the train (a history teacher now getting a posthumous lesson in new media diachrony): the man whose last locomotive minutes of unexploded consciousness Colter tenants in this cybertech invasion of the body snatcher. The gaping "broach" (breach) of temporality under misnomer in *Déjà Vu*, when surfaced in a dismantled suture between hero and villain in discrepant "time frames," returns here across subjectivity's inner divide in three mirror shots of a more extreme recognition even than in *M* (either in Beckert's pivotal sighting of the eponymous chalked "M" or in an earlier scene in which he studies his features in a mirror for signs of psychosis). The mirrors in *Source Code* are, in sequence, functional, accidental, and sculptural: a typical installation in the train bathroom, the reflective surface of the train car window, and finally the polished anamorphic stainless-steel of Anish Kapoor's involuted sculpture, called *Cloud Gate*, in Chicago's Millennium Park. But what they reflect *upon* in regard to the "projective" image—we soon realize—exceeds the plot jolts, and emotional spikes, of their techno-uncanny ironies.

In the case of the terrorist villain in *Déjà Vu*—for whom, as for the rest of us, the future is always a blind spot—the suturing absent one (the retroactive "private eye" of the now-rogue detective) takes shape as fate itself closing in. In *Source Code*, by contrast, the absent one is the surveillant's (either sense: subject or object) own near-dead body forced by POV to countenance the face of himself as other. This happens, first, by the direct suture of shot/countershot in the train's bathroom mirror. It occurs next, flattened to a single frame, in what Slavoj Žižek gravitates to in Krzysztof Kieślowski's cinema as the "interface" effect (marking, as we've seen, the implosion of suture): an effect manifested here in an over-the-shoulder "two-shot" (of self and its dissemblance) in the semi-transparent window of the fated train, time flying past.[9] The third avatar of non-self-coincidence occurs finally (as only more plot can explain, and barely justify at that) once the hero has escaped from his mangled pilot's fate by cybermagic reprieve. It is then that he sees *what has become of him* in the time-warped surface of Kapoor's mirror-faced sculpture, holding hands with the girl he's fallen for on the train, who is at the same time seen reaching across time as well as space to meet the grip of Colter's dead double in his new cognitive (but retained bodily) incarnation as the history teacher.

Okay, it's still Gyllenhaal (at least from the back) deploying for our sake, here and throughout, a star persona as source of his code-induced alter ego. But other narrative perturbations do not so easily dissipate into that mode of metalepsis where aesthetic first cause is inserted as plot effect—where, for instance, we accept the actor's body as that of the character. Even though we know we've been "had," tricked, by seeing his image all along in the laboratory pod, let alone on the train car—pandered to as much as he has been—we're still shocked, late in the film, at the sight of his disemboweled carcass in a holding tank next door to the computer monitors of his mission controllers, with electrodes wired to his eviscerated torso and brain. And shocked, almost more, to find, just before this, that the fact of his disembodiment has been accepted by the manipulative scientific and military personnel running his mission in ways we hadn't foreseen. Suddenly, we realize that the separate camera and mic into which they have been peering and speaking in sutured exchanges with the hero, as registered on more than one visible monitor in his subjective pod, have presumed a living image of him that, quite to the contrary, has been not just virtual but wholly "fictive."

Where the eyeline extremity of suture, turned rupture, was a "terrorist" function in Lang (according to apparatus theory), here instead the terrifying realization is that there has been no audiovisual interchange whatever, no chance of suture. When we finally spot the monitor at which we had assumed the mission operatives were viewing Colter's (albeit simulated) image, and from whose speakers we thought they were following his vocal reports, we see that he has been coming through to them, all along, merely as a text message scrolling across the screen. No attempt at voice-generating software has converted his brain waves into vocal sounds, any more than he has been hearing their commands as actual oral prompts. The time-image—in this grotesque form of bodily effacement within a recycled violence—has evacuated even the movement of sound waves from the space of sheer cyberpresence. Revising a classic case of uncanny voice-over from beyond the grave like that in *Sunset Boulevard* (Billy Wilder, 1950), the vocal trauma in *Source Code* has not just been internalized by the diegesis (as the case of a "talking" corpse) but denied there even the phonics of its own messaging.

It's hard to take this in at first, but there's no getting past it. We've been made to see that the eyes in what's left of the soldier's body twitch behind closed lids. What Colter has thus been "seeing" from the start is merely an electrode feed—bypassing all eyesight—of his military controller, Goodwin, and her civilian boss. The audiovisual monitors in the pod, like the pod itself, are part of the heuristic mirage. They're what would keep him from thinking he was virtually dead, at least until he wises up. (In fact, he often "talks to" his keeper without even looking toward the transmitted image of her that we see in the capsule; the whole thing feels "set up" for us as well as for him.) Only one early clue, minor and passing at that, prepares us for the later disclosure. After the neurological shock and "manifested" physical damage of his first mission, with the virtual monitors spluttering out of commission as a psychic trope for trauma, Goodwin asks a technician whether Colter in his projected space "has a visual signal" again—rather than asking whether, say, he "has image." When the cover of his strictly virtual perception is finally blown, we recognize the true and violent remediation that camerawork and track have until now euphemized in the service both of functional dramaturgy and final surprise: human face as sheer cybernetic interface, voice as mere electronic pulse in orally dubbed transcription. And regarding the latter, there is perhaps a less-marked anticipation at one late turning point of plot, easy to mistake as irrelevant tech gimmickry. This happens when the voice of Colter's father (from a radio interview about his dead and decorated son's heroism) is beamed into the pod as a shameless inducement for Colter to submit one last time to his mission—"beamed," that is, as a mobile graph of sound waves on the sudden manifestation of an oversize screen: the electronic trace, or sonogram, of voice rather than its aural presence, mediated for us at one remove (and all but fully acknowledged as such this time) by a nondiegetic overdub.

The Libidinal Loop

But beyond filial entanglements, there's the further catch, the central emotive hook. Each time the hero is rebooted into the world of his doomed double to scavenge for more information, he grows more and more smitten with the girl he's just (and just again) struck up a conversation with. The rom-com ingredient of the meet-cute gets stretched, by time loop, half a dozen times over, to the length of the entire plot. This is a plot whose last phase is possible only when the pilot-hero's female operator back at Air Force headquarters—where all airborne force is now stratospheric, both computerized and telekinetic—agrees to euthanize him rather than keep him in his electronic straitjacket. She thus allows Colter, against her superior's orders, one last time-lap to catch the (now located) terrorist and thus alter the girl's fate. It's easy to see why one blogger, writing just after the film's release, took *Source Code*, despite its Chicago setting, to be the "first surge film," alluding indirectly to the Iraq troop buildups. Throw more manpower at the problem, keep pumping in the troops, even if it's the same soldier over and over again, and terrorism will be quelled. In the absence, for some reason, of CCTV on the suburban train—a structuring absence again—so-called "human intelligence" must be recruited in disembodied form: the commuter vehicle overtaken by telecommute. With the already doomed hero being blown to bits time after time on the rails of fate, if only digital bits within his new simulated being, the film in this way also indulges the counterterrorist fantasy of a suicide antibomber, surrendering his body again and again to the cause of detection and disposal. As if in a deliberate borrowing not just from *Déjà Vu* but from *Sleep Dealer*, the 2008 sci-fi film by Alex Rivera about Mexican workers jacked-in to remote robot machines operating at a San Diego construction site, in *Source Code* it's not just the fact that reconnaissance has been freakishly technologized but that the War on Terror itself has been outsourced (and disembodied, virtualized) in a sepulchral form of immaterial labor.[10]

The trick of the eventual trick ending is to turn this exploitation of the soldier's overseas casualty, his drastic disembodiment, somehow celebratory, and then to normalize the idea of out-of-body transmit in the familiar form of a supposedly liberated cell-phone link. How strained and thematically contradictory this ends up feeling depends directly on the penultimate plot turn whose logic it sells out. Yet for this dubious last move there has been a digressive setup in smart-aleck banter early on. The repatriated but out-of-step war hero asks the girl on the train at one point if her mobile phone can connect to the Internet, and she mocks him for his anachronistic innocence by saying that no, alas, it's only connected by a long string to her office. Little does she realize that her networked interlocutor is, as digital figment, a kind of humanoid walkie-talkie, whose beamed attention turns her former acquaintance on the train (whose body the hero's reassigned forensic gaze now inhabits) into little more than a ghost, or (again) a zombie, and her as well.

Yet from the hero's own perspective in this iterated electronic transference, it is as if, sent repeatedly into the breach, he is passing each time through the escalating levels of the challenge like a video gamer enhancing his skills (even though in fact he is all avatar, no input). So that in his practiced time travel he is at last empowered—at the very moment when, in parallel montage, the button is pressed to release him from life support—to make a last effort of will and, seizing the moment for a kiss, to precipitate the seizing up of his whole world in a bravura digital freeze of the sort first and most famously seen deep inside the eponymous programmed reality of *The Matrix* (Andy and Lana Wachowski, 1999). What is achieved at this moment is a wholesale arrest of diegetic space, with the time-trapped commuters, himself and the girl included, converted to digital equivalents of trompe-l'oeil mannequins as the camera floats past them, figuring the apparent release of the couple's own *liebestod*.[11]

As the ensuing sentimental coda begins to unroll, we have, that is, every reason to suspect this as yet another cruelly postponed but finally alleviating death-moment fantasy for the electronically resuscitated hero in his last resting tank—this, rather than some unaccountable triumph over a surveillance tech in which instant replay has been continuously manipulated into a brutal time loop. Colter's traumatized subordination to electronics has been too complete for that. We would be further encouraged in this familiar interpretive direction (the death-moment mirage) by the way the final shots of his wired, puppet-like torso in the countdown toward his pending release are intercut several times over—in a prolonged alternating montage—with the emotional amends (filial here, rather than marital, as in *The Sixth Sense*) that the interval allows: a long call home from the train to his estranged father, in the voice of his co-opted double, making up, as otherwise in *The Sixth Sense*, for what he died too soon to set straight. Over against this episode are interspliced images of Colter's mutilated body in wait for its imminent deactivation. And so it is that his preservation tank passes as if from coffin to incubator precisely as his father's acceptance of his death—through an acceptance of the other's voice within him—marks a symbolic second birth into the digitally induced virtuality of a parallel world.

Until then, the whole plot could be seen as shaped around the hero's acquiescence to the fact of his *own* death. And, in turn, around our stunned recognition of it in his unvoiced captioning: "Just send me back in" (five deceptively heard words denaturalized to sixteen electronically decoded ciphers): back "in," as if the mission were now wholly internalized, subjective, its detective operation an entirely *inside* job—even while the "me" is an anachronism and a misnomer. It is only "in" the system, navigating the coded program, where there might be one last chance to complete the genre mission and not just identify the culprit but save the girl—all this (as we've heard talked about beyond his artificial earshot) needing to transpire before the scheduled "memory wipe" that will ready him (or in computer lingo "refresh" him), after some threatened "data crunching" rather than further mutilation, for yet another telepathic ordeal.

Apart from this unfeeling artificial animation, the historical wish fulfillment of such a plot is palpable. Released the year after the 9/11 attacks, Steven Spielberg's *Minority Report* (2002) certainly didn't succeed in establishing a surveillance paradigm for its decade. As *Déjà Vu* makes obvious by contrast, fantasizing the next disaster (by "pre-cog" wiring) is less narratively appealing—even if equally compelling as prevention—than wishing away the last catastrophe through the imagined use of established spycams and satellite streams. This retroaction is what the hero insists on accomplishing in *Source Code* with respect to the girl's death, against the wisdom of his controllers—yet at an ontological cost that no putative happy ending can defray. Once cut loose from his computerized life-support system, the plug mercifully pulled—or so we see on camera—the freed hero, hand in hand with his retrieved dream girl, comes out the other side of that digital freeze, the onboard arrest of all locomotion, released to an embodied second life in the person of the former unsuspecting stranger on the train.

One vector of plot might seem momentarily rectified. With Colter never having been more to the agents in his control room, at least during their surveillance relays, than an intermittent flow of electronic signals, not a comatose face but a mere coerced interface, he announces his triumph now in more of the same data streaming. He does so using a cellphone text to let his controller, Goodwin, know that her prosecution of the top-secret code has in fact sourced, despite its intended use as sheer reconnaissance, a "whole new world"—and, for recent Hollywood scripting, yet another individualist way out. One thinks back to the electronified text memo as first experiment in teleportation through the "surveillance window"—two *l*s—of *Déjà Vu*. Here, in *Source Code*, the e-text comes through from the "other side": that is, from a postmortem branching reality that not only still has "connectivity" within its own alternate world but that works to trope the narrative's preternatural loophole—through disembodied telepresence—with a last gesture of everyday commercial tech. But this messaging comes through, more unnervingly yet, not just spelled out but doubled in a voice-over that—however routine in a normal narrative context—is by now thoroughly alienated and uncanny. More is at stake than just the fact the Colter's voice, the same for us in the pod as for the girl on the train—despite its nonexistence in the control room—is borrowed (we've been forced at the end to remember) from the reanimated larynx of another corpse. Further, the "irrational cut" thus triggering the final voice-over breaks with sensorimotor and acoustic conventions to pry open the space for filmic thought—and indeed thought in part about film's inherent (and irrational) "ventriloquism," preternaturally vexed in this one sci-fi instance: in short, the normal track-based throwing of voice into separately imaged body.[12]

Loquo ergo sum. Cogito aside, I speak, therefore I am. Another individualist way out, yes. Which is to say another digital myth, where the dystopian plot has its own Esc button. And another way, too, whereby the "numeric image," portending such an uncertain future at Deleuze's last writing, has been contorted to offer, rather than a direct time-image, a time-looped one. All under the attenuated reign of a Deleuzian virtual, which contradicts the actual but remains part of the real. For the war casualty in *Source Code*, the virtual has been for the entire film the only on-camera real. Hence the perfectly smooth (if logically slippery) move from somatic mirage in the first place to alternate reality in another: another place, another time frame. Here lies the real and pervasive fantasy element of this and many another recent film in global circulation: in Todorov's terms again, a kind of backsliding from the instrumental marvelous to the uncanny, the daemonic, the hallucinatory (even if digitally afforded). Long before his film's trick ending, the technology that can beam Colter vast distances into the past scene of attack is the same technology that can digitize an optical image of his lost body to give him the proprioceptive orientation that any gamer or VR test pilot needs. Quid pro quo: you lose some (reality), you win some, win it back by digital figment. And once again in the twist-finish mode, one must ask whether resolution comes with a logical swindle—or a swivel with genuine narrative grip.

Such is the recent plot syndrome even in films calling up digital technology only in technique, not plot, from *Donnie Darko* through *The Butterfly Effect*, as well as in an explicit computer thriller like *Source Code*. Even here, though, when the status of *homo electronicus* has been fiercely and explicitly abused, the human form snared by cyber circuits, technology may still, we're to think, help us *out*: service our desire, make emancipatory connections, in this case transmute a macabre allegorical disembodiment into its more standard-issue version in remote messaging. This can happen only, that is, when the nightmare of disincarnate voiceless texting is converted in the end to the convenient wireless proof of a computer-triggered afterlife rather than a hybrid cybernetic limbo. In genre terms, fused in this way are the separate narrative thru-lines of a film like Alejandro Amenábar's *Tesis*, so that now, in *Source Code*, the live recording of sadistic (and here terrorist) murder and the subsequently accessed security-cam images of incrimination are collapsed into the same preternaturally mediating body. At which point, as in *Enemy of the State*, with the state itself turned inimical, we come again upon the myth of little guy pushing back, manipulating the cybernetic system, turning it against itself with sheer pluck rather than expertise. Yet the victory in *Source Code* is not just meretricious but unusually Pyrrhic.

Computopia

To see why, we need only audit again that final moment of phantom voice-over tracked past on the strip in association with the scrolling of its identical e-text. As supposed proof of Colter's vindicated individuality from within the snares of cerebral signaling, his final triumphant debriefing begins in just this voice-over—his image profoundly "off camera" within the same alternate reality, we come to realize, from which he assures his mission controller that the computer's "Source Code" program has indeed originated a "new world" of branched and uncoded virtuality. But even back in the "real world," to which we think at first we've been reliably returned, counsel is to be taken from the near future. In this final voice-over we hear what the (equally) artificial intelligence of a smart phone scrolls out as silent text: "If you are getting this e-mail, you will soon hear that a terrorist attempt has been thwarted." What? What's happening? Where are we? And when? In our mental lurch to grasp this further tricking of closure, we realize that Colter is somewhere far off camera within the same parallel universe we are now watching: making contact not with the space of his at last alleviated corpse but with an identical lab where, by temporal paradox, all missions are still in the offing for his humanoid broadcast platform.

Colter's last remote message is not more remote or electronically generated than the world in which it is received, and by the time we figure this out, we realize that this final trick is itself figurative. For how real can this recognized voice be felt to be, a voice that has all along been a mere figment of poetic (and narratively deceptive) license? And how upbeat can this ending seem when the speaker's former operator—receiving the likes of an i-Phone message from the organic android "I" of this incarnate biotech app—is still standing just a room away from a body not yet euthanized after all, still on hold for this continued militarization of Homeland Security? This is the body about which the offscreen voice now speaks in third person, urging compassion when a next mission does call "him" back to action. With a further "time reassignment" still pending for this post-Cartesian subject, his mind split irrevocably from body by digital intervention, there is only the cold comfort of a self-renewing fantasy, communicated in absentia (absentia from his own pronoun): "Promise me you'll help him and, when you do, do me a favor, tell him everything's gonna be okay." That's because each brave soldierly triumph may well sponsor another parallel universe. Regardless of how many deaths you are compelled to die for your country—itself an allegorical trope for how many enlisted bodies Command Central assigns to the mission—there's the hope of a new (and amorous) afterlife each time. It's the stateside counterterrorist answer to a jihadist's harem in the sky. This geopolitical irony aside, the deeper pattern is familiar. With the hero's closing recourse to the quotidian wonder of remote messaging—even after his own exploitation as an imprisoned data stream—we note yet again, as in so much sci-fi, that normal technology has thus been extrapolated to perverse marvel. Disembodied alphabetic communication offers in this case the kind of everyday wizardry from which the astonishments—and monstrosities—of dystopian science are derived by exaggeration. And indexed by technique: technique, that is, when narratographically registered.

In both of Jones's features, in fact, the surveilled clone and the living surveillance drone—the replicant and the cyborgian brain scanner—each submit to its own exposed artifice from within the denaturalized logic of montage as it is pressed back to the discontinuities of the track itself. In *Moon*, a prolonged barrage of New Wave–style micro-jump cuts punctuates the clone's manic search for proof positive of his derivative status as serial duplicate, reminding us in the process that all continuity of screen character, too, is a reduplication of the image from frame to frame: not just a cloning of the original by photomechanics but an imprinted repetition with minimal difference in the time-based frame line. And in *Source Code*, the repeated explosion of the train from different angles, eight minutes apart and many times over, paced by the hero's forensic reentry into that detonated past, serves to lay bare the ordinary montage of such a showpiece explosion, with its gestalt of separate camera angles. By these respective fractures and decompactions of the track in *Moon* and *Source Code*, the technical construction of cinema underwrites even while unraveling the simulated reality of its dystopian protagonists. The genre signature of sci-fi once again: an image of the near or far future about precisely the future of human imaging, where in these cases so-called life, under conditions of total surveillance, may devolve into the madness of permanent replay.

Whether cloned and robotic, or programmed and renavigated in the purely virtual, life in such plots has become a presence only on demand of the other: all life being that of the "spiritual automaton" (Deleuze) by which cinema once extended rather than substituted for the very processes of becoming. Such narratives leech from their own technical premises to fuel their technophobic plots. This includes not just the technical premises of the surveillance subgenre but even the underlying technological aesthetic of the medium. One is faced with a question already anticipated in discussing Gyllenhaal's role as, in effect, a mirage understudy for the hero in *Source Code* (Colter's electroneural "manifestation" as living body): What's the difference whether an actor is playing a character "himself" or his identical twin, his clone, even his digitally composited mere image? How soon we forget that human figures never enter their screen plots, daredevil or otherwise, in propria persona. It's only natural that we suspend our disbelief, along with the pod-bound hero, in assuming that he is really there in bodily form in the encapsulated space on which we spy unseen.

Thus does this one protagonist, like any other screen actor—giving us the visual image of a character he only provisionally embodies, and then getting put through his assigned script via multiple takes of the same action—underscore the condition of cinema's own optical as well as narrative performance. And not least in an age of digital affordance when the manifested body is no longer necessarily an index of the filmed one to begin with. Colter's digital figment may be the future fate of all bodies on screen. Then too, with every combatant, not just every actor, pressed into service more as a role than a person, technique verges again on critique through that belatedly divulged "reading" (rather than actual seeing) of the slain but still "reenlisted" soldier as a sheer apparatus of retroactive deterrence. As always in the so-called war machine—that machine increasingly identified with the computer—the soldier is indeed faceless. But at the moment of the hero's actual defacement as image in *Source Code*—time and again, with each computer propulsion into the past—the plot is saying one thing, the movie, as film, something more.

Sheets of Presence: From "Synaptic Map" to Bitmap

In thinking through plot to medium in *Source Code*—or, rather, in thinking plot through at the level of its mediation—we find suggestive points of comparison with both other digitally executed fantasy and with a whole range of electronic sci-fi. In that earlier cycle of temporal recursion in the puzzle-film mode, teen heroes escape their troubled present by one fantastic form or another of digital whoosh or cosmic zoom, letting framed space and its textures figure time under distress—en route to temporal restitution. In *Source Code*, when the order comes to "charge the computer drivers," the military hero is vacuumed out from presence (temporal and spatial both) in much the same electronically disintegrated way, via a similar digital chute, though more explicitly technological in this case: his whole bodily mass fracturing into gridded digital bits along the cross-veined fissures of its tessellated form—and then instantaneously reconstituted as human image on the speeding vehicle of the montage counterplot.

Like recent time travelers before him, albeit in a sci-fi rather than fantasy mode now, Colter is cybernetically dis-integrated by the same screen technique that has become, this time, explicitly incorporated as a diegetic technology. In the cross-mapping of the "synaptic" network from Colter's brain to that of his "alter self," visual form and machinic function are so inextricable that we readily read the raster graphics of his bitmap image, obliterated and rezoned, as the very medium of temporal transit. In the microtriangular webwork that "nets" him each time for transmit, the shivering of his image is not exactly like the pixel checkerboard underlying these digital F/X (of the sort we might see in an accidental DVD breakup of the same shot)—but close enough to figure it in passing. But there is a further narrative irony in this, one also delivered by the medium itself—and emerging most clearly by contrast with the later tour de force of the digital freeze. That bravura turn, again, is the stop-action (rather than stop-motion) effect, the camera still seemingly in play, that no sooner signifies a cancelled life support than it also serves to figure—with no pixel static this time—the hero's gateway to a branching reality. Such a mobile but stop-action shot is the CGI upgrade of photomechanical cinema's classic punctuation in the freeze-frame, familiar to us most recently from the last dated (rather than datelined) shot of *Déjà Vu*: the iteration of the single frame-line cell that flattens out diegesis into a quasi-photographic fixity.[13] At the climax of *Source Code*, however, the diegetic space remains negotiable in depth by the camera, though frozen in its own ontology. The result operates somewhere between a metaphorical gesture and a neurological rupture. So, too, with those earlier computerized decimations of Colter's image in teleportation rather than arrest. They are no mere metaphors either.

Nor are they strictly narrational transitions. Operating there, over and over, is not just a case of digital breakdown as scene change—as if we were seeing for a few split, splintered seconds into the bowels of the new hybrid medium's own pixilated generation. That's only the half of it. Any such potential for a self-reflexive recuperation of the F/X involves its own ontological relapse for the hero—which, one may say, *changes the picture* of this digital transit entirely. Given that Colter is as much a heuristic "manifestation" to himself as he is, on screen, to us, it is therefore his virtual presence rather than just his image that is all but instantaneously decomposed and recomposited: as if it, as if "he," were no more than the digital effect which in fact, even inside the plot, he is. Certainly the notion that all montage is *trucage*—Metz's resonant dictum once more—anticipates perfectly, by way of hypertrophic special effects, the digital morphing of the image plane in the several variants of this shot (and its many familiar predecessors from digitally edited fantasy over the last couple of decades). But the sci-fi premise runs deeper this time, however manifestly shallow in the planar effects of its raster dispersion. *Source Code*'s dismembered and now dispelled hero is disintegrated across a montage gap that shatters to a vanishing electronic collage. With human agency constituted in this way—beyond its mortal remains—as pure code, no fully incarnate source left, the result is stylistically overdetermined. All screen presence is manufactured, digitized, virtual. All personage has become *trucage*.

And, in just such moments of spectral transition and technical disclosure, the montage of *Source Code* deposits certain further inlaid visual fragments that end up traversing the whole vector of plot in reverse, future to present. So deeply ingrained, that is, does the mind-game logic seem that an independent motif in this vein—or is it so separate after all?—can be run alongside the main parallel-universe plotting. When the railroad bomb first goes off, propelling Colter back to his virtual cockpit, and then at various points in his later ejection from present to past, lab to train, there's an unaccountable overload of image. Besides pixel breakdown, the temporal malleability of the montage interspace involves flash-forwards to shots of that optically distorting stainless-steel sculpture visible in "real time" (scare quotes indeed) only at the end, when the hero walks toward it in Millennium Park with the girl he's retrieved from death. One result is that the gleaming anamorphic surface of Kapoor's *Cloud Gate* is visible at that final point (for Colter too, not just for us) with a glint of recognition. What we also see in its bent planarity, of course, is that the man holding her hand before the sculpture's warped mirror is Colter's dead double from the train, whose leased body is all that is now available to our hero in this new parallel life.

Two puzzle pieces seem to be falling into place within the same mirror shot—having to do, inextricably, with somatic and temporal displacements alike. Yet questions nag. The flash-forwards to this moment do seem rounded out here in something more than a mere formal symmetry; they appear part of the fable, an inbuilt déjà vu. But engineered for what purpose? And by any mechanism, perhaps, other than cinema's own? Under the immediate spell of the scene's double-take, a quizzical Colter asks the saved girl: "Do you believe in fate?" In the same mood, he had previously asked Goodwin if she ever fantasized about her life taking a different path—of the sort he was at the moment hoping for according to "branching universe" possibilities. No, neither woman is the dreamer he is, a fact that may seem designed in the end to humanize his technological breakthrough as mental disposition (at the expense, nonetheless, of his predecessor's dead body).

But there is another reading of the flash inserts in their intermittent clairvoyance—yielding a different sense of the twist ending. Or inducing another level of trick altogether. For the prefigurations could well insinuate that the happily-ever-after finale was programmed by the Source Code all along, leaking through with split-second hints of destiny rather than confessed machination. Programmed, precoded—this, so that each of the soldier's uploadings onto the scene of terror would be laced with appeasing free associations of potential escape: some glimpsed indeterminate place, that is, beyond pod or doomed passenger car. These would then be anodyne images (utopian in the root sense of unplaced) generated electronically in each sequential reality and offered up there as the unconscious warrant, traumatic time and again, for yet another forking bypass of his death.

Dramatic tone at the end, however, along with orchestral uplift, does strongly suggest the former upbeat assumption: techno-miracle rather than anodyne implant. It is as if Colter's foreseen if unrecognized dream has come genuinely true, an unconscious scene of desire (almost subliminal in its fragmentation) getting realized by dint of heroic faith and persistence. Yet it is typical of such computer phantasmagorias that anything seemingly beyond the cyborgian horizons of the machine may be delusional, may be programmed in its matrix rather than released from the virtual into some autonomous real: a vision deviously uploaded rather than liberating the off-loaded self. Does Colter boast a libidinal sixth sense, or an electronically instilled seventh? Who is to say? Are the loose ends extraneous and implausible—or motivated and psychological, more like figures of desire than fateful prefigurations? In any case, within the rushed blur of such transtemporal shifts, we've seen how the digital virtuality of the hero's image, confirmed by bitmap disintegration at the very seams of montage—and dispelling the simulated exchange of suture—is continuous with the third (and fourth) dimensions of the film's branching reality plot.

Closure is in this sense clarifying—at least as to the broadest social canvas on which the film would make its mark. For, ambiguities aside, the dead end of a narrative tendency seems manifest. Some cycles, like some genres, innovate frenetically to the point where they do more than tie themselves up in knots. They turn themselves inside out. Flamboyant electronic gadgetry on film has for years scrambled to keep at least a little ahead of current real-world technology in order to bring ever-zingier anxieties to bear on the dehumanized space of surveillance and its invasion of all privacy, public, domestic, even somatic. The next step: beyond the mediation of all human activity, the *reduction of the human itself to sheer medium.*

An antiterrorist fantasy of bringing the mass dead back briefly to life—so as to debrief them on the scene of lethal terrorism—might have become, in some routine scripts, a selected victim's post-mortem brain swipe as real-time surveillance in computerized replay: an unmanned (trans)mission. Instead, the surveillance cycle goes one step further in *Source Code* to turn another and previous victim of mortal wounds, a soldier still in rank, into the scanning agency itself. You couldn't kill the messenger in such a case, since he's already as good as dead—and thus not only uniquely instrumental as medium (it takes a dead brain to know one) but also ultimately invulnerable in his telepresent spying. His wasted body is simply rewired as long-distance surveillance feed. If this somatic recycling functions as an impacted gothic allegory of a new military mentality—where the stop-loss program's need to keep boots on the ground is replaced by somatically-rooted drone surveillance and ballistic interception—it also seems a prescient if perverse fable of disclosures about NSA surveillance within a couple of years of its release. It's not just that counterterrorist data are stored passively for activation on a need-to-know-basis. In the fantasy at hand, so, too, can dead heroes be held in abeyance for targeted break-ins to one posthumous cerebral data bank or another.

Mediation Called to Task

With everyday digital convenience in *Source Code* touting (even spouting in final voice-over) its triumph over malign paramilitary contrivance, Friedrich Kittler's paradigm of martial innovation preceding commercial media is openly inverted by this sci-fi denouement. So it is that a popular development in the latter media sphere (the boom in remote electronic messaging) can be maneuvered to naturalize and even ameliorate the potential depredations of the former realm of military surveillance.[14] The era of computerized telephonics, gone over to a nightmare of electro-telepathy and recursive temporality, seems bent on its own fantasized repair. Yet the digital fix, in only one sense, remains. The combat casualty lingers unreleased, dying to fight another day—even while his off-frame avatar is looking back on, and out for, himself in a message from the far side of his latest mission, with its last-minute magic vector from the neutered to the virtual body.

But this is where this trick ending—one so arcane in its double cross that we may barely notice it—can still bite its own tail. The fact that the utopian alter-world doesn't in fact alter the mortal trauma, the macabre half-life, of the hero's artificially sustained heart, lungs, and brain—vestigial organs not finally shut down after all in the galvanic burst of his neuro-electronic escape—is a quirk of the storyline that can scarcely squirm free from the broader aura of biopolitical paranoia that rims the film. There's no escaping the death of one's body. And as soon as we warm to the contrived fantasy of the ravaged soldier's doing so, we're back in the lab with his version of an immobilized rat on the computer treadmill, jerked back there by the double helix of plot itself. The hero's final forecast of a thwarted terrorism still to be announced by the media (in the future perfect of preemption) might as well come by encoded bleeps from some still-wired cranial recess of a complete psychotic break—rather than from his supervisor's handheld mobile inbox—for all the good it does his degraded human remains.

Tonally, the film dodges this recognition in the attempted uplift of its final download, its message from the recursive ever after. But logically, the narrative is caught up in its own time-loop paradox. Hardly without precedent, the genres of sci-fi and so-called puzzle film implode on each other. In the eight minutes left to, and of, our hero, it is only a recent catastrophic past, fled to after averted disaster, that his exploit has redeemed. The present still awaits his continued, his recurrent, vigilance—or let's say that of his inert somatic platform—with more threats coming, as it were, by the minute. By heroic *convention*, the doomed war hero on screen routinely stands in for a host of other soldiers lost in battle. Here instead, by high-tech *invention*, only one death would ever be necessary, at least given just the right recyclable scapegoat, whose wired crypt would become an unforgiving altar for this new military-industrial science of human sacrifice.[15]

That's a symptomatic reading of the film's fantasy. What about its cinematic fact? That too can be symptomatically read, as we've amply seen—regarding, for instance, the technical construction of montage (in jump cuts and iterated camera angles), the premises of the diegesis as fiction (the embodiment of role by the body of the actor), and the mating of voice to that body (on the double-tracked strip). Such are the familiar, self-demarcated media shunts of mediation itself. Such, also, are the elements of a projected scene and scenario undermined by this one sci-fi departure into simulacral presence and repetition. Part of this departure is, of course, the digital turn both of technique as well as plot. So far, discussion has retraced the mesh of plot and theme. Cyberoptic technology gone too far: that's what the film seems to be *about*, or tacitly about. What it's *after*, however, and through precisely a cognate technology, is the commandeering of *our* specular attention, not the hero's. In the sci-fi genre, a general battery of special effects is deployed to effect some special crux from film to film. And here is where sci-fi repeatedly cashes out its imagery separate from its plots, or the former as the inference of the latter. Here, in other words, is where picture and fiction redouble each other even in parting company.

For in this aspect of the film's CGI-enhanced diegesis, the effort of the spectacle, as with so much F/X, is not just to feature or fetishize its technique but to narrativize it as magic, black or white. If this is the first "surge film," it is also one of many splurge films, though more modest in budget than some. Throwing more manpower at the problem may save the world. But in Hollywood, and here the allegorical cinch of this one film is pulled tight, a different logic prevails, not just quantitative but economic. Throwing enough money at the problem, funding enough computer-rendering time (as allegorized in *Déjà Vu* as well), can, as usual in this industrial system, create a "whole new world." And the electronically funded energies of the hero, in outsourced and virtual combat against terror, intersect aptly enough—from within this new martial economy and its "program"—with the soft(ware) rather than hard labor of the F/X technicians. It is at this level of apprehension that the invested capital behind such computer input is to be returned at compound *interest* (both sorts) in ticket sales.

And yet another case of medial disclosure by exaggeration, alluded to briefly above, comes to the fore in *Source Code*. Speaking of recent film style, as especially prominent in the F/X of apocalyptic blockbusters, Steven Shaviro has coined the term "post-continuity editing" for, at least in part, the jaggedness and arbitrary cross-cuts of so much CGI-dominated action cinema—rendered by too many flashpoints of disaster at once for continuous orchestration, a sequencing uncontained by a coherent montage stream, an editing in the end thus liberated from classic protocols of the movement-image.[16] *Source Code* recalls this norm precisely by shrinking it to a bare minimum: a serial recursion rather than disjunctive spectacle, where the normal resources of montage are denied the variant camera angles necessary, say, to fully dynamize the train blast. Instead: the same explosion over and over again, with a "digital pyrotechnician" credited in the end titles, to be sure, but not given free rein to vary his computerized toolkit in the full brandishing of a knockout effect. Certainly the ignited train scene, as *iterable* computer matrix for the surveillance operative rebooted time and again into its fatal momentum, exceeds all narrative continuity and its norms of editing, but only by being backed up to the rudimentary motive for the narrative all told—and hence neutered as climactic visualization. Its image, as such, seems instead isolated as a field of study—exactly what it is within the diegesis: an electronic file for synaptic access rather than a crowd-pleasing spectacle.

Exacerbated almost beyond recognition, the surveillance cycle enacts here its own dubious recycling. It's not that the film navigates a way out of its intractable human impasse. Instead, it divides against itself, its very premise, and seizes e-text voice-over from the locked jaws of abject electronic defeat. Die to live another day, the tagline might run. And may yet—since Colter's rewired body is on hold for another kind of seriality as well, a run of future missions programmed in a different sense. For at this writing, the film is rumored to be going into production as a "weekly procedural" on CBS TV. But how much of the brain-battered torso stashed away inert in a demonic military hospice can one audience, let alone one corpse, endure?[17] Yet the myth persists: in escape from the computer fixations of a surveillant state, some loner hero's private digital fix.

POSTFACE: ON MEDIATION AS INTERFACE

This study began by tabulating some of the returns expected from a retrieval of lapsed or dormant theoretical concepts from the legacy of film theory. Returns not only for a new screen dispensation (digital production and projection) and a new cultural project (electronic oversight) but returns for—and to—the genealogy of a narrative mode, the surveillance plot, reaching farther back into film history. Sufficient results are already in, even as evidence keeps coming—and certain philosophical losses are ready to be tallied. For one thing, a contemporary mode of postfacial encounter in mediated social interactivity is typified by the biometric recognition so often a part of the current spate of surveillance films, so much in the news lately apart from cinematic treatment, and so wholly a sign of our times in a posthuman culture not of identity but of identifying features. These are features (often generic and "profiled") that get circulated in various modes of automatized recognition or remote detection. They serve to replace interpersonal give and take with a telemetric circuit, the intimacy of encounter with digital tracking, private presence with mediated trace. A good deal of human exchange is aggregated, not congregated, in this limbo of interface.

Once upon a time, suture theory arose in part to account, one might say, for the "postfacial" alignment of subject positions in screen editing: an alignment always playing catch-up on the heels of a serial and reciprocal absence and its displaced frontal gaze. And yet finding in this play, this interplay, the medium's bid for its greatest intimacy. In contrast, the new and regularly desutured scan of the technopticon in narrative film tends to evacuate the Deleuzian "affection-image"—typified by the exchangeable frames of specular action and its resulting close-up reaction—into a mere forensic application of the digital zoom instead. Broad philosophic parameters may grow cramped or inoperable before our eyes in this new ocular climate. And the more the gap narrows between a cinema digitally recorded, edited, projected, and sometimes even generated—between this new computer-age (postfilmic) cinema and other modes of electronic interface beyond the theater lobby—the more urgent (because all too familiar) seem the inset frames of surveillance screening, via sci-fi near futurism, in films like *Déjà Vu* and *Source Code*.[1] What cinema, and by association the screened picture more generally, might do, might once have done, in testing one's faith in the existence of the world (Cavell, Deleuze), and this precisely by the gauntlet of the world's enframed sheer image, has been leveled in the surveillance plot to the conceptual flatlands of a forensic epistemophilia.[2] The impetus of *belief*, or call it suspended disbelief, has been supplanted by the tactics of *verification*. Film's ability to think the world at a distance—an *acceptable* distance, eliciting affective investments delinked from proof—turns narrowly evidentiary on the embedded surveillance screen. Cavell's analysis, for instance, of the many ways human doubt can refuse the world on the world's own terms is no longer worked through by this subsidiary view-finding. Quite the reverse. The philosophical problematic of skepticism takes shrunken and potentially lethal form in the statistical probabilities of the properly identified human target.

Under surveillance, which is to say under the law of surveillance, the images constituting a Cavellian "world viewed" are no longer in-themselves or for-themselves. And hence not for us in philosophy's therapeutic sense. Within the narrative, they are strictly for use. Another facet of film philosophy is thereby summarily eroded. Alain Badiou is among the latest writers drawn to Deleuze on cinema, in Badiou's case (as philosopher) not for the effort to fashion some new ideas of the image (as in a medium-specific film theory) but rather to forge some new images of the idea, some new mental pictures of thought itself and its syntheses.[3] The desire for such a conceptual passage through image to idea explains for Badiou the return to Bergson in Deleuze's work, where, once movement is defined as primarily an image rather than an event, a kind of space/time optic ratio, then—when modernist cinema subsequently removes the priority of dramatic action as spatial difference and transition—one is left instead with the time-image and the potentially legible concepts about human temporality it generates. Under surveillance, however, we have seen this vitiation of the action-image degraded instead to the time-coded image of perused duration in the strictly instrumental search for an event (with a lower-case e).

Regarding this co-optation of the optic field by the machines of state, their rogue counterparts, or the international cartels that may secretly control either or both, film examples show no sign of abating. The latest mainstream surveillance film at this writing, finding for itself a title almost unaccountably lying in wait all these years, finds in turn an equally predictable tag line (especially in its plot's British context of CCTV saturation). *Closed Circuit*: "They See Your Every Move." Or, more accurately, the technoptic "they" see movement (which is image to begin with) at the further remove—whether time-delayed or real-time—of sheer interface. Time's integral relation to motion has become motion's new subservience to the manipulated and recursive temporalities of inspection. This isn't philosophical; it is expedient: a wielding not of ideas but of power. Or of "control"—as we are about to see Deleuze name and rethink it.

The narrative formats that reflect such armatures of power aren't just a litany of e-spionage ingenuities; they are a societal litmus test. The variants of a narrative cycle are once again, as they so often are, available for cultural generalization. Even when not seeing eye-to-eye, we don't often go head-to-head these days. It is as if the final reversion to mano-a-mano combat in the thriller mode, so common in these surveillance films, isn't just a sop to the action-hero crowd but a measure of what is otherwise surrendered to remote-controlled violence. As these screen narratives repeatedly work to suggest, if by the same electronic facilitations they bemoan when in the wrong hands, the so-called global village is more like a mass deracination. We inhabit for the most part a post–face-to-face culture, within which, just for instance, the metonymic Facebook of social mediation is a flagrant dead metaphor. Everywhere this same "see change" in modes of perceived otherness, this zeitgeist of disembodied sight lines. And anywhere, at any time, the potential of such mediation for its tactical deployment by forces—and from a vantage—unseen. A vantage from which "homing" is no nostalgic trajectory of the sheltering impulse but rather the technical term for an electronic access (by drone targeting) to any and all supposed havens. Given the atmospheric pressure in narrative resulting from numerous ramifications of this new satellite-linked regime of the ionosphere and its ether streams, girded from below by a buried fiberoptic webwork, the paranoid thriller plots of surveillance cinema offer no more than the overt instrumentation of a furtive violence lurking behind all such "securitized" visibility.

To have concluded with sci-fi versions of this disembodied surveillance crux has, therefore, far more than recent screen frequency to recommend it, where installments of the genre have increasingly taken up the critique of vigilant electronic overreach. For the very pace of digital advance tends to erode the fact/fiction divide between audiovisual emplacements in contemporary cultural space and their futurist extrapolations in dystopian screen narrative. One result is that postfilmic cinema typically reflects on the very medium it shares with other electronic implementations. And there lies, from case to case, the true narratographic hook of these sci-fi screen treatments. In their optical illusions, including fabricated electronic marvels of surveillant teleportation, the wired specular portals of digitial F/X operate again and again by optical *allusion* to the techne they share with an extracinematic inspection in daily social commerce.

Subjected to View

Lang's cinema, where we began, depends on an entirely different materialist platform. What we are made to see ourselves watching by proxy in *M*—it's as complicated as it sounds—is the indexical interchange of photofilmic increments in picturing the stalked subject seeing himself seen. What, instead, we are made to see ourselves entrammeled in by proxy with *Source Code* is the received world as mere electro-cortical data, mediated through a cognitive (rather than sensory) focal point: a world (past, recorded, investigable) whose indexicality has (for "him," what's left of the hero function) gone entirely digital, a matter of racing electronic signals rather than captured integral images. Colter is a wired agent, not a sighted one. Representing biological subjectivity itself in truncation, as he does, his psychosomatic miseries are part of the simulation, the only thing visceral left of his human stump.

A reductio ad absurdum of spectation, this focal center in *Source Code* is not a human function so much as a vicarious transit point for detective evidence: a sheer computer-driven interface. Again theme and its sutured diegetic space come bearing down on the medium itself. The mass killer that the hero's own purely transmissive status is meant to locate and identify—as if Colter were a disembodied GPS—could only materialize for him as a pixilated cerebral figment. Same, too, though at a more primary diegetic level this time, with the "reverse shots" of Colter "himself" (from the deceptive vantage of his in fact unseeing handlers) in the solely electronic materialization of his VR pod, where the once-human subject, turned data stream, is only a digital configuration *even to himself*. Beckert, instead, was for the viewer of *M* (never for the Berlin police) that rapid series of photographic traces one knew then as a film image—and for himself an all-too-human and wholly cornered victim, no sooner spotting his own stigma than spotted doing so. In short, at the level of screen projection, the process of surveillance—as narrative mode, as optical mandate—is one name for the angle of vision (or its electronic simulation) that we inherit from the plot in process.

In this way technique is also commandeered and remastered at the level of *muthos* rather than incidental *opsis* (Jacques Rancière again). For what *Source Code* as much as *Déjà Vu* accomplishes, in its coached irruption of medial conditions, is the immediate conversion of these to sci-fi extravagance rather than flaunted visual finesse. Parallel montage is computerized in each film so as to spring its quantum leap into a parallel universe. Here is where, in a reading back-to-front of my book's subtitle, it should be clear how (c) *surveillance* can take (b) *narrative* shape in the (a) *screening* process as a new kind of instrumental or operational "editing": a cybernetic program within the diegesis, rather than just the mechanical propulsion of screen syntax. And this is where it is also clear that suture comes back into the picture: the picture it articulates. Across the history of screen projection (in and beyond its cinematic function), a presutured *jouissance* must submit to various forms—and themes—of *puissance* in the move from a seen that changes (moving image) through scene change (narrative in embryo) to that technology of motion-triggered surveillance in which all changes, and only changes, are seen—or conjured in this regard by the detective motors of plot. Suture comes back into the picture, that is, by being outdistanced at last (in every sense) by the unseen cyclopic viewpoint of remote CCTV.

Deviation, disequilibrium: once the instigation of plot, now the trigger of automatic record in the motion-sensors of spyware. Even time-travel sci-fi can be reduced to the retroactive installation of a humanoid spycam. Electronic espionage—as a director like Lang could almost have foreseen—has entered yet another feedback loop with montage. As with free indirect discourse under the lens of linguistic analysis, narratography is at least one way to engage—so as more fully to gauge—the ethical friction of such screen plotting from the very grain of cinematographic technique. Technique, mediation: that's what such films are there for. What they are therefore *after*, even half-consciously at times, is a complicit viewing of their invented worlds. This is a viewing that takes place with or without our recognizing the unbroken spectrum that, ironically enough, includes both a paranoia about advanced technological mediation and a parading (without parody) of the narrative techniques that forecast it. Again, Kittler's historical model is confirmed by reversal in the new tech fables. Where previous military innovation has fed back commercially into every important media advance, here instead—as narrativized in a given screen plot—showy initiatives in media, not least the digitization of diegesis by CGI, anticipate the paramilitary aberrations they also invent and picture.

We have reached a point in media history and its "fantasies" (alluding again to Paul Young's account) that constitutes another plateau in how cinema "dreams its rivals" in the mode of nightmare. The vicious circle of surveillance is tightened to a mutual evacuation of each pole. Disembodied telepresence—a rival, at least in less morbid forms, for theatrical cinema, and not just as fantasized magical visualization but as video game model for a programmed avatar—involves in the case of *Source Code* a paranormal transference from the dead subject of surveillance, in perceptual limbo, to its dead object on the train. At which point the former is in turn objectified under debriefing as the mere "screen" (cortical rather than fully optical) of past violence. Whereas in "normal" surveillance the subject in question, the suspect under scrutiny, is reduced to object, in *Source Code* the wholly coded residuum of an intermediary subject (the bomb victim's dead brain)—once his synaptic map had been reconstructed—is absorbed into the primary investigative subject as a shared conduit of cognitive signals awaiting upload in the continued search for his killer. In the process, the antiterrorist operatives don't really "inter-view" the hero back in the lab in the course of his debriefings—as we know from that bitter peripety where the audiovisual void of his arrested subjectivity is revealed in the form of disembodied texting. Instead, they pick his brain more directly in exactly this encoded electromagnetic form. The hero isn't just wired; he *is* the wire in the most literal sense. If they don't really see through his eyes, it's only because he doesn't either. Instead, he transliterates the electronically revisited past into simultaneous record and transmit in his (now externally accessed) mind's eye.

In *Source Code*, then, the virtuality of image concerns the once-human body not just mediated but *mediatized*, made sheer means of electronic transfer. Again: that ontological arc from the modernist *M* toward the laboratory of a postmaterial man as cybernetic figment. So that in *Source Code* any and all reflexive analogs to new modes of cinematic production—at the level of computerized effect or digital record, either one—do not in some narrow way point round on themselves to the cinematic process we're caught up in, here in genre terms a sci-fi narrative of coerced out-of-body prosthetics: the new Frankenstein's creature getting wired into life from his *own* charnel discard (instead of from grave-robbed anonymous body parts). Rather, the disclosures of production delimit in this instance, as in many others lately, the shared technological condition at once of cybernetic optics in the culture at large and of computer-boosted fantasies in F/X thriller films: invisible surveillance and narrative spectacle brought to you equally by newly digitized channels of audiovisual display and cognition. The tipped hand of computerized "production values" in the industrial big-budget film, on the underside of a given dystopian plot of techno excess—instead of bracketing the artifice of its F/X devices (in the sense of suspending in parenthesis our attention to their raw technique)—can't help but put them forward as such. This works so as, in the other sense, to bracket or frame the entire operation in its commercial valence.

The "fictions" of sci-fi are poised to extrapolate from the wonders of such pay-per-view (or pay-purview) technologies to mediations yet unseen. What this amounts to, in *Déjà Vu* and *Source Code* both, is a cooptation of cinematography by a new digital temporality in which the past is as transparent to detection as the scrolling through of the now. Authorized within plot by an asymptote of forensic tech on its way to total surveillance, the result is a railroading of montage aesthetics into a diegetics of instrumental scene-shifting, cutting across time as much as space, but also between present- and alternate-world space. And shredding suture in the process, even when surreptitiously. Openly, though, at least at the level of parallel montage, the former mutual virtualities of narrative alternation become real and operational. And this is marked most obviously in the way their interplay coincides with an epistemology of surveillance at the plot level. Here and elsewhere in this continuing cycle, cinema ends up performing the interface operations from which it recoils.

And the prehistory of this technical irony has moved on, after *M*, not only to the long legacy of Orwell's dystopian telescreen—and the many paranoid thrillers of a military-industrial, political, or corporate technopticon (including *The Conversation* and *Blow Out* on the way toward *Enemy of the State* and beyond)—but to the more satiric social phobias of *Look* and *The Nine Lives of Tomas Katz*, as linked in turn to the psychodrama of voyeurism and violence in a tradition running from *Rear Window* and *Peeping Tom* to *Tesis* and *The Skin I Live In*. Explicit political allegories like *The Lives of Others* and *Caché*, even while muting (or refiguring) the subtext of narrative's own invasive camera, only serve to erode the negotiable divide between medium and theme even further, as is equally the case with the current round of sci-fi thrillers. For these latest time-travel fantasies (or phobias) are digitally enhanced screen productions that all but explicitly foresee the imploded future of the electronic image as a boundary-blurring collapse into an englobing and nonfiction surveillant cinema: one indistinguishable stream of image without activating human vision. In the meantime, under the postcontinuity aesthetic of drag-and-zoom editing, subgenre and medium can often seem to converge on each other in mutual capitulation.

And this caving in of form upon content has ever-newer manifestations. In the ongoing Netflix series *House of Cards*, concerned explicitly in its first season with covert US Congressional dealings, internal surveillance, and political sabotage by planted cell-phone leaks as well as incriminating paper trails, certain private text messages between conspirators pop up as miniature cellular screens within the narrative frame—like something between cartoon thought bubbles and subtitles for a secretly coded communiqué. Narration does not just film the act of texting but relays it directly on the image track. The threefold effect of this fits exactly the paradigm we've seen develop in narrative enunciation on the digital screen. In all its difference from the datelined captioning of narrative scene changes elsewhere typical of espionage networks and their mimetic intercutting, the impact of such internal "windows" still partakes of the surveillance mentality: first by flattening the narrative screen to a planar field continuous with sampled digital monitors, then by replacing even vocal suture with off-frame receipt and reply, and then, if only implicitly, by yielding up to the potential regimes of dataveillance this last residue from the former intimacies of face-to-face (or even telephonic) dialogue. Here is a machinated new version of free indirect discourse crossing unimpeded between third- and first-person treatment in the same optical register, with our literally seeing on screen what characters would otherwise say in their own voices, remote or in person, but carried now not by audio but by strictly visual—graphic—narration. And the very latency of intercept in such hardly inviolate transmissions makes this discursive effect a further and unique sign of our surveillant times.

Beyond Discipline: Frame / Screen / Interface / "Control" Panel

Five years after his second film book ended in uncertainty (1985) about what computerization ("the numeric image") would do to cinema—and to the time-image in particular—Deleuze looked at what it had done to life itself in the intervening half decade of real-time connectivity. He did so by way of fulfilling Foucault's latent forecast for the inevitable edging out of the panoptic model by a state of affairs (no longer necessarily state-determined) that would supplant the long-dominant order of disciplinary norming by dispersed and postinstitutional "societies of control."[4] Deleuze begins by rehearsing Foucault's account of how the era of sovereignty, defined by the ruler's divine right over life and death, gave way to an Enlightenment disciplinary culture in which policing was internalized across such structuring "enclosures" as home, school, military barracks, factory, hospital, and jail, each analogous to the others in their ultimately imprisoning logic. Deleuze then presses against these dwindling bastions of the "discipline" paradigm in denominating, instead, the more disembodied social "control" of a looming century, now ours: a whole battery (or, more to the point, web) of control mechanisms abetted by electronic monitoring of an only incidentally visual sort.

Already taking rapid shape as Deleuze was writing in the early 1990s, the new order goes well beyond the Benthamite model of a single focal point of carceral inspection and reciprocal self-regulation, replacing "enclosure," in the process, with networked routings. Or call them, as Deleuze doesn't, interfaces. In his summary, the "watchwords" of cultural value have been replaced by the "passwords" of access (5), the "molds" of behavior by "modulations" (4), "the time frame of a closed system" (4), by the simultaneities available to "code" rather than "signature or number" (5). Closed spaces have been de-placed, so to say, by a planetary encirclement. At which point a new regime of containment is the reverse face of facilitation through *wwwired* access.

Paul Virilio, alone among contemporary theorists besides Foucault, is cited by Deleuze (4) in regard to the new velocities of vision and data management. But Régis Debray's sense of a postwar videosphere also comes again to mind. For long after, the logosphere that authorized the reign of sovereignty by derivation from the godhead, even the graphosphere of text, of representation, of bureaucracy (including its late cinematographic realizations), gives way to continuous audiovisual streaming in a postmodern electronic circuitry. As in Deleuze's cursory account as well, script capitulates to code. Faced with uneven developments in the matter of social engineering and its technological armatures, let alone in the theories that rise to anatomize them, it isn't always as easy to map one template onto another. Still, it seems fair to say that, for Debray, the graphosphere yields to the postwar videosphere in much the way that the former spheres of institutional disciplinarity (from pedagogy to prison) have, for Deleuze, ceded place to the pervasively "numeric" (or digital) webworks of a control society.

But what resists a closer overlay in such attempted theoretical matchups, given its entirely residual status according to Deleuze, is the very master trope of Foucault's argument in the first place: the metaphor of super-vision enshrined in the ocular shibboleth of the panopticon. Yet in contemporary mediations, despite there being no particular emphasis on this in Deleuze's late position paper, it is surely the case that, beyond any merely figurative sense of a centralized oversight and its radiating cones of vision, an actual globalized optic has come to pass in newly computerized and scopic forms.[5] It isn't just that the Earth is now trademarked by Google but that its surfaces are encompassed by the ballistic as well as informatic parameters of remote "delivery systems." Thus has a figurative mechanical panoptics become an online digital technoptics.

Let's assume for a moment that my intuition above is at least partially right: namely, that clichés of the high-octane thriller, with its requisite chase scenes, shoot-outs, even hand-to-hand showdowns—when grafted onto a climactic turn in the surveillance plot, and even when under simultaneous inspection from long-distance control rooms—may seem mobilized mainly to win back for screen action a form of vulnerable human embodiment tested on its own fleshed terms. If so, then there might be other ways, too, in which the current screen narratives of a coercive digital ecosystem are transposing one kind of social discomfort into an alternate key of action. So let's further assume it to be no mere happenstance, just at the historical point where various peripheral fundamentalisms were flaring up amid, and in resistance to, globalist modernization, that it should be simultaneously the case—in our own postimperial centers—that an already tattered social fabric was rent further by an epidemic of niche news and preprogrammed electronic input serving in its own way to beat a defensive retreat from the daunting new possibilities of global informatics and its continuous streamed data.

But with what effect on screen mythography? If a newly facilitated curiosity about international entanglements seems to have fled instead into alternate and more manageable channels of selective, biased, self-controlled reception, how might narrative cinema reflect this? If we grant such fractured viewing or reading publics separately catered to lately by the media for their ingrained cultural preferences, a split civic sphere for which the dense weave of data in our electronic environment often seems too "world wide," too destabilizing—including an audience that would prefer an ideological hall of mirrors to the disorienting scope of too great an influx of otherness—what of it for action cinema? How might this flight from information overload be exactly what the screen narratives we've been looking at have indirectly plotted out? Perhaps even the paranoid thriller template, whether sci-fi or not quite, in which satellite command and global positioning are heroically evaded or foiled by encrypted escape routes and private hideaways, has tended to inscribe as much a fear of unchecked information flow in general as of individuated surveillance. Seen from this angle, the raw exclusion of data, its summarily occluded view, gets refigured as heroic resistance. It's not just that I am too often sighted and too thoroughly known in my monetized desires; it's that there is too much, altogether, for me to see and know. Repeating the pattern of a previous disciplinary regime, then, this reaction-formation would constitute the equally perverse sign of a subsequent control society already gone internal via the self-blinkering filters of information management in a selective and partisan mode of mediation and networking. On this model, one seeks at least to control one's own data panels, TV and computer both—while thus buying into the abiding ideology of marketed free choice.

But even so. . . . Even if these plots read out in part as fables of computerized and televisual onslaught and entrenched resistance, the narrative vehicle of this figurative tenor remains, in some important measure, threateningly technopolitical and paramilitary: an overhead arsenal as well as a neutral aerial oversight. *Pace* Deleuze on the waning of Foucault's archetype, some such basis for a panoptics of cultural acquiescence (of acculturation itself), including political wariness or submission, has certainly not been rendered wholly obsolete. This is because the cybernetic (rather than manned) panopticon lingers in an audiovisual regime by no means entirely replaced (yet) by coded dataveillance. It has been, in effect, a developing inference of this book that machinic surveillance is a crucial common denominator between a former panoptic model and a new technoptic reality of interfaced agency: between, that is, an internalized discipline and a multifarious, if tacit, control.

Anchoring the transition again in Deleuze's post-Foucauldian terms, such is the replacement—by the surveillance system all told—of disciplinary "enclosure" by what I've been calling the electronic closed circuits of remote optic record or its real-time access. If capitalist production, according to Deleuze, has been supplanted by distribution in the society of control, factory by corporation, capital accumulation by financial flow, national by global interests—and this in the final break from the institutional architectonics of demarcated social loci—what has in turn replaced the centric overlook and its monitored enclaves is, as everywhere recognized, the cyberlinked video feed and its vertiginous open field. What results in part is the emplaced view rather than the enclosed spatial site, epitomized (though scarcely exhausted) by the prying subjectless eye of CCTV. This is especially clear in cinema when, often confounding suture, this cyber-eyeline is set into manifest tension with narrative's own cam—if only until the authority of the latter is conflated with it.

Surveillancinema

One word, no longer two—in a sometimes merely inferred but worrisome continuum. The narrative mechanisms of surveillant cinema can in this way close upon themselves as a new valence of the medium all told. We might put it this way, in a final speculation. If Deleuze had kept cinema more on his mind in his "Postscript on the Societies of Control" (this postscript, in effect, to the hegemony of script itself and to the graphosphere at large), he might have made less sharp a demarcation between regimes. As he remarked on Lang's *Mabuse* sequence: "Occult power is confused with its effects, its supports, its media, its radios, its television, its microphones."[6] Where better than in this confusion, or displacement, to spot the mutation of circumscribed "disciplinary" institutions, in all their montaged alternation, into scenarios of a more encompassing "control"? One recalls in particular the locked evacuated throne room of a centralized criminal power—in its entirely remote-controlled telephonic transmission—from 1933's *The Testament of Dr. Mabuse,* whose "enclosure" was in fact the fabricated site of a more mediated system of coercion. If Deleuze had been thinking, more than half a century later, not so much about "American sci-fi" (in which genre he showed a serious interest elsewhere, yet whose screen narratives on this topic, along with related surveillance thrillers of an electronic stripe, were mostly to come), but thinking more broadly, in that late essay on "control," about the gradual shift in postfilmic cinema's own medial support—from celluloid materiality to digital scan—his perspective might have altered. He might well, in that case, have noted the final ascendancy (or codeification) of the videosphere in exactly its ties to nonaesthetic, and indeed invasive, forms of digital visualization. Given his earlier view of 1970s New American cinema (in the paranoid lineage of Lang, and from the same passage just cited about the *Mabuse* prototype)—an American cinema preoccupied, in its diegetic apparatuses, with "the system of reception, surveillance and transmission" (210)—he might thus have been disposed to address, in short, the not inconsiderable place of newer optic platforms in what would thereby appear more like an electronic mutation of the panopticon than a definitive break with its scopic figuration of the social order.

Certainly this is what many of the films Deleuze didn't live to see have had to say about his late concerns, first about the future of the image, then about the electronic society of control. And not least in regard to the afterlife of the time-image. Though Deleuze never articulated it this way, the replacement of panoptic compartmentalization by a rhyzomatic cyberoptic network—in an update of just that systemic "reception, surveillance, and transmission" he notes in post-'68 American filmmaking—seems to travesty his recurrent sense of film as an "open whole" rather than to inaugurate some radical realization of this philosophical view. So too, in particular, with the time-coded image of surveillance tech, which offers only an overt deformation, rather than a productive adjunct, of his own aesthetic benchmark in the subordination of action to legible duration. And worse. Although in the trajectory of Foucault's thought, sovereignty's original autocratic power over death as well as life was superseded by the ideology of private discipline and its policing, and then more recently by the technologies of transpersonal control, it is the direct power of death that returns, automated now, in the logic of remote presencing—and its concomitant logistics—for the multichannel control panels of the on-camera drone strike. With predator replacing sovereign, the panoptic turned technoptic, death has become entirely *digitaleyezed*.

Then, too, short of this ballistic dimension in the new electronics of image rather than vision, there is a curious historical loop to the wired infrastructure of the "societies of control"—what with control's seeming inversion in the presumed autonomy of elective affinity and voluntary access. The fantasy of private agency can, in the grip of distracted fascination or sheer concentration, whether in video streaming or routine e-mail, put from mind how the "information highway"—given the systems of dataveillance that patrol it—is always more of a two-way commute than we tend to realize. Yet one's submission to the circuits of control is more deeply internalized even than that. Where once the rotary cinematic engine converted industrial labor into a precision aesthetic in its distraction factories, through the conveyor belt of montage itself as well as its in-frame moving parts (as the Frankfurt school might have put it, especially in the work of Siegfried Kracauer), now labor and respite are often performed at the same electronic keyboard, all avenues of distraction under one's own supposed (and sometimes protective) management in the protocols of Ctrl and Alt, Del or Shift. Not just with the leisured bypass into video surfing or computer gaming, however, but even in standard negotiations with electronic globalism, one is impelled—even in the best of epistemological faith—to alternate, shift, delete, and reconfigure a data flow that in fact traverses us, under reverse-Ctrl, as much as we transact with it. Born of the modernist distraction industry, cinema has lasted long enough to record and critique (from within film's own internal eclipse by the digital) this postindustrial world order of electronic filiations and automatized visual policing.

This book began in heuristic resistance to a simplification: all montage is espionage. By the time of the seventh chapter we had reminded ourselves of Christian Metz's claim that all montage is *trucage*. (And since then, in the case of *Source Code*, that even personage can be all *trucage*.) How, by now, might the separate proposals consort? A film like *Look* half spells it out by exaggeration: by biting, as it were, the feeds it is handed. In that film, in a complementary reversal of a cinematic norm, every fixed and predetermined camera angle offers an illusion (a "perceptible" *trucage* in Metz's sense) of surveillance footage—but only as if to remind us that every carefully chosen "transparent" framing, in cinema generally, is an edited selection from an excess of unusable images, the selective "cut" of an optic overkill. In regard to screen narrative, to see is always someone else's tactical decision. The fact that Georges's TV talk show in Haneke's *Caché* is being processed through the digital editing apparatus even as we cut into it makes this point inescapable at one remove, with Georges taking charge, where possible, of his own control panel.

Look, by contrast, pretends to the condition, from first to last, of sheer automatic interface. But as we've noted in the far larger number of screen plots thematizing spywork rather than wholly mediated by its "look"—and operating in this way repeatedly, since *M,* at undisguised narrative pressure points—covert surveillance in film has once again coincided, in the latest time-travel narratives, with the film spectacle we're privy to. Given this, and in light of Deleuze's extension of Foucault on the societal armatures of control rather than discipline, *M* has indeed offered more than a point of departure for this study; it has been a seedbed for social mechanisms as well as, and in their association with, cinematic technique. Immersed in the implacable cross-cutting of Lang's double-dragnet plot, with an interchangeable law and violence convergent on the target, as well as the entire apparatus of the graphosphere in requisition—newspaper headlines, wanted posters in mass-print circulation, archived fingerprints, police graphology, teletype messaging—it is hard not to sense, from the networking of these manhunt tactics by montage alone, how a society of control is anticipated from the very eve of the videosphere. Prognosticating technologies less monolithic than Orwell's, Lang pictures a system of cross-webbed oversight that hardly inoculates, in prospect, the mobility-valorizing prefix of today's *Inter-net* against its surveillant double in the nonelectronic *dragnet.*

And, of course, the whole technological succession in automated sighting-without-the-gaze since *M,* the proliferation of images without primary visualization, may soon incur its own brand of mordant nostalgia. We may one day think back, through the filters of loss, on those lenses, mechanical even when no longer anatomical, by which we were at least once looked for *in persona* if not in person, looked *at*—even when the actual looking had grown mediated, forensic, and ex post facto. Lang's Beckert had to be seen to be known, or at least to be identified—and at first by a fellow human, indeed a fellow marginal, from across an inhabited civic space. Since then, a juggernaut of images without vision. Since then, in turn, a flood of dataveillance without images—under the very claim of impersonality and sheer aggregation. To the extent, therefore, that *specification* may still threaten, "singling" one out, it can come now without optics, let alone panoptics, of any sort. In this way has the visual subjectivity removed from the gaze by the electronic totalizations of (remote) control been lately removed as well, and by continuing numeric reduction, from the very "profiles" thus searched and tabulated. Orwell outstripped: all "screening" now statistical and informatic, no "tele-" needed. In evolution from the anthropomorphic POV to and beyond the anamorphic lens: digital humanity indeed, by any other name.

But our more particular subject has been cinema's complex and unstable place in any such devolution. And on this score, given the mostly phobic plotting down to the present, one could scarcely say, at least not yet, that *any* being-looked-at is tacitly valorized across the multiple layerings of camerawork. The role of the unacknowledged spectator has been more emphatically compromised than that. In film after film since *M*, the motor of plot, including its motivated machines of oversight, has tended to meet the narrative view not halfway exactly, and not by accident, but by full medial coincidence—including its frequent (almost generically determined) ironies of inspection. More and more often on the fictional screen, we thus watch watching by an implied license hard to forget with any steady confidence in the face, the interface, of convergent and suspect technologies, especially when surveillant spyware and spectacle can seem so closely aligned in contemporary production within the same narrative frame. Again: the cross-medial blur or collusion of *surveillancinema,* whose electronically marked camerawork, in a pivot beyond suture, can often *turn on you,* the spectator, in a twofold move, adjusting the point of view to insinuate a further point about unreturned viewing.

This narratography of surveillance plotting has followed the century-long event of screen camerawork in negotiating its options, its contradictions, and its compromises, faced in the end with an antithesis it can battle only by further contamination. Cinema, once filmic, now digital, has, through the regularly portrayed medium of chip camerawork, reverted to origins with a vengeance. The movement-image of classic narrative, transfigured into the time-image, emerges here in the time-coded video file. The art of montage has thus devolved into a repurposed version of the fixed-framed *actualité*—or its equivalent in the automated pan. No longer as a cinema of attraction, however, motion capture is narrowed to the electronics of detection. Via traditional narrative suture, the apparatus goes unseen in the exchanged agencies of the embodied gaze; via surveillance, the apparatus does all the sighting without necessarily seeing, let alone being seen. In narrative montage, suture opens reciprocal visibility to an occupied space on view; in automated video reportage, surveillance telescopes space to electronic trace.

Yet in narrating surveillance, even under the sign of critique, montage takes on its antithesis only by way of an inevitable scopic taint—and its multiple attempted antidotes. In prosecuting its own omniscience, that is, cinema has grown too close for comfort to the machinations it would eschew. This digital fit (together with its imagined fixes within certain narratives) is all but indissoluble whenever cinematic plots find their own high-tech footing on such epistemologically uneven and often ethically shaky terrain—or, in other words, and even before robotic imaging, whenever a given film finds itself, in plot and its optic alike, and precisely via their linked closed circuits, screening narrative surveillance.

NOTES

PREFACE

1. See Stanley Cavell, *The World Viewed: Reflections on the Ontology of Film*, enlarged ed. (Cambridge, MA: Harvard University Press, 1979).

2. Cavell, *The World Viewed*: "A world complete without me which is present to me is the world of my immortality. This is an importance of film—and a danger. It takes my life as my haunting of the world" (160).

3. Stanley Cavell, *Disowning Knowledge: In Six Plays of Shakespeare* (Cambridge, MA: Harvard University Press, 1987), 179–91.

4. See William Shakespeare, *Hamlet*, 3.1.36–37. And on Shakespeare's place in an early modern discourse of espionage within the proliferation of print culture, in which the term "intelligence" first took on (in the sixteenth century) its connotations of covert knowledge, with the etymological sense of "reading between the lines," see Benjamin Miele, "'The Conscience of the King': Theatrical Insight, Moral Judgment, and the Surveillance of Iniquity in *Hamlet* and *King Lear*," in "God's Spies: Reading, Revelation, and the Poetics of Surveillance in Early Modern England" (PhD diss., University of Iowa, 2014).

5. See "About John le Carré," *John le Carré* [4 January 2013], http://www.johnlecarre.com/author: "Artists, in my experience, have very little centre. They fake. They are not the real thing. *They are spies*. I am no exception" (emphasis added).

6. Roland Barthes, *S/Z: An Essay*, trans. Richard Howard (New York: Hill and Wang, 1974), 56.

7. See Jerome Christensen, *America's Corporate Art: The Studio Authorship of Hollywood Motion Pictures* (Stanford, CA: Stanford University Press, 2012). A signal exception, from within the ranks of production studies, appears in this striking work by Christensen, himself a literary scholar working on narrative cinema, when he trains the gaze of his analysis on the means by which studio branding and corporate signature effects are inscribed and thematized by American film.

8. Garrett Stewart, *Between Film and Screen: Modernism's Photo Synthesis* (Chicago: University of Chicago Press, 1999) and *Framed Time: Toward a Postfilmic Cinema* (Chicago: University of Chicago Press, 2006).

INTRODUCTION

1. See, for instance, Rachel E. Dubrofsky, *The Surveillance of Women on Reality Television: Watching "The Bachelor" and "The Bachelorette"* (Lanham, MD: Lexington Books, 2012)—"on" such television, not *in* its narratives—thus foregrounding the first-order mediation of the broadcast camera rather than any plot structures of invaded privacy or optical investigation developed on screen. By contrast, the real-world and often documented "*CSI* effect," based on the long-running CBS narrative series *CSI: Crime Scene Investigation*—with its frequent

digital forensics in the implausible decryption of security-cam images—has bedeviled the surveillance industry, in the marketing of their products, with unreasonable public expectations as to fidelity, field of view, and storage capacity.

2. See Mark Andrejovic, *iSpy: Surveillance and Power in the Interactive Era* (Lawrence, KA: University of Kansas Press, 2007). Stressing in its own way the interactivity of digital optics is Thomas E. McGrath, *Loving Big Brother: Performance, Privacy, and Surveillance Space* (New York: Routledge, 2004), where the author's previous work as theater director disposes him to the experimental aspects of optical capture and feedback in auditorium or gallery space—and away from any phobic stress on camerawork's invaded privacy in its deployment for crime prevention and/or detection. Whereas McGrath stresses the interactive construction of a transactional space for participatory aesthetics, my emphasis in this book, via suture and its short-circuits, falls on the construction of narrative space in screen renderings of the robotic camera's ambit and the deciphered ambience of its purview.

3. For a convenient summary of these developments, see Stephen Herbert and Luke McKernan, eds., "When the Movies Began . . . ," Who's Who of Victorian Cinema, July 2011, http://www.victorian-cinema.net/when_chrono. And for my own fuller distillation of this historical moment in connection with cinema's place in recent early modernist studies, see Garrett Stewart, "Curtain Up on Victorian Popular Cinema; Or, The Critical Theater of the Animatograph," *BRANCH*, http://www.branchcollective.org/?ps_articles=garrett-stewart-curtain-up-on-victorian-popular-cinema-or-the-critical-theater-of-the-animatograph.

4. See Luke McKernan, "The Soldier's Courtship," July 25, 2011, *Bioscope*, accessed August 8, 2011, http://thebioscope.net/2011/07/25/.

5. On this phase of early screen appeal, see the influential account by Tom Gunning, "The Cinema of Attraction: Early Film, Its Spectator, and the Avant-Garde," in *Film and Theory: An Anthology*, ed. Robert Stam and Toby Miller (Oxford: Blackwell, 2000), 229–35.

6. A point made by McKernan in "The Soldier's Courtship."

7. This emphasis on the military tryout of media innovation is a recurrent burden of Friedrich A. Kittler, *Film, Gramophone, Typewriter*, trans. Geoffrey Winthrop Young and Michael Wutz (Stanford, CA: Stanford University Press, 1999).

8. Vladimir Propp, *Morphology of the Folktale*, trans. Laurence Scott (Austin, TX: University of Texas Press, 1968).

9. D. N. Rodowick, "An Elegy for Theory," *October* 122 (Fall 2007): 91–109.

10. The most suggestive and compact formulation of this process—Jean-François Lyotard's description of stylistic defaults or distortions at the representational level getting recuperated at the narrative level—is one I revisit in *Framed Time*, 29–30 (see Stewart, Preface, n. 8), and which the rest of my study builds on in its attention to the narratographic register of cinematographic technique.

11. Friedrich Kittler, *Optical Media*, trans. Anthony Enns (Cambridge, UK: Polity, 2010), where film as "hybrid medium" operates only as it "combines analogue or continuous single frames with a discontinuous or discrete image sequence" (162).

12. And one doesn't need to line up behind the full-bore Lacanian restitution of this systemic critique attempted by Slavoj Žižek in his punningly titled chapter "Back to the Future," *The Fright of Real Tears: Krzystof Kieślowski Between*

Theory and Practice (London: BFI, 2002), 31–54, in order to agree, about the fading of the concept, that "one is tempted to read it as an indication of the decline of cinema studies" (31). Be that as it may, however, the challenging theoretical backlog remains easy to consult, beginning with Daniel Dayan's foundational essay, "The Tudor Code of Classical Cinema," *Film Quarterly*, 28, no. 1 (Autumn, 1974): 22–31, followed by the influential three-part "Dossier Suture," in *Screen* 18, no. 4 (1977): 24–76, comprised of articles by Jacques-Alain Miller, Jean-Pierre Oudart, and Stephen Heath. Among many follow-up commentaries over the next decade, see Kaja Silverman's fifth chapter, "Suture," in *The Subject of Semiotics* (New York: Oxford, 1984), 194–222. And among the more or less dismissive critical responses (especially in resistance to its psychoanalytic paradigm), see William Rothman's, following hard on the heels of Dayan's initial position paper in the same journal: "Against 'The System of the Suture,'" *Film Quarterly*, 29, no. 1 (Autumn, 1975): 45–50.

13. Thomas Y. Levin, "Rhetoric of the Temporal Index: Surveillant Narration and the Cinema of 'Real Time,'" in *CTRL [SPACE]: Rhetorics of Surveillance from Bentham to Big Brother*, ed. Thomas Y. Levin, Ursula Frohne, and Peter Weibel (Karlsruhe, DE: Center for Art and Media, 2002), 578–93. As representative of more recent work indebted to Levin's influential catalog essay, see Catherine Zimmer, "Surveillance Cinema: Narrative between Technology and Politics," *Surveillance & Society* 8, no. 4 (2011): 427–40, and Dietmar Kammerer, for a special CCTV issue of the same journal, "Video Surveillance in Hollywood Movies," *Surveillance & Society* 2, no. 2/3 (2004): 464–73.

14. Among Levin's many closely read instances of "surveillant enunciation" in the 1990s cinema in which it proliferates—from *Thelma & Louise* (Ridley Scott, 1991) and *Sliver* (Philip Noyce, 1993) to *The Truman Show* (Peter Weir, 1998) and *8mm* (Joel Schumacher, 1999)—is included even the more or less unthematized surveillance of *Snake Eyes* (Brian De Palma, 1998), a conspiracy thriller in which, following much security-cam scrutiny in the routine tailing of an assassination-plot suspect, a bravura crane shot tracks from above across one ceiling-freed hotel room after another as if operating, in its all but absurdist send-up of narrative oversight, as "a wet dream of surveillant omniscience" (590). Levin closes with Mike Figgis's *Timecode* (2000) as what amounts to an aesthetic recuperation of real-time optics in a nonsurveillant context.

15. Appearing just as my book was going to press, Sebastien Lefait's *Surveillance on Screen: Monitoring Contemporary Films and Television Programs* (London: Scarecrow, 2013) draws on the sociological framework of "surveillance studies," with its emphasis on new protocols of "watching"—this with a sustained debt to Thomas Mathiesen's "The Viewer Society: Michel Foucault's 'Panopticon' Revisited," *Theoretical Criminology* (May 1997): 215–34, where Mathiesen's argument has it that panoptic oversight, long after Bentham's carceral architectonics, is effectively inverted by a video culture in which the many watch the few, rather than the few the many. It is within roughly this difference between disciplinary models and broadcast media that Lefait locates the new self-consciousness about surveillance devices and their narrative manifestations in such TV shows as *24* and *Lost* as well as in numerous contemporaneous films, including the screen adaptation of *1984*.

16. See Christian Metz, "Identification with the Camera," in *The Imaginary Signifier*, trans. Celia Britton and Annwyl Williams (Bloomington, IN: Indiana

University Press, 1982), 49–52. It is a later piece by Metz, "Impersonal Enunciation, or the Site of Film (In the Margin of Recent Works on Enunciation in Cinema)," *New Literary History* 22, no. 2 (Summer 1991): 747–72, that Lefait (*Surveillance on Screen*) takes up in his conclusion, gravitating to Metz's own emphasis on works in which film "diegetizes the cinematic apparatus" (203) by incorporating a "second" (or internal) screen as touchstone of visual enunciation, inducing in the process what I have called a "tertiary" identification. When that reframed visual plane is put into the service of commenting on a hypermediated culture of data and surveillance screens, then cinema's structure of "reflexivity," according to Lefait—further thematizing what Metz diegeticizes—"now applies to reality as a whole" (209).

CHAPTER ONE: THE PRYING "I" OF MONTAGE

1. The courtroom use of film footage in *Fury* is discussed in Stewart, "Filmic Witness for the Prosecution," *Between Film and Screen*, 58–63 (see Preface, n. 8).

2. Friedrich Kittler, *Optical Media*, trans. Anthony Enns (Cambridge, UK: Polity Press, 2010), where film as "hybrid medium" operates only as it "combines analogue or continuous single frames with a discontinuous or discrete image sequence" (162).

3. See Mary Ann Doane, *The Emergence of Cinematic Time: Modernity, Contingency, the Archive* (Cambridge, MA: Harvard University Press, 2002), 33–68, where discussion of Marey's and Bergson's objections to early film are triangulated with Freud's.

4. Tom Gunning, *The Films of Fritz Lang: Allegories of Vision and Modernity* (London: British Film Institute, 2000), where his analysis is especially suggestive on the "topographical portrayal of city space" (175), whose "gridded and integrated" (175) zones of action, including whose rationalized "charts and maps" (177), are primed for the work of surveillance—as figured at times by overhead establishing shots of the investigative terrain in scenes of police forensics.

5. Jacques Rancière, *Film Fables* (Oxford: Berg, 2006), 1–19.

6. For the most widely available survey of this movement, see Sergiusz Michalski, *New Objectivity: Painting, Graphic Art and Photograph in Weimar Germany 1919–1933* (Koln: Benedikt Taschen, 1994).

7. Jean-Pierre Oudart, "Cinema and Suture," *The Symptom: Online Journal for Lacan.Com*, http://www.lacan.com/symptom8_articles/oudart8.html, unpaginated. This text was published in French in *Cahiers du Cinéma* 211 and 212, April and May 1969, its English version (trans. Kari Hanet) appearing almost a decade later in *Screen* 18 (Winter 1978).

8. This, again, is the method defined in contrast with a deliberately more abstract and medium-blind narratology both in my study *Framed Time: Toward a Postfilmic Cinema* (see Preface, n. 8) and, in respect to a different time-based (syntactic) medium, in *Novel Violence: A Narratography of Victorian Fiction* (Chicago: University of Chicago Press, 2009).

9. See Slavoj Žižek on Kieślowski in *The Fright of Real Tears* (see Intro., n. 12), with its understanding of the "interface" having been discussed previously in Stewart, *Framed Time*, 272–73, n. 19.

10. Alexander R. Galloway, *The Interface Effect* (Cambridge, MA: Polity, 2012), 101–119.

11. See *M*'s place in this post–WWI psychosocial paradigm, amid a fuller dis-

cussion of Lang, in Anton Kaes, *Shell Shock Cinema: Weimar Culture and the Wounds of War* (Princeton: Princeton University Press, 2009). This is a contextual framing of Lang's film that is usefully pursued as well in the joint commentary by Kaes and Eric Rentschler for the Criterion reissue of *M* (2004). The Dix image, and of course the famous close-up of the kneeling, cowering Lorre—as well as most of the subsequent paintings and photographs mentioned from the New Objectivists—are readily visible on the web.

12. David Trotter, *Cinema and Modernism* (Oxford: Blackwell, 2007), 4–13, where he distinguishes his approach (politely but firmly) from my own in *Between Film and Screen*, 4–8 (see Preface, n. 8), stressing as he does an objectivist fixity over flicker.

13. Kittler, *Optical Media*, 211.

14. Roland Barthes, in the posthumously published essay "Right in the Eyes," in *The Responsibility of Form: Critical Essays on Music, Art, and Representation*, trans. Richard Howard (New York: Hill and Wang, 1985), 238.

15. The effect seems to me more complex, *pointed*, and indeed *cutting* than the way it comes across in Gunning's glancing look in *The Films of Fritz Lang* at the moment when Beckert "turns and stares—briefly, but directly—into the camera. This look at the camera (a rarely used device in this film until the final scene) does not claim enunciatory power over the lens and audience, but rather expresses the embarrassment of visibility, being caught in the gaze of the camera" (186). All true—though one would want to say worse than "embarrassment"—but for me it is the way the viewer is made to "claim enunciatory power" over the *surveillance* that is the most purposefully unnerving moment of the film.

16. Gilles Deleuze, *Cinema 1: The Movement-Image*, trans. Hugh Tomlinson and Barbara Habberjam (Minneapolis: University of Minnesota Press, 1986), 155–56.

17. Two years later, in *The Testament of Dr. Mabuse*, Lang finds another variant of this elided face-off when the asylum head Dr. Baum, having internalized the posthumous anarchic madness of Dr. Mabuse, enters the cell where his own victim from the police force, one Hoffmeister, is locked away in a post-traumatic mania. With the door of the cell left open, we hear only the loud violence of confrontation, without being privy to the scene itself, until Hoffmeister emerges seemingly cured of his dementia and, in a separate shot, Baum is now recognized imprisoned by his own, shedding the notebooks of his guru Mabuse. Wholly unsutured, the duel is more like a psychic transfusion, an exchange of derangement, in the attempted normalization of closure.

18. See Deleuze, *Cinema 2: The Time-Image*, trans. Hugh Tomlinson and Barbara Habberjam (Minneapolis: University of Minnesota Press, 1989), 215. Together with the raw interruption of movement, it is thus "the point–cut, relinkage and the black or white screen" that, comprising the three purely "cerebral components" of cinema, form together a whole "noosphere."

19. This is one more example that Michel Chion, in *Film, A Sound Art*, trans. Claudia Gorbman (New York: Columbia University Press, 2009), might have perked up his ears over in discussing certain earlier moments in *M* when a sound bridge precipitates—by voice-over—a distant visualization so autonomous that "the film will then 'forget to close the quotation marks'" (70–71).

20. Walter Benjamin, "The Work of Art in the Age of Mechanical Reproduction," in *Illuminations: Essays and Reflections*, ed. Hannah Arendt (New York:

Harcourt Brace Jovanovich, 1968), where he paraphrases a received view about Atget's deserted streets: "It has quite justly been said of him that he photographed them like scenes of crime" (226).

21. See Michel Foucault, *Discipline and Punish: The Birth of the Prison*, trans. Alan Sheridan (New York: Pantheon, 1978). It is this Foucauldian perspective, with its emphasis on the inscribed and measured rather than publically mutilated body, that informs the essays of Tom Gunning's immediately preceding his Lang book—as, in effect, yet another gathering thesis on surveillance. One article stresses the emergence of cinema's detective genre (including a 1904 film, *A Subject for the Rogue's Gallery*, that we might think of as structurally derived from the 1896 *Arrest of a Pickpocket*) in intimate relation with the police mug shot and its narrativization in early film: "Tracing the Individual Body: Photography, Detectives, and Early Cinema," in *Cinema and the Invention of Modern Life*, ed. Leo Charney and Vanessa R. Schwartz (Berkeley: University of California Press, 1995), 15–44. Such, of course, is exactly the police photograph that does *not* exist of Beckert, and for which the letter *M* itself must substitute. Another of Gunning's essays in this line fills in the prehistory of such photomechanical evidence on screen in the marketing shift, within the preceding phase of "still" photography, from the "detective" to the "hand" camera, with this revised branding meant to detox the portable camera's potential for private surveillance: "Embarrassing Evidence: the Detective Camera and the Documentary Impulse," in *Collecting Visible Evidence*, ed. Jane M. Gaines and Michael Renov (Minneapolis: University of Minnesota Press, 1999), 46–64. The present chapter goes on to suggest that there is something about the missing mug shot of Beckert, vacuumed out from the dragnet apparatus of the manhunt, whose palpable "detective" absence sends reverberations across the entire photomechanical subtext of Lang's montage.

CHAPTER TWO: TELESCREEN PROSE

1. Benchmark studies in this mode of Foucauldian narratology, for eighteenth- and nineteenth-century British fiction, respectively, include John Bender's *Imagining the Penitentiary: Fiction and the Architecture of Mind in Eighteenth-Century England* (Chicago: University of Chicago Press, 1989) and D. A. Miller's *The Novel and the Police* (Berkeley: University of California Press, 1984), followed by Miller's return to questions of free indirect discourse and authorial power in *Jane Austen, or The Secret of Style* (Princeton: Princeton University Press, 2003).

2. "About John le Carré" (see Preface, n. 5)

3. George Orwell, *1984* (New York: Signet Classic, 1961), 5.

4. George Orwell, "Politics and the English Language" (1946), in *Essays by George Orwell* (New York: Harcourt, 1981), 156–170.

5. Albert Glinsky, *Theremin: Ether Music and Espionage* (Urbana, IL: University of Illinois Press, 2000), 261.

6. On the broader question of "syllepsis" and its destabilizing effects, including examples from the prose of John le Carré, see Garrett Stewart, "Syllepsis Redux and the Rhetoric of Double Agency," *Partial Answers* 10, no. 1 (January 2012): 93–120.

7. Tzvetan Todorov, *The Fantastic: A Structural Approach to a Literary Genre*, trans. Richard Howard (Ithaca, NY: Cornell University Press, 1975), where the

parameters of "the fantastic" materialize "because we take a figurative sense literally" (75–76).

8. See Žižek, "Back to the Future," in *The Fright of Real Tears*, 39 (see Intro., n. 12).

9. John le Carré, *A Most Wanted Man* (New York: Simon and Schuster, 2010), 47.

10. John le Carré, *A Delicate Truth* (New York: Viking, 2013), 25.

CHAPTER THREE: FEEDBACK LOOPS OF THE TECHNOPTICON

1. Deleuze, *Cinema 1: The Movement-Image*, 210 (see chap. 1, n. 16).

2. Stewart, "The Photographic Regress of Science Fiction Film," in *Between Film and Screen*, 189–223 (see Preface, n. 8).

3. Giorgio Agamben, *What Is an Apparatus? And Other Essays*, trans. David Kishik and Stefan Pedatella (Stanford, CA: Stanford University Press, 2009), 24, where this "profanation," this "restitution to common use," must operate in the face of acknowledged odds: "While a new European norm imposes biometric apparatuses on all its citizens by developing and perfecting anthropometric technologies invented in the nineteenth century in order to identify recidivist criminals (from mug shots to fingerprinting), surveillance by means of video cameras transforms the public space of the city into the interior of an immense prison" (23).

4. For a fuller comparison of the newest Bourne film with the *Total Recall* remake, see, with illustrations, Garrett Stewart, "Surveillance Cinema," *Film Quarterly* 66, no. 2 (Winter 2012): 5–15.

5. Perhaps the clearest, if ethically muddied, case of this, as discussed (in terms of digital simulation rather than surveillance dissimulation) in my *Framed Time*, 91–92 (see Preface, n. 8), comes in Jonathan Demme's 2004 remake of *The Manchurian Candidate* (John Frankenheimer, 1962). In a closed circuit of roundabout justice, once a high-tech digital implantation produces a mind-altered assassin who takes his own life just before implementing the intended treason, his security-cam image at the political convention is digitally replaced by the FBI before international broadcast—doctored with the likes of everyday Photoshop technique—so as to incriminate, instead, a known henchman of the nefarious international cartel behind the attempted political coup. In sum, according to the sci-fi rather than political template of this remake, routine technology, even in the form of quotidian surveillance cameras, can be tampered with in defiance of a futurist dystopia of remote-controlled cyborgs sent into action not by the apparatus of state violence but by an international corporate entity (see Deleuze on "societies of control" in this book's Postface).

6. Cavell, *The World Viewed* (see Preface, n. 1).

7. See discussion of *The Final Cut* in Stewart, *Framed Time*, 184–93 (see Preface, n. 8).

8. See Garrett Stewart, review of *Death Watch*, *Film Quarterly* 37 no. 1 (Fall 1983): 16–22, which thus records a first interest on my part, I now see in looking back, in the metafilmic machinations of the surveillance motif.

CHAPTER FOUR: IN PLANE SIGHT

1. "A Collective Text by the Editors of *Cahiers du Cinéma*: John Ford's *Young Mr. Lincoln*," in *Narrative, Apparatus, Ideology*, ed. Philip Rosen (New York: Columbia University Press, 1986), 444–82.

2. See Deleuze, *Cinema 1: The Movement-Image*: "Including the spectator in the film, and the film in the mental image, Hitchcock brings the cinema to completion," 204 (see chap. 1, n. 16).

3. See Jacques Rancière, *Film Fables*, 115 (see chap. 1, n. 5).

4. Paul Young, *The Cinema Dreams Its Rivals: Media Fantasy Films from Radio to the Internet* (Minneapolis, MN: University of Minnesota Press, 2005).

5. One might in fact add this logging in of the logo's corporate signature to the list of such reinvestments in a given film's internal narrative economy—or at least its cinematic self-reflex—so persuasively brought to view by Jerome Christenson in *America's Corporate Art* (see Preface, n. 7). Though unmentioned by Christenson, this seems especially the case here since, on his own evidence, the film opens with the auteurist imprimatur of "Alfred Hitchcock's *Rear Window*"—marking the first of a five-picture deal negotiated by Lew Wasserman with Paramount: a contractual arrangement that would, as with *Rope* just before it, guarantee Hitchcock a "possessory credit" before the main title, with no individual "producer" enshrined in the subsequent credits (234). But it's never over till it's over, and the "closing curtain" (with internally disclosed logo) may be Paramount's way of getting a little of its own back in lieu of a personified "producer" claim.

6. Michel Chion, "Alfred Hitchcock's *Rear Window*: The Fourth Side," in *Alfred Hitchcock's "Rear Window,"* ed. John Belton (Cambridge, UK: Cambridge University Press, 2000), 110–17.

7. Laura Mulvey, "Visual Pleasure and Narrative Cinema," *Visual and Other Pleasures*, 2nd ed. (New York: Palgrave Macmillan, 2009), 14–30.

8. The impulse toward "Too Close Reading" is exemplified, with quite different but comparably reflexive evidence, by D. A. Miller in "Hitchcock's Hidden Pictures," *Critical Inquiry* 37, no. 1 (Autumn 2010): 106–30, and again in "Hitchcock's Understyle: A Too-Close View of Rope," *Representations*. 121, no. 1 (Winter 2013): 1–130. My sense of the filmic "undertext" of all such photomechanical cinema (developed across my last two film books) could be thought of as the medial counterpart to Miller's auteurist intimacies.

9. Laura Mulvey, audio commentary, Michael Power, *Peeping Tom* (New York: Criterion Collection, 1999).

10. Laura Mulvey, *Death 24x a Second: Stillness and the Moving Image* (London: Reaktion, 2006), 79–80, where she engages in passing with previous work of mine on the topic.

CHAPTER FIVE: THE OTHERING OF LIVES

1. Slavoj Žižek, *In Defense of Lost Causes* (New York: Verso, 2008), 63.

2. As discussed in Stewart, *Framed Time* (see Preface, n. 8), Haneke broke from his normal 35mm practice to record *Caché* in high-definition video, thus narrowing the gap between our visual narrative and the tapes Georges watches within it. A point to stress here is that the gap between our film and his tapes is further closed by the sequential nature of their content in its exchangeable relation with the plot as it might otherwise have been filmed. Apart from this particu-

lar issue of metanarrative pacing (discussed by Levin and Gilberto Perez—see n. 3 and 4 below), among the considerable writing on this film in the context of Haneke's work, see Catherine Wheatley, *Michael Haneke's Cinema: The Ethic of the Image* (New York: Berghahn, 2009) and *On Michael Haneke*, ed. Brian Price and John David Rhodes (Detroit: Wayne State University Press, 2010).

3. It seems almost as inevitable as it is welcome that Thomas Y. Levin, given his work on "surveillant enunciation" ("Rhetoric of the Temporal Index," see Chapter 1, n. 13), would have later trained his sights on this film and its progressively absorbed monitoring operations. Indeed, precisely the shift from a taped and path-marking progress down the apartment hall, then rewound, to its twofold reiteration in real time is deployed to rehearse Levin's general sense of the gradual irrelevance of playback anxiety in the film, subordinated ultimately, in the final shot, to a real-time discourse of hermeneutics as surveillance. See "Five Tapes, Four Halls, Two Dreams: Vicissitudes of Surveillant Narration in Michael Haneke's *Caché*," in *Function/Fiction: Utilitarian Images Reconfigured*, eds. Vincent Bonin and France Choinière (Montreal: Dazibao, 2008), 59–70. Levin's powerfully observed but ultimately dim view of this process leaves him with a sense of the film's famously "polysemous" last shot as nonetheless a "narrative enunciation whose aesthetic politics are entirely complicit with the very surveillance so pejoratively connoted by the film's thematic concerns" (70). My own difference from the logic of this argument, as from the similar and more recent approach by Gilberto Perez (n. 4 below), depends in part, as should soon be clear, on retaining a sense of this final fixed-frame shot in closer relation to that second dream of Levin's title (finally moral nightmare) that precedes it. So that when I have said that the surveillant frame has been "internalized," I meant not as a rhetorical power play by Haneke's camera, but rather by Georges's unconscious.

4. See Gilberto Perez, "Bourgeois Nightmares," *London Review of Books* 34, no. 23 (December 6, 2012). I had drafted this chapter before the appearance of Perez's essay, which travels the same route—tape by tape, equivalent for him, as from a different angle for Levin as well (n. 3 above), to the film's own "narrative path." Perez makes the point that solving the prolonged mystery of the taping agent would be a kind of structural redundancy, since "the filmmaker's camera has from the start been working in alliance with the culprit's video to uncover a different culprit" (37). To this extent operating parallel to Levin's sense of the film as gradually validating the surveillant narration it would seem at first to eschew, Perez's reading mounts a considered resistance to numbering *Caché* among those recent "puzzle films" discussed in my next chapter. Where I would depart from his plausible sense of metanarrative irony involved in how the tapes are made to double for narration per se concerns only the way this development abrogates, for Perez, any sense that the film is really "all about the fear of surveillance," since "if that is so, then surveillance is a villain that Haneke identifies with" (37). What I have been suggesting is that being made aware of yourself in the eye of the other, from whatever vantage point—and, for much of the time, actually being made to share that optical perspective—turns surveillance not so much into a personified "villain" (somehow party to the director's own sadistic epistemology) as into a figure for the self-"exposure" that video itself figures in its technical dimension.

5. See Agamben, *What Is an Apparatus?* (see chap. 3, n. 3).

CHAPTER SIX: DIGITAL RECONNAISSANCE AND WIRED WAR

1. This cognitive horizon of war—annexing unseen ranges of conflict in its vision of "totality"—reflects one line of argument in Jan Mieszkowski's *Watching War* (Stanford: Stanford University Press, 2012), where an enlisted European "spectatorship" for armed conflict on the world stage has, at least since the Napoleonic era—such is the study's main claim—rendered war a concept remote, "mediated," and "hyperreal" (4) well before modern technological innovations of either long-distance weaponry or broadcast. Complementing this historical legacy of war as remote spectator sport, my emphasis, given the new digitized battlefield, falls on the inverted role of the spectator as devolved upon that of the mediated participant-witness. Material in this chapter is developed in part from Garrett Stewart, "Digital Fatigue: Imaging War in Recent American Film," *Film Quarterly* 62, no. 4 (Summer 2009): 45–55, illustrated with frame captures from the many films taken up.

2. Paul Virilio, *War and Cinema: The Logistics of Perception*, trans. Patrick Camiller (New York: Verso, 1989).

3. Elisabeth Bronfen, *Specters of War: Hollywood's Engagement with Military* Conflict (Rutgers, NJ: Rutgers University Press, 2012).

4. See Ken Provencher, "*Redacted*'s Double Vision," *Film Quarterly*, no. 1 (Fall 2008): 32–38. These compounded and even self-embedded layers of mediation are carefully charted in this article, suggesting that we never know what perspective the film's own "narration" is coming from. More obviously than ever in a film like this, hypermediation runs the risk, in thus fracturing perspective, of hobbling critique. Hence, no doubt, the perceived need for the slow montage of impersonal photographs at the end, its terrible dossier of the Iraqi dead: an unflinching archive of incrimination rather than a shunt of subjective or editorialized POVs (and thus lending in retrospect a further weight to the film's last line, discussed below, about traumatic "snapshots"). This ending, in relation to the distancing scenes that precede it, is also explored more recently, amid other war films contextualized in Bush-era politics (including a couple that are discussed at greater length in the current chapter), by J. Hoberman in *Film after Film: Or, What Became of 21st Century Cinema* (London: Verso, 2012), 160–62, a book which, despite being named by wordplay for the digital eclipse of photochemical imaging as well as for the author's serial commentaries issue after issue in *The Village Voice* (mostly from 2000 on), puts no particular stress, in summarizing these Iraq War films, either on secondary electronic transcription or its relation to digital ballistics.

5. A further historical irony comes into view, from an argument already adduced in connection with Lang's *M*. In *Shell Shock Cinema: Weimar Culture and the Wounds of War* (Princeton, NJ: Princeton University Press, 2009), Anton Kaes notes the vocabulary of cinema in Weimar psychology, where the disjuncture of film editing was an explicit metaphor for the replay of war trauma under hypnosis (49). In the aftermath of Iraq War combat, however, including films about it, the metaphor would offer no potential therapeutic distance. War trauma can now be optically recorded on the spot, at point of origin, returning later in the form of "recovered" video footage quite apart from actual psychic scars—or say, in cinematic treatments, as a strictly figurative marker for them.

6. Jacques Aumont, in *Montage*, trans. Timothy Barnard (Montreal: Caboose,

2013), singles out a residual trace of Eisenstein's discontinuous technique in *The Hurt Locker* when "the bomb disposal expert is fitted out with his helmet" in three discrepant shots "at the cost of a slight temporal overlap at the moment the matched cuts are made (we go back a fraction of a second each time)" (36). For Aumont it is a "gripping" instance of a "routine gesture . . . broken down, no longer natural," in something of the Russian formalist sense "made strange" (36). Without emphasis on its exemplary status here, it is also one of those postclassical innovations of the new digital editing that prompt his closing summary: "We have entered into a period in which the reign of vision has become contested by that of the image, with the result that editing has changed nature, because its job is no longer to regulate a succession of shots as much as it is to regulate a succession of images," adding that "while the shot has a responsibility toward reality, the image is responsible only to itself" (41). In a very specific sense, this toppled "reign of vision" is most often a "device" variously "motivated" in the war film (in another formalist pattern)—though precisely not here in Bigelow's treatment—by the impersonality of surveillance montage. And though "suture" gets no emphasis in Aumont's brief history of montage theory, it is certainly the first casualty of the usurpation of vision by image.

7. Fredric Jameson, "War and Representation," *PMLA* 124, no. 5 (October 2009): 1532–47.

8. I have in mind Jameson's most prominent use of this heuristic grid in *The Political Unconscious: Narrative as a Socially Symbolic Act* (Ithaca, NY: Cornell University Press, 1981), where the social symbolism flagged by his subtitle is often worked out as an ideological blind spot through an application of the semiotic square.

9. See Stewart, "Screen Memory in *Waltz with Bashir*," *Film Quarterly* 63, no. 3 (Spring 2010): 58–62, reprinted without illustrations in *Killer Images: Documentary Film, Memory, and the Performance of Violence,* ed. Joram Ten Brink and Joshua Oppenheimer (New York: Columbia University Press, 2012), 120–26. It is, in part, to resist just this ethical enervation of *vérité* that Ari Folman's remarkable 2008 animated film on the Israeli-Lebanon war of the early 1980s must build up, through layers of exposed repression on the autobiographical protagonist's part (in "cartoon" graphics), toward the recovered video footage of a documented atrocity and its powerful revalidation of suture, however figurative. Folman's character operates as what we might call a marginalized surveillance agent, having once stood sentinel, lighting flares, at the outskirts of a mass execution of Lebanese civilians: a character brought only at the end into an eyeline suture with the carnage and grief in which, until then, he remembers being only distantly complicit—yet which in fact, as a kind of panoptic lighting engineer, he facilitated. His very disavowal of the memory until the end is couched in the language of an electronic surveillance cache: "not stored in my system."

CHAPTER SEVEN: RETROSPECTIVE EYES

1. This 1980s computer-phobic era of Hollywood's cross-media dialectic, as discussed in the last chronological phase of Paul Young's *The Cinema Dreams Its Rivals* (see chap. 4, n. 4), was roughly initiated, according to Young's examples, with *Tron* (1982). Young's is an argument mentioned above in connection with the suppression of commercial TV in the apartment-life ambience of *Rear Win-*

dow. Since that postwar phase of media rivalry, he notes a strain of "informatic voyeurism" (203) in more recent digital cinema that also pits it against computer electronics on the commercial spectrum of mass culture.

2. Christian Metz, "*Trucage* and the Film," *Critical Inquiry* 3, no. 4 (Summer 1977): 672. "Montage itself, at the base of all cinema, is already a perpetual *trucage*, without being reduced to the false in usual cases." Yet it is the "falsity" of the shot exchanges at the center of *Source Code* that has "tricked" the very premise of montage in its limning of the diegesis.

3. See Thomas Elsaesser, "The Mind-Game Film," in *Puzzle Films: Complex Storytelling in Contemporary Hollywood*, ed. Warren Buckland (Oxford: Blackwell, 2009), 13–41, where Elsaesser discusses many of the films I had previously taken up in *Framed Time* as variants of Tzvetan Todorov's "fantastic." See especially Stewart, *Framed Time*, chapter 4, "Temportation," 122–63 (see Preface, n. 8), with discussion of not just the teen hero films of psychotic temporal regression (rather than laptop escapism) like *Donnie Darko* or *The Butterfly Effect* but related films with adult protagonists like *Frequency*, *The Thirteenth Floor*, and *Eternal Sunshine of the Spotless Mind*.

4. See Todorov, "Literature and the Fantastic," in *The Fantastic*, 157–75 (see chap. 2, n. 7).

5. This is the name given by Todorov in *The Fantastic*, 56, to the equipmental cousin of general science fiction ("the scientific marvelous") within the "supernatural" rather than "uncanny" pole of (often ambiguous) plotting.

6. See Stewart, *Framed Time*, 153, 226–27.

7. See André Bazin, "The Ontology of the Photographic Image," in *What Is Cinema?*, trans. Hugh Gray (Berkeley: University of California Press, 1967), 1: 195–99.

8. See Peter Brooks's borrowing from Todorov on this point in Brooks, *Reading for the Plot: Design and Intention in Narrative* (New York: Knopf, 1984), where crime and inquest are found comparable to story and its (re)structuring (fabula and *syuzhet*), rendering the detective story "the narrative of narratives" (25).

9. Scott's film is cited, along with *Source Code* and others, as instancing the "parallel universe" archetype (or "metaverse," or "multiverse") in David Wittenberg's *Time Travel: The Popular Philosophy of Narrative* (New York: Fordham University Press, 2013), where the wrench to monolilthic narrative becomes in its own right a metacinematic function that Wittenberg associates in passing with surveillance oversight (and theorizes at the start in terms of Nietzsche's "eternal return," 17). Wittenberg alludes to the "thematic linking of film-viewing and surveillance technology that has preoccupied mainstream cinema from Hitchcock's *Rear Window* through a recent spate of hyperbolic world-viewing fantasies" (199) where time travel becomes in effect a narratological crux: "a multiplex surveillance of *fabular* lines" (199). The very ideas of narrative autonomy and coherence are thus, as Wittenberg's subtitle would have it, philosophized in their artifice (their arbitrary and equivocal status) by popular plotting. In this narratology of temporal branching, the acknowledged place of the pivotal "montage sequence" (171) is exactly what narratography, in this book's last two chapters, seeks to specify in a comparable metafilmic framework—one rendered unstable by the particular deformations of suture.

CHAPTER EIGHT: PARALLEL WORLD EDITING

1. In distinguishing the "logosphere" as the ancient time of the idol ("the gaze without a subject") from the "graphosphere" as the era of art (where, for instance, perspective painting situates "a subject behind the gaze"), the overview of Debray's "mediology" identifies the third epoch, the modern "videosphere," as a regime which again removes the subject as aesthetic focal point. See Régis Debray, "The Three Ages of Looking," trans. Eric Rauth, *Critical Inquiry* 21 (Spring 1995): esp. 532, 550, the tripartite division being also rephrased—with particular relevance for the films under discussion in these last two chapters—as "the *supernatural,* the *natural,* and the *virtual*" (538).

2. Besides considerable blogging about the time-loop paradox of the film, and insightful conference attention (see n. 10 below), there is a multifaceted "Dialogue: De-Coding *Source Code,*" in *The Oxford Handbook of Sound and Image in Digital Media,* ed. Carol Vernallis, Amy Herzog, and John Richardson (New York: Oxford University Press, 2013), 465–516, where a threefold exchange of articles includes Garrett Stewart, "Sound Thinking: Looped Time, Duped Track," 465–82, concentrating (more fully than here) on anomalies of the sound track in the tension between score and a digitally disincarnate but still diegetic "voice."

3. The question for Gilles Deleuze in *Cinema 2: The Time-Image* (see chap. 1, n. 18) is whether the "electronic image," alternatively called the "tele and video image" and the "numerical image," is destined to "transform cinema or to replace it" (265), which means, for the "time-image" in particular, whether electronics "spoils it or, in contrast, relaunches it" (267). For my treatment of those narrative films in which temporal effects may be said to fall somewhere between these options in their digital ironies, both expanding and unwittingly parodying the time-image at once, see *Framed Time,* esp. 166–71 (see Preface, n. 8). More recently, in *The Neuro-Image: A Deleuzian Film-Philosophy of Digital Screen Culture* (Stanford, CA: Stanford University Press, 2012), Patricia Pisters sets out in her own (very different) way to imagine the digital aftermath of Deleuze's time-image in the wake of celluloid film, based mostly on schizoanalysis in his work with Félix Guattari. In a chapter called "Surveillance Screens and Powers of Affect," emphasizing such an anomalous experimental example as the Dogme project *Red Road* (Andrea Arnold, 2007), Pisters finds an "intense level of affect" in the "blurry CCTV images" (109) that punctuate the narrative, their very grain supposedly haptic, palpable, intimate. Her other chief exhibit, the experimental video *Evidence Locker* (Jill Magid, 2004), epitomizes this performance and installation artist's preoccupation with surveillance in the form, this time, of an answering-back to the security personnel of Amsterdam's CCTV network in eroticized epistles addressed to "Dear Observer." The Deleuzian "affection-image" (according to Pisters) in both screen works would appear to mark a departure from the rule of neutrality in such security-cam automaticity. For me, it is the affectless and time-coded image of round-the-clock record that delineates a more immediate contrast to (rather than continuity with) Deleuze's principles, at least in his cinema books. Then, too, Pisters's study also contains a later chapter on contemporary war and its video remediation, named in allusion to Paul Virilio—"Logistics of Perception 2.0: Multiple Screens as Affective Weapons" (9)—in which she highlights how this weaponizing of the image involves a "desubjectification" (289) of combat linked at once to a cultural "cinemania" (287) and "the technodelirious aesthetic of militarism" (284). Differences aside in our

deployment of Deleuzian cinema theory, and putting it as simply as possible for "digital screen culture" (Pisters's subtitle): electronic surveillance and war, however many chapters they divide between them in anyone's book, are no longer separate topics.

4. An article by Sean Cubitt as wide-ranging as its subtitle, "*Source Code*: Eco-Criticism and Subjectivity," in *The Oxford Handbook of Sound and Image*, 483–501, is expertly alert early on to the transition from photomechanical to digital record, without relating his technological precision directly to the logic of temporal transit and transformation in the plot of *Source Code*. He suggests, for instance, that "from a hermeneutical perspective, chip cameras differ from film almost exclusively in that each frame contains a temporal account of itself" (495)—by which he means that each "shot" is built up over microtime as a calibrated series rather than taken in whole. This, as it happens, is the "hermeneutical perspective" on which I have found whole plots inclined to draw, that of Jones's film included.

5. See Deleuze, *Cinema 2*, 17.

6. I summarize here an array of enumerated parallels between the late-modernist time-image and its millennial modifications discussed more fully in *Framed Time*, 166–70.

7. See Giorgio Agamben, *Homo Sacer: Sovereign Power and Bare Life* (Stanford, CA: Stanford University Press, 1998).

8. *The Jacket* discussed in Stewart, *Framed Time*, 239–41.

9. See Žižek, *The Fright of Real Tears*, 39 (see Intro., n. 12). Beyond his discussing these claims of Žižek's as part of the whole spectrum of film theory under contemporary revision, a genuine further contribution of Seung-Hoon Jeong's powerfully synoptic *Cinematic Interfaces: Film Theory after New Media* (New York: Routledge, 2013) is the way it helps us (in a film Jeong doesn't take up) comprehend the hero of *Source Code* as no longer person, subject, even agent so much as sheer "interface," one whose articulation sheds light precisely on the nature of cinematic projection "after new media" and its different screen protocols.

10. Pitched somewhere as it is—impossibly, "supernaturally" (if not for long, given the pace of neurobiology)—between immaterial production and physical risk, *Source Code* has been suggestively read alongside Jones's *Moon* by Joshua Gooch, in "Allegories of Labor's Liminality and Elite Corruption in Contemporary Film" (a paper presented at the SCMS conference in Boston, MA, March 2012) as the heavily capitalized case of an enslaved workforce of one. Beyond this (as developed in the present chapter), given the new martial economy the film portrays, its "program" to get surplus value out of encorpsed labor overlaps directly in on-screen manifestation (even if connecting only indirectly in the bioeconomic subtext) with the brandished labor of the F/X technicians.

11. Cubitt's "*Source Code*: Eco-Criticism and Subjectivity" submits this digital freeze to a close technical analysis while stressing its use in returning informatic and coded reality back to an image of "the commons," a Capraesque community momentarily remade and held together—artificially cemented?—before the hero's exit into what Cubitt sees as a private heteronormative utopia, but one not entirely dismissible (for him) under the lens of biopolitics and environmentalism. He thus reads the ending more as parable than as irony, with the lost subjectivity suffered by the dematerialized hero getting rescued for an "ecological" fantasy in which the former self, no long self-identical, becomes one with his

(now wholly cybernetic) "environment"—as figured in material terms, for Cubitt, by Kapoor's *Cloud Gate* sculpture: an object disappearing into the ambience it reflects (496). This is possible, for Cubitt, because the posthuman agent is understood in his article—as from a less sanguine position here too—as a medium per se rather than an autonomous entity under mediation.

12. See Garrett Stewart, "Sound Thinking," for my more extended treatment of the sound track and its ironies, including the film's violent disjunction of voice and body—and this in connection with Michel Chion's emphasis on acousmetric voice, Sergei Eisenstein's sound/image syncopations in the notion of "vertical montage," and Deleuze's semiotics of the *sonsign*. In "Moving Lips: Cinema as Ventriloquism," *Yale French Studies* 60 (1980): 67–79, Rick Altman proposes a yet more constitutive dialectic (rather than any inherent priority). "Image and sound: as long as each reinforces the other's lie, then we will not hesitate to believe them both" (70). What we believe in, ultimately, is their coincidence. Such is the dialectic brought digitally up to date—and turned to ontological crisis—in *Source Code* when the "lie" of the *discours* is no longer maintained to protect the *histoire* of the diegesis (as in Altman's model, 74) but exposed in fact to disintegrate it.

13. Discussed at length in Stewart, "Frame of Reference," in *Between Film and Screen*, chap. 3, 117–50 (see Preface, n. 8).

14. I allude to an argument prosecuted frequently by Kittler and threaded fairly continuously through both his *Gramophone, Film, Typewriter*, trans. Geoffrey Winthrop-Young and Michael Wutz (Stanford, CA: Stanford University Press, 1999) and *Optical Media*, trans. Anthony Enns (New York: Polity Press, 2010).

15. *Pace* Cubitt ("*Source Code:* Eco-Criticism and Subjectivity"), the pattern seems decidedly phobic, especially in this sci-fi narrative. In the loosely demarcated cycle of "irreality films" (485) like *Inception, The Adjustment Bureau,* and *Déjà Vu* within which Cubitt wants to locate *Source Code,* including its multiple debts, he later mentions, to *Groundhog Day* (495)—films where (unlike *The Matrix,* for instance) there is no final contrast between the virtual universe and its supposed alternative in the real—Cubitt's point is that such narratives realize thereby the deep logic of the posthuman; rather than media offering a means of communication between subjects under the abiding sign of "knowledge," instead the human body is redefined, under the newer sign of alienated "information," as merely the conduit for data transfer. But *Source Code*, it seems to me, grasps this possibility most fully not in the mode of "utopia" (490, 499) but in that of anxiety, despite its closing escape clause. Hence the place of the surveillance motif (or, say, the intersection of the irreality cycle with the surveillance cycle): according to which the all-but-discarded body is involuntarily disappeared into mediation only under state coercion.

16. Steven Shaviro, *Post Cinematic Affect* (Alresford, Hants, UK: O-Books, 2010), 123, where the Bourne trilogy and the films of Tony Scott are among the exhibits.

17. What was forecast at that drafting has not yet, at this printing, come to pass. Maybe the iteration was after all recognized as too bleakly internal to the original plot for further multiplication.

POSTFACE: ON MEDIATION AS INTERFACE

1. See in this respect the sustained rereading of film theory through the rear-view mirror of digital optics and its platforms—carried out under the retrospective framework of computer interface—in Seung-Hoon Jeong, *Cinematic Interfaces: Film Theory after New Media* (see chap. 8, n. 9).

2. A comparison of Cavell and Deleuze on this point closes Stewart, *Framed Time*, 264–66 (see Preface, n. 8).

3. Alain Badiou, *Cinema*, trans. Susan Spitzer (Malden, MA: Polity, 2013), 202: "Cinema transforms philosophy. In other words, cinema transforms the very notion of idea." Badiou's chapter, "Cinema as Philosophical Experimentation," culminates with "A Tribute to Gilles Deleuze," 222–232, where the distinction between the movement-image and the time-image is revisited.

4. Gilles Deleuze, "Postscript on the Societies of Control," *October* 59 (Winter 1992): 3–7; orig. pub. *L'Autre Journal*, no. 1 (mai 1990).

5. It is no accident that the ambitious 22-minute screen essay made about Deleuze's "Postscript" by the video collaborative Liquid Theory TV (Gary Hall, Clare Birchall, and Pete Woodbridge) introduces traffic-cam footage (unmentioned by Deleuze) of a crowded urban street corner at the moment they begin to elaborate on the computerized basis of the control society; nor are they at all far from the mark, in another interpolation of their own, when they note how the encounter with serialized information in codex form, always to be begun again in a culture of self-disciplined personal industry, is superseded by "liquid reading" in an entirely open field. See, from within the very network of data flow under critique, http://www.youtube.com/watch?v=GIus7lm_ZK0.

6. Deleuze, *Cinema 1: The Movement-Image*, 210 (see chap. 1, n. 16); here Deleuze makes the direct link between Lang's narrative schemata and post-Vietnam "surveillance" narratives in American cinema.

INDEX